BUDDHIST RITUALS OF DEATH AND REBIRTH

In Buddhist thought and practice, death has always been a central concept. This book provides a careful and thorough analysis of the rituals and social customs surrounding death in the Theravāda tradition of Sri Lanka. The author describes the rituals of death and rebirth and analyses social issues of the relationship between monks and lay people in this context. This aspect is of particular interest as death rituals are the only life cycle ritual in which Theravāda Buddhist monks are actively involved. The author then embarks upon an investigation of the ancient origins of these rituals. Drawing on early Vedic sūtras and Pāli texts, as well as archaeological and epigraphical material, this book establishes that Sri Lankan rituals are deeply rooted in their pre-Buddhist, Vedic precursors. Whilst beliefs and doctrines have undergone considerable changes over the centuries, it becomes evident that the underlying practices have largely remained stable. As the first comprehensive study of death rituals in Theravāda Buddhist practice, this is an important contribution to the fields of Buddhist studies, indology, anthropology and religious studies.

Rita Langer is Lecturer in Buddhist Studies at the University of Bristol, UK. Focusing on Southeast Asia (Thailand and Laos), she is continuing her research into Theravāda death rituals as part of a larger AHRC funded project, 'Buddhist Death Rituals of Southeast Asia and China'.

ROUTLEDGE CRITICAL STUDIES IN BUDDHISM

General Editors:
Charles S. Prebish and Damien Keown

Routledge Critical Studies in Buddhism is a comprehensive study of the Buddhist tradition. The series explores this complex and extensive tradition from a variety of perspectives, using a range of different methodologies.

The series is diverse in its focus, including historical studies, textual translations and commentaries, sociological investigations, bibliographic studies, and considerations of religious practice as an expression of Buddhism's integral religiosity. It also presents materials on modern intellectual historical studies, including the role of Buddhist thought and scholarship in a contemporary, critical context and in the light of current social issues. The series is expansive and imaginative in scope, spanning more than two and a half millennia of Buddhist history. It is receptive to all research works that inform and advance our knowledge and understanding of the Buddhist tradition.

A SURVEY OF VINAYA LITERATURE
Charles S. Prebish

THE REFLEXIVE NATURE OF AWARENESS
Paul Williams

ALTRUISM AND REALITY
Paul Williams

BUDDHISM AND HUMAN RIGHTS
Edited by Damien Keown, Charles Prebish and Wayne Husted

WOMEN IN THE FOOTSTEPS OF THE BUDDHA
Kathryn R. Blackstone

THE RESONANCE OF EMPTINESS
Gay Watson

AMERICAN BUDDHISM
Edited by Duncan Ryuken Williams and Christopher Queen

IMAGING WISDOM
Jacob N. Kinnard

PAIN AND ITS ENDING
Carol S. Anderson

EMPTINESS APPRAISED
David F. Burton

THE SOUND OF LIBERATING TRUTH
Edited by Sallie B. King and Paul O. Ingram

BUDDHIST THEOLOGY
Edited by Roger R. Jackson and John J. Makransky

THE GLORIOUS DEEDS OF PURNA
Joel Tatelman

EARLY BUDDHISM: A NEW APPROACH
Sue Hamilton

CONTEMPORARY BUDDHIST ETHICS
Edited by Damien Keown

INNOVATIVE BUDDHIST WOMEN
Edited by Karma Lekshe Tsomo

TEACHING BUDDHISM IN THE WEST
Edited by V.S. Hori, R.P. Hayes and J.M. Shields

EMPTY VISION
David L. McMahan

SELF, REALITY AND REASON IN TIBETAN PHILOSOPHY
Thupten Jinpa

IN DEFENSE OF DHARMA
Tessa J. Bartholomeusz

BUDDHIST PHENOMENOLOGY
Dan Lusthaus

RELIGIOUS MOTIVATION AND THE ORIGINS OF BUDDHISM
Torkel Brekke

DEVELOPMENTS IN AUSTRALIAN BUDDHISM
Michelle Spuler

ZEN WAR STORIES
Brian Victoria

THE BUDDHIST UNCONSCIOUS
William S. Waldron

INDIAN BUDDHIST THEORIES OF PERSONS
James Duerlinger

ACTION DHARMA
Edited by Christopher Queen, Charles Prebish and Damien Keown

TIBETAN AND ZEN BUDDHISM IN BRITAIN
David N. Kay

THE CONCEPT OF THE BUDDHA
Guang Xing

THE PHILOSOPHY OF DESIRE IN THE BUDDHIST PALI CANON
David Webster

THE NOTION OF *DITTHI* IN THERAVADA BUDDHISM
Paul Fuller

THE BUDDHIST THEORY OF SELF-COGNITION
Zhihua Yao

MORAL THEORY IN ŚĀNTIDEVA'S ŚIKṢĀSAMUCCAYA
Barbra R. Clayton

BUDDHIST STUDIES FROM INDIA TO AMERICA
Edited by Damien Keown

DISCOURSE AND IDEOLOGY IN MEDIEVAL JAPANESE BUDDHISM
Edited by Richard K. Payne and Taigen Dan Leighton

BUDDHIST THOUGHT AND APPLIED PSYCHOLOGICAL RESEARCH
Edited by D.K. Nauriyal, Michael S. Drummond and Y.B. Lal

BUDDHISM IN CANADA
Edited by Bruce Matthews

BUDDHISM, CONFLICT AND VIOLENCE IN MODERN SRI LANKA
Edited by Mahinda Deegalle

THERAVĀDA BUDDHISM AND THE BRITISH ENCOUNTER
Religious, missionary and colonial experience in nineteenth century Sri Lanka
Elizabeth Harris

BEYOND ENLIGHTENMENT
Buddhism, religion, modernity
Richard Cohen

BUDDHISM IN THE PUBLIC SPHERE
Reorienting global interdependence
Peter D. Hershock

BRITISH BUDDHISM
Teachings, practice and development
Robert Bluck

BUDDHIST NUNS IN TAIWAN AND SRI LANKA
A critique of the feminist perspective
Wei-Yi Cheng

NEW BUDDHIST MOVEMENTS IN THAILAND
Toward an understanding of Wat Phra Dhammakāya and Santi Asoke
Rory Mackenzie

BUDDHIST RITUALS OF DEATH AND REBIRTH
Contemporary Sri Lankan practice and its origins
Rita Langer

The following titles are published in association with the *Oxford Centre for Buddhist Studies*

Oxford Centre for Buddhist Studies

a project of The Society for the Wider Understanding of the Buddhist Tradition

The *Oxford Centre for Buddhist Studies* conducts and promotes rigorous teaching and research into all forms of the Buddhist tradition.

EARLY BUDDHIST METAPHYSICS
Noa Ronkin

MIPHAM'S DIALECTICS AND THE DEBATES ON EMPTINESS
Karma Phuntsho

HOW BUDDHISM BEGAN
The conditioned genesis of the early teachings
Richard F. Gombrich

BUDDHIST MEDITATION
An anthology of texts from the Pāli canon
Sarah Shaw

REMAKING BUDDHISM FOR MEDIEVAL NEPAL
The fifteenth-century reformation of Newar Buddhism
Will Tuladhar-Douglas

METAPHOR AND LITERALISM IN BUDDHISM
The doctrinal history of nirvana
Soonil Hwang

THE BIOGRAPHIES OF RECHUNGPA
The evolution of a Tibetan hagiography
Peter Alan Roberts

THE ORIGIN OF BUDDHIST MEDITATION
Alexander Wynne

BUDDHIST RITUALS OF DEATH AND REBIRTH

Contemporary Sri Lankan practice and its origins

Rita Langer

Routledge
Taylor & Francis Group
LONDON AND NEW YORK

First published 2007
by Routledge
2 Park Square, Milton Park, Abingdon, Oxon, OX14 4RN

Simultaneously published in the USA and Canada
by Routledge
270 Madison Ave, New York NY 10016

Routledge is an imprint of the Taylor & Francis Group, an informa business

Transferred to Digital Printing 2009

Typeset in Times New Roman by
Graphicraft Limited, Hong Kong

British Library Cataloguing in Publication Data
A catalogue record for this book is available from the British Library

Library of Congress Cataloging in Publication Data
A catalog record for this book has been requested

ISBN10: 0–415–39496–1 (hbk)
ISBN10: 0–415–54470–X (pbk)
ISBN10: 0–203–96073–4 (ebk)

ISBN13: 978–0–415–39496–3 (hbk)
ISBN13: 978–0–415–54470–2 (pbk)
ISBN13: 978–0–203–96073–8 (ebk)

FOR RUPERT AND LEONARD

CONTENTS

ACKNOWLEDGEMENTS

This book is a revised version of my PhD dissertation ('Death and funerary rites in Sri Lanka: a study of contemporary Buddhist practice and its origins') submitted to the University of Hamburg in 2004.

Before I embarked on the PhD I was priveleged to study at three great institutions under exceptional teachers. At the Institut für Kultur und Geschichte Indiens und Tibets (Hamburg University) I am indebted to PD Professor Dr Erb, Professor Dr Schmithausen, Professor Dr Seyfort-Ruegg, Professor Dr Srinivasan and Professor Dr Wezler, for their inspirational classes. I was very fortunate to meet in my first week at Hamburg university a group of students who would during the course of the next twenty years become my colleagues, advisors and closest friends: Dr Mudagamuwe Maithrimurthi, Michael Pahlke, Burkhard Quessel and Professor Dr Alexander von Rospatt. I also spent a period of 18 months at SOAS in London where I studied under Professor Piatigorsky, Dr Skorupski, Professor Wijayawardhana, and Dr Denwood. I would also like to thank Professor Indira Chowdhury and Dr Ulrich Pagel for making my time in London truly memorable. Last but not least, I spent a year at the Postgraduate Institute for Pāli and Buddhist Studies in Sri Lanka where I attended classes with Ven. Dr K. Dhammajoti, Professor Karunadasa, Professor Wijebandara and Professor Tilakaratana. During that period I frequently went to Colombo University to consult Professor Wijayawardhana and Professor Disanayaka whose enthusiasm always stays with me.

I would like to express my gratitude to the Deutscher Akademischer Austauschdienst (DAAD) in Germany for funding two extended periods of study in Sri Lanka: my postgraduate studies at the PGIPBS as well as my subsequent field work in 1998/99. Both stays were made enjoyable by my friends in Sri Lanka, particularly Mahinda Fernando, Jasmin Mangalika, Upali and Indrani Perera, Ravi and Achala, Khanti Ratnayaka, Nanda Senanayaka, Priyanthi and Sarath Wijesinghe. I cannot thank them enough for all these years of unwavering friendship and support. I would also like to thank Ven. R. Devananda, Ven. M. Ratanajoti and Ven. H. Vimalananda for their time and patience as well as Nimal Sriyaratne for his help with the transcripts and translations of the sermons. I am particularly glad to have the opportunity to thank the people in the village for opening their homes and hearts to me at a particularly difficult time when their lives were touched by death. For reasons of privacy I will not name individuals. During the extended period of writing I was sustained by my friends in Britain and Germany. To mention but a few: Rolf and Adelheit Buschner, Oliver Cooper, Michael Houser, Dr Ken Robinson Dr Thomas Langer, Dr Maria Schetelich and Bill Pruitt all helped me in various ways including reading and editing my work. Special thanks also to Dr Mürmel (Leipzig University) for agreeing to be one of the examiners of my PhD dissertation and for his bibliographical hints. Finally my gratitude goes to Professor Damien Keown for accepting my dissertation for the 'Critical Studies in Buddhism' series.

Three people have been central to my efforts and supported me in ways that go beyond the call of duty and friendship. I cannot begin to find the right words to adequately express my deep-felt gratitude and affection for my supervisor Professor Dr Lambert Schmithausen. It will be near impossible to find anyone who would devote more time and energy to students than he did (many apologies to his lovely family). Professor Wijayawardhana has been incredibly generous with his time and patient with my insistent questioning, from the first day we met in SOAS and throughout the years. My understanding of the subject matter would be greatly diminished without him. Dr Maithrimurthi, apart from being a faithful and supportive friend, has advised me on all aspect of Sri Lankan life, and in his role as a former monk gave me invaluable insights into the dynamics of Buddhist practice. It goes without saying that any mistakes in this study are entirely my responsibility.

This book is dedicated to my husband Rupert and son Leonard who encouraged me from the very beginning, accompanied me on my field trips, and put up with me during the years of research. Rupert displayed extraordinary patience in reading every page of every draft and explaining the finer points of Abhidhamma while Leonard's charming presence opened many doors and hearts for me in Sri Lanka.

INTRODUCTION

1. General

Sri Lankan Buddhists, if at all possible, prepare for death. A monk is called to the death bed, the dying person takes the refuges and precepts and close relatives join in. When the person has died the corpse is sent away to be embalmed before it is returned to the house in a coffin.

On the third or fourth day after the death the funeral takes place. A number of monks are invited to the house of the deceased and offered a new, white piece of cloth. There is a short sermon and more chanting. The merit of the offering is given to the deceased. The burial or cremation takes place at the cemetery. Afterwards people return to the house of the deceased where a meal is shared by family, friends and neighbours.

On the sixth day after the death a monk is invited to preach. Again a great number of people are expected. The spirit of the deceased is encouraged to come and listen to the monk who preaches for exactly one hour. Merit is given to the deceased. The monk leaves and the guests are treated to a feast. The next day a number of monks are invited to the home for the midday meal. They enter the house in single file, with a layperson in front carrying a reliquary on his head. After a short sermon the meal is served to the monks. Scraps of food are taken to the garden for the hungry ghosts. Utensils wrapped in brown paper are offered to the monks. And again the merit is offered to the deceased. When the monks have left, the guests once more share a meal. After three months, one year, and then annually, the process is repeated: monks are invited for a meal; small scraps of food are left in the garden; utensils are donated; merit is offered to the deceased.

* * *

This sequence of events—death, funeral, post-funerary rites—forms the basis of the three main chapters of the present study. Each chapter is presented by way of three 'levels': (1) description of contemporary practice, (2) commentary and (3) historical roots. First-hand accounts based on my own fieldwork constitute the first level (I.1, II.1 and III.1) with a longer discussion of specific aspects added where appropriate in the form of an excursus.

The accounts give rise to various immediate questions: What do monks chant at a deathbed and why? How is the merit thought to be received? What is the 'spirit' of the deceased which is invited and why is it fed on the sixth day? Why is the deceased offered merit but not food on the seventh day? What is the function of feeding the hungry ghosts (or crows and dogs) in the funeral context? Consideration of these questions forms the second level or 'commentary' (I.2, II.2 and III.2) which again includes the occasional excursus where appropriate.

The third level (I.3, II.3, III.3) is devoted to the historical background and constitutes the most elaborate and detailed of the three levels. A wealth of material is found scattered in the ancient Pāli sources,[1] but my research embraces also the Vedic *sūtra*s, Brāhmaṇas and Upaniṣads which formed the cultural and ritual backdrop to the rise of Buddhism and Hinduism. How the Upaniṣads and Brāhmaṇas give particular significance to the time of death, which is something echoed in the Pāli sources, is considered in section 1.3. The Vedic *sūtra*s contain detailed prescriptions of the handling of a dead body and the remains left after cremation that supply details absent from the Pāli material. This literary evidence considered alongside certain archaeological evidence provides the basis for a discussion in section II.3 of ancient Indian and early Buddhist funerary practices. Finally, the origins of the custom of giving merit, which developed into the main feature of the Sri Lankan funerary rites and which provides a good example of the inclusivist nature of Buddhism, are traced back to the Upaniṣads in section III.3.

There is, of course, a certain overlap between the three chapters as well as between levels. For example, the Vedic post-funerary rites (II.3.1.3) are included in the general discussion of the Vedic sources in chapter II (Funeral) rather than in chapter III (Post-Funerary Rites), where the focus is on the giving of merit. Furthermore, the division into these three main chapters was adopted for the benefit of comparison with other cultures, but is not entirely suited to the Sri Lankan context, where the seventh day is a turning point. Finally there is a topic—hungry ghosts (*prētas*) and ancestors—which cuts across the categories and comes up in a number of places as indicated by subtitles ('On *prētas*', 'More on *prētas*', 'Yet more on *prētas*').

The approach of the present study is predominantly textual and philological with emphasis on the history of ideas and practices. This reflects my professional training (as an Indologist) as well as personal interests. Sri Lanka lends itself to this kind of approach: it is part of the pan-Indian culture (like other countries on the periphery, such as Nepal, Pakistan, Bangladesh), which brings with it all the advantages of shared linguistic roots and cultural heritage (as well as the danger of assuming that terms have retained their original connotation over the centuries). Besides, Sri Lanka has had a more or less unbroken history of Buddhism, which allegedly goes back to the time of emperor Aśoka (third century BC).[2] Even though the chronicles report frequent invasions from South India, Sri Lanka has not been Hinduised in the way Nepal has, for example. It is furthermore linked to ancient India and the beginnings of Buddhism by a commentarial tradition (Pāli) containing Indian as well as Sri Lankan material on local customs. And finally, it would have been impossible for me to even consider anything resembling a field trip had it not been for the constant support of my friends in Sri Lanka (particularly in the village).

Given the same starting point, a set of ceremonies in a particular village, other avenues of research were possible: a study comparing funeral rites in different parts of the island, different religious communities in Sri Lanka (Buddhist, Hindu, Muslim, Vedda, Burgher), or different Theravāda Buddhist countries (Sri Lanka, Thailand, Burma).

On the basis of the same set of ceremonies, one might have investigated the relationship between the Buddhist *saṃgha* and laity, or systematically analysed the different sermons and preachings in Sri Lanka. One could have inquired into the problem of what people mean when they speak of 'Buddhist' or 'non-Buddhist', or compared the differences between village and urban set ups, Sinhala or English-speaking environment.

Given the same starting point, death rites, one might have concentrated more on the wider meanings of death for Theravāda Buddhism (death imagery, corpses as an object of meditation, etc.), or one might have inquired further into the concept of intermediate state (*antarābhava*), which is of great importance in Tibetan Buddhism.

These different approaches—to name but a few—will suffice to illustrate the extremely versatile nature of the topic and material, while at the same time outlining the limitations of the present study. But there are also the limitations of the researcher to be considered: my degree is in Indology, and I do not have any formal training in anthropology, sociology or archaeology. I nevertheless hope that the ethnographic and archaeological material adds a dimension important enough to excuse any shortcomings in its presentation. Gombrich (1971 (1991), 3) vividly describes the reasons for and problems of venturing into disciplines beyond one's initial academic training and expertise:

> Academic boundaries are artificial: the realities are the problems. Problems have a way of crossing these boundaries; while chasing one the hapless researcher may wander, alone and unarmed, into the territory of a foreign and possibly hostile discipline. If he keeps quiet, he may escape unobserved; if he is fool enough to raise his voice he will be apprehended, and must throw himself on his captor's mercy. I am in this unfortunate position. By education a philologist, far less of a historian, and devoid of anthropological training, I have been chasing the problem of religious change, and found myself far from home, deep inside the territory of the social sciences, far from Oxford libraries in a village in central Ceylon.

A further shortcoming of the present work is that it does not include Sinhala textual and secondary sources. While my proficiency in Sinhala is sufficient to conduct interviews, read pamphlets and (with some help) transcribe and translate the sermons given at the ceremonies, I do not read literary Sinhala. My experience is that interviews conducted in Sinhala produce very different material from the ones conducted in English, and I should think that the same might be true for Sinhala secondary sources. Regrettably, I have to leave this to others to discover.[3]

Finally, there is the question of where the present study fits into the contemporary study of Buddhism. If we go back in time for a moment: in the late nineteenth century, European Indology represented by scholars such as Rhys Davids and Oldenberg turned its attention to the translation of Buddhist texts. The style of translation and choice of texts and topics was, of course, in keeping with the interests of these scholars and the intellectual approach of their time. The result was, as could be expected, a somewhat one-dimensional picture of Buddhism or as Seneviratne (1999, 2f.) puts it:

> For these early Western interpreters of Buddhism, there was no question or ambiguity as to the object and focus of their study, which was a select corpus of Buddhist texts. To them any material that did not conform to the imagined Buddhism of this Euro-Buddhist canon was outside Buddhism. Such material were labelled and classified away as pagan cults, animism, folk supernaturalism, idolatry, and so forth. By the process of biblification in the form of printed translations into Western languages, they fixed and placed boundaries on this canon, paving the way for a new Buddhist scriptualism.

While I agree in general with Seneviratne, it has to be said, however, that Western scholars were by far not the first to translate Buddhist texts and thereby 'fix and place boundaries' on it. The Tibetans and Chinese had done that long before the Western scholars, and then as now, quite extraordinary scholarship was displayed. The idea of a canon is by no means a Western invention; it is found already in Buddhaghosa who lists and groups the various texts.[4] These early attempts construe a form of Buddhism in keeping with the intellectual needs and fashions of the late nineteenth century have to be seen in their context. Modern scholarship, too, is inevitably influenced by intellectual fashions and will be judged some day in the (maybe not so) remote future.

Besides, I am not sure what precisely Seneviratne (1999, 3) means when he speaks of the 'essentialized, sanitized, cleansed, scriptualized, and objectified Buddhism of these texts'. Maybe it is time to revisit the texts? It seems to me that the Buddhist texts are as varied and rich as the practice: reaching from doctrinal lists to anecdotes and stories. They incorporate ghosts, demons and other supernatural beings; they record the performance of miracles, the display of supernatural powers, and very moving stories. They give advice on how to reach meditational achievements as well as how to deal with everyday problems.

That is not to say that there is no more to Buddhism than is found in the canon, and a more recent generation of scholars has recognized not everything that is outside the canon is also outside Buddhism. A number of studies in different Theravāda countries (Tambiah 1970; Gombrich 1971) came to similar conclusions: different types of Theravāda Buddhism share a common core of concepts and ideas, but are distinguished by local differences. However, these local variations of Theravāda are now looked on as coherent in themselves, rather than aberrations from some norm.

Again, building on this new and more colourful picture of Buddhism, a number of scholars began to consider questions of the different religious approaches found within Buddhism: syncretistic Buddhism/compartmentalized Buddhism (Terwiel 1975) or cognitive/affective (Gombrich 1971) nibbānic/kammatic (Spiro 1982). At around the same time the term 'protestant Buddhism' was coined by Obeyesekere (1970).[5]

Seneviratne 1999, 7 goes one step further:

> I contend that the anthropological categories such as 'Thai Buddhism', 'Burmese Buddhism', and 'Sinhalese Buddhism' need to be expanded beyond their present connotation of a syncretism between doctrinal Buddhism and folk Buddhism, great or little traditions of mystical belief and practices and so forth, to embrace the broader array of religiously grounded phenomena like 'fundamentalism' and 'ideology'. Such an expanded definition would cover the political, economic, and cultural activities of diverse religious personalities—monk and lay virtuosi, mystagogues, apologists, champions, and various other propagandists. Whereas we can approach in a more or less value-neutral way the different syncretistic Buddhisms on which anthropological focus has been so far nearly exclusive, it would be difficult to do so when it comes to the ideological actors and movements covered by our expanded definition.

The present work has all these phases and studies as basis and background and in a way takes certain scholarly achievements for granted. Differences in approach within Buddhism are well known and assumed as given nowadays. Terms like 'protestant Buddhism' have entered the common vocabulary of scholars researching contemporary South Asian Buddhist societies, and heightened the awareness of issues such as the monk-layman relationship.

This background allowed the focus of the present study to shift again, from a dualistic approach to a complementary approach, which combines material from a variety of sources and disciplines in the manner of Strong's study on Upagupta (1992). Following Strong's example, I look at these different sources as contributing to a greater, more detailed picture. This approach seemed most suited to my interests and questions, but I do not intend to advertise it as superior to other approaches. It seems to me of great importance to treat each source and discipline in its context: an archaeological report, for example, does not answer the same questions as an Abhidhamma treatise, or an interview. I do not regard claims of superiority as conducive to a better understanding of Buddhism at large. My interest has been to explore different viewpoints: how far can the textual, archaeological and epigraphical sources provide better understanding of contemporary Buddhist practices, but also how far can ethnographic material add to a better understanding of the texts, etc.

2. The fieldwork

A word about the village

As I had a grant (genorously provided by the DAAD) that was for six months (Aug. 1998 to February 1999), I could not afford to spend too much time searching for the 'ideal village'. Besides, the purpose of my fieldtrip was not to conduct ethnographic or sociological research in a 'representative' Sri Lankan village reflecting the ethnic overall distribution of the country's population.[6] My interest was merely to provide an account of a Buddhist funeral for the purpose of illustrating and supplementing my research based on the Pāli and Sanskrit texts. It was only in the course of my research that I reversed the viewpoint and made the contemporary practice the starting point and main focus of the study.

I decided not to make up an artificial name for the village, but to call it 'our village' (*apē gama*) which reflects how my informants referred to it and how I came to think of it in the course of my stay. I will refer to other villages and place names by their initial letter. I had been in contact with friends and people from our village for some ten years. Besides, Colombo is not too difficult to reach from there, which was essential for me for practical reasons such as banking, shopping, the use of email facilities, universities etc. I did not conduct a demographic survey, and the following description of the village is based purely on personal impressions and talks with the villagers.

The railway station and a level crossing with a dozen or so small grocery and hardware shops and a doctor's surgery make the centre (referred to as 'town' (*ṭavumēa*) by the villagers). For any shopping or services beyond the bare essentials, people have to go to one of the two towns near by. There are two nursery schools and a junior school; distances to places are short and telephones and cars rare. The residential areas spread out much further, and the percentage of homeowners is high. What appears at first sight to be one 'village' (c.160 houses) covering an area of about a mile to a mile and a half are in fact two, or even three 'villages', but the borders are not obvious to the uninitiated.

There are no factories, offices, hospitals, etc., in the village, and the means of making a living are restricted to agriculture, a handful of shops, carpentry, a couple of hair dressers, and an agency post office. As a result, the number of people commuting for work to surrounding towns or Colombo is high.

There are two Buddhist temples (*pansal*) in the village, a newer 'town-temple' and an older temple at the fringe. The latter belonged originally to the Siam Nikāya tradition, but the abbot affiliated himself to the Rāmañña Nikāya about 100 years ago and subsequently founded the second, younger Rāmañña Nikāya temple.[7] There is no church, mosque or Hindu temple, the population is almost exclusively Buddhist, and the predominant caste (*kulaya*) is Govigama.[8]

Observation of ceremonies

During my stay I observed four 'sets' of funeral ceremonies (each consisting of: 1. burial (*bhūmidānaya*) or cremation (*ādāhanaya*); 2. preaching (*baṇa*) on the sixth day; 3. alms giving (*dānaya*) on the seventh day) as well as a number of miscellaneous ceremonies. My descriptions of the ceremonies are personal and based on individual events (rather than a summary of various ceremonies). They are intended as an introduction for people who are not familiar with Sri Lankan customs.

About a month after my arrival, the husband of the woman cooking for me and my family[9] turned up in our kitchen and announced that a remote relation of his had passed away and that the funeral was to take place in two days' time in a village not far away, referred to henceforward as T. The woman who had died was originally from our village and there was a whole group of people planning to go. This funeral and the follow-up rituals serve as the base of my first description ('A Laywoman's Burial'). The fact that the funeral did not actually take place in our village turned out to be of less importance as the lay people involved were mostly from our village.

The second description ('A Monk's Cremation') is based on the cremation of an eminent abbot of a relatively large temple with a temple school (*pirivena*) for monks in a neighbouring village, henceforward referred to as D. In a way, the descriptions of a simple laywoman's burial and an eminent monk's cremation represent the two ends of the spectrum. I do not, however, intend to make a social statement as cremations for laypeople can be quite grand as well and monks' cremations might come much simpler. Even though in essence the cremation of a monk differs very little from a cremation of a layperson, the former seems to have preserved certain features, such as the spreading out of a white cloth in front of the funeral procession, which used to be customary at every funeral. Besides, the preparations for and the proceedings at a monk's cremation allow some insight into the dynamics of the relationship between monks and laypeople.

Interviews

Other important sources of information were informal discussions with people involved in the funerals and formal interviews conducted during my fieldwork, which mainly dealt with people's beliefs and interpretations. Rather than treating the interview material in a separate section, I drew on it as yet another resource to be utilised and partly included where appropriate in the corresponding chapters (death, funeral, post-funerary rites).

Some questions, however, not related to Buddhist practice but aimed at doctrinal interpretations, were dealt with in a separate, theoretical excursus. The interview material is of a diverse nature and requires a brief introduction with regard to scope and content. I conducted about eighteen formal interviews: some of those interviews were topical, connected with a particular event or ceremony I had observed; others were of a questionnaire type. Since only a handful of people in the village speak English, most of these interviews were conducted in Sinhala. I decided against working with an interpreter because people were generally more at ease and willing to share inside information when the conversation took place without interference in English. This by far outweighed the fact that inevitably I would miss some minor points, which could be checked later with the help of the audio-recordings.

The interviews conducted in English were mostly done with middle-class people from outside the village (some from Colombo) and differed considerably in content from those conducted in Sinhala. This is partly due to the different educational background, but there is yet another factor to consider.

People were more inclined to talk about 'ghost stories', i.e., stories of *prētas*, *bhūtas*, etc., and seemingly 'irrational' explanations of customs. It was noticeable how people opened up when given a chance to switch to Sinhala prompted by a certain expression or clue.[10] The fact that the choice of language had such a great impact on the content and quality of the interviews would deserve a separate study.

After the first tentative attempts, I embarked on a number of specific interviews geared to an interviewee or an event. By that time I had observed (and mostly transcribed and translated) the first set of ceremonies at T., which influenced the quality of the questions. A number of interviews and informal discussions with Professor Wijayawardhana (Department of Sinhala, Colombo University) were aimed at drawing on his wide knowledge of Sinhala customs in general and the specifically Sinhalese understanding of Pāli and Sanskrit technical terms. I am greatly indebted to him for his unfaltering patience with my inquisitiveness and persistence. An interview with Ven. R., who had conducted the funeral in T., was specifically geared to his last visit to the dying laywoman and the 'last rites' performed on that occasion.[11] The last of these topical interviews was conducted with Ven. D. following 'A Monk's Cremation' and aimed at establishing the differences between cremations conducted for laypeople and monks. The interviews at this stage were all conducted in English (with the exception of the last one), but again the Sinhala terminology was double checked.[12]

The last two months of my stay were mostly dedicated to conducting a series of structured interviews in Sinhala and English (a total of thirteen) based on a questionnaire of twelve questions. The questions aimed at providing a link between contemporary Buddhist practice and canonical and post-canonical Pāli texts.

The questionnaire comprises four main sections with three questions each. The first topic discussed was that of giving merit (*pin dīma/anumodanāva*) in order to ease into the discussion by taking a 'positive' topic as a starting point. This was followed by a discussion of the customs during the first seven days after a death has occurred (*märunāṭa passe palaveni davas hata/antarābhava*). The third topic discussed was the death moment (*märena mohota/cuticitta*), its importance and implications for the next rebirth. The last topic was the problem of what constitutes merit or demerit (*pin/pav*; *kusal/akusal*) and is not directly derived from observation of certain events but is of a much broader nature.

It should be borne in mind that the questionnaire served only as a guideline during the interviews. The order of questions, which were deliberately kept very simple and free of technical terms, was changed frequently following the flow of the conversation and there are slight differences in the phrasing of the English and Sinhala questions even though the general content and structure were the same.

The choice of interviewees attempted a wide range with regard to age, sex, educational background, social status, religious status (i.e., monk or layperson), etc., as far as the limited time allowed.[13] The result is a number of interviews, which though based on the same set of questions, vary greatly in length and content. My overall aim was to gain a picture, however sketchy and incomplete, of people's beliefs and interpretations as well as their understanding of certain technical Pāli and Sanskrit terms. It must be borne in mind, of course, that a person might not know the literal meaning of a technical term but might nevertheless be familiar with the concept.[14]

I

DEATH AND DYING

I did not attend pre-death or near-death rituals in the course of this fieldwork, nor did I conduct interviews with recently bereaved people. Unlike the following chapters, this one is, therefore, not based on personal observation.

Contemporary Sri Lankan practice

In the particular case that served as the basis for my description of a funeral ('A Laywoman's Burial') Ven. R. (the abbot of the local Siam Nikāya temple in T.) was called to the deathbed. He later stressed in his sermons, especially at the *baṇa* preaching that despite her old age (mid-nineties) and frail condition she was conscious and able to hold a conversation. He told me that he had preached a little sermon, reminding her of meritorious deeds she had performed in her lifetime and had then chanted protective Pāli *suttas* (Pāli: *paritta*; Sinhala: *pirit*): *Mahāmaṅgalasutta* (Sn 258–269), *Karaṇīyamettasutta* (Sn 143–152) and *Ratanasutta* (Sn 222–238). He also said that he had provided her with a protective 'chanted' piece of string (*pirit nūla*) and given her protective 'chanted' water (*pirit pän*) to drink.

To get a clearer picture of the 'last rites' and the underlying beliefs I included questions about the moment of death in a questionnaire, which I had devised:

> Questionnaire C.1: What do people do if someone is about to die in the home? Are there special customs?

The answers will be analysed with regard to the role of monks and that of laypeople and I will look at the answers of monks and those of laypeople separately.

The role of monks (questionnaire C.1)

All the monks I interviewed agreed that a visit to a dying person's house on the invitation of the family is customary. The invited monk speaks to the ill person and reminds him/her of past, meritorious deeds (such as taking the eight precepts, a pilgrimage, donations, etc.). He then chants *pirit*, ties a 'protective string' around the wrist of the dying person (and everyone present) and gives 'protective water' to drink. The *suttas* named by all the monks in this context were: *Mahāmaṅgalasutta*, *Karaṇīyamettasutta*, *Ratanasutta*, but one interviewee added the *Mahāsatipaṭṭhānasutta* (D II 290–315) to this standard list. All interviewees mentioned that the chanting is done when someone is still conscious and able to take part in the ceremony. The dying person often makes a gift to the *saṃgha* (called *dahampūjāva*), which might be a set of eight requisites (*aṭa pirikara*) or just a packet of tea or sugar, according to the financial means of the family. It is hoped that the memory of this last meritorious deed at the moment of death will take away the fear.

One interviewee said that in the case of a monk nearing death sometimes a *bodhipūjāva*[1] or a *dānaya* is performed on his behalf and that the other monks in the temple might chant in Pāli for an hour. It was, however, not entirely clear if this chanting was part of the *bodhipūjāva* he had mentioned before, or a separate event.

The answers of the laypeople relating to the role of the monks largely conformed with those given by monks with one exception: three of the interviewees (all from Colombo) mentioned that it might actually be counterproductive to call a monk to the deathbed. It would make the dying person realise that his death was near and cause agitation rather than calm.

The role of laypeople (questionnaire C.1)

It is generally regarded as a meritorious deed to visit a sick neighbour or relation, but it seems to be a must when someone is considered to be close to death. It is customary to bring small presents or even money to support the family who might be under considerable financial strain to meet the costs of hospital treatments, medication, and eventually, funeral expenses.

Let us again look at the monks' answers first: most stated that there were no special customs, but two of the interviewees (and one former monk), all three belonging to the Rāmañña Nikāya, did mention the custom of placing a Buddha image (*buddhapratimāva*) or a tray with flowers near the dying person as a visual aid to remember meritorious deeds in the hour of death.[2] They further mentioned that family members would read from a so-called 'book of merit' (*pinpota*), in which important meritorious deeds are recorded. One of the interviewees remembered a monk actually handing out small notebooks to laypeople (approximately 35 years ago) encouraging them to keep such a 'merit diary'. It was, however, not widely known among the people I interviewed, which suggests that the custom has either gone out of fashion altogether or is practised in other parts of the island. The custom of reading a *pinpota* at the deathbed has its origin in the story of King Duṭṭhagāmaṇi and is frequently referred to in secondary literature.[3]

Laypeople, too, generally agreed that there were no special near-death rituals or customs besides providing physical comfort. One interviewee mentioned that the dying person should be given some water to drink. This custom is well documented in secondary sources[4] and, of course, is reminiscent of the Hindu custom of putting *pañcagavya* into the dying person's mouth.[5] Another interviewee mentioned pomegranate juice or bees' honey which is meant to give the dying person a pleasant sensation.[6]

Frequently it was mentioned that it is important to remind a dying person of meritorious deeds to make him happy (*satuṭu*) and to influence his mind in a positive (religious) way. It is generally believed that to think of the Buddha, Dhamma, Saṃgha or a meritorious deed is conducive to a better rebirth. And most people said that laypeople can say the five precepts, chant *pirit* or read from a *baṇa* book in the likely case that there is no monk around. One person told me that she recited the *Karaṇīyamettasutta* for her father who died in her arms of a sudden stroke. Another interviewee said that the family had played a tape of protective chanting (*pirit*) when death was imminent. Yet another person told me of an elderly relation of his, who took donations to the temple on his birthday and died while listening to the monks praising his meritorious deed. This was considered 'the perfect death' and it was generally agreed that he must have been reborn as a god.

The fact that someone died while listening to chanting seems to be a great comfort for family members and friends and is frequently mentioned in a funeral house.

Excursus: **jīvadānaya**

In the context of death preparation, a further two practices should be mentioned: the last alms giving and the releasing of animals.

A terminally ill person might express the wish to invite a number of monks for a last *dānaya* before passing away, and one interviewee, who was very knowledgeable with regard to Sinhala customs (past and present), referred to this as *jīvadānaya*.[7] Another interviewee told me that *jīvadānaya* was rarely practised when he was a child and that it had become more popular in recent years. Other interviewees, however, did not mention the custom (or the term *jīvadānaya*) and I did not find evidence that it is a lively tradition in the village. Ample evidence is, however, found in the secondary literature and according to Ariyapala (1968, 360) the custom goes back to at least mediaeval times in Sri Lanka as it is mentioned in the *Saddharmaratnāvaliya* and referred to as *āsanna karman* (lit. '[death] proximate *kamma*'):[8]

> What is known as *jīvadāna* (alms-giving when still alive) in certain parts of the island today, seems to correspond to what is meant here. *Jīvadāna* is known in some parts of the island as *godāna* (lit. offering of cattle), e.g., in Hatara and Hat Korales, and refers

> to the offering of a piece of cloth to a monk in some places while in others this offering is preceded by an alms-giving. The term *godāna* suggests that cattle were gifted. Whether this was the actual practice it is difficult to surmise.

The above quoted passage is of further interest as it equates the terms *jīvadāna* and *godāna*. Dickson, too, uses both terms synonymously and gives a more detailed description of what is involved under the heading '*The "Jīvadānaṃ," or Pinkama by a man whose end is approaching*'. Dickson's description shows some interesting features that deserve to be mentioned. First, the *pinkama* he describes seems to be quite an elaborate affair, lasting for over two days. It starts with a *buddhapūjāva* at the temple, an evening *dānaya* for the invited monk, and a sermon (*baṇa*) lasting for six hours into the night. On the second day there is an alms giving (*dānaya*), when both morning and midday meals are provided, as well as certain utilitarian items including a 'piece of calico' are given. Second, Dickson's description of the *jīvadāna* is very similar to that of the *matakadānaya* and both are said to be given by the relations of the dying person on his behalf, rather than by the person himself. Finally, the offering of a 'piece of calico' is reminiscent of the *matakavastra* offered at funerals.

The term *godānaya*, which is used as a synonym of the *jīvadānaya*, points to Hinduism/Brahmanism as its possible origin. Tillakaratne (1986, 158) points out that there is evidence in a 'large number of *olas* [palm leaves] of gift styled *godāna patra*, which point to the conclusion that cattle were among the presents given to the monks at this ceremony'. In support of his assumption that cattle were actually given as part of a near-death donation to the *saṃgha* he quotes a *godāna patraya* dated A.D. 1803.

And even if no cattle were offered—in fact very often a substitute is given so that the gift is a *godānaya* only in name—it seems worthwhile looking into the Hindu ritual close to death which was named *godānaya*. Dubois (1906, 483) describes the ceremony as follows:

> The cow is led up to the sick person, who takes her by the tail, and at the same time the *purohita* recites a *mantram* praying that the cow may lead the dying Brahmin by a happy road into the other world. The latter then makes a present of the animal to some other Brahmin, into whose hand he pours a few drops of water in token of a gift. This gift of a cow is called *godana*, and is indispensable if one wishes to arrive without mishap in Yama-loka, or the kingdom of Yama, the king of hell. Bordering Yama-loka there is a river of fire which all men must cross after they have ceased to live. Those, who have made the *godana*, when they come to their last hour, will find on the banks of this river a cow which will help them to pass on to the opposite bank without being touched by the flame.

Pandey (1969, 246), too, describes the *godāna* as important part of the Hindu ceremonies performed when death is near. He points out that in earlier times, what he refers to as the '*sūtra* period', the cow was 'either sacrificed and burnt with the corpse or let loose to run away from the cremation ground'. The custom of presenting the cow to the brahmin and the belief that it will help the dead person to cross the river is, according to Caland (1896, 8), already found in the texts of the Vedic schools.

According to Firth (1997, 62) the *godāna*, though in decline, is still practised today, and her description is remarkably similar to the accounts of Dubois and Pandey. She further adds that a 'silver surrogate image of a cow, or money of equal value, with a ritual statement of intention, is an equally meritorious gift'.

The other near-death custom mentioned above is the releasing of animals, usually birds, but even cows, which is regarded as a very meritorious deed. A vow is often made to free an animal in exchange for one's own life (or the life of a relative or friend).[9] The technical term for the ancient practice of ceremonial releasing of animals is *abhayadānaya* (lit. 'giving of fearlessness').[10] However, in upcountry Sri Lanka (Kandy) it is referred to as *jīvadāna* 'gift (or giving) of life'.[11] The same is true for Nepal where *jīvadānas* are regarded as meritorious and in some way as life prolonging.[12]

To sum up, the near-death customs discussed here have a long tradition and go back to pre-Buddhist rituals. The Buddhist *dānaya* by someone close to death (called *jīvadānaya* or *godānaya*) also involves gifts (even though not cows), but places emphasis on the making and giving of merit, which brings it very close to a *matakadānaya* indeed. The custom of releasing animals (called *abhayadānaya* or *jīvadānaya* 'gift of life') by someone who is near death also has a long tradition and is regarded as highly meritorious. It is not quite clear to me how both customs came to be known under the name of *jīvadānaya* in different parts of the island, but it is clear that they have more in common than the name.

Commentary on the practice

The importance of the moment of death (questionnaire C.2 & 3)

In Theravāda doctrine special significance is given to the quality of the last conscious moments at the time of death as determining the circumstances of the next rebirth. The concept of good and bad deaths is found in other religions as well and it might be more accurate to speak of an Indian concept of good and bad death. One of these concepts is 'untimely death' (*akālamaraṇa*), which is regarded as inauspicious and can result in certain problems for the departed or his family. On the other hand, it is regarded auspicious to die with a religious thought, which in the case of a Hindu might be directed at, say, Vishnu, and in the case of Buddhists at the Buddha, Dharma, and Saṃgha.

Two questions (C 2 and 3) aimed at establishing a clearer picture of 'good' or a 'bad' death in contemporary Sri Lanka.

> Questionnaire C.2: Is it better to die with a clear mind? What happens if someone dies with an angry mind or in a sudden accident?
> Questionnaire C.3: Can a bad person go to a good place because he had a good thought at the moment of death, or can a good person go to a bad place because of a bad thought at the moment of death?

The monks unanimously agreed that the quality of the last conscious moment is the determining factor as to the form or place of the next rebirth. The pre-death customs were explained to me as reminding the dying person of meritorious deeds and to serving in 'purifying the mind', as one English-speaking interviewee put it. It is preferable to die consciously or unconfused, and one monk pointed out that to die unconfused (*asammūḷho kālaṃ karoti*) is one of the eleven advantages of practising benevolence (*mettā*).[13]

So, provided some meritorious deed comes to his mind at the crucial last moment by force of some previous good *kamma* (Sinhala: *karmaśaktiya*, *puṇyaśaktiya*), even a bad person can be born in a good place. The example quoted for this by one of the monks was the case of King Duṭṭhagāmaṇi, who, after having killed many Tamils, was born in the Tusita heaven.[14]

An elderly, exceptionally learned monk mentioned the 'sign of *kamma*' (*kammanimitta*) and illustrated this with a story: an alcoholic on his death bed saw bottles of soft drinks in his room which were meant for the invited monks (as *gilaṃpasa*).[15] Due to his previous bad *kamma* he mistook these for liquor bottles, died overcome with greed and was reborn in a miserable place. His bad lifestyle and bad habitual *kamma* had brought about an unfavourable frame of mind at the moment of death.[16]

Laypeople, too, said that it is better to die consciously and two of the interviewees said that people who die in sudden accidents go to an intermediate state before they can be reborn. Again it was unanimously agreed that the frame of mind at the moment of death is the determining factor for the place of rebirth. To die in an angry frame of mind might—even for very virtuous people—result in rebirth as a *perētayā* or in another low or unpleasant existence. One example for this case was King Aśoka, who was allegedly born as a snake due to anger (*kēntiya*) arising at the moment of death, but was again reborn in a *devalokaya* after only seven days due to his generally good *kamma*.[17]

Similarly, to die in a good, happy frame of mind, remembering meritorious deeds or a word of the Buddha, could, even for a bad person, result in a good rebirth. One interviewee related the story of the mass murderer Aṅgulimāla, who had killed 999 people before he became not only a follower of the Buddha, but an *arahat*.[18] Here one interviewee objected by saying that a truly bad person can never be reborn in a good place straight away.[19]

Moreover, an ex-monk living in Colombo questioned this concept altogether, judging that it was 'unfair' that the dying thought would be the one determining factor for the place of rebirth. Others said that bad people are more likely to die filled with fear, which would bring about a bad dying thought. On the other hand, it was occasionally mentioned that a good dying thought can even cancel out past bad *kamma*, making it disappear (*näti venavā*). In Abhidhamma terms, however, it is not a question of good *kamma* 'cancelling out' bad *kamma*, but rather of certain *kamma* (good or bad) not coming to fruition, as for example all the *kamma* of an *arahat* becomes defunct on his passing away.[20]

However, the general opinion, both on the part of the monks as well as of the laypeople, was that previous *kamma* will come to fruition eventually, which is in agreement with the Abhidhamma. One monk illustrated this with a simile: the dying thought is like an air ticket to a nice place, but without money (i.e., sufficiently good *kamma*) one will not be able to stay there for very long.

Interestingly, one interviewee, a middle-class woman from a suburb of Colombo, told me, 'We pray (*prārthanā karanavā*) every day that our thought at the moment of death may be good.'[21] She explained this to me as a kind of meditative reflection on death and repeatedly used the term *prārthanā*. However, this was not mentioned by anyone else, and I doubt that it is common practice in the village.

Looking at the interview material as a whole, it was striking that there was very little diversity in the replies, which generally conformed very closely to traditional Theravāda doctrine. If we assume that the knowledge of Buddhist matters of ordinary village people is mainly acquired in the *dharma* school and from sermons, we can conclude that this is a topic extensively taught to laypeople.

When things go wrong: on **prētas**

Most people I interviewed agreed that under certain circumstances people can be reborn (or return) as 'ghosts', but it took further probing to get more detailed information. My information about spirits haunting a house, etc., derives almost exclusively from interviews conducted in Sinhala, as there seemed to be a certain reluctance on the side of English-speaking interviewees to talk about this topic. This might be for a number of reasons.

First, it is rather difficult to translate the various Sinhala terms for 'ghost' (and the underlying concepts) into English. Second, it might be felt that it is difficult for a foreigner to enter the world of cosmology with its gods, demons, higher and lesser deities. And thirdly, the English speakers amongst the interviewees tended to be more Western educated and orientated and took a more 'rational approach' to the questions posed. In interviews conducted in Sinhala, on the other hand, the picture was very different and much more in favour of 'ghost stories'. This made it desirable to stick to Sinhala as much as possible.

Terminology: Sinhala yakā/bhūtayā/prētayā/perētayā. The terminology applied in the context of these 'ghost stories' does not seem clearly defined. A rather general term for 'ghost', which is frequently used in conversation, is *bhūta*. There are, however, two terms, which are more specifically used in the context of death: *maḷayakā* (pl. *maḷayakku*) and *prētayā/perētayā* or even *maḷaprētayā*. The *maḷayakku* are the most powerful and can actually harm or help people according to their inclination. One needs a certain amount of merit to gain such a powerful position and not every *bhūtayā* makes it. Merit given to a dead relative who happens to be a *maḷayakā* will actually strengthen his/her position. *Prētas* on the other hand are usually regarded as rather weak and depend for their very sustenance on merit given to them by their living relatives. They can, however, make a small child ill by looking at his food, as one informant told me.[22] This seems to be the basic hierarchy most people agreed on, but, as Gombrich (1991, 188–196) points out, the distinction between these classes of beings is somewhat blurred, and there are differences with regard to usage and understanding of these terms in up country and low country.[23] My informants talked in the context of a troublesome ghost who needed to be dealt with, only occasionally of *bhūtayā* and *yakā* (or *maḷayakā*), but most often of *prētas*.

Terminology: Sanskrit preta/pitṛ; *Pāli* peta; *Sinhala* prētayā/perētayā. Let me briefly outline the development and various stages beginning with Sanskrit: the past participle from the root *pra* √*i*, *preta* (mfn.), which literally means 'gone away', came to mean 'departed, deceased, dead, a dead person'.[24] In the course of time the term acquired another, more specialized meaning, namely, 'the spirit of a dead person (esp. before obsequial rites are performed), a ghost, an evil being' and 'a newly dead' as opposed to 'ancestor' (*pitṛ*, m.).[25] *Preta* can be used generally to mean 'dead', or in a more technical sense, 'newly dead, ghost'.

The Pāli term *peta* seems to have preserved some of the ambiguity of Sanskrit *preta*, ('dead' and 'ghost'), and might even have retained traces of the Sanskrit term *pitṛ*. However, the fact that two terms might be conflated linguistically does not necessarily mean that the underlying concepts are conflated as well. Without the *śrāddha* rites, the deceased would remain *pretas* and dangerous for the living, and Holt (1981, 6) points out that the 'pattern of ritual activity designed to promote the deceased from the status of *pretas* to *pitṛ* was prevalent before the emergence of specifically Buddhist conceptions'. It is therefore difficult to argue that the distinction between *preta* and *pitṛ*, which is of great importance in the Indian context, would not have been known as well. Besides, even though *peta* sometimes only means 'dead' (possibly with the connotation of ancestor), in the majority of cases it refers to a hungry ghost belonging to a particular Buddhist *gati*. It appears that *peta* has historically developed out of the *preta* ('newly dead ghost') and retained certain of its features (perpetual hunger, misery, and need of support).

According to Clough's *Sinhala English Dictionary* (1892), all the connotations discussed so far ('dead, spirit of a dead person, fathers') were still to be found in Sinhala *prēta* at the end of the nineteenth century.[26] However, as Sinhala *prētayā/perētayā* is a loan word from Sanskrit, one might suspect that either Clough (or his source) was influenced by the Sanskrit connotations, or else, some of the connotations may have been lost since the late 19th century.

Whatever the case may be, people referred to *prētas* frequently, either in a rather general way as 'ghosts' or in the more technical meaning of the specific class of beings (*gati*). None of my informants used *prēta/perēta* as meaning 'dead' and there seemed to be no trace of the connotation *pitṛ*.

As far as the connotation of the Sinhala term *prēta* is concerned, the case seems to be reasonably clear cut. Unfortunately, the underlying notions and ideas are more complex as these *prētas* are grouped together or associated with rather different beings (gods, crows, *yakku*) and treated in a variety of ways depending on the context, as we shall see later.[27]

Different types of prētas. When speaking about troublesome ghosts I will only use the term *prēta* unless the specific context requires a distinction. A *prētayā* (or *maḷayakā* for that matter) can cause disturbances in the house like opening drawers, carrying things (pens, etc.) through the room; they are often said to throw stones at a house and even chew betel and spit the red juice into the house. They are usually angry with a member of their family, and follow the person around, making their presence felt.

Wirz (1941, 202) distiguishes between three types of *prētas* according to their dwelling place and behaviour: the *ñati-prēteo* (*ñati*, 'relative') cannot let go of their loved ones; the *maḷa-prēteo* (*maḷa*, 'dead') have as prefered dwelling places cemeteries and crossroads; the *gevala-prēteo* (*geval*, 'houses') are ghosts who cannot bring themselves to leave their previous homes. Wirz (1941, 202) not only provides detailed descriptions but also drawings of male, female, and infant *prētas*.

According to Tillakaratne (1986, 130), *prētas* can cause diseases, which they do if neglected by their relatives, but are generally easy to please. I was frequently told by people that *prētas* are always hungry and thirsty and cannot feed or clothe themselves. Some informants added that this is reflected in their outer appearance as they have long, thin necks and huge bellies.[28] This concept of hungry ghosts is, of course, not confined to Sri Lanka, but found all over South Asia.[29]

How to become a prēta. Most people said that being overly agitated, angry, greedy, envious or malicious at the moment of death is thought to lead to a rebirth in a 'bad place' (*naraka täna*). Some interviewees, however, were more specific and mentioned the possibility that the departed might return as a *bhūtayā*, *maḷayakā* or *prētayā* to haunt a house or a specific family member. The most frequently mentioned cause for becoming a *prēta* was a greedy disposition at the time of death.[30] Being overly attached to loved ones, too, can lead to becoming a *prētayā* or *prētī*, and the classic example here is a mother who dies a sudden, untimely death leaving behind a small child.[31] Obeyesekere 1984, 69 reports the case of a woman who had died failing to say her farewell to her granddaughter and turned into a troublesome ancestor. Tillakaratne (1986, 154) mentions another possible cause for becoming a *prēta*: elderly people seeking revenge after death when they feel they have been neglected during their lifetime. *Prētas* are regarded as particularly pitiable, but nevertheless have to be dealt with as they can cause trouble (see also III.2.1.2).

Excursus: pirit *chanting in contemporary Sri Lanka*

The custom of *pirit* chanting seems to be the most important feature of the pre-death rituals.[32] It is, however, by no means confined to the death context, and indeed, Gombrich (1991, 242) remarks on the 'extremely unspecific nature of the ceremony':

> *Pirit* is used at a sick bed, to commemorate a death, to consecrate a new building, to avert a public misfortune, to celebrate the opening of Parliament, or simply to acquire merit.

According to the occasion, *pirit* ceremonies also vary greatly in length (ranging from one hour to one week) and the number of *suttas* recited. The above-mentioned three *suttas* (*Mahāmaṅgalasutta*, *Karaṇīyamettasutta*, *Ratanasutta*) followed by a few stanzas from the *Mahājayamaṅgalagāthā* form what is referred to as *maha pirita* in Sri Lanka, and either constitutes a complete *pirit* ceremony in itself or the beginning and end of a longer ceremony.

As Gombrich points out (1991, 240), the use of certain *suttas* as *pirit* is canonical. Even accounts of the use of *piritnūla* and *pirit* water, are old, though not canonical, and already found in the commentarial Pāli literature.[33] Three *suttas* are connected with a specific purpose. The first one, the *Aṅgulimālasutta*, is recited for a pregnant woman with the intention of easing her labour pains.[34] The rationale behind this is the concept of ritual power (Pāli, Sinhala: *ānubhāva*) created by way of uttering an important truth (*satyavacana/satyavākya*), which is repeated nowadays by the monks reciting this sutta. The concept of *satyavacana* (the same idea is expressed in Pāli as *saccakiriyā*) is, of course, an old one, dating back to Vedic times as has been pointed out by various scholars.[35]

Palihawadana (1997, 505f.) investigates the Vedic origins and traces back the *pirit* chanting to the practice of *svādhyāya/sajjhāya*:

> The same idea about the power of truth utterance is found in Buddhist texts. An early instance of this is the *Majjhima Nikāya* reference (II 102 f.) to Aṅgulimāla relieving a woman's pains of birth by the simple invocation of the truth of his desisting from violence 'since I was born by the Aryan birth' (i.e., his conversion by the Buddha). But specifically 'truth' in the Buddhist case is the Buddha-word as expressed in the Buddhist Suttas. Re-telling that is a source of protection. That is why bhikkhus recite Suttas. . . . A specifically Buddhist theory of validating ritual recitation is that it has power because it is recited by monks with *mettā* (kindness/friendliness) towards beings, or because it invokes the 'power of *mettā*' of the Buddhas.[36]

The 'ritual efficacy' of truth, which is inherent in the *sutta*s can be applied to various situations, as the example of Aṅgulimāla shows.[37] However, one of the main functions of *pirit* chanting is that of protection (*rakkhā*), especially from evil influences of non-human beings.

The *Āṭānāṭiyasutta* (D III 194ff.) is the second *sutta*, which is connected with a specific purpose: protection from ghosts (*pretas* or *yakṣas*) (see III.2.1.2.). Schmithausen (1997, 36, n.75) observes:

> It is interesting that, e.g., in the *Āṭānāṭiyasutta* . . . —a text called 'protection' (*rakkhā*) consisting of a laudatory hymn and intended to protect monks, nuns and pious lay followers (and especially such as have retired into the wilderness) against malevolent *spirits*, who are doubtless dangerous to humans but not on their part endangered by them—friendship or friendliness is not mentioned as a means to pacify them. It is rather by reminding them of the superiority of the Buddha(s) and because they will otherwise be dishonoured, excluded from their community and even have their heads split by fellow-spirits . . . that these spirits are dissuaded from molesting or attacking pious Buddhists.[38]

Thirdly there is a group of three so-called *Bhojjaṅgasutta*s; Mahākassapattherabojjhaṅga (S V 79), Mahāmoggalānattherabojjhaṅga (S V 80), and Mahācundattherabojjhaṅga (S V 81) which are associated with relief from illnesses. They are found in all the *paritta* collections, constitute part of the overnight recitals and are, according to some informants, recited at the sick bed of a patient.[39] After quoting a number of examples from the Suttas de Silva (1993, 33) concludes: 'There seems to be a belief that attention paid to doctrinal topics, especially the recitation of virtues which one has already cultivated in one's personality, is endowed with healing properties.'

Besides the ritual efficacy of *satyavacana* there is another aspect: *pirit* chanting and listening to *pirit* are meritorious deeds according to the Abhidhamma (in the category of *desanā*).[40] Gombrich (1991, 242) points out that the belief in the positive effect of chanting at someone's sickbed is problematic:

> To earn merit in any way, including this, will improve one's *karma*, but *karma* is a long-range affair, and there is no reason why the merit just gained should take immediate effect, so as to make a sick man well. To say that *pin* can cancel out *pav* is in fact a heresy, discussed at the beginning of Chapter 5. Indeed, if one is thinking in terms of *karma* the presumption must be rather the other way: if a man is ill because of a past sin he will go on being ill till the sin is expiated, despite any *ad hoc* remedial action. In the case of misfortune, to explain *pirit* as 'merit in a hurry' will therefore not wash.

The problem of how the chanting of *pirit* can be explained as effective is intrinsically an Abhidhamma problem, and we shall, as suggested by Gombrich, turn to the Buddhist tradition itself in search of an answer.[41] Cancelling out past bad *kamma* or acquiring 'merit in a hurry' are not the only way to improve one's karmic conditions instantly. According to the Abhidhamma, every being has a store of good and bad *kamma*, and it is rather a question of which particular *kamma* comes to fruition at any given time. By chanting *pirit* or venerating the Triple Gem (which is in a sense the most basic form of *pirit*) one can therefore tip the balance in favour of good *kamma*, which is, according to the Abhidhammatthavibhāvinī Ṭīkā, conducive to warding of dangers, etc. That is to say, favourable conditions are being set up so that good resultants of past deeds can arise.

> Therein teachers elaborate in many ways on the usefulness of venerating the Triple Gem, but they predict in particular the preventing of dangers. Hence the authors of the summaries have stated that by its power dangers are stopped. As to its meaning, veneration of the Triple Gem is the wholesome volition that produces the act of venerating. It is to be experienced in this life as the success of the store of meritorious *kamma* of those venerated and those venerating: by virtue of supporting the *kamma* that is the ground for accomplishments already gained, it inhibits 'obstructive' and 'destructive' *kammas*, which are obstacles to the flow of the results produced by that [wholesome] *kamma*, and brings about the non-occurrence of the obstacles of disease, etc., which block the aforementioned success and have their origin in that [unwholesome] *kamma*.
>
> (Gethin 2002, 3; Abhidh-s-mhṭ 54)

Based on this passage I can see no grounds for assuming that the idea that chanting at a sick bed can bring about improvement is non-doctrinal. However, I am not sure how widespread it is in Sri Lanka to call a monk to chant *pirit* at the sick bed with the intention to make the patient better. The chanting of *pirit* at the deathbed is, on the other hand, very popular. According to the Abhidhamma, cancelling *kamma* is not the issue, but rather which particular *kamma* comes to fruition at the moment of death. Gethin (1994, 11–35 (21)) explains—mainly, but not solely, based on the Abhidhammatthasaṅgaha (p. 24) and Abhidhammatthavibhāvinī Ṭīkā (pp. 130–31)—the karmic process at the moment of death:

> Essentially the nature of *bhavaṅga* for a given lifetime is determined by the last full consciousness process of the immediately preceding life. This last process is in turn strongly influenced and directly conditioned by—though it is, of course, not its *result* in the technical sense of *vipāka*—the *kamma* performed by the being during his or her life. Relevant here is a fourfold classification of *kamma* according to what will take precedence in ripening and bearing fruit. The four varieties are 'weighty' (*garuka*), 'proximate' (*āsanna*), 'habitual' (*bahula*, *āciṇṇa*), 'performed' (*kaṭattā*). This list is explicitly understood as primarily relevant to the time of death. In other words, it is intended to answer the question: at the time of death, which of the many *kammas* a being has performed during his or her lifetime is going to bear fruit and condition rebirth? The answer is that if any 'weighty' *kammas* have been performed then these must inevitably come before the mind in some way and overshadow the last consciousness process of a being's life. But if there are no weighty *kammas* then, at least according to the traditions followed by the *Abhidhammattha-saṅgaha*, some significant act recalled or done at the time of death will condition the rebirth. In the absence of this, that which has been done repeatedly and habitually will play the key role. Failing that, any repeated act can take centre-stage at the time of death.

Provided no bad *garuka-kamma* (such as killing a parent, etc.) comes in the way, and provided the dying person responds by turning his mind to the *pirit*, this could actually make a difference with regard to the next rebirth. The chanting of *pirit*, of course, can only create conditions conducive to a 'positive' dying thought, which in itself qualifies as *kamma* (under the category of *āsanna*). Ultimately, it depends on the dying person himself which *kamma* comes to fruition at the moment of death.

Gombrich (1991, 257) describes a 'positive dying thought' as a *prārthanā*, a religious or earnest wish. These *prārthanā*s are part of most religious and merit-making activities and usually 'granted' by a monk at the end of a ceremony with the formula 'May your wishes be fulfilled . . .' (*icchitaṃ patthitaṃ* . . .). In this case the wishes for oneself are not made publicly and they are not necessarily of a religious nature. They can be made in private as well, without a monk as mediator and even outside the context of a religious ceremony either for oneself or for someone else. Someone might make a religious wish without articulating it after returning from a pilgrimage.

However, in the ceremonies I attended the wish seemed to be pre-formulated by a monk and differed very little from ceremony to ceremony, always wishing for rebirth in pleasant human and divine existences and eventually attainment of *nirvāṇa* in the company of the Buddha Maitreya.[42] This wish was formulated first for the dead, then for the gods (usually the appropriate verse was chanted as well), and finally for everyone present. This was confirmed every time by people saying *sādhu*, *sādhu*, *sādhu*, and sometimes, but not always, followed by the monk reciting the above-mentioned verse (*icchitaṃ patthitaṃ* . . .) to which again everyone responds with *sādhu*, *sādhu*, *sādhu*.

Gombrich (1991, 257) suggests that the *prārthanās* might have originated from the death wish as 'an attempt to mitigate the rigour of *karma*'. Again, as in the case of *pirit* chanting at a sickbed, he raises the question of how far it is justified to assume that the death wish can bring about 'sudden improvement'.

Death, like childbirth, is a potentially dangerous transitional period for which the people involved need protection and guidance. Even if it could be proved that no 'sudden improvement' can be experienced, the listening to chanting might still be ritually effective in the sense of *satyavacana*. Or it might be hoped that the protective aspect (*rakkhā*) of the *pirit* chanting might ward off evil influences from the side of non-human beings (such as *yakṣas* and *pretas*) at a particularly vulnerable moment in one's life.[43]

It seems to me more likely that the various aspects are present as a complex whole in people's minds (with stress on one or the other depending on the occasion) and that it is precisely this complexity that accounts for the high popularity of *pirit* chanting.

Some historical roots: time of death

Inscriptional evidence indicates that the practice of actively preparing for death goes back at least to the time of Aśoka (third century BC), probably further. Aśoka granted a period of three days between the death sentence and the execution of the prisoner specifically for that purpose:

> My order goes even so far that a reprieve of three days is granted by me to fettered persons who are convicted and sentenced to death. Their relatives will plead with someone for their life, or if

> they do not plead, they will offer alms or undergo fasting for their next world. My desire is indeed thus: That they may accomplish the next world, even when the time expires, and that different dharma-practices, self-discipline and distribution of alms increase among people also.[44]
>
> (Guruge 1997, 274, Aśoka's pillar edict IV)

The term 'different dharma practices' (*vividhe dhammacalane*) may refer to different Buddhist practices, or those of other religious groups and in fact nothing in the wording of Aśoka's edict indicates that his ruling is meant for Buddhists only. The most natural reading of this passage seems to be that Aśoka responded to a common need in his subjects to prepare for death, whatever their beliefs.

A post-canonical piece of evidence for the actual customs and ceremonies is found in the Visuddhimagga:

> In another's case, relatives present [objects to him] at the five sense doors, such as a visible datum as object, perhaps flowers, garlands, flags, banners [sic!], etc., saying 'This is being offered to the Blessed One for your sake, dear, set your mind at rest'; or a sound as object, perhaps, preaching of the Dhamma, offerings of music, etc.; or an odour as object, perhaps incense, scents, perfumes, etc.; or a taste as object perhaps honey, molasses, etc., saying 'Taste this, dear, it is a gift to be given for your sake'; or a tangible datum as object, perhaps Chinese silk, silk of Somāra, saying 'Touch this, dear, it is a gift to be given for your sake'.[45]
>
> (Bhikkhu Ñānamoli 1956, 634; Vism 550)

This passage is particularly interesting because it seems very close to what my Sri Lankan informants had told me (presenting flowers, incense, etc., recitation of the Dhamma, etc.). Two former monks had even mentioned honey should be placed on the tongue of a dying man, but could not recollect, where this piece of information had come from. This suggests that my interviewees were partly describing normative behaviour and if this is indeed the case, the Visuddhimagga as a source cannot be excluded. Buddhaghosa's chief work is one of the main reference books that monks in Sri Lanka turn to, and its influence on the Buddhist monks and lay people who listen to the sermons in the temples or on the radio and television in Sri Lanka cannot be overestimated.[46] There are, of course, other sources for sermons and stories, but these are not always easy to trace. Aggacitta Bhikkhu (1999, 37) relates a story which is set 'in Sri Lanka during the heyday of Theravada Buddhism, when there were reputedly many arahants still around'. The story runs as follows: an exhunter is haunted by visions of a fierce black dog on his deathbed. To calm him down, his son, an Arahant, orders that flowers be offered to the Buddha and has his dying father carried to the temple to rejoice in the offering.[47]

The Tibetan tradition, too, has a long history of giving special significance to the time of death (and beyond). Most people will have heard of the so-called 'Tibetan Book of the Dead', a translation of a body of teachings known in Tibetan as Bardo Tödrol Chenmo (lit. 'great liberation through hearing in the *bar do*').[48] Sogyal Rinpoche, a contemporary incarnated Lama (*sprul sku*) of the Tibetan *rnying ma* tradition and founder of a number of Rigpa centres in Europe and North America, put these teachings in a wider context in a readable guidebook for contemporary Buddhists.[49] On a theoretical level Sogyal Rinpoche (1992, 223) seems to go a step further when he talks of actually 'transforming' and 'purifying' one's *kamma* at the moment of death.[50] Death is depicted as providing a unique opportunity to change our fate and make a new start with a better, purer *kamma*.[51]

A similar motif of death as an opportunity for radical change in karmic conditions is found in the Japanese Pure Land tradition, where the reciting of the Buddha's name (*Nianfo*) throughout one's lifetime, but particularly when death is near, is conducive to being reborn in the Pure Land. However, according to Stevenson (1995, 368), not only the recitation, but also meditation (*samādhi*) is crucial in ensuring rebirth in Sukhāvatī, the Buddhist paradise.[52]

These examples show how much importance and weight were given to the time of death by the various Buddhist traditions.[53] However, the picture would not be complete without mentioning another, far less prominent, strand of Indian thought which placed the emphasis on the moment of conception. Here it is the *kamma* of the parents that plays the main role in determining the nature of the being, which is about to be conceived, or to 'enter the womb'. Doniger O'Flaherty (1980, 22) sees this as a 'variant' of the belief described above and observes that the *Garuḍa Purāṇa*:

> places more emphasis upon the consciousness of the father himself: 'Whatever a man has on his mind at the time of impregnation, a creature born of such a nature (*svabhāva*) will enter the womb.' . . . just as, in the Upaniṣads, a man is exhorted to meditate appropriately while begetting his offspring in order to get the kind he has in mind.[54]

However, as this is not a concept, which I came across in Sri Lanka, I wish to return to the more common concept that one's dying thought determines the quality of one's next rebirth. From this originate a number of questions: How far can this concept be traced back? What is the relationship between death and the force of *karman*? What picture can we gain from the canonical and post-canonical Pāli material? How does the Abhidhamma interpretation of the death process relate to these questions?[55]

The Vedic and brahmanical material

When I was searching the Sanskrit texts for material, two things become apparent: first, rebirth, central as it is to Indian philosophy, is not found in the earliest texts; and second, rebirth and *karman* do not appear to be linked together from the beginning. In fact, originally *karman* seems to have been only one of several concepts connected with rebirth, but in the course of time it proved to be more popular than others.[56] One of these 'other concepts' linked with rebirth is a curious notion of 'rebirth according to one's wish', sometimes referred to in the texts as *kāmacāra*. The wish—variously referred to in the texts as *kāma* or *kratu*—is directed to a particular form or place of rebirth and can be spontaneous (at the time of death) or cultivated for a long time. This understanding seems to have some affinity with the Buddhist notion that a mental effort, a positive state of mind, can bring about a good rebirth.

The earliest evidence for the concept of 'rebirth according to one's wish' is found in the Brāhmaṇas (ŚB 10.6.3, GB 1.1.15 and 1.3.22, and JUB 3.28) and Upaniṣads (BĀU 4.4.4, ChU 3.17.6, PU 3,9 and 10), and there is also evidence in the later epic literature (Bhagavadgītā 8.5 and 6). As dating of Indian texts is rather uncertain, I will concentrate on the possible development of the concepts rather than attempt to present the material in a strict chronological order.

A number of scholars have touched upon the problem of 'rebirth according to one's wish'. Edgerton (1924) deals briefly with it in the context of his comparative study on the time of death in all the major religions. Frauwallner (1953, 65) mentions the concept in passing in the context of the history of the various Indian systems and doctrines.[57] Both authors mainly refer to ŚB 10.6.3.1 for the earliest evidence and Bhagavadgītā 8.5 and 6 for the later period. As for the somewhat more recent literature, Horsch (1971, 106) and Schmithausen (1995) both utilize the same set of passages: JUB 3.28, GB 1.1.15 and 1.3.22, SāmavBr 3.8.1, as well as BĀU 4.4.4 and ChU 3.17.6 for a discussion of *karman*.

These few examples will suffice to demonstrate that first, scholars seem to rely on the same set of passages for early evidence, and second, they agree that the concept survived and left traces in the Epos (Bhagavadgītā) and (more importantly for the present study) in Buddhism.[58] I will attempt to trace the concept of 'rebirth according to one's wish' from the Brāhmaṇas and Upaniṣads to Buddhist literature, and finally, to the contemporary Buddhist practice in Sri Lanka.

Vedic background

In earliest Vedic times, as Horsch (1971, 106) points out, burial was customary amongst the Indians and Iranians,[59] and presumably one's destiny after death was thought of as a dark and shadowy underworld, comparable to the Greek Hades. There seems to have been only one underworld without differentiation in terms of rich/poor, initiated/uninitiated, etc. As an alternative to this dark shadowy underworld, the return to one's own family was desirable. It was, according to Schmithausen (1995, 50), widespread not only outside but inside India in pre-Upaniṣadic times and the return was believed to occur automatically and not dependent on special sacrifices or knowledge.[60]

According to Horsch (1971, 107) the picture changed when the belief in a lighter, brighter afterlife (modelled very closely after happier aspects of this life), as expressed in the myth of Yama, came up. He further suggests that this shift is connected with a change in funeral customs from burial to cremation. It is not quite clear, however, if only those who can afford a cremation and the associated rituals ascend to heaven, while those who cannot afford them descend into the underworld.[61]

Besides, the fact that heaven was modelled after this life (and more generally after the cycles of nature) led to the idea that eventually the dead had to 'die again'. The concept of redeath historically precedes the doctrine of rebirth, and it has been commonly assumed so far that there is a historical connection between the concepts of redeath (*punarmṛtyu*) and return (*punarāvṛtti*).[62] Bodewitz (1996, 35), however, doubts that such a causal and historical connection exists. Logically, of course, rebirth can only happen on the basis of redeath, whereas redeath does not necessarily imply rebirth. After examining the passages where *punarmṛtyu* occurs, Bodewitz (1996, 46) concludes:

> It is evident that the concept of *punarmṛtyu*, which is almost exclusively found in passages where its defeat is described, should be interpreted in the context of an antagonism between ritualism and other paths leading to final bliss. The defeat of *punarmṛtyu* is the answer of the ritualists (the Brahmins) to the challenge of the non-ritualists who say that ultimately everybody will die in the heaven promised by the Brahmins.

Whatever the solution (ritual or non-ritual), the common problem was to avoid return (or possibly several returns?) to this world. Alternating between this and the other world constitutes the older stratum of the doctrine of rebirth.[63] Only now the return to this world is not desired any more, but endured as an intermediate state between heavenly existences. Besides, the return to one's own family was only desirable for the few who were comfortably well off, and with the class system becoming more rigid, it became common to aspire to return into a family of higher social status than one's own.[64] People aspired to return to places of their choice and one of the goals for the afterlife was the free choice of and movement between various places of rebirth in both this and the other world. This is, according to

Schmithausen, the first strand of Indian belief, but before I investigate its goal, 'free movement' (*kāmacāra*), I will briefly outline another strand of Indian philosophy.[65]

When the alternating between here and there came to be regarded as unsatisfactory, a new goal finds its expression in the Upaniṣads: the final escape from the suffering of redeath. Here two models are found, both involving a 'doorman' guarding the entrance to eternal freedom from death. Frauwallner (1953, 52–55) named the first doctrine 'water doctrine' (Wasserlehre), because it is largely modelled after the water cycle in nature. According to this doctrine, which is found in the first chapter of the Kauśītaki Upaniṣad, the dead have to get past the moon by answering various questions in order to be allowed into the Brahma world where there is no more death.[66] An extension of this doctrine is the well-known teaching of the two (or three) paths (ChU 5, BĀU 6.2): the dead follow different paths from the start and no guardian or 'doorman' is needed. Only the ones who know or who practise asceticism in the forest will follow the path of the gods (*devayāna*) that leads them by way of the flame of the funeral pyre to the sun and the Brahma world. Those who do not have the required knowledge and those who live in the village follow the path of the ancestors (*pitṛyāna*), which leads by way of the smoke to the moon and back to earth (via wind, rain, and the food chain). The third path is for those who cannot achieve either of the other two and leads to repeated rebirth as worms, insects, etc.

In the second model, named 'fire doctrine' (Feuerlehre) by Frauwallner (1953, 60ff.), the sun (the cosmic equivalent to body heat)[67] has the function of being the door to and guardian of the other world, and only those who know are allowed through into eternal bliss and light.

To sum up, there are two broad strands of belief concerning the afterlife found side by side in the Upaniṣads. The first (JUB 3.28, BĀU 4.4.4) is the belief that the dead go through various stages to the sun or moon, but not beyond that, and the goal of this path lies in freedom of movement between these various places according to one's wish. The second strand (JB 1.17–18; JUB 3.14.1–6 and 4.14; KU 1.1; ChU 5, BĀU 6.2) now opens up the possibility of going beyond the sun or moon, and the goal here is to enter the eternal bliss of the Brahma world.

Brāhmaṇas and older Upaniṣads

As mentioned above, the earliest evidence seems to be a passage in the Śatapatha-Brāhmaṇa, which shall, therefore, serve as a starting point:

> Now, man here, indeed, is possessed of understanding [*kratu*], and according to how great his understanding is when he departs this world, so does he, on passing away, enter the yonder world.[68]
>
> (Eggeling 1966, 400; ŚB 10.6.3.1)

And in another Śatapatha-Brāhmaṇa passage it is said (albeit without explicit reference to rebirth):

> Mitra and Varuṇa, forsooth, are his intelligence and will; and as such belonging to his self: whenever he desires anything in his mind, as 'Would that this were mine! I might do this!', that is intelligence [*kratu*]; and whenever that is accomplished, that is will. Now intelligence indeed is Mitra, and will is Varuṇa; and Mitra is the priesthood, and Varuṇa the nobility; and the priesthood is the conceiver and the noble is the doer.[69]
>
> (Eggeling 1966, 269; ŚB 4.1.4.1)

The key term *kratu* is well documented from the times of the Ṛgveda and the *Monier Williams Sanskrit English Dictionary* gives a wide range of meanings including 'plan, intention, resolution, determination, purpose', but also 'desire, will, power, ability', and 'intelligence, understanding'. Edgerton (1927, 223) comments on Eggeling's translation of *kratu*:

> Eggeling translates it 'understanding', but with an alternative, 'will, purpose.' which is more in accord with the Hindu commentator on the passage, who says *kratu* means *niścaya*, *adhyavasāya*, that is, 'fixed determination'. It seems to mean man's mental constitution as a whole, his total 'frame of mind', but with a strong flavour of will, conscious purpose, or determination.[70]

Schmithausen (1995, 55f.) defines *kratu* as '[meditatively cultivated] will or resolve [to become (or do) something]', and Horsch (1971, 131), too, opting for 'will', interprets the above-quoted passage in terms of an internalisation of ritual, a shift from ritual activities to the underlying intention.

The will (*kratu*) seems to be the driving force in acquiring a particular form of existence from which various questions arise: First, when is the wish made? Would it be effective if one were to cultivate it only on one's deathbed? How long before death does one have to cultivate that will? And second, are there any other conditions or restrictions? Who can cultivate the will and who cannot? What happens to those who have not cultivated a wish?

The Sāmavidhāna Brāhmaṇa prescribes a chant (*sāman*) for those who wish to 'wander consciously through all existences',[71] which has to be practised always (*sadā*) and has to be remembered at the time of death (*antavelāyāṃ* rendered by the commentary as *prāṇaniryāṇakāle*).

> Wer wünscht [*kāmayeta*]: 'möchte ich mit Bewußtsein alle Existenzen durchwandern', der soll immer das Sāman zu 'erwecke uns heute zu Großem' anwenden und in der Todesstunde daran denken: mit Bewußtsein wird er alle Existenzen durchwandern.[72]
>
> (Konov 1893, 76; SāmavBr 3.7.1)

In this passage the term *kratu* is not mentioned and the element of wish is expressed in the finite verb form *kāmayeta*. The quotation is interesting for several reasons: it confirms the aspect of 'rehearsal' by repeated use of a particular chant. Besides, it says explicitly that the chant has to be evoked and remembered at the time of death, and finally, it places the concept of 'rebirth according to one's wish' in the realm of ritualistic and esoteric knowledge.

Let us now turn to what is probably the most quoted passage in the context of 'rebirth according to one's wish':

> 'To what?' 'To the world of *brahman*.' It carries him forth to the sun. 2. He says to the sun: 'Carry me forth.' 'To what?' 'To the world of *brahman*.' It carries him forth to the moon. He thus wanders to and fro between these divinities. 3. This is the end. There is no carrying forth beyond this [limit]. And all the worlds beyond this [limit] of which we have spoken, they are all obtained, they are conquered, in all of them there is unrestricted movement [*kāmacāra*] for him who knows thus. 4. If he should wish: 'May I be born here again,' on whatever family he might fix his thoughts, be it a Brāhman-family, be it a royal family, into that he is born. 'He keeps on ascending to this[73] world again fore-knowing.'[74]
>
> (Oertel 1894, 188; JUB 3.28)

Whereas the previous passage spoke of preparation for the time of death, the scene described here takes place after death. The dead person reaches the sun and moon (presumably by way of the funeral pyre or sacrificial fire) and his quest for the Brahma world remains unanswered (unless sun and moon are representing the Brahma world here), but he has 'unrestricted movement' to go where he wishes (*kāmacāra*, from the root *kam*). However, wish alone is not sufficient; a knowledge referred to in a previous passage (*ya evaṃ veda*) appears to be the prerequisite for this achievement.[75] Those who do not possess this special knowledge have to return to this world in the form of rain, according to JUB 4.14. It is also possible that those who cannot afford a cremation are excluded from having a chance to achieve 'rebirth according to one's wish', as well, but the text does not say so in this passage.

To get a step closer to the possible nature of that knowledge, let us take a look at another passage:

> Verily this same syllable is the firm stand of the three-fold knowledge. [Saying] *om* the *hotar* stands firm, [saying] *om* the *adhvaryu*, [saying] *om* the *udgātar*. 7. Verily this same syllable is the triple heaven (?) of the Vedas. The priests having placed the sacrificer in this syllable carry him up together into the heavenly world. Therefore he should recite the afterverse [saying] *om* only.
>
> (Oertel 1894, 180; JUB 3.19.6–7)

Threefold ritual knowledge is the cause for ascending to heaven, but it is guarded carefully from humans by the gods and is only accessible with the help of the three priests. Again, it is possible that the symbolism of the sacrificial fire indicates a funeral pyre, which would exclude those who are not cremated, from the ascent to heaven.

To sum up the findings from the Brāhmaṇas: first, the achievement of 'rebirth according to one's wish' was based purely on ritual knowledge and action (Sāmavidhāna Brāhmaṇa 3.7.1; JUB 3.28; JUB 3.19.6–7) and the involvement of priests. Ethical criteria for one's destiny in the afterlife have not come into the picture yet, and the concept of 'rebirth according to one's wish' appears to predate the concept of ethical *karman*.[76] It is, however, possible that both concepts coexisted in different traditions for a long time.

Let us now turn to two passages in the Upaniṣads: (1) BĀU 4.4.5, 'A man resolves in accordance with his desire, acts in accordance with his resolve, and turns out to be in accordance with his action.' (2) ChU 3.14, 'Now, then, man is undoubtedly made of resolve. What a man becomes on departing from here after death is in accordance with his resolve in this world. So he should make this resolve.'[77]

ChU 3.14 makes clear reference to the departure from this world (*pretya*), and even though death is not mentioned in BĀU 4.4.5, the preceding paragraph suggests it as the context:

> It is like this. As a weaver, after she has removed the coloured yarn, weaves a different design that is newer and more attractive, so the self, after it has knocked down this body and rendered it unconscious, makes for himself a different figure that is newer and more attractive —the figure of a forefather, or of a Gandharva, or of a god, or of Prajapati, or of *brahman*, or else the figure of some other being.
>
> (Olivelle 1998, 121; BĀU 4.4.4)

In passages such as Sāmavidhāna Brāhmaṇa and BĀU 4.4.5, the wish or resolve has to be cultivated before death; in other passages (such as JUB 3.28) a wish for a particular form of rebirth can even be made after death. It is clear from the various contexts, however, that it takes effect after death with regard to the next rebirth.

The question of possible other conditions requires looking into the wider context of the two Upaniṣadic passages (BĀU 4.4.4, BĀU 4.4.5 and ChU 3.14). BĀU 4.4.5 seems to be concerned with death in general, not just death of the initiated (or cremated), and physical death alone seems to be sufficient to realise the desired existence, as Schmithausen observes.[78] So if it is not knowledge (as in JUB 3.28) that serves as a prerequisite of 'rebirth according to one's wish', what does? BĀU 4.4.5 introduces another factor, namely *karman*. It seems worthwhile comparing the two Upaniṣadic passages BĀU 4.4.5 and ChU 3.14 more closely.[79]

To start with, in BĀU 4.4.5, the emphasis seems to be on desire or wish (*kāma*) rather than on will or resolve (*kratu*). One gets the impression that *kāma* has the connotation of a deep psychological motivation that cannot be controlled here, unlike earlier passages where *kāma* seem to refer to 'choice'. The passage introduces yet another element, e.g., *karman* in the key phrase (*sa yathākāmo bhavati, tatkratur bhavati; yatkratur bhavati, tat karma kurute; yat karma kurute, tad abhisaṃpadyate*). In ChU 3.14, on the other hand, wish (*kāma*) does not feature very prominently and is only mentioned as being contained in *ātman* together with *karman, gandha, rasa*, etc. Here, will or resolve (*kratu*) seems to be seen as the driving force in the rebirth process (*atha khalu kratumayaḥ puruṣo yathākratur asmiṃlloke puruṣo bhavati tathetaḥ pretya bhavati*).[80] This raises the question of the relationship between *kāma* and *kratu*. A number of possibilities come to mind: the two terms might be quasi-synonymous; or *kratu* could be a concrete expression of *kāma* (as psychological motivation); or *kāma* might be a more general term whereas *kratu* is a more technical term for the same process.

Looking at the two phrases, however, one notices first of all that BĀU 4.4.5 (linking *kāma, kratu, karman, abhisaṃpadyate*) reads like a more elaborate version of ChU 3.14 (naming only *kratu* and *bhava*), and second that causal connections are expressed in a style somewhat suggestive of the Buddhist formula of dependent origination (*pratītyasamutpāda*). Arranged in the form of a table the different stages look as follows:

pratītyasamutpāda	BĀU 4.4.5	ChU 3.14
tṛṣṇā	*kāma*	
upādāna	*kratu*	*kratu*
bhava	*karman*	*bhava (as vipāka)*
jāti	*abhisaṃpadyate*	
jarā-maraṇa		

The two descriptions of the rebirth process show similarities: 1. thirst or desire to be reborn; 2. grasping or resolve; 3. actual becoming (*bhava*). According to the commentarial tradition *bhava* has two aspects: 1. karmic conditions for becoming (like *karman* in BĀU 4.4.5), which bring the actual conception into the realm of birth (*jāti*);[81] and 2. the result (*vipāka*) of these karmic conditions, i.e., *bhava* serves as the first moment of the new existence (like *bhava* in ChU 3.14). However, the Buddhist interpretation would be that thirst (*taṇhā*) is responsible for the fact that a being is reborn, and *kamma* i.e., merit or demerit, responsible for the quality of the rebirth.[82] I do not wish to suggest that the commentarial interpretation is in any direct way based on the Upaniṣadic material or vice versa, I wish to merely make an observation of similarity here which may merit further investigation.[83]

In BĀU 4.4.5. 'rebirth according to ones wish' is no longer a direct result of a wish (*kāma*, *kratu*), but of *karman*, which is caused or prompted by the wish. Schmithausen (1995, 57) cautiously interprets BĀU 4.4.5 as an attempt to harmonize the concept that wish determines the after life destiny with the doctrine of *karman*, which in BĀU 4.4.5 might still have the connotation of ritually positive and meritorious deeds.

In the later Upaniṣads a shift from ritual and sacrificial *karman* to ethicised *karman* is apparent, but passages like BĀU 4.4.5 are far from being unambiguous, and *karman* could equally be interpreted as ritual or as retributive action. G. Flood (1996, 86) says: 'In the *Bṛhadāraṇyaka Upaniṣad* retributive action first appears to be a secret and little-known doctrine.' The passage Flood refers to is:

> Yājñavalkya replied: 'My friend, we cannot talk about this in public. Take my hand, Ārtabhāga; let's go and discuss this in private.' So they left and talked about it. And what did they talk about? They talked about nothing but action. And what did they praise? They praised nothing but action. Yājñavalkya told him: 'A man turns into something good by good action and into something bad by bad action.'
>
> (Olivelle 1998, 80; BĀU 3.2.13)

Schmithausen (1995, 56ff.) agrees that what is presented here is indeed the doctrine of ethicised *karman*. Once ethicised *karman* was firmly connected with the rebirth process a number of problems arose, such as the relationship between *karman* and *kāma* (or free-will). W. Doniger O'Flaherty (1980, 13) speaks of *karman* as the 'straw man in the Purāṇas: it is set up to be knocked down' and explains its popularity:

> In the first place, one must not underestimate the value of karma (and fate) as a plot device; karma ex machina explains what cannot otherwise be justified. Thus inconsistencies in character, such as the sufferings of a good man, are explained by reference to karma accumulated in unknowable previous lives—and this also gives the Paurāṇika a chance to drag in another good story, often *bei den Haarn* [*sic*].

We find similar patterns in Buddhist stories. There is, however, an understanding that the most serious offences (harming a Buddha, killing a parent, etc.) produce so-called 'weighty karma' (*garuka-kamma*), which cannot be superseded, but inevitably comes to fruition at the end of the offender's lifetime.

Another question to arise was what serves as the carrier of *karman* from one existence to another. Doniger O'Flaherty (1980, 13) comments:

> At this point, in the classical medical and philosophical texts, the parents are said to retain their role in providing the substance, but the merit is attributed to the soul's previous existence(s); the substance is split off from the code. The Hindus and Buddhists were now forced to postulate a series of mediating elements to connect the body (given by the parents) with its karma (given from the previous life), now that these had been split apart.

To return to 'rebirth according to one's wish', one more passage from Praśna Upaniṣad should be quoted:

> The up-breath is fire. Therefore, when one's fire is extinguished, one returns again to the life breath with the faculties uniting in the mind and whatever thought one then has. United with heat, then, the life breath, together with the self, leads him to the world that accords with his conception.[84]
>
> (Olivelle 1998, 464; PU 3.9–10)

Here the context is clearly the time of death, and the 'thought' or 'thoughts' (*citta*), rather than the wish (*kāma*) or the will or resolve (*kratu*), are the deciding element here when it comes to the place of rebirth. The thought leading to the next place of birth sounds rather Buddhist, and considering that Praśna is said to be post-Buddhist, there might well have been cross influences.

Summary

In the early Vedic period death meant going to the dark underworld, and accordingly, the goal in the afterlife was to return to one's own family. In the course of time the vision of a brighter and more pleasant afterlife destiny came up and the return to this world was seen as an involuntary interim stage. In the Upaniṣads we find two strands with two distinct goals in the afterlife: ascent to the sun and 'rebirth according to one's wish'[85] and the two or three paths (*devayāna, pitṛyāna*) with the ultimate goal of going to the world of Brahman to escape redeath and rebirth.[86] The voluntary intended rebirth in a chosen existence is not to be interpreted as inferior and the means of achieving it was knowledge (most probably ritualistic) imparted by the priest to the sacrificer. This element of an earnest, sometimes rehearsed, wish for a particular existence is referred to in the texts as *kratu* or *kāma*. Some texts (ChU 3.14, ŚB 10.6.3) seem to suggest that the wish for a particular form of rebirth had to be cultivated before death; some texts (JUB 3.28) do not appear to exclude the possibility of making the wish or choice after death.[87]

According to Horsch (1971, 144) and Edgerton (1927, 234), 'rebirth according to one's wish' is historically the older concept and was only later connected with the concept of *karman* (BĀU 4.4.5). At some stage *karman* took on ethical implications and began to be more firmly connected with the rebirth process at the expense of other, competing concepts such as the automatic return into one's family and 'rebirth according to one's wish'. Nevertheless, the concept of 'rebirth according to one's wish' proved extraordinarily resilient, as the textual evidence and contemporary practice show.

The Pāli nikāyas *and some stories from the commentaries*

The continuity of the concept of 'rebirth according to one's wish' from the Upaniṣads to Buddhism and beyond into the epics has already been pointed out. The textual evidence for this concept on the Buddhist side: Majjhima-nikāya (M III 99f.), Jātaka (J I 48), Mahāvastu (MVu I 1), Lalitavistara (Adhy. 3) and Milindapañha (Mil 3,7,2), and for the non-Buddhist side the second-century BC epos Mahābhārata (Bhagavadgītā 8.5 and 6). Considerably more evidence is scattered in a variety of Buddhist texts, but not always easy to locate. The term *kāmacāra* does not seem to occur, nor are there any other obvious key words or technical terms that would facilitate the search. My findings, however incomplete, will suffice to demonstrate that the concept was alive at the time when these texts were composed.

For the Buddhist texts the logical starting point seems to be instances of death in a positive frame of mind followed by a favourable rebirth (in short good death), assuming that was what beings wish for. There are, however, also stories about people getting swept away by emotions and catapulted into a bad existence. I shall, therefore, investigate passages that describe a death accompanied by a bad frame of mind followed by a rebirth in an unpleasant destiny (in short 'a bad death') next. I am particularly interested in finding evidence and explanations of direct causal connection between a person's frame of mind at the time of death and the resulting rebirth. The Abhidhamma interpretation will be investigated in a separate chapter as it represents a particular style and technical language that sets it apart from the Suttas.

Good death

The Saṅgīti Sutta of the Dīgha-nikāya (D III 207–72) which lists, amongst numerous other categories, 'eight kinds of rebirth due to generosity' (*aṭṭha dānuppattiyo*) shall serve as a starting point for an examination of good death:

> [There are] eight kinds of rebirth due to generosity: Here, someone gives an ascetic or Brahmin food, drink, clothes, transport, garlands, perfumes and ointments, sleeping accommodation, a dwelling, or lights, and he hopes to receive a return for his gifts. He sees a rich

> Khattiya or Brahmin or householder living in full enjoyment of the pleasures of the five senses, and he thinks: 'If only when I die I may be reborn as one of these rich people!' He sets his heart on this thought, fixes it and develops it. And this thought, being set (*adhimuttaṃ*) at such a low level (*hīne*),[88] and not developed to a higher level, leads to rebirth right there. But I say this of a moral person, not of an immoral one. The mental aspiration of a moral person is effective through its purity.
>
> (Walshe 1995, 505; D III 258ff.)

One could, of course, argue that this passage is merely about the effect of *kamma*. However, the strong emphasis on the thought (*citta*) of being reborn in a particular existence, which has to be cultivated and developed (*bhāveti*), seems to indicate that this passage is in essence about 'rebirth according to one's wish'. The core is reminiscent of the BĀU and ChU passages discussed above: someone sees an appealing form of existence, such as a rich Kṣatriya, etc. (*kāma* in BĀU 4.4.5 and ChU 3.13), he puts his mind to it (*kratu* in BĀU 4.4.5), and is reborn in that very existence after his death. In the Saṅgīti Sutta 'rebirth according to one's wish' is embedded in the Buddhist ethical framework with good *kamma*—in the shape of meritorious deeds or generosity (*dāna*)—as the basis or starting point and morality (*sīla*) as condition. As we shall see when comparing various passages, generosity may be mentioned before or after formulation of the wish but in any case some form of ethical base seems indispensable.

Resolve: analysis of the Saṅgīti Sutta. I will analyse the structure of the Saṅgīti Sutta and identify the various stages of the 'rebirth according to one's wish': (a) condition(s); (b) prompting the resolution; (c) resolve; (d) assertion of achievement; (e) [additional] condition. This framework will also serve as a base for a comparison with a number of other suttas[89] dealing with the same topic.

First, it seems necessary to give a brief introduction to the Saṃyutta-nikāya as its structure is not always easy to unravel. We are looking at different sets of nearly identical suttas describing how one comes to be reborn as a particular type of *nāga*, *supaṇṇa*, or *gandhabba*. For easy reference and greater clarity I have grouped these as follows:

— *nāga* set 1 (S III 243, i.e., S 29.7–10): describes in almost identical terms how rebirth as one of the four types of *nāga* (egg-born, etc.) is caused merely by seeing and admiring a *nāga* and wishing to be reborn as one.

— *nāga* set 2 (S III 244, i.e., S 29.11–50): consists of almost identical suttas and differs from the first set only in that generosity is practised after wishing for rebirth as a particular *nāga*.

Similarly the Suttas concerning *supaṇṇas*:

— *supaṇṇa* set 1 (S III 247, i.e., S 30.3–6): describes how one might become one of the four types of *supaṇṇa* merely by wishing to.
— *supaṇṇa* set 2 (S III 24–49, i.e., S 30.7–46): differs from *supaṇṇa* set 1 only in that generosity is practised after wishing for rebirth as a particular *supaṇṇa*.

The situation is slightly changed for the *gandhabbas*:

— *gandhabba set* 1 (S III 250, i.e., S 31.2): a short Sutta speaks in general terms of becoming a *gandhabba* merely by wishing to.
— *gandhabba set* 2 (S III 251f, i.e., S 31.3–12): acts of generosity (corresponding to the aspiration) are mentioned after the wish, e.g., to become a '*gandhabba* who dwells in fragrant roots, heartwood, etc., one has to give fragrant roots, etc.
— *gandhabba set* 3 (S III 252f, i.e., S 31.13–22): resembles closely *nāga* and *supaṇṇa* sets 2 in that generosity is mentioned in the form of the standard items that are offered to ascetics.

To facilitate the task of comparing the above mentioned suttas, the different stages that were identified for the Saṅgīti Sutta will serve as a guideline:

(a) The *conditio sine qua non* for 'rebirth according to one's wish' in the Saṅgīti Sutta is generosity (the standard list of items to be offered to ascetics are enumerated: *anna, pāna, . . . seyyāvasathapadīpeyya*) and rebirth in the desired existence is presented as a pay off (*so yaṃ deti taṃ paccāsīsati*). In M I 289ff. the condition is right behaviour and acting in accordance with the Dhamma (*dhammacārī samacārī*); whereas the Saṅkhāruppatti Sutta (M III 99ff.), literally the sutta about 'rebirth according to one's volitions',[90] which is, interestingly, directed towards *bhikkhus*, has a list of five qualities (*saddhā, sīla, suta, cāga, paññā*) required.[91] At S IV 302–304, various tree deities try to persuade the householder (*gahapati*) Citta to make a resolution to become a Cakkavattin (Universal Monarch). They argue that he is *sīlavā kalyāṇadhammo*, and thereby entitled to make such an earnest wish. At *nāga* sets 1 and 2 and *supaṇṇa* sets 1 and 2 the assumption (or condition?) is that the person in question is one 'who acts ambiguously' (*dvayakārī*) through body, speech, and mind. On the other hand, the three *gandhabba* sets take as a starting point a person of 'good conduct (*sucaritaṃ*) of body, speech, and mind'.[92]
(b) An element of prompting the resolve follows next in the Saṅgīti Sutta: someone sees a rich *kṣatriya, brāhmaṇa*, etc., or hears wonderful things about a certain divine form of existence. Almost identical phrasing is found in M III 99, as well as in both *nāga* sets, both *supaṇṇa* sets, and

all three *gandhabba* sets. The exception here is M I 289ff., which does not contain such an element.

(c) The resolution proper is either called *paṇidhi* or *cetopaṇidhi*, or simply *citta*, sometimes glossed as *patthanā* (in the commentaries).[93] In the Saṅgīti Sutta the resolve is expressed in a formula which is repeated verbatim for all eight forms of existence up to the four kings. A similar formula is found in all the suttas, but the lists of the forms of existences differ considerably in length. M I 289 and M III 99 are not only much more detailed in listing different types of *devas*, but Nirvāṇa is named as the final achievement. Other suttas concentrate on only one class of beings (as in *gandhabba* set 1), or even on a particular type of a class of beings (as in *nāga* sets 1 and 2, *supaṇṇa* sets 1 and 2, *gandhabba* sets 2 and 3). S IV 302, too, is rather specifically aiming for rebirth as a *cakkavatti* (rather than a *kṣatriya*).

The formulation of the resolve in the Saṅgīti Sutta is followed by a phrase emphasising the cultivation of the thought (see also M III 99ff.). The importance of the resolve is also emphasised in the commentary to the Saṅkhāruppatti Sutta, where it is stated that the *patthanā* is essential for the achievement.[94] However, none of the suttas explicitly mention the wish as being made at the time of death. Nevertheless, almost all the suttas (with the exception of the Saṅgīti Sutta, and S IV 302) explicitly state that the fulfillment of the wish takes place at death.

(d) Then follows an assertion in the Saṅgīti Sutta, that the rebirth in a particular form of existence, is indeed achieved. The same expression is found at M III 99,[95] while M I 289 merely states that such a 'rebirth according to one's wish' is possible, and the *nāga*, *supaṇṇa*, and *gandhabba sets* again just repeat that the goal is achieved (*upapajjati* rather than *upapajeyya*). In S IV 302, however, the story takes a different turn in that Citta refuses to take the *paṇidhi* and preaches instead to the friends before he dies.

(e) Finally, almost like an afterthought, comes an additional condition in the Saṅgīti Sutta: the resolve *cetopaṇidhi* only works for morally good people due to its[96] 'purity' (*suddhattā*). This formula only changes for the *brahmakāyikā devā*, the lowest of the *rūpadhātu* realms, where overcoming of passion (*vītarāgattā*), which is a requirement for entrance into *rūpadhātu*, is added. The two Majjhima suttas, *nāga* set 1, *supaṇṇa* set 1, and *gandhabba* set 1 do not add any final conditions. However, in *nāga* set 2, *supaṇṇa* set 2, and *gandhabba* set 3 the standard declaration of generosity (*so annam deti . . . padīpeyyaṃ deti*) which occurred at the beginning of the Saṅgīti Sutta is here inserted between the actual resolve and the affirmation. Furthermore, we find an interesting variation in *gandhabba* set 3, where it is said that someone who wants to be reborn amongst the gods who live off scented roots has to give scented roots, which is reminiscent of mimetic magic. One gets the impression that in these last cases the act of generosity is motivated by the ambition to be reborn in a certain form of existence. Furthermore, the fact that generosity is sometimes mentioned and sometimes not might suggest that the formula was added later.

Let us briefly sum up: the framework for 'rebirth according to one's wish' are the three pillars of Buddhist practice: (a) generosity[97] (*dāna*), (b) cultivation of mind (*bhāvanā*) expressed in the resolution, and (c) morality (*sīla*) as additional condition. This suggests 'rebirth according to one's wish' has acquired an ethical twist, as it is said in the Saṅgīti Sutta: 'The mental aspiration of a moral person is effective through its purity'.[98]

The Saṅgīti Sutta stops with the attainment of the Brahma world, but other Suttas (such as Sāleyyaka Sutta, M I 289ff.) not only enumerate many more forms of heavenly existence, they actually end with the attainment of Nibbāna. The phrasing changes in the context of Nibbāna:

> If, householders, one who observes conduct in accordance with the Dhamma, righteous conduct, should wish: 'Oh, that by realising for myself with direct knowledge I might here and now enter upon and abide in the deliverance of mind and deliverance by wisdom that are taintless with the destruction of the taints!' it is possible that, by realising for himself with direct knowledge, he will here and now enter upon and abide in the deliverance of mind and deliverance by wisdom that are taintless with the destruction of the taints. Why is that? Because he observes conduct in accordance with the Dhamma, righteous conduct.
>
> (Bhikkhu Ñāṇamoli and Bhikkhu Bodhi 1995, 384; M I 289)

There are, however, also passages such as S III 154 (= A IV 125–26), which seem somewhat at odds with the concept of a wish with regard to achievements (*āsavakkhaya*). In fact, the simile of the hatching hens seems to illustrate the exact opposite:

> Suppose, *bhikkhus*, there were eight or ten or twelve hen's eggs that were not properly sat upon, not properly warmed, not properly nurtured by the hen. Although the wish might arise for the hen, 'O that the chicks should pierce the eggshell with the points of their claws or with their beaks and break out safely', still those chicks would be unfit to break out.
>
> (Gethin 1992, 245f.; S III 154)

The Sutta makes the point here that the wish is utterly irrelevant to the outcome of the hatching. Other similes follow, illustrating precisely the same point.[99]

The Saṅkhāruppatti Sutta (M III 99–103), too, works its way up the cosmological ladder and finally comes to the attainment of the 'deliverance of mind'. The wording is almost identical with the Sāleyyaka Sutta, but the fact that the final stage is 'non-rebirth' is emphasised. One gets the impression here that in the cosmological hierarchy Nibbāna followed naturally as the final pinnacle. However, as it cannot be achieved without overcoming the hindrances, etc., this caused a break with the formula.[100]

There is, however, another dimension to this. Schmithausen talks about two distinct strands and religious goals coexisting in the Upaniṣads: free movement between the different forms of existence (*kāmacāra*-eschatology) on the one hand, and escaping re-death and re-birth for good (highest-place-eschatology) on the other hand. The Saṅgīti Sutta can be interpreted as a continuation of the Upaniṣadic concept of *kāmacāra*, which was characteristic for the first strand. The concept of *nibbāna*, on the other hand, would come rather close to the goal of the second strand, the escape from re-death and re-birth. By beginning with 'rebirth according to one's wish' and finishing with Nibbāna as final achievement, the Saṅkhāruppatti Sutta seems to combine these two strands in a whole.

So far we have only assumed that the wish must also be present in the person's mind at the time of death, but it is not explicitly said that this is a necessary requirement. It is, therefore, worth looking at other passages, which are more explicit with regard to the time of death even though they might not mention a formulated wish (*pannidhi*). In S V 375ff. we find the story of Sarakāṇi, who, despite being partial to drinking, was declared a stream enterer by the Buddha as a result of his vigorous efforts on his deathbed. At Dhp-a III 170–77 a weaver's daughter was advised by the Buddha to meditate on death and was reborn in Tusita as a result of her efforts. Sometimes the last words take the form of a prophesy about the next rebirth. At Dhp-a I 151–154 Anāthapiṇḍika's daughter Sumanā (destined to be reborn in Tusita) addresses her father as 'younger brother' (*kaniṭṭhabhātika*) on her deathbed. The Buddha explains to Anāthapiṇḍika that she had surpassed him spiritually, which made him 'junior' to her. The implication seems to be that a sign indicating her next rebirth, a *gatinimitta*, had appeared to Sumanā, even though the term is not mentioned here.

Overcoming remorse. At Dhp-a II 203–209 a public executioner offers alms to Ven. Sāriputta on the day of his retirement after 55 years of service but cannot concentrate on the sermon as he keeps remembering all the people he had killed. Ven. Sāriputta tricks him into listening by making him falsely believe that he was not responsible for his bad deeds as he only followed the king's orders. As a result he attains a calm state of mind and when he is killed later that day (by a cow) is reborn in Tusita. This story states two important aspects: first, remorse is spiritually undesirable because it prevents concentration on what is important; second, the importance of a spiritual friend, a *kalyāṇamitta*, is emphasised, and even an element of trickery is condoned.

A more famous example of overcoming remorse is that of King Aśoka (ca. 247–207 B.C.),[101] who ascended to the Mauryan throne in approximately 264 B.C. and waged a brutal war against Kaliṅga.[102] He later became deeply affected by Buddhism and turned into one of its strongest and most generous supporters. According to the Buddhist tradition he was haunted by bad thoughts on his deathbed:

> He gave with joy a hundred millions
> after conquering all the earth,
> till in the end his realm came down
> to less then half a gall-nut's worth.
> Yet when his merit was used up,
> his body breathing its last breath,
> the sorrowless Asoka too
> felt sorrow face to face with death.[103]
>
> (Bhikkhu Ñāṇamoli 1956, 250; Vism 232)

The text does not reveal his afterlife destiny, but according to a popular legend in Sri Lanka King Aśoka was reborn as in the *nāga* realm as a result of regret and ascended to Tusita heaven after seven days.[104]

The description of the death of another king who is legendary in Sri Lanka, King Dutthagāmaṇī (ca. 101–77 B.C.), is rather more detailed.[105] As death drew near six gods were waiting in their carts ready to whisk the king away to their respective heaven and the king, following the monks' advice, chooses Tusita:

> 74. When the most wise king heard these words of the thera, he, casting a glance at the Great Thūpa, closed his eyes as he lay,
> 75. And when he, even at that moment, had passed away, he was seen reborn and standing in celestial form in the car,
> 76. that came from Tusita-heaven. And to make manifest the reward of the works of merit performed by him he drove,
> 77. showing himself in all his glory to the people, standing on the same car, three times around the Great Thūpa, going to the left, and then, when he had done homage to the thūpa and the brotherhood he passed into the Tusita-heaven.[106]
>
> (Geiger 1912, 226; Mv XXXII 74–77)

Both the versions of King Duṭṭhagāmaṇi's death (Mahāvaṃsa and Manorathapūraṇī) describe the king as having only positive visions but according to another popular legend in Sri Lanka he was tormented on his deathbed by regret.[107] The source for this legend might lie in the Mahāvaṃsa itself.

In the last sixteen verses of chapter XXV there is the well-known story that Duṭṭhagāmaṇi expressed remorse at having killed so many people and was reassured by *arahats* that all of them except for one and a half were non-believers.[108] This legend with its death/remorse theme might have been modelled after the death of the Great Aśoka.[109] Indeed, a modern commentary from Myanmar (Paramatthadīpanī-anudīpanī) treats King Aśoka's death together with that of King Duṭṭhagāmaṇi.[110]

There is no indication that King Duṭṭhagāmaṇi's ascent to Tusita had been a long cultivated wish of his: he had to seek advice from the monks on that issue. His rebirth in Tusita heaven appeared, nevertheless, to be a direct result of his directing the mind there. This seems to indicate that concentration on, or possibly visualisation of, a divine existence might fulfil a function similar to the rehearsed wish. Schmithausen (1987, 356) sees a development here (comparing Saṅkhāruppatti Sutta and Saptadhātu Sūtra). The mere intention to be reborn in a particular form of existence is no longer sufficient, but a state of mind which is on a level with that form of existence has to be achieved.

It seems worthwhile looking into the various stages of King Duṭṭhagāmaṇi's death preparation, even though they are likely to represent an 'ideal death scenario' rather than a realistic picture of the customs at the time.

First, he ordered his younger brother to complete the building work on the Mahāstūpa but legend has it that he failed to do so and instead covered the unfinished dome in white cloth to avoid disappointment (Mv 32.1–6). Duṭṭhagāmaṇi was then taken to pay his respects to the Mahāstūpa (Mv 32.7–9), which seems to have been his last observable act of merit recorded in the Mahāvaṃsa.[111] Next he requests the company of a particular monk, Theraputtābhaya who comes flying through the air to his deathbed with 500 bhikkhus and preaches (Mv 32.11–23). Next, the king ordered his scribe to come and read out his meritorous deeds from a 'merit book' (Mv 32.25).[112] The scribe begins to read (verses 26–32), then the king takes over and relates in the first person his meritorious deeds (verses 33–47), and at last Thera Abhaya relates two instances of alms giving (verses 48–55). Finally, the king gives instructions regarding his cremation and the worship of the Great *Stūpa*.

The function of this elaborate reading of an impressive list of meritorious deeds is found in the Abhidhamma: to remember past meritorious deeds can be an act of merit in itself, and to die with one's mind fixed on a meritorious deed is conducive to a positive rebirth. I have not come across any other evidence in the Pāli material for this practice, but the legend of King Duṭṭhagāmaṇi is very popular in Sri Lanka. This might account for the fact that 'merit books' (Sinhala: *pinpot*) were known to my informants even though they did not seem to play any role in contemporary Sri Lankan practice.

Giving up attachment. It is only a small step from acknowledging the importance of the last moment of life to the attempt to influence it for oneself (by way of cultivating a resolve) and for someone else. In the Mahāsudassana Sutta (D II 169–199) the dying king admonishes his queen, who reminds him of all his worldly possessions, of the 'correct' way of speaking at someone's deathbed:

> This is how you should speak: 'All things that are pleasing and attractive are liable to change, to vanish, to become otherwise. Do not, Sire, die filled with longing. To die filled with longing is painful and blameworthy. Of your eighty-four thousand cities, Kusāvatī is the chief: abandon desire, abandon the longing to live with them.'
>
> (Walshe 1995, 288; D II 189)

The repetitiveness of the Sutta, which goes over the long list of royal possessions one by one again and again throughout the Sutta has an almost meditative quality. The keyword here is *apekkhā* (affection, desire, longing) with regard to possessions and life in general, which is encouraged by the queen and rejected by the king. As it happens, most people will not be struggling through long lists of cities, palaces, etc. (84 000 of each!), at the end of their lives, but the basic principle is the same. The way to help a dying relative is to encourage him or her to give up longing as it is not conducive to a good death.

At S V 408 the layman Mahānāma asks the Buddha how one should talk to someone who is dying. Interestingly, the Sutta is very clear that the hypothetical situation involves two laypersons (*upāsaka*), not monks. The Buddha's reply shall be analysed stage by stage, as it might illuminate the contemporary Buddhist practice in Sri Lanka. At first (S V 408) the ill person should be reassured of his trust in the Buddha, Dhamma, and Saṃgha as well as of his own ability. Then he is admonished to withdraw his mind from his relatives (starting with his parents, wife and children, etc.) and his 'possessions', or rather responsibilities. Thirdly, he is encouraged to give up aspirations for future existences one by one, starting with attachment to human pleasures, in favour of the next highest form of divine existence, and so on (S V 408f.). In this fashion, applying the mind to a particular form of future existence only to let go of it, the dying person works his way up the cosmological ladder to the Brahma world (cf. M I 289 and M III 99). In effect by emphasising the embracing and the letting go (*cittaṃ vuṭṭhāpetvā*) of every form of existence individually, the Sutta seems to imply an indirect acknowledgement of 'rebirth according to one's wish'. Finally, he is admonished to direct his mind towards cessation (*nirodha*), which results in liberation of mind equaling that of a monk (S V 410). In other words, he gives up 'rebirth according to one's wish' in favour of Nibbāna. We are not told in this Sutta how a monk should talk to a layperson, or indeed to a fellow monk, but one might venture to guess that it was felt inappropriate for monks to engage in 'rebirth according to one's wish'.[113]

At Vin III 79 some monks speak to a very ill fellow monk and praise death, as they felt sorry for his great suffering. As a result the sick monk starves himself to death and his fellow monks feel regret and doubt. And, according to both the Vinaya text and the commentary, the Samantapāsādikā, they were right to feel bad, as they had committed a *pārājika* offence:

> *Out of compassion*: seeing that he was in great pain as a result of his illness, those monks felt compassion and, wanting his death yet not realizing that his death is what they wanted, spoke in praise of death, saying, 'You are virtuous and have done wholesome deeds. Why should you be afraid of dying? For someone who is virtuous certainly the only thing that can follow from death is heaven.' And as a result of their praising death, that monk stopped taking his food and died prematurely. Therefore they committed the offence. . . . However, a sick monk should be given the following sort of instruction, 'For one who is virtuous the path and fruit can arise unexpectedly, so forget your attachment to such things as the monastery, and establish mindfulness of the Buddha, Dhamma, Saṃgha and the body, and pay attention to [the manner of] bringing [things] to mind'.
>
> (Gethin 2004, 11; Sp 464)

Again the structure is that of 'wrong advice' versus 'right advice', as we had in the Mahāsudassana Sutta. The good advice, the encouragement to let go of attachment, the recollection of Buddha, Dhamma, and Saṃgha, is reminiscent of the advice Mahānāma (S V 408). The interesting issue here is that wrong advice, the 'praise of death' (*maraṇa-vaṇṇa*), even if originally motivated by pity and compassion,[114] could constitute an offence of the gravest class, if the sick monk decided to end his life. A monk when called to a deathbed is, consequently, in a rather precarious position: he has to encourage the sick person to abandon desire but at the same time he must not provoke depression that might lead to suicide.[115]

If a layperson in the hour of death can achieve Nibbāna assisted by another layperson, how much greater would be the chances if one could listen to the Buddha himself preaching the *dhamma*? This is precisely the case at A III 380ff., where the monk Phagguna who is in great pain and agony, was visited on his deathbed by the Buddha and attained Nibbāna (as in the Sutta S V 410). Prompted by Ānanda the Buddha explains the advantages of 'timely hearing of Dhamma' (*kālena dhammassavana*):

> There are six advantages, Ānanda, in hearing the Dhamma in time, in testing its goodness in time. What six? Consider, Ānanda, the monk whose mind is not wholly freed from the five lower fetters, but, when dying, is able to see the Tathāgata: the Tathāgata teaches him Dhamma, lovely in the beginning, lovely in the middle, lovely in the

> end, its goodness, its significance; and makes known the godly life, wholly fulfilled, perfectly pure. When he has heard that Dhamma teaching, his mind is wholly freed from the five lower fetters. This, Ānanda, is the first advantage in hearing Dhamma in time.
>
> (Hare 1934, III 271; A III 380)

We are not told what precisely the Buddha said, whether he preached about letting go of better forms of existence, or whether his *dhammadesanā* to the monk Phagguna was on a different, more technical level. Again, it is possible that hearing the *dhamma* from the Buddha himself would produce an effect almost automatically, with only a minimum of effort on the part of the dying person. After all, Phagguna's great suffering cannot have been particularly conducive to insight and meditation and is not commonly associated with a good death or with higher achievements.

Dying with faith. In the Mahāparinibbāna Sutta it is said that those who die in a place of pilgrimage associated with the Buddha will be reborn in heaven:

> Monks and nuns, lay men and lay women will come thinking, 'Here is where the Tathāgata was born, and here is where he awakened to unsurpassed full awakening, and here is where he turned the unsurpassed wheel of truth, and here is where he attained nirvana by the element of nirvana without any remnant of attachment.' All those who die with faithful hearts while they are on pilgrimage to a shrine will at the breaking up of the body after death be born in a happy realm, a heaven world.
>
> (Gethin, unpublished; D II 140)

Here the key factor seems to be in the compound, *pasannacitta*, (lit. 'glad at heart') which Gethin translates as 'those with faithful hearts', following the commentarial tradition.[116] Incidentally, there is evidence (albeit not in a Sutta) that hearing the Dhamma and being full of faith at the time of death is not only beneficial for human beings but indeed even for animals. One morning while staying in Campā near a lotus pond, the Buddha uttered the following cryptic prediction:

> Tonight, when I am teaching the Dhamma, a frog, while taking my voice as an object (*nimitta*), will die by the works of others and will come with a great retinue of gods while a big crowd is watching; for many there will be a realization of the Teaching.
>
> (Vv-a 217)

And a bit further on we learn about the events, which take place on that evening just as the Buddha begins his sermon:

> At that moment a frog came out of the lotus pond and [thinking] 'This is *dhamma* spoken', with the idea of *dhamma*, he took [my] voice as an object (*nimitta*) and sat down at the outer edge of the assembly. [Just] then a cow-herd arrived at the place and saw the Teacher teaching the *dhamma* and the congregation listening very peacefully to the *dhamma*. With his mind on that he stood [there], leaning on his stick and [because] he did not see the frog he stood on its head, crushing it. The frog with a happy mind because of the idea of *dhamma* died instantly and was reborn in the sphere of the thirty-three gods, in a gold celestial palace twelve *yojanas* in size, as if awakened from sleep and saw himself there surrounded by a group of nymphs. As he was reflecting: 'From where did I come to be reborn here?' he saw his former existence. And as he was thinking 'What did I do, that I [of all frogs] was reborn here, that I obtained such success?' he did not see anything other than the taking the Blessed One's voice as object. He immediately came with his celestial palace, stepped down from it and, while a big crowd of people was watching, approached with a great retinue and great divine power, bowed down with his head at the feet of the Blessed One, greeting him with cupped hands and stood there paying respect.
>
> (Vv-a 217)

The crucial point for us seems to be that the frog did not make a resolution to be reborn in the realm of the thirty-three gods, he did not have any deep insight nor did he make any special effort. He was, however, *pasannacitta*, 'glad at heart' at hearing the *dhamma*. This seemingly involuntary act of faith coincided with the last moments of his existence as a frog, so the Buddha's voice became his *kammanimitta*, the decisive element at the time of his death (see the chapter on Abhidhamma). A similar story is found in the Dhammapada-aṭṭhakathā where it is said that 500 young bats happened to overhear two monks chanting the Abhidhamma in their cave:

> We are told that in the dispensation of the Buddha Kassapa they were little bats. On a certain occasion, as they hung over a mountain cave, they overheard two monks reciting the Abhidhamma as they walked up and down and took their voices as an object. As for the expressions, 'These aggregates of being, these elements of being,' they did not know what they meant; but solely because they had taken their voices as an object, when they passed from that state of existence they were reborn in the World of the Gods. There, for the space of an interval between two Buddhas, they enjoyed celestial glory; afterwards they were reborn in Sāvatthī in the households of families of distinction.
>
> (adapted from Burlingame 1921 III 52; Dhp-a III 223)

The bats did not all die at the same time while listening to the recital (at least it does not say so) but the fact that they 'took the voices as object' seems to have been the deciding element that caused rebirth amongst the gods. There is yet another animal story, this time from the commentary to the Mahāsatipaṭṭhāna Sutta that deals with the topic of recollecting the teaching at the time of death:

> A dancer took on a baby parrot and walked about teaching it. After he had stayed in a nunnery he went away, forgetting the little parrot at the time of his leaving. The novices took him and looked after him. They gave him the name 'Buddharakkhita'. Then one day the principal nun saw him sitting in front of her and said: 'Buddharakkhita?' 'What is it, honorable One?' 'Do you pay any attention to [mental] cultivation?' 'I do not have one, honorable One.' 'It is not right to live as a diffused personality, especially when staying in the vicinity of ascetics, some form of fixed thought is to be desired. If you cannot do anything else, then repeat [to yourself] "*aṭṭhi, aṭṭhi*".'[117] Abiding by the nun's instruction he moved about repeating '*aṭṭhi, aṭṭhi*' [to himself]. One day early in the morning while the morning sun was shining, a bird sat on top of an arch and grabbed him with his claws. He shouted 'Kiri, kiri!' The novices heard that and said: 'Honorable Ones, Buddharakkhita has been grabbed by a bird. Let us free him'. They grabbed clods of earth and such and followed [the bird] and freed Buddharakkhita. The nun brought him back, sat him down in front of her and said: 'Buddharakkhita, when you were grabbed by the bird, what was on your mind?' 'Honorable One, [I had nothing other on my mind than] "Just a heap of bones is leaving having grabbed a heap of bones. Where will he scatter them?" Thus, Honorable One, only a heap of bones was on my mind.' 'Very good, very good, Buddharakkhita, in the future you will have the right condition for the destruction of birth!'
>
> (Sv III 742)

Luckily the little parrot lived to tell the tale, but had he not, one might on the basis of the previous two stories assume he would have been reborn amongst the gods and after intervals in heaven and as a human, become an arahat, as predicted by the principal nun. The commentary is rather precise here in emphasising that this will happen in the future (*anāgate*), as it is impossible for animals to attain arahatship. Again, there might be more stories reporting the events surrounding the death of animals, but these three examples will suffice.

Bad death

I will next examine bad death followed by rebirth in one of the unfortunate states.

Resolve. I have not found any evidence of a bad resolve in the Nikāyas, but there are examples in the commentaries and the Abhidhamma. A particular type of wrong view (or rather clouded vision) seems to be represented at Dhp-a I 47f. Two women, one barren and one fruitful, share one husband and are locked in a battle of hatred. The fruitful wife, now pregnant again, realises that it was her barren co-wife who had previously caused her two miscarriages and is now about to kill her and her unborn third child. She makes a *patthanā* on her deathbed to become a *yakkhinī* and as a result is reborn as a cat and her rival as a hen.[118] Thereby a cycle is started that continues with respective resolutions and killings until the Buddha intervenes.[119] In this story the main motivation for a resolve to be reborn in a powerful, but nevertheless unhappy, form of existence, is revenge.

This is, of course, totally different from the Bodhisattva's conscious decision to be reborn in bad existences in order to relieve the suffering of his fellow beings there as, according to Kathāvatthu XXIII 3, the Andhakas claim he does:

> You maintain that he entered the womb of his own free will. Do you also imply that he chose to be reborn in purgatory, or as an animal? That he possessed magic potency? You deny. I ask it again. You assent. Then did he practice the Four Steps to that potency—will, effort, thought, investigation? Neither can you quote me here a Sutta in justification.
>
> (Shwe Zan Aung and Mrs. Rhys Davids 1915, 367; Kv-a 623f.)

Here the Kathāvatthu makes the interesting point that being reborn according to one's wish would be due to special power (*iddhi*). The opponent agrees that the Bodhisattva can exercise his choice of where he is reborn on the grounds of special powers (*iddhi*) which are resulting from meritorious deeds in the past (*puññiddhi*), rather than from meditation (*bhāvanāmaya*). The Theravādins, however, seem to have upheld the view that a Bodhisattva does not consciously decide to be reborn in a bad existence, as that would bypass his *kamma*.

Remorse. We have already cited two famous examples of overcoming remorse before death, and as we shall see, Aśoka and Duṭṭhagāmaṇi might have had a narrow escape.

In the Dhammapada-aṭṭhakathā is is said that Queen Mallikā, despite having shown great generosity and support for the Saṃgha, was reborn in the Avīci hell due to the incident of indecent sexual behaviour (with her pet dog in the bath) and subsequent deception of the king who had witnessed the act.[120] The reason for her rebirth in Avīci is, according to the commentary, not the incident itself, but the fact that she remembered it at the moment of death (presumably reliving her regret and shame). On the seventh day, however, she is reborn in Tusita due to the amount of merit accumulated by her in the present life.[121]

Another story in the Dhammapada-aṭṭhakathā about regret at the time of death reports longerlasting consequences. The monk Erakapatta once went in a boat and tore off a leaf holding onto an Eraka tree. He registered his deed but thought it was unimportant until many existences later:

> Although for twenty thousand years he performed meditations in the forest without confessing his fault, yet, when he came to die, he felt as though an Eraka leaf had seized him by the neck. Desiring to confess his fault, but seeing no other monk, he was filled with remorse and cried out, 'My virtue is impaired!' Thus he died. Having passed out of that state of existence, he was born a dragon king, the measure of his body being that of a dug-out canoe. At the moment of rebirth he surveyed his person, and was filled with remorse as he thought to himself, 'After performing meditations for so long a time, I have been reborn in a causeless state, in a feeding place for frogs.'
>
> (Burlingame 1921 III 56f.; Dhp-a III 230ff.)

Compared to Queen Mallikā's misbehaviour and deceit, Erakapatta's misdeed seems trivial and the resulting fate rather grim (for the interval between two Buddhas he was reborn as a *nāga* king) considering that the monk in question is a meditator of long standing (twenty thousand years to be precise). The imagery is quite strong and evocative (fast moving boat, the leaf grabbing the monk by the throat) and is reminiscent of the stream of *saṃsāra*.[122] One would be hard pressed to make sense of the story in a literal sense, but the moral of Erakapatta's story is clearly monastic: even the slightest fault left unconfessed might haunt you at the time of death.[123]

Attachment. A rather touching example of the bad consequences of attachment to objects at the time of death, is related at Dhp-a III 341–344. An earnest monk named Tissa takes a liking to his brand new robe, but alas, he dies before he had a chance to wear it. The other monks decide to cut it up and divide it amongst themselves, but the Buddha intervenes and orders them to leave the robe for seven days. Eventually he explains to the puzzled monks:

> Monks, Tissa was reborn as a bug in his own robe. When you set about to divide the robe among you, he screamed 'They are plundering my property.' And thus screaming, he ran this way and that. Had you taken his robe, he would have cherished a grudge against you, and because of this sin would have been reborn in Hell. That is the reason why I directed that the robe should be laid aside. But now he

> has been reborn in the Abode of the Tusita gods, and for this reason I have permitted you to take the robe and divide it among you.[124]
>
> (adapted from Burlingame 1921 III 121; Dhp-a III 343)

The danger of dying with attachment to an image on one's mind is vividly illustrated in the Nikāyas:

> It would be better, bhikkhus, for the eye faculty to be lacerated by a red-hot iron pin burning, blazing, and glowing, than for one to grasp the sign through the features in a form cognizable by the eye. For if consciousness should stand tied to gratification in the sign or in the features, and if one should die on that occasion, it is possible that one will go to one of two destinations: hell or the animal realm. Having seen this danger, I speak thus.
>
> (Bhikkhu Bodhi 2000 II 1234; S IV 168)

This passage illustrates just why it is so important to assist a dying person in giving up attachment at the time of death.

Wrong view. A number of Suttas deal in a more general way with karmic retribution and it is often repeated that wrong view (*micchādiṭṭhi*) leads to rebirth in either hell or the animal realm. I will, however, concentrate here on two passages that deal with the time of death. At S IV 308ff. a mercenary holds the wrong view that a soldier dying in battle will be reborn amongst the so-called battle-slain gods (*parajitānaṃ*[125] *devānaṃ sahavyataṃ*). The Buddha explains that the mind of a soldier in battle is already low and evil as it is intent on killing beings, but to further hold the wrong view that he will be reborn amongst *devas* makes it doubly wrong:

> But should he hold such a view as this: 'When a mercenary strives and exerts himself in battle, if others slay him and finish him off while he is striving and exerting himself in battle, then with the breakup of the body, after death, he is reborn in the company of the battle-slain devas'—that is a wrong view on his part. For a person with wrong view, I say, there is one of two destinations: either hell or the animal realm.
>
> (Bhikkhu Bodhi 2000 II 1335; S IV 308ff.)

One gets the impression here that the hateful thought at the time of death might have sufficed to cause rebirth in hell and that the wrong view is only an additional factor. Furthermore, it is not actually said explicitly that the *micchādiṭṭhi* occurs at the time of death.[126] However, as a result of the Buddha's preaching the soldier takes refuge for life, but does not ordain or become an *arahant*.[127]

General explanation

An entire Sutta, the Mahākammavibhaṅga Sutta (M III 207–215), is devoted to the workings of *kamma*. The Buddha explains that there are four categories of people:

(a) those who do not keep the precepts, etc., hold a wrong view and find a miserable after life destiny;
(b) those who do not keep the precepts, etc., hold a wrong view and find a happy after life destiny;
(c) those who do keep the precepts, etc., hold a right view and find a happy after life destiny;
(d) those who do keep the precepts, etc., hold a right view and find a miserable after life destiny.

In categories (a) and (c) *kamma* is presented as cause for bad or good results, whereas in categories (b) and (d) the exact opposite is proclaimed, which appears to override *kamma*.[128] This description of the four categories of people is then repeated with slightly different emphasis (a recluse or brahmin with a divine eye observes the above four cases). The following explanation centers around two main aspects: first, the quality of the next rebirth might be caused either by deeds in the present existence or by right or wrong views at the moment of death (*maraṇakāle*); and second, good or bad *kamma* will not necessarily come to fruition in the very next existence.

The first part of the explanation seems to suggest that wrong or right view at the time of death can override a lifetime of good or bad *kamma* respectively. The fault with this suggestion is that the brahmin watching with a divine eye only sees a certain moment in peoples' life. This snapshot might give him the completely wrong idea about the moral quality of the person in question and the seemingly unfitting rebirth. Similarly, the death moment is like a snap shot of the mental disposition of a person at any particular moment: it is likely to be in keeping with someone's general disposition, but might reflect a momentary lapse and appear 'unfitting'. The second part of the explanation then is a straightforward assertion that there is indeed karmic retribution and right or wrong view at the time of death can only temporarily override (but not eradicate) *kamma*. The commentary on the Mahākammavibhaṅga Sutta quotes a rather interesting example of *micchādiṭṭhi* ('Skanda is the best! Śiva is the best! Brahmā is the best!' or 'The world is created by Īśvara, etc.').[129] The belief in a creator God, even though not included in the standard formula of the ten wrong views as it appears in the Nikāyas and Abhidhamma, is nevertheless not out of keeping with it.[130] It is just possible—but this is pure speculation—that there might be a hint of a warning here. Even those who turned to Buddhism during their lifetime might on their deathbed instinctively revert to the god(s) of their childhood.

At least that seems to me more likely than getting entangled in wrong views such as '*natthi ayaṃ loko, natthi paro loko*' on the deathbed.

At A I 31 wrong view and right view in general (not necessarily at the time of death) are singled out as by far the most important factor in determining the quality of the next rebirth. In the next two Suttas (A I 32f.) *micchādiṭṭhi* and *sammādiṭṭhi* serve as the basis on the one hand for *kamma* and on the other hand for *cetanā*, *patthanā*, *paṇidhi* and *saṅkhāra*. The latter must refer to wishes for a specific afterlife, which might become acute as death draws near (see Saṅkhāruppatti Sutta).

At A I 8–9 the death context is explicit, but the terminology is slightly changed as the Sutta speaks more generally of a person with a corrupt mind and with a pure mind (*paduṭṭhacittaṃ/pasannacittaṃ*):

> Now here, monks, with my own thought embracing his, I am aware of a monk whose mind is corrupt. If at this very time he were to make an end, he would be put into Purgatory according to his desserts.[131] Why so? Because of his corrupt mind. In like manner, monks, it is owing to a corrupt mind that some beings in this world, when the body breaks up, after death are reborn in the Waste, the Woeful Way, the Downfall, in Purgatory (*and similarly for good destinies*).[132]
>
> (Woodward 1932, I 6; A I 8f.)

This should suffice to demonstrate that there is evidence in the Nikāyas and commentaries that the frame of mind at the time of death is one of the factors influencing the next rebirth. So what should be aimed for is a frame of mind that is pure (*pasanna*), free of hate (*adosa*), and firmly grounded in *sammādiṭṭhi*. One method of achieving this is the cultivation of friendliness (*mettā*) throughout one's lifetime:

> Monks, eleven advantages are to be looked for from the release of the heart by the practice of amity, by making amity grow, by making much of it, by making amity a vehicle and basis, by persisting in it, by becoming familiar with it, by well establishing it. What are the eleven? One sleeps happy and wakes happy; he sees no evil dream; he is dear to human beings and non-human beings alike; the devas guard him; fire, poison or sword affect him not; quickly he concentrates his mind; his complexion is serene; he makes an end without bewilderment; and if he has penetrated no further [to Arahatship] he reaches at death the Brahma-world.[133]
>
> (Woodward 1936, V 219; A V 341f.)

The connection between 'friendliness' and conscious death is not immediately apparent. Perhaps cultivating *mettā* towards unpleasant or dangerous beings prepares one for the death moment in that it prevents hatred, fear, regret etc., coming up at that crucial time. There is, however, yet another aspect to this: the ritual efficacy of *mettā* in warding off evil spirits at the time of death, when one is particularly vulnerable. As mentioned above, the Karaṇīyametta Sutta (Sn 25–26) is always amongst the Suttas chanted by monks at the deathbed.

At A III 84, 'mindfulness of death' (*maraṇasaññā*) is recommended amongst other meditation practices, such as 'perceiving the foulness of the body'.[134] The terminology is similar to that of the previous sutta, but the tone is rather different. The advantages of 'cultivating *mettā*' reflect engagement with the world and society in an attempt to gain happiness here. Cultivating 'mindfulness of death' on the other hand, aims at the opposite: the final liberation, disengagement from society, which, of course, does not necessarily happen at death.

Summary

On the one hand, people strive to improve their situation in this or the next life; on the other hand, the highest goal is to escape this *saṃsāra* altogether. This tension which is reminiscent of the two strands in the Upaniṣads, seems to run through Buddhist scriptures and has frequently been commented on by Buddhist scholars.[135] I would not exclude the possibility that there is a certain continuity (even though not in terminology). The Upaniṣadic concept of 'rebirth according to one's wish' seems to have become embeded into the ethical framework of Buddhism.

However, the picture is changed somewhat when we look at instances of bad death, which mostly stem from the stories in the commentaries. The general mood is one of warning, almost threat, and the listeners are told to keep striving in order to avoid disaster. While it would be dangerous to make general claims, it might still be worthwhile to share ideas about possible developments or shifts in emphasis from the Nikayas to the commentarial literature.

First, the passages dealing with good death could belong to an earlier stratum which is still close to the Upaniṣads and not yet systematised, whereas passages describing bad death might be in some way secondary, either logically derived from, or construed in parallel to the instances of good death.

Second, change in tone might have to do with a different target audience: the positive tone of the 'rebirth according to one's wish' for ordinary laypeople and monks, a more systematised approach aiming at liberation for highly accomplished forest monks. Unfortunately it is not always mentioned in the suttas who is addressed and who is spoken of.

And finally it might simply be a matter of a carrot-and-stick approach: a positive rebirth as the reward of ethically good behaviour, bad death being used as a warning. The intention in both cases is to incite behaviour in accordance with the ethical norm of Buddhism, which is conducive to a better rebirth and eventually Nibbāna.

The Abhidhamma interpretation

In the previous chapters I used the term 'time of death' rather loosely in a non-technical sense because the texts I was quoting (Nikāyas and commentaries) did so. However, in this chapter I will speak of either final 'conscious moments' (plural) or the consciousness process (*cittavīthi*) to reflect the language of the Abhidhamma. In order to gain some understanding of the thought process at the crucial time of death, let us first take a look at 'normal' thought processes.[136]

Ordinary thought processes

In the Abhidhamma understanding a 'thought process' (*citta-vīthi*) refers to the process by which the mind becomes aware of a particular object and reacts to it in some way with greed or with aversion or with wisdom and compassion, for example.[137] Each thought process consists of a series of separate (yet connected) 'arisings of consciousness' (*cittuppāda*) or 'moments of consciousness' (*citta-kkhaṇa*). A typical thought process comprises seventeen such moments and involves the mind in changing from its karmically passive state, known as *bhavaṅga*, to a karmically active state, known as 'impulsion' (*javana*) which makes up seven of the seventeen moments. What a being would consciously experience as a particular memory or feeling of desire, greed, or remorse, is understood to be made up of an unspecified number of these 'thought processes' (each with seventeen moments of consciousness). In the course of even the simplest experience or 'thought', the mind flicks back and forth between the 'active' (*javana*) and 'passive' (*bhavaṅga*) mode a number of times, or, to put it differently, by various stimuli the mind is continually shaken out of its passive mode only to lapse back into it. Gethin 1994, 15 explains:

> This basic switching between passive and active state of mind is understood to apply not only to the consciousness of human beings but to that of all beings in the thirty-one realms of existence, from beings suffering in *niraya* to the *brahmās* in the pure abodes and formless realms; the only exception is the case of 'unconscious beings' (*asañña-satta*), who remain without any consciousness (*acittaka*) for 500 *mahākappas.* In other words, to have a mind, to be conscious, is to switch between those two modes of mind.

In both modes the mind has an object, but whereas the object of the mind in 'active' mode changes all the time depending on the stimulus and beings are generally aware of what it is, the object of the mind in *bhavaṅga* remains the same throughout a given lifetime, and beings are unaware of its nature. The question is: What is the relationship between these active and passive modes of mind, and what determines the nature of one's *bhavaṅga*? As for the first question, we have already seen that the mind rests in *bhavaṅga* as its 'natural abode', and it is continually shaken out of that state. Again, according to Gethin (1994, 19) this means:

> [I]t is the nature of *bhavaṅga* that defines in general what kind of being one is—it gives one's general place in the overall scheme of things. However, as the implications of this understanding are drawn out, I think it becomes clear that we need to go further than this: *bhavaṅga* does not simply define *what* one is, it defines precisely *who* one is.

If *bhavaṅga* represents what and who we are, our nature and character, it also defines our potential and limits or shortcomings, which means that however hard some beings may try, they may never achieve certain attainments in their given existence, as they are 'simply beyond their capabilities'.[138] The fact that the nature of one's *bhavaṅga* does not change during one's lifetime and defines one with all its limitations makes it all the more crucial to explore the second question: How and by what is the nature or object of one's *bhavaṅga* determined?

According to developed Abhidhamma theory, *bhavaṅga* and its object only change substantially in the process of death and rebirth: a new *bhavaṅga-citta* (with a new object) arises at the moment of 'relinking' (*paṭisandhi*) to a new life and will remain the same throughout the next existence. The new *bhavaṅga-citta* is the immediate result (*vipāka*) of the *kamma* constituted by the final thought process (*citta-vīthi*) of one's previous life, which in establishing the new *bhavaṅga-citta* sets the tone for the new life (Gethin 1994). In technical terms, the last *bhavaṅga* moment of the old existence is called *cuti-citta* or 'decease consciousness' and still takes the 'old' object. This *cuti-citta* is immediately followed by the first *bhavaṅga* moment of the new existence termed *paṭisandhi-citta* or 'relinking consciousness' and already takes the 'new' object. The object of the new *bhavaṅga* is that of the last 'impulsions' (*javana*)—active moments of consciousness that constitute *kamma*—of the final consciousness process of the previous existence. What is crucial in determining the nature of rebirth is the frame of mind immediately preceding the actual moment of death (*cuticitta*). On the basis of this La Vallée Poussin (1911) suggests: 'Death, then, is the transformation of this "fundamental thought" called *bhavaṅga*, "limb of existence," into "emigrating thought" (*chyutichitta*).'

Even though the *paṭisandhi* strictly reflects only the nature and content of the five (identical) 'impulsions' (*javanas*) of the final consciousness process, it is perhaps understood that in most cases the general quality of the experience close to the time of death is likely to be more or less consistently of one type and that this general quality is what will be reflected in the new *bhavaṅga*. However, it should be noted that strictly speaking, although such images as a 'reflection' and 'echo' are used for relinking (Vism 554), the new *bhavaṅga*, even in the case of a being reborn in an unhappy destiny (*duggati*) as an animal or hungry ghost, is not understood to be *directly* associated with such qualities as greed (*lobha*) or regret (*kukkucca*); in such cases the function of *bhavaṅga* is said to be performed by some form of the mind consciousness element (*mano-viññāṇa-dhātu*) that is the result of unwholesome *kamma* (*akusala-vipāka*) and in normal circumstances performs the function of investigating (*santīraṇa*) (see Abhidh-s 23). This is conceived of as a rather basic form of consciousness, only associated with ten 'mental factors' (*cetasikas*): the seven universals and three of the particulars, namely 'thinking of' (*vitakka*), 'examining' (*vicāra*) and 'decision' (*adhimokkha*) (see Abhidh-s chapter 2). Indeed, while it seems to be implied that *bhavaṅga* is in some way the vehicle for latent unwholesome tendencies, even in the case of someone reborn in a happy destiny, the precise mechanisms for this do not seem to be specified in the *aṭṭhakathās* (Gethin 1994, 30), though it is possible that more is said on this matter in the largely unstudied (in the West) Abhidhamma *ṭīkās*.

Near death thought processes

The analysis of the thought process near death differs very slightly from the analysis of the 'normal' thought processes that occur during one's lifetime, in that the former has five instead of seven *javanas*. This variation is, however, not unique to the death process, but also occurs in dreamlike states of diminished consciousness, etc., and need not concern us here. We shall concentrate here on the thought process as occurring near death.[139]

As mentioned before, every consciousness process begins with an 'object' (*ārammaṇa*)—typically a sense impression, past thought, or concept (*paññatti*)—that, as it were, shakes the mind out of *bhavaṅga*, and brings it into active mode. As the last thought process is crucial in that it determines the next *bhavaṅga*, it is treated with special attention in the Abhidhamma, and the objects at the time of death are divided into three different technical categories, namely *kamma* or 'action', *kamma-nimitta* or 'sign of action', and *gati-nimitta* or 'sign of destiny'. These expressions are only used for the specific purpose of describing the objects of mind processes near death. Herein, *kamma* is always a past complex of *citta* and *cetasika*; *kammanimitta* is either a past or present sense impression (a visible object or sound, etc.), or a concept; and *gatinimitta* is a present sense impression and only occurs for beings in the *kāmadhātu*.[140] The Sammohavinodanī defines *kamma*, *kammanimitta* and *gatinimitta* as follows:

> In brief, rebirth-linking has three kinds of objects, kamma, the sign of kamma and the sign of destiny. Herein, kamma is accumulated profitable and unprofitable volition; the sign of kamma is that thing (*vatthu*) by taking which as its object kamma was accumulated. Herein, although the kamma was performed a hundred thousand *koṭis* of aeons ago in the past, yet at that moment the kamma or its sign comes and makes its appearance.
>
> (Bhikkhu Ñāṇamoli 1987, I 190; Vibh-a I 156f.)

This is immediately followed by a story illustrating *kammanimitta*:

> Here is a story concerning the appearing of a *kamma* sign. Gopaka Sīvali, it seems, had a shrine built in the Tālapiṭṭhika monastery. The shrine appeared to him as he lay on his deathbed. Taking that sign, he died and was reborn in the divine world.[141]
>
> (Bhikkhu Ñāṇamoli 1987, I 190; Vibh-a 156f.)

The Visuddhimagga treats *kamma* and *kammanimitta* together:

> For example, first in the case of a person in the happy destinies of the sense-sphere who is an evil-doer, when he is lying on his deathbed, his evil kamma according as it has been stored up, or its sign, comes into focus in the mind door. For it is said, 'Then [the evil deeds that he did in the past] . . . cover him [and overspread him and envelop him]' (M III 164), and so on.[142]
>
> (Bhikkhu Ñānamoli 1956, 631ff.; Vism 548)

And indeed the difference between *kamma* and *kammanimitta* is very subtle, as one gets the impression that *kamma* is a non-conceptualised memory of a past deed, whereas *kammanimitta* is a memory based on or prompted by a concrete image or object. This is why the Visuddhimagga devotes another paragraph to *kammanimitta*:

> In another's case, relatives present [objects to him] at the five sense doors, such as a visible datum as object, perhaps flowers, garlands, flags, banners, etc., saying 'This is being offered to the Blessed One for your sake, dear, set your mind at rest'; or a sound as object, perhaps, preaching of the Dhamma, offerings of music, etc.; or an odour as object, perhaps incense, scents, perfumes, etc.; or a taste as object perhaps honey, molasses, etc., saying 'Taste this, dear, it is a gift to be given for your sake'; or a tangible datum as object, perhaps Chinese silk, silk of Somāra, saying 'Touch this, dear, it is a gift to be given for your sake'.[143]
>
> (Bhikkhu Ñānamoli 1956, 634; Vism 550)

It is difficult to determine if this passage, which has been discussed in some detail in the introductory part of the present chapter, reflects the actual practice at the time the Visuddhimagga was composed, or if it described an ideal situation, which was, and possibly still is, aspired to. An example for a *kammanimitta* for someone to be reborn in a bad destiny is an object that might trigger greed (*rāgādihetubhūtaṃ hīnārammaṇaṃ*).[144]

Gethin (1994, 22) interprets the somewhat difficult concepts of *kamma* and *kamanimitta* as follows:

> What seems to be envisaged, though the texts do not quite spell this out, is that this memory prompts a kind of reliving of the original *kamma*: one experiences again a wholesome or unwholesome state of mind similar to the state of mind experienced at the time of performing the remembered action. This reliving of the experience is what directly conditions the rebirth consciousness and the subsequent *bhavaṅga*. A *kamma-nimitta* is a sense-object (either past or present) or a concept. Again what is envisaged is that at the time of death some past sense-object associated with a particular past action comes before the mind (i.e., is remembered) and once more prompts a kind of reliving of the experience.

Another point that seems worth mentioning here is that the Sammohavinodanī (156) goes to some length to assert that even in cases of 'dying in confusion' (*sammūḷhakālakiriyā*) and 'rapid death' (*lahukamaraṇa*) there is an object of death consciousness, namely either *kamma* or *kammanimitta*.[145]

And finally the signs for rebirth (*gatinimitta*) are described in the Visuddhimagga (for the bad forms of rebirth):

> In another's case, owing to kamma of the kind already described, there comes into focus at the mind door at the time of death the sign of the unhappy destinies with the appearance of fire and flames, etc., in the hells, and so on.
>
> (Ñāṇamoli 1956, 632; Vism 549f.)

And (for the good destinies):

> In another's case, owing to blameless sense-sphere kamma, there comes into focus in the mind door at the time of death the sign of a happy destiny, in other words, the appearance of the mother's womb in the case of the human world or the appearance of pleasure groves, divine palaces, wishing-trees, etc., in the case of the divine world.
>
> (Ñāṇamoli 1956, 633; Vism 550)

To sum up the main points: all three categories of objects (*kamma*, *kamma-nimitta* and *gati-nimitta*) involve a *kamma* occurring at the time of death by way of 'reliving' some past experience. The object of this experience can be a past action (*kamma*), or some 'sign'—a past or present sense-object, or a concept—that is associated with or reminds one of a past action (*kamma-nimitta*); or it can be a present vision (*gati-nimitta*) of the fires of hell or the mansions of heaven. It is not arbitrary what comes to mind at the time of death: it is affected by one's past tendencies and actions, but can also be influenced by the actions of friends and relatives.

Kamma *at the time of death*

Various Abhidhamma works describe (with regard to the moment of death) a classification of four types of *kamma* arranged in an hierarchical order according to which one takes precedence at the time of death. In the Visuddhimagga this reads:

> Another fourfold classification of kamma is: weighty, habitual, death-threshold, and kamma [stored up] by being performed. Herein, when there is weighty and unweighty kamma, the *weightier*, whether profitable or unprofitable, whether kamma consisting in matricide or kamma of the exalted spheres, takes precedence in ripening. Likewise when there is habitual and unhabitual kamma, the *more habitual*, whether consisting in good or bad conduct, takes precedence in ripening. *Death-threshold* kamma is that remembered at the time of death; for when a man near death can remember [kamma], he is reborn according to that. Kamma not included in the foregoing three kinds that has been often repeated is called *kamma [stored up] by being performed*. This brings about rebirth-linking if other kinds fail.[146]
>
> (Ñāṇamoli 1956, 697; Vism 601)

To put this in perspective, *garuka-kamma* takes absolute precedence over all other categories of *kamma* and cannot be superseded. However, this will effect only very few beings as we can gather from the examples given in the above extract from Visuddhimagga. Unwholesome *garuka-kamma* is matricide, for example, and wholesome *garuka-kamma* is attainment of *jhānas*, neither of these types being particularly common occurrences. At the other end of the spectrum is 'performed' *kamma* (*kaṭattā*), which seems rather vague and only comes into play as a kind of last resort in case no other *kamma* comes to mind, which, again is unlikely. In practical terms this leaves a choice of either 'habitual *kamma*' (*bahula āciṇṇa*) or 'proximate *kamma*' (*āsanna*) for most beings. If the habitual *kamma* (either good or bad) is sufficiently strong, it will define the time of death, and rebirth will then be more or less in keeping with one's character or nature. Only if that fails and no strong habits have been developed during one's lifetime will the first thing that comes to one's mind at the time of death come into play.[147]

The question of what takes precedence is, as we have seen above, rather crucial for the individual at the time of death, as it will define the new *bhavaṅga*, which in turn sets the tone for the future existence. But it seems that the question of what *kamma* comes to mind at the time of death is not merely a personal one but one which has been discussed in Abhidhamma literature. Both the Visuddhimagga (601) and Abhidhammāvatāra (117) follow the order given above: weighty (*garuka*), habitual (*bahula āciṇṇa*), death-threshold or 'proximate' (*āsanna*) and finally (in the absence or the other three) *kamma* [stored up] or 'performed' (*kaṭattā*). However, the Abhidhammatthasaṃgaha (24) seems to give death-threshold or 'proximate' *kamma* (*āsanna*) precedence over habitual *kamma* (*bahula āciṇṇa*). This is acknowledged and illustrated by a rather nice simile in the Abhidhammatthavibhāvinī Ṭīkā:

> As when the gate of a cowpen full of cattle is opened, although there are steers and bulls behind, the animal close to the gate of the pen, even if it is a weak old cow, gets out first. Thus, even when there are other strong wholesome and unwholesome *kammas*, because of being close to the time of death, that which is proximate gives its result first and is therefore given here first.
> (Gethin 1994, 21 n. 35; Abhidhammatthavibhāvinī Ṭīkā 131)

In giving precedence to 'habitual' *kamma*, the Visuddhimagga and Abhidhammāvatāra seem to advocate that it is one's good or bad habits, one's nature and, in a way, the sum total of one's good or bad deeds that carries the weight at the time of death. The Abhidhammatthasaṃgaha and Abhidhammatthavibhāvinī Ṭīkā, on the other hand, in giving precedence to 'proximate' *kamma*, open the way for 'out of character' dispositions of mind at the time of death. To be sure, there is still a chance that habitually practised good or bad acts might also be the ones that feature at the time of death but precisely because they have become second nature, it is no longer certain. There is a real possibility that a long life of good habits might be overridden by a bad thought process at the end, or vice versa ('the weak old cow' being in the right place at the right time).

Summary

Even though the texts are not explicit, it seems to be the case that the concept of *bhavaṅga* has been perceived at a later stage as serving as the carrier of the kammic blue print of a person, a 'balance sheet' to use Gethin's term.[148] However, this description does not tally with the stories of unexpected and atypical rebirth (such as Mallikā, Erakapatta), which precisely thrive on the fact that the quality of the next rebirth, and therefore the new *bhavaṅga*, is 'out of character'. It is precisely this snapshot idea that is exploited as a narrative device to encourage (it is never too late) or to warn people (you never know when death might strike).

How does this relate to the contemporary Sri Lankan practice? Flowers, incense, chanting, etc., at the time of death may trigger the memory of, say, a visit to a Buddhist temple. As such it could provide an object of class (a) *kamma* or class (b) *kamma-nimitta*, and would either come under the category of 'habitual' (for a religious person) or of 'proximate' *kamma* (someone remembers one visit to a temple). Here the need to help a dying relative or friend takes over and the rigid law of karmic retribution and the self-responsibility is pushed into the background. Aspiring to or visualising a certain form of existence ('rebirth according to one's wish') could be interpreted as an attempt to induce a certain kammic experience at the time of death.

The *bhavaṅga/cuticitta/paṭisandhi* theory of the Abhidhamma gives authority to the notion of the importance of the last moment of one's life as determining the future rebirth, but this is not without problems. The tension between the desire to assist loved ones at the time of death and the rigid law of *kamma* is still there as reflected in the different orders of *kammas*.

II

THE FUNERAL

Contemporary Sri Lankan practice

A laywoman's burial

1. At about 10.00 a.m. a group of six people start out from the village. Near the station we buy milk powder and sugar. A short train ride is followed by a longer bus and three-wheeler ride. White flags along the roadside signal the way to the funeral house.[1] A white poster across the road states in large letters: 'All conditioned things have the nature of decay'.[2] More white posters and rows of metal chairs are in the front garden.[3] Metal posts covered with a roof of corrugated iron provide shade. A group of men are sitting there, chatting and chewing betel.[4] The men wear white sarongs and white shirts. Our arrival arouses a certain amount of interest. Women in white sarees come closer to watch us. The immediate family lines up in front of the house to greet us formally. The dead woman's daughter and son-in-law are in their seventies. The daughter gives a brief account of the death of her mother. We are told the mother was about 94. We enter the front room, which is bare of all furniture. In the centre is a wooden coffin, folded open.[5] An awning has been put up over it. The deceased is dressed all in white, her hands folded over her chest. Arching over the coffin are two enormous, artificial elephant tusks. At the head end a tall oil lamp is burning. We spend a few minutes in silence in the front room. Then we move on to the adjoining kitchen where women are gathered. The presents of milk powder and sugar are placed on the kitchen table.[6] A door leads to the garden behind the house. Fields with trees slope down. The house is small; the walls have never been plastered. Only extended family and close friends are present. The dead mother came originally from our village. Apart from the daughter there are several sons in their late sixties. The granddaughters walk around with trays of fizzy orange drinks.

2. It is nearly noon. Preparations start in the courtyard behind the house. Men build an awning as protection from the sun. Women bring out utensils for cooking. Jobs are allocated and a certain amount of light-hearted banter accompanies the work. Enormous pumpkins and an impressive quantity of beans are washed. The women cut the pumpkins up, sitting on the floor, holding long knives between their toes. Big slabs of dried fish are washed and cut. Bowls of red lentils must be picked through for small stones.[7] Men prepare small fireplaces made out of bricks. Soon there is the smell of spices being roasted and ground. Women take turns scraping out coconuts. More and more huge clay pots turn up and get filled.

At lunchtime a break is announced and men and women walk over to the neighbours' house. The house is bigger and comfortably furnished. The funeral party is welcomed by the neighbours. Most of the surrounding houses belong to the extended family. A lunch has been prepared and the variety of dishes is great. People sit down wherever there is space and eat together. After lunch everyone walks back to the funeral house. Work is resumed with more concentration and less banter. Behind the house the actual cooking starts. The front of the house is being prepared for the monks' arrival. A white cloth is tied underneath the corrugated iron roof. A floor mat is spread out under the roof. Four metal chairs are covered with white cloth. They are put on the mat facing the house. To the side, a small table is set up and covered with a tablecloth. Four bottles of fizzy orange and a parcel wrapped in a brown paper bag are placed on it. A tray with betel leaves and other utensils is arranged. In front of the chairs a rug is rolled out. In the meantime the place starts to fill up. The immediate family straighten their sarees and sarongs. The newcomers are mainly outsiders or remote relations. By about 3.00 p.m., a crowd of approximately one hundred people has gathered. Elderly people wear the traditional Sri Lankan formal clothes in white.

3. At about 3.45 p.m., four monks arrive in a van.[8] People move closer and stop chatting. The monks approach the house, the most senior first. One by one they step onto a coconut mat in front of the house. A male family member squats down in front of them. He pours water from a plastic bowl over their feet and pats them dry with a towel. They take their seats on the four arranged chairs. The family kneels down in front of each monk to pay their respects. The rest of us remain standing. Inside the house the coffin is now closed. Six men lift it up and move near the door. The exact time to carry the coffin out of the house has been determined astrologically. Someone checks his watch and signals that it is the right time. The coffin is carried over the threshold and put down on the stand outside. The monks are facing the closed coffin and the house. On the other side of the coffin a floor mat is being spread out. The immediate family sits down. A jug with water and an empty bowl is put in front of them. The layman who conducts the funeral proceedings greets the monks and visitors.[9] The ceremony proper starts and people sit down on the floor. The salutation to the Buddha is chanted, followed by the Three Refuges and the Five Precepts. The abbot of the local temple says a few words. Instructed by him the daughter kneels down in front of the monks. She offers the brown parcel containing a white piece of cloth. While she is doing this everyone chants together three times:

imaṃ matakavatthaṃ bhikkhusaṃghassa dema!
We offer the 'cloth of the dead' to the community of monks!

This is followed by:

tambūlagilānapaccayadānaṃ bhikkhusaṃghassa dema!
We offer this gift of betel and refreshments to the community of monks!

Immediately afterwards the monks chant twice in a sombre voice:

aniccā vata saṃkhārā uppādavayadhammino
uppajitvā nirujjhanti tesaṃ vūpasamo sukho.[10]
Impermanent are conditioned things; it is their nature to arise and fall;
having arisen they cease; their complete stilling is happiness.

The abbot, the most senior monk present, dedicates the merit to the dead mother. He instructs the relatives to pour the water into the bowl. The family members take hold of the jug and start pouring very slowly. The abbot chants; everyone repeats after him:

Idaṃ me ñātīnaṃ hotu! Sukhitā hontu ñātayo![11]
May this be for my relatives! May the relatives be happy!

The family continues to pour the water. All four monks chant together:

Yathā vārivahā pūrā paripūrenti sāgaraṃ,
evam eva ito dinnaṃ petānaṃ upakappati.
Unname udakaṃ vaṭṭaṃ yathā ninnaṃ pavattati,
evam eva ito dinnaṃ petānaṃ upakappati.[12]

Just as the rivers full of water fill the ocean full,
even so does what is given here benefit the dead.
Just as water rained on high ground moves [down] to the low land,
even so does what is given here benefit the dead.

The bowl begins to overflow. The monks continue the chanting:

Icchitaṃ patthitam tuyhaṃ sabbaṃ eva samijjhatu,
pūrentu cittasaṃkappā maṇi jotiraso yathā.

(repeated and followed by:)
Icchitaṃ patthitam tuyhaṃ khippaṃ eva samijjhatu,
sabbe pūrentu cittasaṃkappā cando paṇṇaraso yathā.

May all whatever is desired and wanted quickly come to be.
May all your wishes be fulfilled like a radiant wish-fulfilling gem.
May all whatever is desired and wanted quickly come to be.
May all your wishes be fulfilled like the moon on the full moon day.

Everyone says, '*Sādhu! sādhu! sādhu!*' The abbot begins the sermon. A quotation from the Pāli scriptures provides the theme for his talk. The concluding part consists of religious wishes. 'By the force of this merit may the next rebirths be good ones! May *Nirvāṇa* be attained!' The dead mother and all who are present are included. Everyone says, '*Sādhu! sādhu! sādhu!*' The funeral conductor conveys everyone's gratitude. Permission is given to the monks to leave. The brown paper bag and the four bottles of fizzy orange are packed into the waiting van. The monks leave at about 4.30 p.m. The funeral conductor introduces various speakers next. About six to eight people give short speeches. They are friends and colleagues of family members. At the end the dates of the two follow-up ceremonies are announced: the sixth-day preaching and the seventh-day alms giving. For a brief moment the coffin is opened. The granddaughters start weeping. People jostle closer to take a look. It is the final farewell for the women. The daughter touches her dead mother's face lightly.

The coffin is closed and the bearers swiftly carry it away.[13] A white parasol is held over it. Grains of puffed rice are thrown. Only men walk in the procession; the women and some men stay back. Two men make preparations in the deserted front room. A small fireplace is built out of bricks on the floor. The fire is lit. A new clay pot is filled with milk. The milk is brought to the boil. It overflows and spills onto the floor. A sprig from a lime tree lies nearby. Very little attention is paid to the proceedings.[14] The women have gone back to the courtyard. Banana leaves are cut into circular 'plates' and washed. The funeral meal requires the finishing touches.

4. The distance from the funeral house to the cemetery is about one kilometre. The country road to the cemetery is marked with white flags. At the entrance to the cemetery an arch has been erected. A poster like the one at the entrance to the funeral house hangs from it. A path is marked by a fence made of young coconut leafs. It leads to the open grave where the gravediggers are waiting. The coffin is carried clockwise around the open grave three times. The procession follows still holding the white parasol and throwing puffed rice. The coffin is placed alongside the open grave, head to the west.[15] Once more it is opened. The white tassles are hanging down into the open grave. The sun is very low now, the shadows are long. Men pay their last respects in silence. One of them addresses the group, 'If anyone has anything to say he should speak now.' Everyone remains silent. The coffin is closed for the last time and lowered into the open grave. Two of the gravediggers stand in the open grave and receive the coffin. After they have climbed out people start throwing handfuls of earth on to the coffin. The gravediggers finish off with spades, forming a mound.

Decorations are being cut from the flowers of young coconuts. Two king coconuts are cut open. One of the gravediggers jokingly takes a sip before placing them at the head and foot of the mound. Two oil lamps are lit and placed in protective bamboo pipes on the grave. People leave the cemetery collecting the white flag sticks on their way to the house. Sunset is close. Back at the funeral house a small table has been prepared in front of the house. Bottles of liquor, soft drinks and biscuits are arranged, all covered with a table cloth. This is the gravediggers' 'payment'. The women begin to serve the funeral meal on the banana leaves. Some people start eating; others discuss transport arrangements. As dusk is brief people are anxious to be on their way before dark.

A monk's cremation

1. For days death notices at the station had announced the time and date of the cremation. They show a picture of the dead monk, the abbot of a temple in a neighbouring village. At about 2.00 p.m. we walk into town to the level crossing. A number of three-wheelers race along the main road, each of them taking two or three monks to the temple. Orange flags along the roadside mark the way over a little river and through the paddy fields.[16] Turning off the main road we pass small groups of people heading for the temple. Hundreds of flag bands across the road have turned the lane into an orange arcade. The entrance to the temple premises is marked by a tall orange gate. At the top is written 'All conditioned things are impermanent'. Before we go to the temple we turn right into the playing-field nearby.

At the far end, the funeral pyre has been erected in the east-west direction.[17] Four layers give it a stepped pyramid shape. It is made out of wooden poles and orange fabric. Each layer is decorated with a curtain and has tassles at all four corners. It looks surprisingly solid and resembles a temple. We cross the field to take a closer look. No one is near the pyre.[18] There is an opening of about a square metre at the west end covered with a curtain. A fence surrounds the pyre leaving a gap where the opening is. Eight silver-painted clay pots are placed upside down on the poles of the fence.[19] At the other end of the playing-field a stand for the coffin has been put up. It is covered down to the ground with a red cloth. At both sides mats are spread out on the floor. There is a sun roof made of corrugated iron on metal poles. A white cloth has been tied underneath. It is decorated with strips of orange plastic. At the west side is a wooden lectern with a number of microphones. Big loudspeakers look down on the place from lamp posts.

About 150 to 200 metal chairs have been arranged in an L-shape around the stand for the coffin. They, too, are under corrugated iron sun roofs. We turn back and enter the temple premises. There are a great number of posters (printed on orange and white cloth). The temple is relatively large with a temple school for monks (*pirivena*) attached.[20] A big crowd of about 300 to 400 hundred people has gathered. Groups of monks in orange robes mix with groups of laypeople in white. The wooden coffin is already closed when we arrive. Two monks sit near the coffin.[21] The slight delay of the proceedings is due to the fact that some monks from Kandy have not yet arrived. Upon their arrival a processions begins to form.[22]

2. Young men smartly dressed in white trousers and shirts walk in front. They wear orange sashes over their shoulder and carry long poles with a round-shaped disc at the top.[23] Two groups of six are walking in single file. A senior monk holding a fan and a picture of the dead abbot leads the procession. He, too, has an orange sash added to his robes and a strip of cloth serves as a belt. He is followed by six laymen carrying the coffin. An orange canopy is held over it and puffed rice is thrown all along the way. The monk walks very slowly on long strips of white cloth spread out in front of him. A number of young men behind the coffin collect the cloth. They rush to the front of the procession and skilfully throw it to their colleagues in front who spread it out again. Their sarongs are tied up, they are sweating. The coffin bearers are careful not to step on the white cloth between them.[24] The most senior monks are the first to follow the coffin; then come the junior monks.[25] The older laypeople, dressed in formal white sarees and sarongs, walk behind the monks. Some people walk alongside the procession; others join up after it has passed.[26]

Very slowly the orange and white procession starts to move clockwise around the temple. After the third circumambulation it leaves the temple premises. The entrance to the school grounds is just across the road. A schoolboy in uniform holding a picture of the dead abbot welcomes the procession. He is joined by nursery-school children waving white flags. The coffin bearers turn left and put the coffin down on the stand. A folded orange shawl is put across it like a sash. The senior monks take their seats facing the coffin and the pyre. A group of about fifteen monks of different ages sit down on the mat at the west end.[27] A jug with water and an empty bowl is placed in front of them on the mat. To the side is a small table with several brown paper parcels containing white pieces of cloth. A tray of betel leaves and bottles of fizzy drinks are covered with a cloth. A group of lay people dressed in white sit down on the mat at the other end. Some photographers and a couple of people filming for a local TV station are waiting nearby.

3. A middle-aged monk acts as the funeral conductor. His introductions are broadcast over the loud speakers. Various monks come forward and say a few words. People are settling on the floor or remain standing. An elderly senior monk begins with the salutation to the Buddha. The Three Refuges and the Five Precepts are chanted by everyone after him. This is followed by a short speech ending in religious wishes (*prārthanā*). The brown paper parcels are handed to the monks on the mat. The parcels are subsequently placed on the coffin. A monk's voice over the speaker chants three times:

imāni matakavatthāni bhikkhusaṃghassa dema!
We offer these 'clothes of the dead' to the community of monks!

This is followed immediately by senior monks chanting. The other monks repeat after the broadcasted voice:

aniccā vata saṃkhārā . . . (as above)

Then the monks and laypeople on both ends of the coffin get up and take the parcels. They offer them side by side to the senior monks sitting nearest to the coffin. The senior monk at the microphone dedicates the merit to the dead abbot. Now the monks settle back on the mat where they are joined by two of the laypeople. They sit or kneel in a circle around the bowl and all take hold of the jug. They begin to pour very slowly while the chanting begins:

Yathā vārivahā . . . (as above)

The bowl begins to overflow. The monk speaks for a little while. Eventually he chants the 'blessing' for everyone present:

Icchitaṃ patthitaṃ tuyhaṃ . . . (as above)

All the laypeople say '*Sādhu! sādhu! sādhu!*' The funeral conductor takes his place at the microphone to introduce the speakers. First, a number of senior monks give their speeches. Meanwhile, laypeople and junior monks walk around with trays of bottled soft drinks. They are offered to the senior monks first, then to other junior monks and eventually to children and the foreigner. The speeches continue. It is now the turn of junior monks to speak. Various printed papers are being distributed amongst the laypeople: death notices, a poem and A4-sized colour prints with a picture of the deceased. The pictures are especially popular. The speeches continue. It is now the turn of the laypeople. The main supporters of the temple and other 'important' laymen speak, amongst them a well-known politician. Two noisy dogs are being chased off the school ground. People begin to get bored and start chatting. After the speeches are over the coffin is briefly folded open. The body is dressed in robes; an orange cloth is wrapped around the head.[28] There is a lot of motion as people jostle closer. Press photographers take their last pictures of the dead abbot. The coffin is closed again and carried the short distance to the funeral pyre by six laymen.

4. People rush to find a place as close to the funeral pyre as possible. The coffin bearers circumambulate the pyre three times clockwise. A poem is sung and broadcasted over the speakers. People settle down and go quiet. The curtain covering the opening of the funeral pyre is lifted and the coffin is pushed in. Two employees of the funeral house climb inside. Large planks of wood are passed inside and stacked around the coffin.[29] Bottles of kerosene are being poured onto the wood. The two professionals climb out and light two long wooden torches. Two men wearing white sarongs and vests are standing by. A white piece of cloth is tied around their heads. They take the torches and hold them behind their backs. Starting from the west end they circumambulate the pyre three times. One is walking clockwise, the other anticlockwise. As they meet again at the west end they throw the torches over their shoulders into the opening in the pyre. They take off their head cloths and throw them into the pyre as well.[30] Again the professionals take over. Five planks of wood are nailed to the opening. The curtain is let down again and tied with ribbons at the side. Almost immediately the first people start leaving. The majority stays until the top of the pyre begins to burn and smoke rises up into the early evening sky. By the time the first flames are visible more than half the people have left the place.

Excursus: treatment of the corpse and its disposal

I did not observe the customs at the time of death (or immediately before and after) personally and have to rely for this aspect on interviews and secondary literature. I was told that as soon as death occurs the body is straightened, fingers and toes tied together and the corpse is laid out with the head to the west.[31] The next step in the treatment of the corpse is embalming, which is historically well documented.[32] Its practice, however, seemed to have been restricted to certain cases, e.g., when permission of the king was awaited. Robert Knox's colourful description of the preservation of the body runs as follows:

> [T]hey cut down a Tree that may be proper for their purpose, and hollow it, like a Hog-trough, and put the body being Embowelled and Embalmed into it, filled up all about with Pepper. And so let it lay in the house, until it be the king's Command to carry it out to the burning. For that they dare not do without the King's order, if the Person deceased be a Courtier. Sometimes the King gives no order in a great while, it may be not at all. Therefore in such cases, that the Body may not take up house-room, or annoy them, they dig an hole in the floor of their house, and put hollowed tree and all in and cover it. If afterwards the King commands to burn the Body, they take it up again in obedience to the King, otherwise there it lyes.
>
> (Knox 1681, 116 (1966, 219))

Indeed, ordinary people with no special relationship to the king were, according to Knox, disposed of rather soon after death and it was not necessary to embalm them. A very learned, elderly man told me that even in his youth embalming was not commonly practised. It has become increasingly popular nowadays, especially when relatives residing abroad are expected for the funeral.[33] The body is then dressed in white, festive clothes in the case of laypeople or orange robes in the case of a monk, and returned to the house in a coffin. There is no difference in design between the coffins used for cremations and those used for burials.

It is difficult to determine with any certainty when coffins first came to be used in Sri Lanka, but one might suspect Western influence during colonial times here. Robert Knox (1681, 116 (1966, 219)) does not mention a coffin in his description of a cremation of an official of the king nor in his description of a burial for 'Persons of inferior Quality' on the previous page. Tillakaratne (1986, 164) observes:

> It is striking that no reference to a coffin is found in the Sinhalese literary works written prior to the advent of the Europeans. The usual practice was to lay the corpse on the bier after wrapping it up in a strip of cloth or a mat. The *Mandāram pura puvata* says that the body of King Sri Vijaya Rājasiṃha was wrapped in costly silk cloths 'in accordance with the ancient custom' before it was placed on the bier.[34]

According to Tillakaratne (1986, 174, n. 76), the simplest form of a bier was a stretcher made of two bamboo poles, whereas people of higher standing would be carried to the cremation ground on costly grand bedsteads or couches. Going back in time, Ariyapala (1968, 308), based on the Saddharma Ratnāvaliya (thirteenth century), says that traditionally no coffins were used. He further quotes Martin Wickramasinghe, who is unfortunately not very specific at all as to the period he is referring to:

> Martin Wickramasinghe makes the following observation: . . . The coffin was not a feature of ancient Sinhalese civilization. In my opinion burying a dead body in a coffin was also not an ancient Sinhalese custom. They cremated the dead; if not, threw it into the cemetery. One can see this ancient custom persisting yet with the Tamils and the Muslims of India.[35]

This leads us to the question of different ways of disposing of the body, preferences and historical changes. The picture we gain from Wickramasinghe is that the 'ancient' methods were throwing the corpse into the charnel ground (for poor, ordinary people) and cremation (for people of higher social standing and monks). Disanayaka (1998, 90), unfortunately without producing evidence and solely on the basis of his observation of Sinhala idioms, points out:

> In rural areas, the phrase used to denote burial is '*kälē gahanava*' (to throw into the jungle), a phrase reminiscent of an old custom when the dead body was left in the forest (*kälē*).

This is reminiscent of the ancient Indian practice of leaving dead bodies in charnel grounds. Basham (1967, 178) points out that cremation was practised by 'the upper classes in ancient India' but co-existed side by side with other forms of disposal. Particularly interesting is his observation that there might have been a certain overlap in practices:

> In most literary references the *śmaśāna*, or cremation ground, is described as covered with putrefying corpses and haunted by dogs and vultures, rather than as a scene of cremation. The description of such places show that many people in ancient India did not cremate their dead, but, like the Zoroastrians of Persia, merely abandoned their bodies to the wild beasts. No doubt economic considerations played a big part in this practice, especially in those parts of the country where timber was scarce; even to this day the poorer Indians must be content with exiguous funeral pyres, and their bodies are often not completely burnt.

The different practices are also reflected in the different Pali words for 'cemetery': the term *āḷāhana* (derived from the √*ḍah*, to burn) refers to cremation ground, whereas the term *sīvathika/sivathika* (derivation uncertain) appears to be used for a charnel ground.[36] The former is relatively rare and hardly ever occurs in the Nikāyas, whereas the latter is quite common in both the Nikāyas and commentarial literature. The term *susāna*, however, is the most commonly used term and, like its Sanskrit counterpart *śmaśāna*, is not restricted to cremation grounds but seems more generally used for a place of disposal of the dead.[37] The practice in our village, too, was to have cremations at one end of the burial ground, and it is only to be expected that, particularly in the case of small villages, there should be only one designated place for the disposal of the dead, whereas larger (or richer) towns might have two or more places.[38]

Graphic descriptions of charnel grounds are also a familiar motif in the context of certain meditation practices (*aśubha-bhāvanā*), and feature in the Mahāsatipaṭṭhāna Sutta (D II 290–315) and elsewhere.[39] Schmithausen (1982, 71) raises the question of why in the course of this meditation technique real corpses are replaced by mental images and suggests a possible change of funeral customs (increasing popularity of cremations) as a contributing factor.[40]

To return to Sri Lanka, Ariyapala (1968, 309) points out that even in literature as late as the thirteenth century a distinction is made between a cremation ground (*sohona*) and a charnel ground (*amu sohona*), where corpses are cast. This might be an indication that both practices were still known and possibly even practised at that time. And according to Tillakaratne (1986, 173, n. 72) 'this custom [leaving corpses for wild animals] may have prevailed to a certain extent in some of the out-of-the-way places such as Ūva, for here the term *miniya kälē gahanavā*, "throwing the corpse into the jungle", is still frequently used even in reference to burial'. It seems quite possible (and plausible) that the custom of leaving corpses out in the open survived in Sri Lanka much longer than on the subcontinent. It may have even been the prevalent form of disposal of the dead and could have co-existed with cremation (for the more privileged), just as burials coexist with cremations today.

Burials, according to Wickramasinghe (see above), came into the picture at some later stage, but unfortunately he, too, does not adduce evidence nor does he give any indication when that would have been. Of course the line might be very fine between 'throwing a corpse into the jungle or cemetery' and burying it 'without any more ado' as described by Knox (1681, 116 (1966, 218)). However, there seems to be general agreement in the secondary literature that then and now cremation was reserved for socially higher-ranking people and monks, whereas leaving the body in a charnel ground or burial was for ordinary people.[41]

Tillakaratne (1986, 163), commenting upon the above quoted 'embalming passage' in Robert Knox (1681, 116 (1966, 219)), adds another factor, a special tax on cremation:

> Codrington mentions yet another tax levied by the king before the cremation of a dead body was allowed. This was known as *bim-puluṭu*, literally 'Soil-burning'. The king was considered the 'lord of the earth' (*bhūpati*), and the fee *bim-puluṭu* was levied for 'burning the king's soil at the cremation of a dead body'.[42]

The mention of a special tax on cremation is of great interest, because it indicates that even in the seventeenth century cremations were for the well-to-do. For the early nineteenth century, Davy (1821, 291) states that the low castes were prohibited from cremating their dead.

Disanayaka (1998, 89) sums up contemporary practice:

> The corpse will be disposed of in one of three ways: burial (*valalanavā*), deposit in an underground chamber (*tänpat karanavā*), and cremation. Buddhist monks are always cremated, and laymen are cremated, only if they are of some social standing. However, a layman will not be cremated if any of his elder siblings are still alive.

Unlike monks, who are always cremated, lay people have a choice between burial and cremation. I was told that cremations are more costly than burials, and this is one factor that obviously influences the choice.[43]

No funerals are conducted on Tuesdays or Fridays, and this rule seems to be strictly observed in the case of both monks and laypeople, although no one could offer any explanation for this.[44] Quite a few people dismissed this rule as nonsense and one monk reasoned that if there is no bad day for dying, why should there be a bad day for funerals.[45] In searching for an explanation, a good starting point might be to look at other beliefs and practices with regard to certain days of the week. One hint might be found in the rules for rituals devoted to the gods and demons taking place on certain days of the week.[46] Gombrich (1991, 228) says that *devāles* are open only on special days called *kemvara* (sic!).[47] The *kemvara* days vary from area to area (or even from deity to deity), and he mentions Sundays, Tuesdays and Fridays for the *devāles* in his area, but Saturdays and Wednesdays for the low country. Gombrich further mentions a certain ceremony held for the Twelve Gods (involving dancing and becoming possessed), which takes place on Tuesday or Friday nights. Certain ceremonies performed for the deities (especially those involving being possessed) are not performed on *pōya* days.[48] This is, of course, not a satisfactory explanation of why certain days of the week and not others are singled out for the worship of deities (and there does not seem to be total agreement about which days they are). It does, however, hint at the possibility that certain days of the week are 'reserved' for worshipping deities in the same way that certain days of the month (*pōya*) are 'reserved' for specific 'Buddhist' rituals.

Commentary to the practice

Early Buddhist texts do not offer explanations in the manner of, for example, the Vedic Gṛhya- and Śrauta-*sūtra*s which will be discussed below, nor are they *prescriptive* in nature. What little we find on funerary rites in the Pāli texts is in the form of *description*, such as the account of the Buddha's cremation in the Mahāparinibbāna-Sutta and its commentaries. When asked on his deathbed how his body should be treated after death, the Buddha famously replied that it should be treated like the body of a universal monarch. There is no hint of an attempt to establish a new, 'Buddhist' cremation ritual. As Holt (1981, 1) states:

> Buddhist interpretations of death did not originate in an historical or cultural vacuum. Conceptions of the after-life, and the prescribed behavior relating to the dead, were modified adaptations of prevailing Brāhmaṇical patterns of belief. This is especially apparent when we examine the beliefs and practices of the early Buddhist laity.[49]

This raises the question: does it make sense at all to speak of 'Buddhist' death rituals? Most of my informants did, indeed, distinguish between 'Buddhist' and 'non-Buddhist', and there seems to be a clear idea, even though the content might vary from person to person, that some ceremonies are 'Buddhist' while others are 'non-Buddhist'. They used the term *bauddhāgama* in this context, but only in the negative form and clearly with a negative connotation of 'not worth bothering about' (*mēvā Bauddhāgama nemeyi, mēvā siritvirit vitarayi*).

The question of 'Buddhist' versus 'non-Buddhist' and indeed the term *bauddhāgama* again link in with a wider discussion of religious self-identity and require some explanation and definition. The term *āgama*, of course, is an old one, but Carter (1993, 19) tries to prove that it has undergone a change in meaning and that its usage in the sense of 'religion' is relatively young and influenced by a series of debates between Buddhists and Christians which started about 1865 in Sri Lanka:

> It is probable that the use of the terms *āgama* and *buddhāgama* to represent 'religion' and 'Buddhism' respectively antedates these debates. By how many years? I would suggest by about 100 at most.

Unfortunately, Carter does not adduce any evidence why it should be a 100 years and not more or less. Bechert (1976) on the other hand argues that the use of *āgama* and Buddhadharma as synonyms is much older:

> . . . denn wie man im Śrī-Sumaṅgala Śabdakoṣaya leicht finden kann, kennt schon der älteste erhaltene singhalesische Prosatext (*Dhamapiyā Aṭuvā Gäṭapadaya*, ed. D.B. Jayatilaka, Colombo 1933, S.17) *āgama* im Sinne von Buddhadharma.[50]

To sum this up, at some point, either as a result of colonial influence or much earlier, a Buddhist identity developed. This manifests itself in modern Sri Lanka more often than not in a derogatory way of perceiving the other, 'non-Buddhist', which is, as was repeatedly pointed out to me, not worth studying. I had originally adopted the distinction in my dissertation (using inverted commas) in order to reflect my informants' point of view but have since decided to give it up.[51] First, I would argue that rituals which have been practised and incorporated into a Buddhist framework probably from the beginning (there must have been funerals of followers of the Buddha around the time of the Buddha) makes them 'Buddhist'. Second, some of the ceremonies described here may not have been started or 'invented' by the Buddha, but it does not necessarily mean they are 'against the spirit of Buddhism'. I shall refer to these as 'general customs'. Thirdly, some of these ceremonies have been given a 'Buddhist twist' such as the custom of offering a *matakavastra* to the monks.

The general customs

Any attempt to categorise the customs surrounding the funerals is necessarily a simplification, but in view of the great number of major and minor customs it seems to be necessary. The funeral customs will therefore be summarized under three main categories: respect for the departed, death pollution and customs connected with the spirit of the departed. Starting with a summary of the customs in contemporary Sri Lanka, I shall then turn to secondary literature for the corresponding contemporary Hindu customs.

Respect for the departed

The first two categories (Respect and Pollution) could be regarded as two sides of the same coin, as the corpse is, according to Firth (1997, 73), considered in the Indian context to be 'highly inauspicious and auspicious' at the same time. To start with the auspicious aspect, respect for the departed finds expression mainly in three ways: 'paying last respects', the funeral procession and circumambulation.

After the coffin is brought back to the house, neighbours and friends come to 'pay their last respects' (*salakanavā*) to the departed by visiting the funeral house and spending some time near the body. Respects are paid at certain stages, i.e., before the procession begins and at the cemetery near the open grave. Disanayaka (1998, 90) says there is also the custom of scattering flowers or perfume on the corpse which 'is known as "*miniyata katā karanava*" literally, "speaking to the corpse"'.[52] I have not witnessed this custom personally, but the scattering of flowers or flower petals on the corpse is, of course, very common in contemporary Hindu rituals (see Firth 1997, 84f.) and might have its origin in the concept of the body being offered into the fire as a sacrifice.

The clockwise circumambulation (*pradakṣiṇā*) is a common Indian way of veneration—for example when visiting sacred or religious sites—and as such not confined to Hindus or Buddhists. The circumambulation of the corpse is of particular importance in the contemporary Hindu funeral context and Firth (1997, 74) sums up its function as follows:

> The circumambulation seems to have several functions. There is the discharge of debt (*ṛṇa*), which would be especially important if the deceased is a parent or grandparent. Second, like the circumambulation of a god, the mourners take *darśana*, receiving the blessing of the deceased, by being 'in his sight'. At the pyre the circumambulations create a boundary around the corpse, which protects the newly released soul (*bhūta-preta*) and the body from ghosts on the one hand, and separates the mourners from the *bhūta-preta* on the other, as it may still be attached to the family. Finally, they may be a rite of separation of psychological significance to the mourners.[53]

I did not observe circumambulation of the corpse in the Sri Lankan funeral context, but rather the circumambulation of the grave/funeral pyre.[54] In Sri Lanka the coffin is carried three times clockwise around the open grave (or funeral pyre) before it is finally placed inside. At the monk's cremation described above, the coffin was carried clockwise around the temple complex as a sign of respect for his achievments.

There is also circumambulation of the funeral pyre after the coffin has been placed in it. In Sri Lanka two nephews of the deceased circumambulate the pyre in different directions before lighting it.[55] Firth (1997, 76) also refers to the circumambulation of the funeral pyre in contemporary Hindu rites:

> A number of informants said that the circumambulation here had to be clockwise (*pradakṣiṇā*), indicating a view of the body as sacred. . . . Other informants said emphatically they should be anti-clockwise, suggesting that the body was impure and inauspicious.

This statement regarding the ambiguous status of the body provides a clue to an understanding of the curious double circumambulation in Sri Lanka. But it should also be added that the 'normal' *pradakṣiṇā* is life-affirming as it follows the movement of the sun, whereas the *apradakṣiṇā* is the negation of life.

Another expression of respect in Sri Lanka are processions (*perahära*). Best known is the annual Kandy *perahära*, but most temples hold an annual procession. In fact almost every time the relic receptacle (*dhātukaraňḍuva*) is taken out of the temple, a small procession is formed with one person carrying the relic receptacle, another person holding an umbrella over it. At the funeral procession, too, an umbrella is held over the coffin and grains of puffed rice and sometimes even small coins are thrown onto the coffin all the way to the cemetery. As was pointed out to me, the custom of throwing puffed rice is also part of certain rituals performed for gods at a *devāle*.[56] Disanayaka (1998, 90) further mentions that drums (*mala bera*) and other musical instruments are played in the funeral procession, but I did not observe this at the funerals I attended. The description by Tillakaratne (1986, 164) suggests that in the past, too, somewhat more elaborate processions took place than the ones I witnessed:

> The funeral procession was then formed consisting of the body on the bier, preceded by the drummers and pipers and followed by the relatives and friends of the dead carrying different articles such as canopies, small earthen vessels containing fried paddy (*vilanda*) and scented water. Usually the funeral procession proceeded along a specially appointed route, which was sometimes strewn with white sand.

The custom of strewing white sand seems to be a precedent for or variation of the custom of the coffin bearers walking on a white cloth, which, I was told, was the usual practise at every funeral in the past.[57]

The coffin bearers changed twice on the way to the cemetery, which was explained as follows: for the first stage the immediate family carries the coffin, for the second stage the more remote relations carry it and the third and last is covered by friends and neighbours of the departed, i.e., the geographical distance from the house mirrors in some way the distance by relationship. In Sri Lanka women sometimes prefer not to walk in the procession but stay at home, especially when they are pregnant.[58] As mentioned above, cremations seem to attract bigger crowds, and in my judgment, the number of women is also higher in this case. According to Disanayaka (1998, 90), in most parts of the island monks are not supposed to walk in the procession.[59] In our area the ceremony conducted by the monks takes place at the funeral house, and the monks do not come to the cemetery at all but leave before the procession starts. An exception here was the funeral procession described in 'A Monk's Cremation', which formed a part of the ceremony.

By attending a funeral one shows one's respect for the deceased himself as well as for the bereaved family, which makes it a social duty and accounts for the fact that funerals are rather big affairs. By no means are all of the people who attend the funeral or walk in the procession personally acquainted with the departed.

Death pollution

As well as being regarded as an object of veneration, the corpse is also a source of pollution.[60] The Sinhalese term for instances of pollution (such as death, birth and menstruation) is *kili*, which Wijesekera (1949, 194) defines as 'forbidden, not allowed, polluted, unclean and hence to be segregated and avoided'.

Parry (1994, 216) shows that there are certain parallels between death and birth pollution in the Indian context:

> [B]oth are also brought about by the—one might say purposeful, even violent—separation of bodies. Death pollution is triggered at the point at which the vital breath evacuates the body, which, according to one theory at least, is the point at which the chief mourner cracks open the cranium as the corpse lies burning on the pyre. Birth pollution is triggered by cutting the umbilical cord.

As one would expect there are certain restrictions regarding food. From the moment a death occurs, all cooking stops in a house, and meals for the family are provided by friends and neighbours. Firth (1997, 80) observes that for contemporary Hindu practice, too, cooking stops in some households immediately after a death occurs (not after the breaking of the skull). A funeral house is regarded as polluted and therefore not an appropriate place for preparing food. But there might be another reason for these food restrictions: death pollution is, according to Parry (1994, 217), spread by sharing meals.

As in other cases of temporary pollution, certain rituals are performed to mark the end of the period of impurity. After the coffin is taken to the cemetery, a new clay pot of milk is made to boil over in the front room where the coffin was kept, which is meant to cleanse it ('to take the fumes away'). On New Year's day a similar ritual is carried out at a particular, astrologically determined, moment but in the case of a funeral there does not appear to be any rule about the time other than that it happens after the coffin has been removed. Even now cooking activity cannot be resumed straightaway; seven days have to pass after the death occurred.

Not only the funeral house is in need of cleansing, but also, or foremost, the people visiting it. Milk is sprinkled on the people returning from the cemetery with a sprig from a lime tree (*dehi*).[61] It is also customary to rub lime leaves on one's head when returning home from a funeral and this is done especially for children.[62]

Other rules relating to a funeral house suggest spiritual pollution as well. *Yantras* and amulets are supposed to lose their power and should be left at home and put back on only after one has had a bath on return from the funeral house. For the Indian context, too, bathing (along with a number of other purificatory rites) seems obligatory and is well documented after return from a funeral house.[63] Pregnant women or people with open wounds or certain illnesses are not supposed to visit funeral houses.

The spirit of the departed

Certain customs were explained to me in terms of the presence of the spirit of the departed (*malagiyaprāṇakārayā*). Pictures, mirrors and shiny objects, even betel leaves, are turned around or removed from the house in order not to confuse the spirit when it sees its own reflection (or in order to not scare the family, who might see the reflection of the spirit in the mirror). Furthermore, doors and windows are kept open in a funeral house so as not to restrict the spirit's movement.

I was told that it is regarded as 'dangerous' to leave the body (or an open grave or funeral pyre) unattended, but no specific reasons were given. For up to seven days, and at the very least until the funeral day, there will always be people in the house, and a night vigil is kept next to the coffin. Women do not participate with the exception of elderly women in the neighbourhood who provide coffee, tea and snacks throughout the night. I was told that in the past the Sinhala version of the *Vessantarajātaka* was recited in a sorrowful voice on such occasion.[64] Nowadays one is more likely to find a group of young men (friends and neighbours of the family) playing games such as *käram* and drinking arrak. The coffin has to be taken out of the house at a particular astrologically powerful moment to prevent the spirit from returning to the house. Even the clockwise circumambulation around the grave was interpreted as confusing the spirit so that it will not find its way home.[65]

Unlike the customs described under the first two categories (Respect for the Departed and Death Pollution) the customs subsumed under this category are of a more subtle nature and not easily observable. Again, as in the case of ghosts haunting a house or a particular family member, people were rather self-conscious and reluctant to offer information about these customs. It is therefore not surprising that in the secondary literature on Sri Lankan customs nothing much is found, which makes it necessary to turn elsewhere for clues.

In brahmanical Hinduism, physical death is not the absolute end, but the beginning of a liminal period, which ends when the spirit of the departed (*preta*) becomes an ancestor (*pitṛ*). The different stages the soul goes through (from death to its final destiny as an ancestor), as well as the accompanying rituals, are well defined and described in brahmanical and contemporary literature.[66] Even though the literature on contemporary Hindu rites does not provide us with close parallels to the customs mentioned above, there are some valuable clues as to the possible motives.

Parry (1994, 173) points out that from the moment of death, the corpse needs to be protected from evil spirits trying to take possession of it:

> A lamp is lit near the patient, and is kept alight until the corpse is taken out of the house. Its flame is a sign to the soul that it should go straight up, and also affords protection against the evil spirits which threaten to invade the corpse (and which are also kept at bay by the women who continually surround and touch it).

Some more insight into the dangers for the liminal being can be gained when examining the nature of the first six offerings (*piṇḍa*). According to Ghosh (1989, 155) the predominant motive behind these first six offerings (of which only one is meant as food for the spirit) is to secure protection from evil spirits:

> Thereafter, i.e., between the time of death and till cremation is over, six *piṇḍas* are to be offered 'to deities and to the evil spirits.' . . . The first *piṇḍa* is meant for Mother Earth, the deity presiding over the site of death; the second (at the door-step) is provision (*pātheyam*) for the journey; the third (in the courtyard) is for all who move in the sky (*khecara*) including the sun: 'with this one stroke crores of evil spirits fade away.' The one offered in the living room is meant to ward off *Piśācas*, *Rākṣasas* and *Yakṣas* floating in the air in different

> directions, while the *piṇḍa* placed in the cremation ground helps the departed soul to attain a state of spirithood (*pretatvam*). This last one also bars evil spirits from the residual bones collected and stored for the time being. (V.31-36).[67]

To my knowledge it is not customary in Sri Lanka to make offerings to the deities or demons on the day of the funeral. However, the custom of keeping a lamp burning near the open coffin, etc., indicates that the belief in evil spirits hovering around the corpse might also be present in Sri Lanka.

But according to Parry (1994, 173) it is not only the evil spirits that attempt to invade and take possession of the corpse, but the soul itself tries to re-enter it:

> My priestly informants are clear that as soon as the soul leaves the body, the *yamdut* (messengers of death) take it straight off to the court of their master with a noose around its neck. There they show it the torments of the various hells, which await it before returning to earth. . . . Finding himself back home, the deceased tries to re-enter the body he has recently vacated, but is held back by the *yamdut*'s halter. For the next ten days the disembodied soul hovers miserably about the scene of its death searching for a house to inhabit.

The spirit is confused and has yet to realize the fact that he is dead and has to let go of his attachments and bonds to this world, if he has not already done so before his death.[68] Consequently, one definition of a bad death is an 'unprepared death' (such as death by sudden accident or childbirth) which necessitates additional rituals.

The intermediate being, the *preta*, is further described in the Hindu literature as naked, hungry, thirsty and totally dependent on his family for support. He is the size of the thumb and lacks a physical body, which has to be ritually created limb by limb by way of offerings of rice balls, etc.[69] According to Ghosh (1989, 157) (based on the *Garuḍa Purāṇa*) failure to perform these offerings might result in a bad destiny for the departed (presumably he will not turn into a *pitṛ*) and misfortune for his relatives. Parry (1994, 175), too, points out the dangerous nature of the spirit:

> Up until the ritual of *sapindikaran* on the twelfth day after death, at which the deceased is transformed into an ancestor, his ghost represents a positive danger to those who survive him. Unable to reconcile itself to the separation of death, it beckons others to follow. The bus which carries the corpse and the mourners to Kashi has a crash; the pressure lantern which lights the funeral procession's way in the dark explodes; a funeral attendant is pulled into the pyre by

> a sexually predatory female ghost and badly burnt about the groin. The living must therefore put a safe distance between themselves and the departed, and as we shall find their disjunction is ritually marked at various points in the subsequent sequence. At no point should any relationship with the ghost be acknowledged—by, for example, using a kinship term or caste title to refer to it.[70]

Since the spirit is generally regarded as dangerous for the living, it is not surprising that preventive measures are taken on the day of the cremation or burial which falls into the 'liminal' period of ten days (in contemporary Hinduism) to stop it from returning home.[71] Parry (1994, 175) describes how mustard seeds are scattered during the procession on the way from the home to the cremation ground:

> Mustard seed attracts ghosts and ancestors. After cremation the disembodied *pret* will try to find its way back home; but in retracing its steps it is greedily distracted by the seeds and will hopefully never arrive.

I did not come across this particular custom of scattering mustard seeds at the funeral procession, but Wirz (1941, 205f.) refers to the scattering of mustard seeds at the end of a ceremony involving an offering for *prētas* who are haunting a house in order keep them away.

In contemporary Hinduism there is discussion about whether the death takes place when a person takes his last breath or when the skull of the burning corpse is split open by the chief mourner. Parry (1994, 177 and, 181) also says, that the splitting of the skull is important as it releases 'some crucial aspect of a person's life-force' (named *atma* or *pran* by Parry's informants) and enables it to move away from the gross body unhindered.

Even though this is not practised at cremations in Sri Lanka (and would, of course, not be possibe in the case of burials), one informant told me that there is a belief that the 'skull breaks at midnight'. However, all the other informants thought it very funny and complete nonsense whenever I mentioned this during my interviews. Nevertheless, the idea that the free movement of the spirit must not be obstructed by closed doors or windows is somewhat reminiscent of the notion that the spirit must be released.

To sum up, a number of Sri Lankan customs were explained to me either as preventing the spirit of the dead person (*maḷagiyaprāṇakārayā*) from returning to the house or as being signs of respect for the dead person. These preventative measures seem to be taken routinely, not prompted by signs that might indicate that the dead person has actually turned into a *prēta*. On the contrary, during this preliminary period of seven days the spirit is referred to as *maḷagiyaprāṇakārayā*, but never as *prēta* (*preta* would be the appropriate term in the Hindu context); in fact, the term *prēta* is positively avoided. Signs that indicate that a relative has actually turned into a *prēta* usually manifest themselves at a later stage and will therefore be discussed in the chapter Post-funerary Rites.

Excursus: intermediate state (questionnaire B.1–3)

The belief in a liminal period in contemporary Hinduism is grounded in the authoritative Sanskrit scriptures, which describe and prescribe accompanying ceremonies and rituals. In Buddhism the situation is more complex: some of the early Buddhist schools (such as the Sārvāstivādins) accept the concept of an intermediate state (*antarābhava*); others like the Theravādins do not. In Sri Lanka (and Thailand) there appears to be a gap between the official Theravāda doctrine of instantaneous rebirth, and popular practices which seem to suggest the belief in a liminal period after death.

However, the fact that certain customs are preserved for seven days in a funeral house and occasional mention of a spirit of the departed are not conclusive evidence of a well-defined concept of an intermediate period. In order to find out more about people's beliefs a set of three questions (B.1–3) was included in the questionnaire. The first question is of a more general nature:

> Questionnaire B.1: Why is the light kept on in the house, and why are people always awake in a funeral house until after the seven-day *dānaya*?

This time the answers of the monks were not unanimous. Two of the interviewees stated that the customs described above are not Buddhist (*bauddhāgama nemeyi*) but have their origin in the belief that the spirit of the departed is still around for seven days after the death. This belief was then attributed to Hindus and 'ancient people' respectively. They also mentioned that the custom of keeping doors and windows open in a funeral house is meant to protect against the bacteria (*visabīja*) of the corpse, an argument frequently brought up by laypeople as well.[72] Interestingly, one monk said that the customs observed in the funeral house of a layperson were largely observed in a temple as well after a monk has passed away.

Laypeople's opinion was divided: the majority of the interviewees, some in very certain terms, said all these customs are nothing but nonsense (lit. 'lies': *boru väḍa*), with no deeper meaning, and that they are 'non-Buddhist'. Others denied that they have any deeper meaning or relevance, but believed these customs were meant to comfort the bereaved or show respect for the departed. Again, the argument of bacteria (*visabīja*) from the corpse was adduced to explain the custom of not cooking (and not sweeping) and of keeping doors (and windows) open in a funeral house. Other people said that the spirit of the departed was still around in the house, and its movements should not be hindered. Interestingly, the idea that the spirit might get confused when looking into a mirror, etc., was mentioned, but only as 'people's belief' rather than the interviewee's own opinion. There seemed to be a certain reluctance to speak about pollution and spirits during the interviews that were conducted in English, so most of the information about these topics actually comes from interviews conducted in Sinhala.

The following two questions aim at establishing whether a link is made between the customs during the first seven days after the passing away and the (non-Theravāda) belief in an intermediate state.

> Questionnaire B.2: Are people reborn immediately after death, or later, after seven days or more?
> Questionnaire B.3: If people are not reborn immediately, do they exist as a kind of ghost, and would they be called *perētas* or something else?

Two of the monks strictly denied the existence of an intermediate state (*antarābhava*) but made reference to Ven. Ñāṇasīha and Ven. Balangoda Ānanda Maitreya, who wrote in favour of this concept.[73] The explanation by one very learned monk was rather technical and completely in line with Theravāda Abhidhamma in referring to the rebirth process in terms of *javanas*, *cuticitta* and *paṭisaṃdhi*. Another monk explained to me that it was a Buddhist belief that for seven days the consciousness of the deceased is wandering in space and therefore the spirit of the deceased is invited to come and listen to the *baṇa* preaching and to attend the seven-day *dānaya*. He called this the '*gandhabba* state' and after further probing he said that *antarābhava* was another name for it and that a being in that state would be called *gandhabba*, *bhūta* or *prēta*. Furthermore, he made the point that *prēta* is a general term for any dead person, even though ordinary people associate a particular class of miserable beings with this term. The fact that he thought people needed to be taught the 'original meaning' itself is interesting. Another interviewee said that the spirit of the departed is still present in the house for seven or eight days (according to the *karma* of the departed) and that this intermediate state is called *gandhabba avasthā*. Yet another monk mentioned the belief that a corpse should not be left alone in order to prevent the spirit of the dead (*malagiyaprāṇakārayā*) from returning to the house later as a ghost (*preta* or *bhūta*). It was not clear, however, how far he actually shared this belief and if he in fact meant that the departed had entered an intermediate state.

For laypeople, however, opinion was unanimously in favour of the existence of an intermediate state. About one third of the interviewees claimed that rebirth takes place at the earliest on the seventh day itself, which marks a kind of turning point, or any time after that.[74] The other two-thirds stated that depending on the *karma* of the deceased, rebirth might take place immediately after death (if the *karma* is sufficiently good) or after an intermediate period of undefined duration.

One elderly interviewee with rather academic knowledge of Buddhism, named this state as *antarābhava*, defined its duration as up to seven times seven days and said that beings in this state possess a subtle body (*sūkṣmaśarīra*), which recalls the description in Vasubandhu's Abhidharmakośa (AKBh 121ff.). He then went on to explain that people who die a sudden and unexpected death ('without time to think') have to endure that state for a certain amount of time. As an 'example' he quoted a newspaper story about an American airpilot who died in a plane crash but was seen afterwards by his wife and children before the family got the news of his sudden death. Another interviewee accepted the existence of an intermediate state but said there was no special name for it as it was not a proper form of existence (*gati*), which recalls the argument found in the Kathāvatthu (Kv viii.2). The other interviewees were less specific in describing this state, but did name it as *gandhabba avasthā* and the intermediate individual as a *gandhabba*. Three people said beings in that state were called *prāṇakārayā* or *malagiyaprāṇakārayā*, which one person translated for me as 'the one who has the life (of the deceased)'. None of the laypeople interviewed actually denied the existence of an intermediate state and most agreed that the duration for this state is not fixed, but dependent on the *karma* of the departed.

To sum up the findings, it was striking that the majority of people (including monks) stated that the spirit of the departed is still around for some time after death. Most people explicitly named this state *gandhabba avasthā* or *antarābhava*. In at least one case the concept was very structured and closely resembled the Sarvāstivāda concept of *antarābhava* as described in the Abhidharmakośa.

Offering of the **matakavastra**

The custom of donating a piece of new white cloth along with other items such as betel (*dähät*) and refreshments (*gilampasa*) can be observed at every funeral in Sri Lanka today and is well documented in the secondary literature.[75] The donation is made by the close relatives and accompanied by the chanting of the verses *imaṃ mataka-vatthaṃ*, etc., as described above. The cloth is referred to in secondary literature as either *mataka-vastra* ('cloth of the dead' or 'cloth [offered on behalf of] the dead') or as *paṃsukūla* ('refuse rag') and the act of offering it to the *saṃgha* is called *mataka-vastra-pūjā* or *paṃsukūla-pūjā* accordingly.[76] And Kariyawasam (1995, 44) says, 'The cloth, called a *paṃsukūla*—literally, a dust-heap cloth—is intended to be cut into pieces and then stitched into a robe.'

It appears that two, or even three, practices and the respective underlying concepts have been fused here which has led to certain inconsistencies in terminology.

mataka-vastra. The contemporary Sri Lankan practice of offering a piece of new white 'cloth of the dead' is reminiscent of a custom described in the Vedic sūtras. The body is covered with a new, uncut piece of white cloth that is meant to serve the departed as a new garment to wear when entering the world of Yama. Caland (1896, 16f.) describes that before the cremation a piece of this cloth is cut off, honoured and worn by the relatives for at least a day and finally offered to the priest.

On the basis of the scarce literature it can be said that there is certain evidence that in Sri Lanka, too, it was the custom to cover the body with a cloth. Ariyapala (1968, 360) relates an incident from the *Saddharma-ratnāvaliya* (thirteenth century):[77]

> Another prevalent custom seems to have been the spreading of a piece of cloth, the corners of which were tied on to four sticks, on the grave (*sohon kaḍa*) (Pjv 613). In the Maṭṭakuṇḍalī story, the SdhRv describing the father lamenting the loss of his son after he had been buried, says: '*vasālū kaḍa reddaṭa lōbhayen hañḍannāsē hañḍayi*', cries as if crying for the cloth that covered the dead body (48). This may refer to the shroud used to cover the dead body.

There is, however, no mention of this, or any other cloth, being donated to the *saṃgha.* Tillakaratne (1986, 146), too, mentions that the corpse was covered with a cloth and adds the interesting detail that it was the duty of the washerman caste to provide a strip of cloth to cover the face.[78] And Knox gives evidence that in the fifteenth century a cloth was used to cover the dead body:

> But Persons of greater quality are burned, and that with Ceremony. When they are dead they lay them out, and put a Cloth over their Privy Parts, and then wash the Body, by taking half a dozen Pitchers of water, and pouring upon it. Then they cover him with a Linnen cloth, and so carry him forth for burning.
>
> (Knox 1681, 116 (1966, 218))

J.F. Dickson seems to be the first to mention that the cloth that covers the body is 'presented to the priest':

> When a man dies he is buried by his friends quietly; a priest awaits the arrival of the body at the grave; the body is dressed in the ordinary dress of the deceased, and is placed on sticks on the top of the grave. The cloth which covers it is removed and presented to the priest who says: *Aniccā vata saṅkhārā* . . . The priest departs, taking with him the cloth; the friends of the deceased remain to bury the body.
>
> (Dickson 1884, 233)

However, the body is described as dressed in ordinary clothes and not 'wrapped in' but merely 'covered with' a cloth (like the earlier instance descibed by Knox in the context of cremation of the well-to-do). It seems to me that the difference between covering and wrapping is of some importance. The modern Sri Lankan practice, like its Vedic counterpart, involves the covering of a body as a symbolic act ('to dress the departed in a new garment for his new life') and the subsequent removal (or partial removal when a piece of the cloth is cut off) before the body is cremated or buried. It is an honoured item, handled with respect by the relatives and subsequently offered to the priest or monk.

paṃsukūla. The term *paṃsukūla* refers to the ancient ascetic practice of monks wearing robes made of rags thrown away.[79] One of the places those rags were found is the charnel ground, where bodies wrapped in a cloth were left for wild animals to eat (see above II.1.3). This practice goes back at least to the time of the Buddha, but became optional during his lifetime when the Buddha himself gave permission to accept robes donated by laypeople. Rahula (1966, 153) writes:

> Bhikkhus originally used to wear only *paṃsukūla cīvara* 'rag-robes', i.e., robes made of pieces of cloth thrown away as useless. But later, at the request of Jīvaka, the famous physician, the Buddha allowed monks to accept robes from the laity. When this opportunity was provided, people began to make profuse gifts of robes to the bhikkhus.

The incident quoted here by Ven. Walpola Rahula is related in the Vinaya where two interesting facts emerge: first, until Jīvaka's request the monks wore only robes made of rags; second, even after that time it was still an option for the monks to wear *paṃsukūla* robes made of rags—the other option being *gahapaticīvara* (lit. laypeoples' robes) which were donated by the laypeople.[80] Wearing *paṃsukūla* robes is one of the thirteen ascetic practices (*dhutaṅga*) discussed in the Visuddhimagga as occurring in three different grades, from very strict to weak. This shows that this practice was still known in Buddhaghosa's time, even though it is difficult to tell how widely practised it was.[81]

How does this fit in with contemporary Sri Lankan practice? It seems that the *paṃsukūla*, being a refuse rag, is quite the opposite of the new piece of cloth donated by laypeople at funerals. First, something, which is thrown away, can be picked up by anyone (including monks) and there would be no need to offer it formally. It might even have been considered the monks' right to take *paṃsukūlas*, but I do not have any evidence for this. Second, a refuse rag would not be regarded as fit to serve as a formal offering to the *saṃgha*. From my observation of contemporary practice it is evident that laypeople offer the best they can afford, but not something that has been thrown away. In short, one would assume that something cannot be refuse and an offering at the same time.[82] Thirdly, the ascetic practice only indicates that the monks picked up the rags from the charnel ground after the bodies were left there and eaten by the animals, but there is no mention of their involvement with the actual funeral rites.

As far as contemporary practice is concerned, most of my informants knew the term *paṃsukūla* and referred to the ancient ascetic practice of wearing only robes made of rags. The notion of *paṃsukūla* robes is further kept alive by the custom of offering unsewn cloth at the *kaṭhina* ceremony which marks the end of the rainy season retreat as described by Kariyawasam (1995, 48).[83]

dānaya. Gombrich (1991, 283) comments on the problem of 'rag' versus 'offering' as follows:

> The modern *paṃsukūla* ceremony is a curious fusion of this with a *dāne*. By picking up the cloth from the coffin the monk is symbolically taking the winding sheet, or some other item of the corpse's clothing, and thus conforming to the letter of the *paṃsukūla* practice. On the other hand the dead man's next of kin are giving the cloth, which therefore is the best new white cloth, to enhance the value of the gift; they have made the funeral an occasion for transferring the merit earned by a gift to the Sangha, thus destroying the spirit of the *paṃsukūla* idea so that the original meaning of the term has been completely lost.

Even though Gombrich's definition of *paṃsukūla* as 'rags picked up in a cemetery' seems a bit narrow (already in the Visuddhimagga the definition is widened); I agree with him as far as the 'curious fusion of the *paṃsukūla* ceremony and a *dāne*' is concerned. The offering of the *mataka-vastra* to the *saṃgha* falls under the category of *dāna*, but unlike a meal, which is prepared and offered on behalf of the dead person, the *mataka-vastra* could be viewed as the last offering actually done by him. There might also be another aspect to it, that of a 'payment' to the monks for rendering their services. It is customary and expected that Brahmins are paid for their services. The 'payment' consists of some old items (possibly also items of clothing of the departed) as well as new items and gold, and it is said to benefit the departed in some way. Here the priests act as mediators in accepting the items on behalf of the departed and receive compensation for their services at the same time. One cannot avoid the impression that this custom has also influenced the attitude of Buddhists in Sri Lanka to this day. It does not seem to me out of the question that the *mataka-vastra*, or indeed any offering to the monks, could be viewed in the light of a symbolic 'payment' for the monks' services at the funeral.[84]

To sum up: there are two distinctly different practices, which have become fused and mixed up. On the one hand, there are the Vedic rituals performed in the context of cremations, which include the symbolic 'covering of the body' with a new, uncut white piece of cloth, treated as a precious item belonging to the departed and later offered to the priests.

On the other hand, there is the custom of 'wrapping corpses in a cloth' and leaving them in charnel grounds for wild animals to eat. Here the cloth is a refuse rag, something that the wild animals would leave behind after they have eaten the corpse, and which could be picked up by ascetics and made into clothing. In the course of time the two practices seem to have been fused in people's minds. In addition, an element of *dānaya* or even 'payment' has left its mark on the modern Buddhist practice in Sri Lanka. Like a Vedic priest, the monk might in some way be seen to represent the departed and to receive goods on his behalf.

Considering the range of ideas and associations attached to the piece of new white cloth, it is not surprising that the custom of offering the *mataka-vastra* is so popular in Sri Lanka. And as modern practice shows, the offering the *mataka-vastra* does not require cremation as a context, but is part of burial ceremonies as well. Cremations as well as burials lend themselves to a certain ceremonial decorum, which brings us to our last point, the involvement of monks. The offering of a piece of cloth does require a recipient, a priest or a monk to act as mediator between the living and the dead. And, at least in modern practice, it constitutes the only formal involvement of the monks that is specific to the funeral rites (other than chanting and giving of merit, which are both rather unspecific and occur in post-funerary and other contexts).

If the involvement of monks in funeral rites is indeed bound up with the practice of offering the *mataka-vastra*, as I suspect it is, it might be worth exploring when it became an intrinsic part of Sri Lankan funeral rites. It is hard (even though not impossible) to imagine the practice of a ceremonial offering of a piece of cloth in the context of leaving bodies in charnel grounds. A more natural and presumably original context for the offering of a piece of cloth is the cremation and, by extension, the burial. Our earlier assumption was, that then (as now) cremations were only for the well-to-do and leaving bodies in charnel grounds (then) or burial (now) were for the majority. This would mean that while the offering of a white piece of cloth might have been part of the cremation ceremony from very early times, it became widespread practice only when burials became the norm and leaving the body in a charnel ground went out of practice.

Some historical roots: handling the remains

Much of what has been observed in contemporary Sri Lankan funeral rites appears to have resonances of the ancient Indian practices. Of course, caution is needed. The mere fact that a ritual which is prescribed in Vedic or Brāhmaṇical texts is also found in contemporary Sri Lanka does not necessarily mean that there is a connection or that the ritual needs to be interpreted in the same way. On the other hand, it is also neither impossible nor improbable that a more or less unbroken continuity in practice can be found. For the Hindu funeral rites Knipe (1977, 111) makes two observations, which are relevant here:

> With few exceptions, the Hindu rites at the time of death and the procedures for cremation (*antyeṣṭi*) are fairly uniform throughout the regions of India. Similarly the series of rites for the departed (*śrāddhas*), where it has been retained, is performed according to traditional archaic standards. The basic structures of the *antyeṣṭi* and the *śrāddha* rites proceed from Vedic models, models prefigured in the *saṃhitās* and *brāhmaṇas*, detailed in the *gṛhyasūtras*, and then conveyed with continuing elaboration in two thousand years of *dharmaśāstra* literature. This conformity in ritual across Vedic, epic, purāṇic, and āgamic periods, and on into modern practice, is remarkable considering that the answer to the question, 'Where does a Hindu go when he dies?' had varied considerably within each one of these periods.

If we accept Knipe's statement, it does not seem far-fetched to make a link between the funeral rites of Theravāda Buddhists in contemporary Sri Lanka and the rites described in Vedic sūtras.[85]

It is appropriate then to begin this chapter with a brief survey of the extensive literature, both descriptive and prescriptive, from the Vedic sūtras to the *dharmaśāstra* and Purāṇa literature, followed by a brief summary of the funerary rites as depicted in the Vedic sūtras. With this approach it is hoped to some extent to fill the gap that the total lack of prescriptive, ritual literature in Theravāda Buddhism has left. By providing a condensed picture of Vedic funerary rites I will further put the fragmentary Sri Lankan rituals in a wider framework. Many details of the brahmanical or Hindu rites practised in India will, unfortunately, only be mentioned in passing.

The lack of ritual literature in Theravāda Buddhism does not mean that there is no textual evidence at all for the ancient Buddhist funeral practices in the Pāli sources. But the information is scattered in a variety of texts, hidden in stories or commentaries, and studies devoted to the investigation of funeral practices in the Pāli sources are scarce. In part two of the present chapter I therefore hope to present a representative (though by no means exhaustive) selection of passages relating to these practices.

The third part of this chapter will take into account archaeological evidence of funeral practices. This material has so far not attained the attention it deserves, as has been pointed out by scholars such as Gregory Schopen,

Trainor and Coningham to name but a few. Schopen's work in particular has added a much-needed archaeological dimension to the study of Buddhism while still taking account of the ancient texts.

For the Vedic material, I rely mainly on Gonda (1977 and 1980), and Kane (1941–1953) for the general intoduction to the Vedic material. For the details of the Vedic funerary rites Caland (1896) is still unsurpassed as a work of reference. In his foot-steps followed Evison (1989, unfortunately unpublished) and Firth (1997). For archaeological material I have to rely mainly on Schopen (1997) and, to a degree, Coningham (2001).

The Vedic and brahmanical material

The Ṛgveda, particularly the tenth *maṇḍala*, contains a number of hymns dealing with death, e.g., the god Yama (10.14), cremation (10.16) and even burial (10.18), etc. To give a flavour of their beauty I shall quote a verse of the burial hymn:

> (Addressing the earth) Open up, earth; do not crush him. Be easy for him to enter and to burrow in. Earth, wrap him up as a mother wraps a son in the edge of her skirt.
>
> (Daniger O'Flaherty 1981, 52; ṚV 10.18)

However, we will have to leave the evocative hymns of the Ṛgveda and turn to the rather less evocative ritual literature of the Vedic *sūtras*.[86]

Brief survey of the sources

Vedic sūtras

Approximate dating of material

The oldest systematic texts dealing with funeral rites in India are the sūtras of the Vedāṅga, which constitute the beginning of the *Smṛti* (tradition) as opposed to *Śruti* (revealed). These sūtras were composed by brahmins for brahmins over a rather long period of time (approximately from the sixth or seventh century BC to the second century AD according to Gonda (1977, 476)). They are composed in a short elliptic style that facilitated memorisation and fall broadly into four categories (*śrauta*, *gṛhya*, *dharma* and *śulva*), but for present purposes only *śrauta* (dealing with great solemn rites) and *gṛhya* (dealing with domestic rites) are relevant. Gonda (1977, 468) describes them as follows:

> The complicated *śrauta* rites are carried out—on the invitation, at the expense and for the benefit of the patron or 'sacrificer' (*yajamāna*),

> a well-to-do member of the high classes—by specialized officiants (up to sixteen in number) and need three sacred fires, the formulas being taken from the *saṃhitās*. The domestic rites require one fire (the domestic, *gṛhya*, fire) and are as a rule performed by the householder himself using a formulary taken from a special collection. . . . The domestic rites, which are more often closely related to everyday life, are brief ceremonies in which milk, butter or grain is offered. . . . The most characteristic *gṛhya* rites are the so-called sacraments (*saṃskāra*), the Indian variant of the 'rites de passage'.

Gonda (1977, 478) gives a guideline for the relative dating of the sūtras, but subsequently warns the reader that the period cannot be strictly separated.[87]

Different schools
Apart from the broad divide into *śrauta* and *gṛhya*, there are other categories, such as the various schools of the Veda, each belonging to the tradition of one of the four *saṃhitās* (Ṛgveda, Sāmaveda, Atharvaveda and Yajurveda, respectively). There does not seem to be any certainty about how many of these schools existed, but they commonly derive their names from famous teachers or *sūtrakāras*. Unfortunately, not much is known of these teachers, and according to Gonda (1977, 475): 'Generally speaking, all of these *sūtrakāras* are very shadowy figures'.

pitṛmedhasūtras
The texts dealing with the rites for the deceased, the so-called *pitṛmedhasūtras*, constitute a distinct category of ritual texts in each of the various schools.[88] While some schools have a separate work called *pitṛmedhasūtra*, others attach a separate chapter either to their *śrautasūtras* or to their *gṛhyasūtras*.[89] It appears that in many cases the difference between *śrauta* and *gṛhya* is rather one of scale, expense and the number of priests involved than one of content. The *pitṛmedha* has yet another aspect to it: the question of whether the dead person was a so-called *āhitāgni* (one who maintains the three sacred Vedic fires) or an *anāhitāgni* (one who maintains the domestic fire). The *śrauta* rituals are performed exclusively by (and for) the former, whereas the *gṛhya* rituals are performed by (and for) the latter. Gonda (1977, 616) seems to imply that the schools who include the *pitṛmedha* in the *śrauta* section, such as the Kātyāyana and Śāṅkhāyana schools as well as the Mānavas, grant these rites only to the *āhitāgnis*. Unfortunately he does not explain what rites are granted to the *anāhitāgnis*, and it would go beyond the scope of the present study to investigate those details any further.

Garuḍa Purāṇa (GP). With the Purāṇic literature a new epoch begins in Indian literature. Mylius (1983, 146) says that the importance of the Pūraṇas for 'Hinduism' equals that of the Vedas for Brāhmaṇism and points out their accessibility to and popularity amongst the lower classes of society. Amongst the Purāṇas, the Garuḍa Purāṇa, or to be precise its Uttarakhaṇḍa section (UttK, also referred to as Pretakalpa or Pretakhaṇḍa), has acquired special importance as a guide and handbook for all things concerning death, ghosts and funerals, even today in modern Hindu communities.[90] It has attracted much attention in the secondary literature and has been regarded as one of the most important sources for the study of Indian funeral rites.

Rocher (1986, 177) gives a brief overview of the rather complicated textual history and various editions which differ considerably in length and, presumably, also in content. Considering the vast popularity of the Garuḍa Purāṇa it is difficult to determine how many versions or editions of the text or parts of the text exist. Besides, there are certain problems concerning the textual history of the Garuḍa Purāṇa. On the basis of stylistic criteria, Hazra (1975, 144) comes to the conclusion that the Uttarakhaṇḍa section, the Pretakalpa, was originally composed as an independent work and added to the Garuḍa Purāṇa at a later stage. Considering the encyclopaedic nature of the Garuḍa Purāṇa (Mylius 1983, 155)—covering a number of different topics, such as astronomy, medicine, grammar, etc.—it is not unlikely that the Garuḍa Purāṇa might have an older core that over time attracted other previously independent treatises on special topics.

Considering the heterogeneous character of the purāṇic material in general, any attempt at precise dating is virtually impossible. Mylius (1983, 145) states that it can be assumed that the greater part of the purāṇic texts were composed between 300 and 800 CE. Hazra (1975, 144) dates the composition of the older parts of the Garuḍa Purāṇa, the Pūrvakhaṇḍa, between 800 and 1000 CE. However, that still does not tell us when the Uttarakhaṇḍa might have been added or even composed for that matter.

Other sources. Another source for concepts on death and dying are the older Upaniṣads (BĀU 4.4.4; ChU 3.28; etc.), which have briefly been discussed in the chapter on death, as they were important in forming certain concepts of salvation as well as an afterlife dependent on *karma* and retribution. Interestingly, the changing concept of the afterlife does not seem to have had much effect on the actual practice, i.e., the performance of the rituals, and shall therefore not be discussed further in this chapter.

The Bhagavadgītā, too, has exercised great influence on the Indian thinking about death and rebirth. To name just a few examples: 2.22–24 (the soul casting off the old body and taking a new one); 2.8–11 and 8.5–6 (focusing on Kṛṣṇa at the time of death); 8.24 (the northern path to the absolute for yogins); 8.22–23 (the southern path of darkness for ordinary people).[91] As in the case of the Upaniṣads, however, these notions and concepts seem to have little bearing on the actual practice.

The Epics also contain some detailed accounts of funerals, which Caland (1896, 168) induces as examples of practice (as opposed to the theory of the

Vedic ritual literature). It has to be taken into account that these epical, royal funerals are probably fictitious accounts and do not reflect the everyday practice of ordinary people at the time the Epics were composed. It seems nevertheless worthwhile looking at them. The Mahābhārata relates a great number of bloody battles and is, consequently, a great source of funeral descriptions: the group cremation of the soldiers killed in battle (MBh XI.26.39); the funerals of Bhīṣma (MBh XII. 169. 10), Vasudeva (MBh XVI. 7. 15–31) and Dhṛtarāṣṭra (MBh XV. 39) to name but few. In the Rāmāyana two accounts are particularly interesting: the funeral of Rāvaṇa on the island of Laṅkā (VI, 113, 102) and the funeral of Daśaratha (II. 64. 77). Unfortunately, the details of the descriptions are too numerous to give here.[92]

The present study is concerned with brahmanical material mainly as the historical background to the Sri Lankan Buddhist practice; I shall therefore concentrate on the funeral rites as depicted in the Vedic sūtras, or, to be precise, on Caland's 'digests' of the relevant texts. Caland utilised the texts and ritual *sūtra*s of thirteen schools, which are named as follows: Baudhāyana; Bhāradvāja; Āpastamba; Hiraṇyakeśin; Vaikhānasa; Mānavas; Kaṭhas; Mādhyandinas; Kauśika; Gautama; Kauthumas; Āśvalāyana; Śāṅkhāyana.[93] I will not go into detail regarding the different schools as this is not only irrelevant for present purposes, but positively distracting. Any later developments, as found in the Garuḍa Purāṇa and the epic material, will only be indicated in footnotes if they appear directly relevant to a better understanding of the Sri Lankan practice.[94]

Vedic funeral rites

Caland (1896, 171f.) identifies two recurring themes at the heart of the old Indian funeral rites: the fear that the soul of the departed might return to create trouble and the concept of cremation as sacrifice of and for the dead.

It is worth bearing these two main aspects in mind when looking at the great number of details of the various stages of the funeral rites. I will concentrate on the description of the practices (based on Caland) and leave out all references to the Vedic hymns to be chanted in the rites. I will roughly, keep to the division employed in the description and interpretation of the Sri Lankan material, but apart from that the Vedic material will be presented in its own right.

The funeral house. When a death occurs in a house two main tasks arise: first, the corpse has to be prepared and made fit to serve as the object to be offered to the fire of cremation,[95] and second, certain changes are to be made due to the notion that the relatives and the house have become impure.[96]

The person in charge of the sacrifice (who this is in any individual case depends on the relationship with the dead and who is available) prepares himself by shaving his head and body, bathing and changing the direction of his sacrificial cord. His first duty is to prepare the expiatory ritual (*prāyaścitta*), which is an offering outside the house. The body is laid out with its head to the east or, according to other schools, to the south.[97] The other relatives also change the direction of their cords, but unlike the person in charge, they do not shave, but untie their hair and smear it with dust. Now the corpse is washed, nails and hair are cut and ointments are applied to it. According to some schools this should take place at the cremation ground where the hair and nails are buried in the ground.[98] Some sources prescribe tying the thumbs and the big toes together with a white string, or tying a piece of string around the left big toe. Caland (1896, 175) provides two possible explanations for this custom: first, it might be an analogue of the act of tying the sacrificial animal with a rope (especially where only the left toe is tied, just as only the left leg of the animal is tied), or, alternatively, the motivation could be to immobilise the dead and keep him from returning to the home. There is also mention in the sūtras of opening up the corpse to take out the inner organs, etc., but this is explicitly dismissed by the composers of the *sūtras*. The corpse is then placed on a goat skin on a stretcher and covered with a new, white piece of cloth for a new existence in the realm of Yama. His old clothes or—according to other schools—a small cut-off of the new cloth, is supposed to be worn by the son or brother until it is old, or at least for a day.[99] After the corpse has thus been prepared and made fit to serve as a sacrifice, a number of other preparations are made and utensils arranged before the procession to the cremation ground can begin.

The second aspect mentioned above, the notion that pollution is incurred by the presence of the corpse, brings with it a host of rules and restrictions. Depending on the degree of relationship and on the status of the dead (very small children hardly cause any pollution when they die), the family members are impure for a period of between twelve days and one year. They are not supposed to eat anything on the first day and only one meal a day after that (but nothing salty). They are not allowed to study the Veda while impure, nor to shave or cut their hair, but are supposed to sleep on the floor and practise celibacy. Not only the relatives, but the house itself is polluted, and cooking in the house is not allowed until purificatory rites have been performed at the end of the fixed period of pollution. At the same time, it is the duty of the relatives to provide food, water and clothing for the newly dead (see below under post-funerary rites). Cremations take place within a day, but these restrictions and practices continue after the corpse has been removed at least until the eleventh day.

The funeral procession. The fear that the dead person might return to the home is clearly the driving force behind a number of customs surrounding the procession.[100] The sacrificial fires (including the domestic fire) are carried in the front, followed by the body (carried by elderly family members);[101] next come the sacrificial animals (old and vicious, tied with a rope by the left leg) and finally the relatives of the departed (with loose hair) and the four priests (*hotar*, *adhvaryu*, *sāmaga*, *brahman*). No-one is supposed to look backwards as the procession moves to leave the town[102] by the eastern (or according to other schools western) gate.[103] According to the different schools, there are three or four stops to be made on the way; each time a succession of ritual acts is to be performed: the stretcher is put down; one of the three or four animals is slaughtered and offered to the south of the head of the body (or a spoonful of a special rice dish serves as a substitute). Then the relatives circumambulate the body three times in the auspicious (*pradakṣiṇā*) and three times in the inauspicious way (*apradakṣiṇā*) while fanning the body with the ends of the garments.[104] A clay pot of food is brought along and half its contents thrown on the ground; the other half is offered to the deceased after arrival at the cremation ground. The clay pot that contained the rice dish is smashed after the last offering has been made.[105] The later custom of offering rice balls (*piṇḍa*) at certain points on the way (beginning with the first *piṇḍa* to be offered at the house) is already prescribed by at least one of the schools.

Preparatory rituals. The place for the cremation has to fulfil certain conditions and is carefully chosen according to rather strict instructions.[106] An area is marked and ritually cleansed; eight poles (in accordance with the eight directions) are secured in the ground and connected with ropes. Inside this area special types of wood are to be arranged in a prescribed way, and the sacred fires are placed at certain places outside the area. The utensils for the sacrifice are arranged one by one (not in pairs as for sacrifices to the gods) and placed upside down. The pieces of string tying the thumbs and toes are cut. Everything is sprinkled with water before the stretcher is placed on the pyre.[107]

The next important stage is that the widow (if the dead person was male and married, which is the scenario that the Vedic *sūtras* seem to assume as the norm) is led to the pyre, usually by the *adhvaryu*, and lies down next to her husband. She is subsequently brought back to the living by her husband's brother or by a brahmin. She then gives a gift of 'a thousand', but it is not clear from the *sūtras* what this consists of nor to whom it is given (to the *adhvaryu* or to the person who brought her back to life). Any gold ornaments are removed from the corpse and handed over to the eldest son.

Now the seven openings of the head (eyes, ears, nostrils, and mouth) are closed with pieces of gold or melted butter and some schools prescibe the pouring of butter, honey, milk, etc., as well as certain herbs and incense onto the corpse. The sacrificial utensils, which the deceased used throughout his life, are arranged on and around him. According to Caland (1896, 176), this has two functions: to equip the departed for the Yamaloka and to dispose of the utensils.

The last step of the preparations is the sacrifice of a cow (*anuṣṭaraṇī*), which is either freed or slaughtered (the description of the actual killing is rather gruesome). The kidneys are placed in the hands of the departed as a means of pacifying Yama's dogs (Caland 1896, 177). Other parts such as the heart, tongue, and skin (with feet) are placed on the corpse to protect the departed from the fire (in this context Agni is only the mediator, but not the receiver of the sacrifice). Caland refers to this throughout as 'wrap-around-animal' ('Umlegethier', sic!). Into the hands of the departed, two pieces of rice are placed which are meant for Mitra and Varuṇa. The deceased is now equipped for the journey, and the corpse is ready and in a fit state to be sacrificed.

Cremation. The cremation ceremony begins with relatives circumambulating the pyre three times and fanning it with the ends of their garments.[108] The widow or son takes a pot of water with a hole on her or his head (or left shoulder) and circumambulates the pyre anticlockwise (*apradakṣiṇā*) three times, beginning at the foot end. Every time the feet are reached, another hole is made in the pot until the pyre has been watered properly. Finally, the pot is smashed.

There are basically two different ways to light the pyre. To start with the rite for *āhitāgnis*, three rows of dried grass are strewn, leading from the three sacrificial fires to the pyre, like a fuse. It has a certain significance, the three fires represent the realms of the gods, fathers, and *gandharvas*; the one that reaches the pyre first is regarded as an omen that the departed is on his way to that realm. The rite for *anāhitāgnis*, who only have the domestic fire, differs in that the youngest son places the fire on the shoulder of the departed. Here the way the smoke moves (straight up, up and to the side, or downwards) represents heaven, the ether or the earth respectively and is taken as an omen.

Now a goat is freed and runs away. This is followed by a sacrifice to Agni, offered into the burning fire. Various schools add offerings to other gods, such as Yama or Sarasvatī, and some schools have the water poured around the pyre at this stage. All schools, however, prescribe some chanting to the effect that Agni is asked to protect the departed and not to burn him.[109]

Purificatory rituals. When leaving the cremation ground, no one in the procession is supposed to look back.[110] A number of precautions are taken to ensure the spirit of the dead cannot follow: between cremation ground and village three ditches are cut and filled with water for the mourners to step into. Two branches of a particular tree are made to form an arch through which the mourners walk. They all go to a place where there is water. They fully submerge themselves underwater with loosened hair and then make an offering of water to the dead. In some schools it is prescribed that new clothes have to be put on after the bath. The relatives and friends then have to spend the time until dusk under a shady tree while the elders tell stories from the epics to console the grieving family. When returning to the house the mourners should touch water, or fire, smoke, cow dung, stone, etc. The doorway to the house has to be sprinkled with water. Finally the priests have to be paid in the name of the departed. They receive gold, clothes, brass vessels, jugs of water, etc., which are said to benefit the soul of the departed (*preta*) in some way because it is still in a liminal stage and in need of clothes, food and drink.

Vedic post-funerary rites

To complete the Vedic picture, a very brief summary is given of the disposal of the bones and the offerings to the dead even though this falls, strictly speaking, under the category of post-funerary rites.

Collecting the bones. The date and timespan between the cremation and collecting the bones does not appear to be fixed, and the various schools differ widely as to when this important first post-funerary rite should take place.[111] Some schools prescribe that before the collection of the bones an uneven number of priests should be fed.[112] Then the relatives set out for the cremation ground, where a space is cleared and prepared south of the place where the actual cremation had taken place. Some embers are taken from the funeral pyre and used to start the fire into which certain offerings are made. This is followed by a sprinkling of the pyre with water and milk from an uneven number of pots. The verses chanted on this occasion leave no doubt that the act is meant to extinguish, cool and calm the funeral fire.

The collecting of bones is supposed to be done by postmenopausal women, preferably five (or some other uneven number) who position themselves around the extinguished funeral pyre: one woman at the head end and two women each in the region of the shoulders and legs. The bones to be collected are the teeth, skull, shoulder-bones, arm-bones, ribs, hip-bones, thigh-bones and leg-bones. Some schools prescribe that the remaining ashes are to be made into a dough and shaped like a human form. Other schools state that a human shape has to be made from flowers. In any case, an offering is now made to the departed, as well as to Yama and Rudra. Next the bones are washed, sprinkled with perfume and put into an urn with a piece of gold, honey, butter, etc. Opinions as to where to deposit the remains differ widely: some say the urn should be buried somewhere in the vicinity (or at the root of a tree, or in a forest) or that it should be enshrined. Again, others say it should be thrown into a river or the sea.

Offerings to the departed. We have already mentioned in the section on the funeral house that offerings are made to the departed.[113] The relatives provide rice balls (*piṇḍa*), milk, water, scents, ointments, lamps, etc. A bowl of water is hung up outside to provide the opportunity for the dead to bathe. The first of these *piṇḍa* offerings is made before leaving for the cremation ground, others are made on the way to and in the cremation ground itself and, finally, offerings are made in the house of the departed. Some say these offerings are to be performed twice a day, morning and night, for ten days and are meant to restore the body of the departed.[114] On the eleventh day an offering (*ekoddiṣṭaśrāddha*) is performed for the departed, as well as for certain deities.[115] At the same time offerings to the priests are made in the name of the departed, with the number of priests invited increasing as the days go by with each offering, reaching twelve offerings on the twelfth day. The priests also receive their compensation (*dakṣiṇā*), which consists of some old articles of every-day use, such as a bed, pillow, etc., as well as more substantial ones such as an ox, brass vessels or a new piece of cloth.[116]

The offerings, which are made to the deceased directly, culminate in a ceremony called *sapiṇḍīkaraṇa*, which merges the offering for the newly dead with those for his father and grandfather and is meant to make him an ancestor.[117] Nevertheless, the relatives continue to make offerings to the dead person even after the twelfth day in certain intervals until the first anniversary of the death, by which time the dead person has completed his journey to the Yamaloka. There is a certain ritual inconsistency here as well as conflicting motives, such as the desire that the household return to normal, on the one hand, and the need to remember the dead, on the other.

Summary

To sum-up the findings from the Vedic *sūtras*, one can say that the three aspects—honouring the dead, death pollution and fear of the spirit of the dead—which were strong and recurring motives in the Sri Lankan contemporary practice, all have their roots in Vedic times. The character of the dead is multifaceted: on the one hand, the corpse is to serve as an offering (washed and anointed); on the other hand, certain elements in the ritual suggest an almost bodily entry into the Yamaloka (providing the dead with utensils, 'protecting him from the fire'). The circumambulation, too, shows the ambivalent nature of the sacrifice, as it is done in both directions. Participation in a funeral procession is an honour, but it is also polluting to be in close contact with a corpse, and special care is taken to ritually cleanse family members (touching fire or water, etc.) and the house on the day of the cremation.

The spirit of the dead is still lingering and needs protecting, feeding and building up, but at the same time, precautions are taken to prevent it from following the relatives home. This tension is perceivable in a number of rites on the cremation day. The corpse is under threat from flying demons, etc., and in need of protection on its way to the cemetery. The spirit is also dangerous, and when leaving the place of cremation, arches and ditches are made to prevent it from returning home. Nevertheless, back home, the next offering of rice balls is made for the departed, which, as we just heard, was not supposed to follow there.

In the Sri Lankan funeral practice the same tension is tangible: precautions are taken (such as removing the coffin from the house at a particular astrologically fixed moment) to keep the spirit away from home, only to invite it back on the sixth day and provide it with food, drink, a sleeping mat and pillow. Details might differ (as they do from one Vedic school to the next), but it appears that all the main elements of the Vedic funeral rites are still represented in the Sri Lankan contemporary practice, albeit in a rudimentary form and possibly perceived differently (perhaps less in terms of a sacrifice). However, the one great difference is the fact that no animal sacrifices are made at funerals in Sri Lanka. But then again, the Vedic sūtras themselves give instructions as to how rice or other offerings can be substituted for a live animal, and it would be interesting to know just how often an actual animal sacrifice was carried out.

The Pāli **nikāyas** *and some stories from the commentaries*

The most famous of all Buddhist funerals is the cremation of Gotama Buddha as described in the Mahāparinibbāna Sutta (D II 72–168). As it was a cremation fit for a Cakkavatti, however, it represents an idealised version of what might have been practised at the time of the Buddha. Let us first look at the formulaic instructions given to Ānanda in the Mahāparinibbāna Sutta:

> 'Ānanda, the Tathāgata's body should be treated as people treat the body of a wheel-turning king.'
> 'And how, lord, do people treat the body of a wheel-turning king?'
> 'First they wrap the body in unused cloth, then in teased cotton, then again in unused cloth. And when in this manner they have wrapped the body in five hundred double layers, they place it in an iron coffin full of oil. This they cover with another iron coffin [as a lid]. Then they make a funeral pyre of all kinds of incense and cremate the body. Afterwards they build a stupa for the wheel-turning king where four roads meet. This is how people treat the body of a wheel-turning king. As people treat the body of a wheel-turning king, so the Tathāgata's body should be treated. A stupa should be built for the Tathāgata where four roads meet.'[118]
>
> (Gethin, unpublished; D II 142)

Reading carefully through the different stages and events that were reported to have taken place after the Buddha passed away, one can, however, build up a more detailed picture of the proceedings. For each stage, the corresponding passage from the Mahāparinibbāna Sutta will be discussed first, and then further material from the Pāli sources will be adduced.

Funeral rites

The funeral house. No funeral house is named in the Mahāparinibbāna Sutta, as the Buddha reportedly passed away on his way to Kusinārā at a place called Upavattana in the sal grove of the Mallas.[119] However, the Mallas of Kusinārā are invited to come for a last audience with the Buddha and to pay their respects, as this important event is taking place in the vicinity of their village (*gāmakkhette*). Like all major events in the life of a Buddha (birth, awakening, etc.), the actual death moment is marked by an earthquake.[120] Immediately afterwards, Brahmā, Sakka and Ven. Anuruddha utter verses.[121]

Wailing, cosmic and personal grief

First, those monks who 'had not yet got rid of greed' broke into expressions of grief and 'threw out their arms and called out; they fell to the ground, broken, and rolled back and forth.'[122] The reaction of some of the gods and of the Mallas, after they have been informed by Ānanda of the Buddha's final passing away, is described in exactly the same phrases with the added detail that their hair is dishevelled (*kese pakiriya*).[123]

There are numerous other accounts of cosmic grief in the Pāli material (mainly in the commentaries), but three examples shall suffice. The earth trembled, drums sounded, flowers rained down, and the gods lamented the death of the Buddha's aunt and stepmother Mahāpajāpatī.[124] All six divine worlds were in shock over the death of Mahāmoggallāna.[125] But the greatest lament of all—at least according to the commentary—was felt at Ānanda's death when a feeling of utter desolation took over:

> The populace wept and wailed. Like the sound of the earth splitting open was the sound of their lamentation; yet more pitiful even than that was the sound of lamentation at the death of the Teacher. For four months men went about wailing and lamenting, saying, 'So long as he who held the Teacher's bowl and robe remained, it was as if the Teacher himself yet remained; it was as if the Teacher himself yet remained among us. But now the Teacher is dead.'
>
> (Burlingame 1921, II 161. Dhp-a II 100)

Personal grief, too, is well documented in the Pāli sources. Ānanda is often portrayed as showing emotions such as grief and despair (cf. D II 143), but the best known, and probably most moving account of personal grief, is the story of Kisā Gotamī nearly losing her mind over the loss of her infant son.[126] What follows is the well-known parable of the mustard seed: the Buddha prescribes as medicine for her son mustard seeds procured from a house where no-one ever has ever died. After hours spent knocking at people's doors and searching, the truth dawns on her and she attains the first stage of the Buddhist path (stream entry), eventually becoming an arahant.

In other stories, too, deep-felt grief leads to the realisation of the truth, for example, in the case of a weaver who is inconsolable at the accidental death of his daughter. He is comforted by the Buddha and led to higher realisations, which ultimately result in arahantship.[127] Queen Ubbarī was so overcome with grief that she did not leave her husband's funeral pyre and circumambulated it at night.[128] She, too, was fortunate enough to be instructed wisely (in her case by the Bodhisatta), became a nun and cultivated friendliness (*mettā*) as a result of which she was reborn in the Brahman world. King Muṇḍa's mourning over the death of his wife, Queen Bhaddā, is described in somewhat more tangible terms: 'He neither bathed, nor anointed himself, nor partook of any food, nor concerned himself with any affairs, but day and night clung in grief to her body as though a-swoon.'[129] This is reminiscent of the restrictions in a funeral house that we find in the Vedic *sūtra*s, which also mention rules with regard to eating and bathing.

Night vigil

The Mahāparinibbana Sutta mentions that after the Buddha passed away 'Venerable Anuruddha and Venerable Ānanda spent the rest of the night in discussion of the teaching and practice'.[130] There is no mention of a night vigil after this first night, but it may be assumed that with so many beings from different worlds nearby there would always have been someone near the body. One might also assume that a similar situation arose in the case of the cremations of other eminent monks (even though I have not come across any evidence for that). However, it is most likely that the cremations usually took place the same day, as seems to have been the intention in the case of the Buddha's cremation, which was postponed every night (see below).

Paying respects to the body

In the morning Ānanda set out for Kusinārā to inform the Mallas, who, in turn, gathered together all that was needed for the worship of the Buddha's body: incense, garlands and musical instruments, and five hundred sets of garments.[131] Then it is said that they spent the whole day worshipping the Buddha's body (*sārīraṃ . . . pūjentā*), but did not quite manage to wrap it in the cloth and garments which they brought along with them:

> There they paid their respects to the body, honouring, revering and worshipping it with dances, songs, music, garlands and incense, making awnings and preparing pavilions. In this way they passed the day. Then the Mallas thought, 'It is too late to burn the Blessed One's body today, we shall burn it tomorrow.'
>
> (Gethin, unpublished; D II 159)

This is repeated the next day, and so on until the seventh day. It is quite interesting that the Mallas do not simply fix a date for the cremation, but intend to hold it the same day and then postpone it every day, but not beyond the seventh day.[132]

Again, singing and dancing are mentioned in the context of the other cremations of eminent people, such as Mahāpajāpati and her 500 fellow *bhikkhunī arahants.*[133] A Jātaka story in which a king conducts the funeral for a *paccekabuddha* is also of interest. Following the Bodhisatta's advice, the king does not make a sacrifice (*yañña*) but orders the release of the animals prepared for the sacrifice and holds a seven-day festival (*sādhukīḷa*) instead.[134] From the fact that the Bodhisatta advises against *yañña*, one might conclude that the term refers in this context to animal sacrifices. Somewhat less grand but still royal are the funeral rites, which King Bimbisāra arranges for an unseen friend of his, King Pukkusāti. The description of his funeral is of particular interest as it goes into some detail over the preparation of the body:

> He lamented and arranged for the son of a good family to be brought on a bed, which was placed in an appropriate place. As he did not know how to treat someone who had not undergone higher ordination [yet had attained certain insights], he summoned the washer and barber, arranged for the son of good family to be washed [from] head [to foot], for new clothes to be put on, [for him] to be adorned in royal dress and to be placed on a palanquin. Then honoring him with all kinds of music, perfume and garlands, he had him taken out of the city. Then he had a funeral pyre built with many [different types] of scented woods, performed the *śarīrakicca* and had a *cetiya* built for the remains.
>
> (Ps V 63)

The washing of the corpse is of course familiar from the Vedic sūtras, and I suspect the mention of the 'correct place' (*yuttokāse ṭhapetvā*) might have its origin there. We also find the familiar elements of music, garlands and procession, and the passage will be discussed again later in the context of the term *śarīrakicca.*

The funeral procession. Next, eight people of rank prepare themselves by bathing and donning clean clothes to carry the Buddha's body to the cremation ground, but they are not able to lift the Buddha's body.[135] This sparks an interesting conflict with regard to the route of the funeral procession. The humans want to head straight to a place south of Kusinārā and thereby avoid entering the city altogether.[136] The gods, on the other hand, want to enter the city by the north gate, lead the procession through the centre and out of the east gate, because the assembly hall of the Mallas, called Makuṭabandhana, is situated there.[137] But there is, according to Waldschmidt's Sanskrit text and the Chinese translation (1951, 416–417), another suggestion: the procession should enter the city by the west gate and leave by the east gate.[138] In the end, the route of the gods is followed; a procession through the city is made, going to the cremation place east of the city.[139]

Stages of the procession

Both humans and gods intend to make the procession while continuing the worship with song, dance, etc.[140] Caland (1896, 171) describes how in the Vedic *sūtra*s music, singing and dancing was originally meant as noise to chase the soul away. One has to assume here that the interpretation had changed from frightening noise to an expression of honour.[141] The procession is not punctuated by ritual stops for offerings to the deceased and gods like its Vedic counterpart, but the commentary relates an event occurring in the centre of the town. Mallikā donates a rare and precious ornament to the Buddha and makes an earnest wish:

> She placed the ornament on the body of the Blessed One. The ornament enveloped the body from the head to the soles of the feet. The gold-coloured body of the Blessed One adorned with that ornament made of seven kinds of gems shone forth brilliantly.
>
> (An 2003, 193; Sv II 597)

This is reminiscent of the Vedic ritual covering of the corpse with the skin of a sacrificial animal ('Umlegethier' sic!) as protection against the fire of cremation.

The description of the funeral procession of Mahāpajāpati and her fellow *bhikkhunīs* (Thī-a 155f.) contains other interesting details: apart from music, etc., she and her fellow *bhikkhunīs* are placed on couches inside a 'golden pinnacled building';[142] the gods serve as coffin bearers; flags are raised, flowers cover the ground. Interestingly, the order of the procession is also given: the 500 *bhikkhunīs* are taken out first, carried by the gods; followed by Mahāpajāpati, carried by the four guardians of the world (*cattāro lokapālā*); finally the Buddha (with the *bhikkhus*), pays his respects to his stepmother. The final two verses compare this occasion to the cremation of the Buddha:

> The final quenching of the Buddha was not equal to the final quenching of Gotamī. [Hers] was a much more wonderful occasion.
> The Buddha did not prepare the bhikkhus for the Buddha's quenching the way the Buddha and Sāriputta, etc., did for the quenching of Gotamī.
>
> (Pruitt 1998, 199; Thī-a 156)

Another interesting story is found in the Jātakas, where the king orders that the Bodhisatta (in his incarnation as a monkey king) be cremated with all the honours of a human king, and he summons his ministers to what could be interpreted as a procession. The women of the harem are told to turn up with dishevelled hair, wearing red garments and carrying torches.[143] The dishevelled hair, of course, is familiar, but the order to wear red clothes and carry torches is somewhat unusual.

Preparatory rituals. At this stage in the proceedings, the question again arises about how to treat the body of a Buddha, and Ānanda answers with the same standard formula. The body is finally wrapped and placed in an iron coffin full of oil and closed with a lid.[144] The commentary interprets the iron vessel as 'golden',[145] and An (2003, 158) suggests, that 'when Buddhaghosa comments on it as gold, it is assumed that iron had become, in his time, a metal which he might consider too base for the purpose proposed'.[146] The problem of which metal might be referred to here attracted an extraordinary amount of attention in secondary literature, but the question of what purpose a metal coffin serves in a cremation remains yet to be solved.[147]

If, just for a moment, we take the Sutta literally: a body wrapped in cotton, soaked with oil is put in a closed iron vessel and placed on a funeral pyre. The near air-tight environment would result in a much gentler way of combustion than an open air cremation. The many layers of cotton serve as padding and keep air in the coffin to a minimum. The oil ensures that the cotton, and the remaining oxygen trapped in the cloth, is burnt off first.[148] The extinguishing of the pyre (which in the Vedic ritual is meant as cooling or calming the body) has a vital function in stopping the process of decomposition before the bones are totally destroyed. Of all the proposed metals, only iron would be strong enough for the purpose. The fact that Buddhaghosa, as well as the Chinese version (Waldschmidt 1951, 411), assume a golden coffin, suggests that either this procedure was no longer known or practised or that the commentary chooses to ignore the laws of physics.

The only other case of an iron vessel with oil in connection with bodies that I could locate in the Pāli material was that of Queen Bhaddā (A III 58). The grieving king orders that her body should be placed in an iron vessel, 'so that we shall see her body longer'.[149] The main purpose of the oil vessel in this case seems to be the preservation of the body. This is familiar from the Vedic sūtras, which prescribe putting the body of an *āhitāgni* who has died abroad in an oil vessel before it is transported home. The case of King Daśaratha (e.g., Ramāyaṇa II 64.77), who died while his sons were in exile, is similar. His body is kept in a vessel filled with oil (*tailadroṇyām*) until one or all of the sons have returned to tend to their filial duties.[150] More importantly, it is also said that, after the arrival of his son Bharata, the body of King Daśaratha is taken out of the oil vessel and put on a stretcher, which reinforces the impression that the purpose of the oil was purely to preserve the body.[151] In the case of the Buddha's cremation, the opposite seems to be the case: the body is put in an oil vessel just before and solely for the purpose of cremation, and therefore cannot have anything to do with preservation.

This leaves two possible explanations: first, a gentle form of combustion, with the exclusion of air, preserves the bones better. Considering that every bit of bone, even the size of a mustard seed, is of great value for the faithful who worship relics, this is of no little importance. Second, burning the body in an enclosed receptacle preserves the purity or rather authenticity of the relics. And indeed, the sutta makes a special point of asserting that the bones were pure and devoid of all residue.[152]

Purificatory rites

The same purificatory rites that are required of those who carry the body in the procession are also required of those who light the pyre, and the text explains how four eminent Mallas prepare themselves to light the pyre.[153] Now everything is ready: the body is wrapped, the coffin closed and placed on the pyre, the four Mallas are ritually pure to light the fire, but just as in the case of the procession, there is a hold up.

Śarīrapūjā. The lighting of the pyre is prevented by the gods who perceive that Mahākassapa is on his way with 500 monks to worship the Buddha's body:

> Then venerable Mahākassapa arrived at Makuṭabandhana, the shrine of the Mallas at Kusinārā, and approached the Blessed One's funeral pyre. Then he arranged his outer robe on one shoulder, bowed with cupped hands and, keeping it to his right, walked three times round the funeral pyre. Then he bowed down, touching the feet of the Blessed One with his head.[154]
>
> (Gethin unpublished; D II 163)

The commentator obviously felt that an explanation was needed and states that the feet of the Buddha appeared miraculously within the coffin and hundreds of layers of cloth presented themselves to Mahākassapa for worship and then disappeared again, without any damage to the coffin.[155] This is, however, not the only explanation of how Mahākassapa might have worshiped the feet. Both the Sanskrit and the Chinese version of the Mahāparinirvāṇa *sūtra* present a different story (Waldschmidt 1951, 428): Mahākaśyapa unwraps the body and worships it. He then makes the decision to do *śarīrapūjā* himself and wraps the body in the same way as before in fresh cotton and oil and erects a new pyre. This resolves the issue of how the feet were worshiped without resorting to a miracle.

The statement that Mahākassapa performed the *śarīrapūjā* is more problematic than might appear at first sight. Earlier the Buddha had admonished Ānanda, not to get involved with *śarīrapūjā* (*śarīrapūjā*):

> Ānanda, don't concern yourselves with the Tathāgata's funeral (*śarīrapūjā*). You should strive for the true goal, you should be devoted

> to the true goal, you should live applying yourselves to the true goal, ardent, without being neglectful. There are knowledgeable princes, knowledgeable brahmins and knowledgeable householders too who are committed to the Tathāgata—they will conduct the Tathāgata's funeral (*śarīrapūjā*).
>
> (Gethin, unpublished; D II 141)

This has led some scholars to assume that monks should not get involved with *śarīrapūja* at all.[156] This only poses a problem in the Sanskrit version where Mahākassapa is said to conduct a *śarīrapūjā*. Schopen (1997, 107f.) resolves the conflict by suggesting that not all monks, but only the spiritually junior ones (like Ānanda) were meant to refrain from involvement with funeral rites. He adduces Mahākassapa's example (but unfortunately no others) as evidence that monks of high rank and long standing were indeed involved with *śarīrapūjā*.

Apart from the question of who was allowed to engage in *śarīrapūjā*, there is the issue of what precisely the term *śarīrapūjā* refers to. Rhys Davids (1910, 154) translates the term in this passage as 'honouring the remains' (*sarīrāni* in the plural). Schopen (1997, 105ff.), on the other hand, argues on the basis of a number of passages that the term *śarīrapūjā* originally referred to the 'worship of the body' (sg. *sarīraṃ*), and that the meaning 'worship of the relics' (pl. *sarīrāni*) was in fact a later misunderstanding (Mil 177ff.).[157] Assuming that *śarīrapūjā* refers to the handling of the body prior to cremation—and Schopen's evidence (mostly from the Mūlasarvāstivāda Vinaya) seems to leave little doubt that it did—the problem remains that very little is known about what this actually involved. In the Pāli material *śarīrapūjā* usually refers to the Buddha, and in only two commentarial passages to an arahant:

> A great crowd performed the worship of the body for seven days, put together (piled up) scented fire wood, cremated the body and built a cetiya with the relics.[158]
>
> (Ps V 92)

Here *śarīrapūjā* seems to refer to the seven-day pre-cremation celebrations, which were even in the Mahāparinibbāna Sutta (see above) described in the same terminology (*sarīraṃ . . . pūjentā*).

Schopen (1997, 104) comes to the conclusion (based on passages from the Tibetan and Sanskrit sources), that the term *śarīrapūjā* refers to 'funeral activities that began with the wrapping of the body and ended with cremation and constructing the *stūpa* and had . . . nothing to do with relics.' He quotes examples from the Mūlasarvāstivāda Vinaya that monks were not allowed to distribute the robe and bowl of a departed fellow monk unless they had performed the *śarīrapūjā*. Schopen (1997, 107) further points out that in the Mahāparinirvāṇa *sūtra* the term is used to describe a very short sequence of activities:

> Having thought this he brings other clothes, wraps the body with them, puts it back into the vessel, closes the lid, makes a(nother) pyre, and stands to one side. That is all. It is apparently just this sequence of activities that the text intends by the term *śarīra-pūjā.*

There are, however, several problems with Schopen's interpretation. Schopen does not adduce any other passages that would mention these elements (layers of cotton, oil, iron vessel) and associate them explicitely with *śarīrapūjā*. Unless we assume that this rather elaborate procedure is followed in each of the other examples Schopen mentions, one might conclude that these elements were the distinguishing feature of the funeral rites of a *cakkavatti*. This still leaves us in the dark as to what the term *śarīrapūjā* entails or, for that matter, what the common funerary practice was at the time of the Buddha.

But *śarīrapūjā* is not the only term used in the context of funeral rites; far more common, at least in the commentarial literature, is the term *śarīrakicca*. It seems to refer to a similar stage in the proceedings, somewhere between death and collecting the bones and occurs most frequently in the formula *sarīrakiccaṃ kāretvā dhātuyo gahetvā cetiyaṃ akāsi* (or slight variations of it). Occasionally we glimpse a detail, such as that *śarīrakicca* takes place at the cemetery (Ja IV 51). In the case of kings, it is is done by a priest, a *purohita* (Ja III 238) or by the ministers, *amacca* (Ja IV 125), and in the case of ordinary people by family members, mother, son, etc. (as at Ja III 37); but in the case of monks, it is done by fellow monks (Dhp-a III 342 mentions a grieving sister, but the *śarīrakicca* is nevertheless performed by fellow monks). Many passages describe a king or queen as performing *śarīrakicca* or ordering it to be performed for a *paccekabuddha* (Mp I 174; Ap-a 2595etc.) or for the Bodhisatta—even in his incarnation as a monkey (Ja III 374) or horse (Ja I 180; Ja I 182).

Finally, a hint might be found in Ps v 63, where a sequence of the events is described: '[Bimbisāra] summoned the washer and barber, arranged for the son of good family to be washed [from] head [to toe], for new clothes to be put on, to be adorned in royal dress, and to be placed on a palanquin. Then honoring him with all kinds of music, perfume and garlands he had him taken out of the city. Then he had a funeral pyre built with many [different types] of scented woods, performed the *śarīrakicca* and had a *cetiya* built for the remains.' This suggests that *śarīrakicca* is performed immediately before the collection of the bones, but what else could there be left to do to the body? Let us briefly remind ourselves what the Vedic ritual works prescribe at this late stage in the proceedings when the deceased is already on the funeral pyre: they call for the removal of gold ornaments from the body, closing the seven apertures of the head, and a rather gruesome slaughter of a sacrificial animal ('Umlegethier'). There is, however, no evidence that the term *śarīrakicca* refers to any of these specific activities and the slaughter of an animal especially seems very unlikely (though not impossible) in a Buddhist context.[159] There is, nevertheless, a second possibility: the term *śarīrakicca* might simply be a euphemism for the actual act of burning the body. Whenever the term occurs in a sequence of events, it is always the activity just before the collecting of the bones. Some texts actually use the term 'burning' in that sequence (Ps V 92 and Ja III 434: *sarīraṃ jhāpetvā dhātuyo ādāya cetiyaṃ akāsi.*) where Pv V 63 has *sarīrakiccaṃ katvā* (as do other passages). There is a further indication that *śarīrakicca* actually refers to the burning of the body, or that at least it was interpreted as such by the commentarial tradition. At Mp I 282, when the Buddha gives instructions for how to treat the body of Bāhiya Dāruciriya, the term *sarīra-jjhāpana-kicca* clearly means cremation. This leaves two possible interpretations: either *śarīrakicca* was a euphemism for burning the body, or it was simply a short form for *sarīra-jhāpana-kicca*—at least this is how the commentary understands it.

Schopen (1997, 213f.) points out another important connection, namely, the one between the performance of the funeral rites and the inheritance. It appears that in this respect the Buddhist Vinaya rules do not diverge very much from the Dharmaśāstra, where it is stated that the person who performs the funeral rites has the claim on the inheritance.[160] This casts a different light on the Mahākassapa episode. His performance of *śarīrapūjā* would make him one of the rightful heirs of the Buddha, alongside the Mallas (see above), who performed the first *śarīrapūjā*. What is more, it would make him the only monastic heir, and indeed Mahākassapa emerged as a leading figure after the death of the Buddha, presiding over the first council at Rājagaha. However, there is a serious flaw with this theory. Mahākassapa is, as far as I know, never declared to be the official successor of the Buddha. On the contrary, the suttas seem to make a point of not naming an official successor (D II 100). Besides, as was apparent from Dhp-a II 100, it is Ānanda who inherits the Buddha's robe and bowl, and who—at least from the point of view of the commentary—was looked upon by the other monks as the successor to the Buddha.[161] It appears that Mahākaśyapa's performance of *śarīrapūjā*, which appears in the Sanskrit version, but not in the Pāli sources, and its implications would require more investigation.

Cremation. The funeral pyre, which could not be lit by the four Mallas (who had bathed and prepared themselves for the task), now ignites by itself.[162] The way the pyre catches fire is, in the Vedic context, regarded as an omen of the whereabouts (in the various realms of the fathers, gods, *gandharvas*, etc.) of the deceased.[163] The fact that the pyre ignites spontaneously is, therefore, appropriate for a Buddha as he is not being reborn in any of the realms. Another example of spontaneous ignition is Ānanda's self-cremation in mid-air over a river (Dhp-a II 99). People on both sides of the river had been quarreling over where Ānanda should pass away. By making his body split in two, Ānanda made sure that both parties received a share of his relics.[164]

A cremation on a funeral pyre consisting of all kinds of scented wood, perfume and incense, even though it is not an exclusive privilege of Buddhas, is obviously not an everyday event. It is, therefore, interesting to look for descriptions covering the other end of the spectrum, the cremation of ordinary people, or even paupers. At Ud 8 the Buddha returns from his alms round to see the dead body of Bāhiya lying at the roadside. He gives simple instructions of how to dispose of a dead fellow monk: the body is to be placed on strecher, taken away and burnt, finally a *stūpa* is to be built. This seems to represent a standard formula that we find in many passages in the commentaries.[165] For more detailed and rather colourful descriptions of the cremation grounds, the Dhammapada-aṭṭhakathā is a good source. In one story it is said that those who want to take residence in a cremation ground should inform the authorities about their intention, they should abstain from certain food items such as fish, meat, sesame, etc., and exercise the highest willpower. The keeper of the cremation ground appears to make a pact with a monk, who resides there:

> In case, reverend Sir, while you reside in this burning-ground, you succeed in reaching the goal of the religious life, and if they bring a dead body and cast it away, I will place it in a bamboo structure covered with woolen cloth (*kambalakūtāgāraṃ āropetvā*), rendering the usual honours with perfumes and garlands, I will perform the funeral rites over the body. If you do not succeed, I will place [the body] on a funeral pyre, light a fire (*citakaṃ āropetvā aggiṃ jāletvā*), drag the body along with a stake, throw it outside, chop it to pieces with an axe, throw the pieces into the fire, and burn it.
>
> (adapted from Burlingame 1921, I 186; Dhp-a I 69)

The monk accepts the challenge and some time after, relatives bring in the body of a beautiful woman 'of good family' together with firewood, oil, etc., and 'paying the keeper the usual fee, they turned the body over to her and departed'.[166] This indicates that some people did not perform the necessary rituals themselves but employed someone else to do it.[167] Furthermore, it provides a clue as to the two very different treatments of the body, which are the subject of the challenge. After the relatives left, the keeper can, presumably, either perform all the rituals dutifully, i.e., build a bamboo structure covered with woollen cloth,[168] use the perfume and garlands, etc., (scenario A) or take a short cut by lighting a simple fire and throwing the chopped up corpse onto it to save on firewood (scenario B). There is no mention of the keeper using any of the other utensils (*dārutelādīhi saddhiṃ*) and presumably she would keep or sell them. Accordingly, the challenge for the monk is by attaining arahantship to get the keeper of the cremation ground to give up her dishonourable practice in at least this one case. Scenario B is reminiscent of the rather graphic description of a pauper's cremation at Dhp-a I 99 (involving piercing and turning over of body parts), which is a far cry from the pyres made of 'all kinds of scented wood and perfume' that we saw were used for the Buddha's and Mahāpajāpati's cremations.

Purificatory rituals. The extinguishing or cooling of the funeral pyre is an important stage in the Vedic ritual and also gets special mention in the Mahāparinibbāna Sutta, too:

> And when the Blessed One's body had been burnt up, a shower of water came from the sky and extinguished the funeral pyre, and water also burst forth from the sāl trees to extinguish the pyre, while the Mallas too extinguished it with perfumed water.[169]
>
> (Gethin, unpublished; D II 164)

The sutta itself mentions no purificatory rituals, but the commentary states very briefly:

> Thus the royal Mallas extinguished the pyre and cleaned the council hall with four kinds of perfume, and scattered a cluster of flowers with puffed rice as a fifth thing.
>
> (An 2003, 207; Sv II 604)

This is immediately followed by a description of the decorations and preparations for the worship of the relics.

Post-funerary rites

Collecting of the bones. As the relics are contained in the iron vessel, no collection as such takes place.[170] The Mahāparinibbānasutta emphasises strongly the purity of the relics:

> Now when the Blessed One's body burned, no cinders or ash at all were formed from what had been the layers of skin, flesh, sinews and oil of the joints, only the bones remained as relics. Just as when ghee or oil burns no cinders or ash at all are formed, in exactly the same way when the Blessed One's body burned, no cinders or ash at all were formed . . . only the bones remained as relics. Of the five hundred double layers of cloth only two—the innermost and the outermost—were not burnt up.[171]
>
> (Gethin, unpublished; D II 164)

Here the term *sarīrāni* (the plural of *sarīra*, 'body, corpse') denotes 'relics, bones' and *chārikā* and *masi* denote 'ashes' and 'soot' respectively. This is later repeated verbatim and illustrated with the simile of butter or oil burning down without leaving any kind of residue, not even the smallest particles of soot. It would be interesting to investigate if in the context of ordinary people, too, the term *sarīrāni* was used, or if this term has acquired the connotation of 'relics' rather than 'bones' (for which the Pāli would be *aṭṭhi*).[172]

Three interesting aspects emerge here: first, bones and 'ashes' are not only linguistically distinguished, but defined as essentially different substances. Second, only the 'bone-matter' was distributed, enshrined in *stūpas* and venerated. Thirdly, remains of the flesh or body fluid, even in the form of 'ashes', might have been regarded as 'polluting' with regard to the relics.

The Buddha's relics (now in a golden casket) are then worshipped for seven days and taken into the city in a procession on an elephant before they are enshrined and *stūpas* are built.[173] In a Jātaka story it is related how the king arranges a royal funeral and seven-day worship of the relics (*dhātu*) of the Bodhisatta in his incarnation as a monkey:

> The king caused a shrine to be built at the Bodhisatta's burial place, torches to be burnt there and offerings of incense and flowers to be made; he had the skull inlaid with gold, and put it in front raised on a spear-point: honouring it with incense and flowers, he put it inside the king's gate when he came to Benares, and having the whole city decked out he paid honour to it for seven days. Then taking it as a relic and raising a shrine, he honoured it with incense and garlands all his life.
>
> (Cowell 1895–1907 III 227; Ja III 375)

There are three different types of worship here: a *cetiya*, seven-day festivities in honour of the skull and the enshrining of the skull. This is reminiscent of and possibly modelled after the treatment of the Buddha's relics in the Mahāparinibbāna Sutta as described next.

Division of the relics

Eight parties now request the relics, and the situation turns political when the Mallas assert their territorial rights and exclusive claim to the relics (D II 165). Finally, a Brahmin named Doṇa is asked to perform the task of dividing the relics and in turn is allowed to keep the urn.[174] When another interested party, the Moriyas of Pipphalivana, turn up after the relics have been divided, they are granted the charcoal from the pyre.[175] The statement that the urn and the charcoal were venerated too, clearly places the Buddha outside the realm of pollution. The commentary gives more details of relics:

> These seven relics were not distributed;[176] four teeth, the two collar bones, the *uṇhīsa*. The rest were distributed. Among them, the smallest relic was the size of a mustard seed; the bigger relics were the size of a rice grain broken in the middle; the biggest was the size of a kidney bean broken in the middle.
>
> (An 2003, 206; Sv II 604)

The Buddha's relics are now referred to as *dhātu*, or sometimes as *sarīra-dhātu* (bodily relics) and with their distribution begins a rather long-winded history of worship, deceipt, power struggle, legends, *nāga* kings, smuggling, rain making, miracles, etc. To name but one legend which is very popular in Sri Lanka: it is said that the Buddha's relics will move out of all the different *stūpas* in Sri Lanka and reassemble at the Mahācetiya before moving on towards the Mahābodhipallaṅka. The same will happen everywhere there are relics (in India, in the realms of nāgas, devas and brahmas) until they are all assembled at the great Mahābodhipallaṅka one last time, before a second *parinibbāna*, the so-called *dhātuparinibbāna*, will occur and they disappear altogether:

> Having come together at the Mahābodhipallaṅka (in India) they will join together as a lump of gold and shed forth the sixfold radiance throughout the systems of ten thousand worlds. Then the deities of all those worlds will assemble and express their sorrow more intensely than they did when the Buddha passed away. None excepting the Anāgāmins and the Arahants will be able to remain unmoved. At last fire will spring from the relics and, blazing forth as far as the world of the Brahmas, will burn the relics entirely.[177]

In the Mahāparinibbāna Sutta (D II 166), each group, when staking their claim to the relics, promises to build a *stūpa* and to hold a festival. At Sv II 611–614 we read that Mahākassapa commissions the secret building of a *stūpa* in Laṅkādīpa that is to house the relics. Other information on how a *stūpa* is to be built is rare in the Pāli material, and seems confined to the *stūpas* for former Buddhas.[178] In the Mahāparinibbāna Sutta the Buddha explains that only four types of people are worthy of a *stūpa*:

> These four are worthy of a stupa. Which four? A Tathāgata who is an arahat and perfectly awakened buddha is worthy of a stupa, a one-off buddha, a realized disciple of a Tathāgata, and a wheel-turning king are worthy of a stupa.[179]
>
> (Gethin, unpublished; D II 142)

The commentary to this passage might explain why there is virtually nothing to be gleaned from the Pāli sources on *stūpas* or *cetiyas* for ordinary people:

> A universal king (*rājā cakkavattī*): why here did the Blessed One give permission to build a monument (*thūpa*) for a king who lived a household life, not for a virtuous unenlightened monk? Because he [the king] is rare. If monuments for unenlightened monks were allowed, there would be no more space for monuments in the island of Tambapaṇṇi, and the same goes for other places. So he did not allow them because he thought they would be unexceptional. Universal kings come into being one at a time: his monument is therefore rare. However, it is surely right to do as great honour to a virtuous unenlightened monk as to a monk who has attained *parinibbāṇa*.[180]
>
> (adapted from An 2003, 158; Sv II 583)

Otherwise there is little more in the commentaries than a formulaic expression and only occasionally is it added that the *stūpa* was built at crossroads (*cātumahāpathe*).[181] I did not come across any passages that would reveal more about the shape, size, material, content, treatment, etc., of these monuments.

The curious fact that the Pāli Vinaya seems to be the only Vinaya that lacks a section on how to build and worship a *stūpa* has been commented on by Bareau (1962) and Roth (1980, 186):

> The Pāli tradition apparently did not include such a section, as the compilers of the ancient Pāli canon were governed by a tradition according to which the construction and worship of a *stūpa* was the concern of laymen and not of monks. Therefore, there was felt to be no need for a particular *stūpa*-section to be included in the *khandhaka*-section of the Pāli *Vinaya*.

Schopen (1997, 86–98; originally published in *JPTS*, vol XIII (1989)) sets out to refute this and claims that the Pāli Vinaya did in fact contain such a section. In response, three articles appeared in *JPTS*, vol. XV (von Hinüber 1990, Gombrich 1990, Hallisey 1990) convincingly refuting Schopen's claim. It is unnessecary to repeat the arguments of the two sides.

Schopen developed further theories about the disappearance of the *stūpa* section from the Pāli Vinaya, which, again, met with serious objections: there is no commentarial evidence that there might be a gap in the Vinaya itself (von Hinüber 1990, 128); in Ceylon Vinaya texts were copied and distributed, which makes accidental and simultaneous disappearance of whole sections unlikely (Hallisey 1990, 199); other examples prove that additional rules can appear in commentarial literature without anyone claiming that a section of the Vinaya must have gone missing (von Hinüber 1990, 137). Finally the question is: who benefits from a conspiracy against *stūpa* worship?

Whatever the case may be, as von Hinüber (1990, 138) puts it, 'The astonishing fact pointed out again by Schopen remains that not much is found in the Theravāda Vinaya about duties in respect of *cetiyas*, in complete contradistinction to the Vinayas of other schools.' So what do the scholars mentioned above offer as possible explanations for this fact? Hallisey (1990, 208) advises more caution with regard to the conclusions to be drawn from Vinaya material but does not offer a solution. Again von Hinüber (1990, 127) alludes to the suggestions of Bareau and Roth:

> The explanation given by both these scholars is that the Theravāda Vinaya reflects a very early stage of the development of Buddhist ecclesiastical law, when there was no need felt for the respective regulations, or, alternatively, that it had been the concern of laymen rather than monks to care for *stūpas*. In the end both interpretations may complement each other: for during the early times of Buddhism monks may have left matters of worship to laymen.

Finally Gombrich (1990, 143) questions the assumption of a lay origin of the *stūpa* cult, but agrees with Bareau as far as the first argument, the early closing date, is concerned:

> The Pali Vinaya, on the other hand, is plausibly recorded to have been written down in Sri Lanka in the first century B.C. . . . One does not have to posit that it received no further additions after the first century B.C., but merely that the Pali tradition had left the main stream and naturally failed to record later developments on the Indian mainland.

Gombrich does not spell out what these 'later developments on the Indian mainland' are, but we know that one of them is a great growth in *stūpa* building from about 150 BC.[182] If we assume that this prompted the compilation of rules regarding the worship of the *stūpas* in other Vinayas, we now have several possible scenarios for Sri Lanka: *stūpa* building in Sri Lanka might not have taken off in the same way, or at the same time, or, only *stūpas* dedicated to the historical Buddha were built but did not attract a host of smaller mortuary *stūpas* in the way their counterparts on the mainland did (see also II.3.3).[183]

There might be yet another aspect to it. If we assume that mortuary *stūpas* only make sense in a cremation context, the lack of mortuary *stūpas* in Sri Lanka might be due to different funerary practices. Unlike in India, in Sri Lanka (now as then) cremations were the exception and other forms of disposal of the body (charnel ground, burial) the norm. Could it be that for ordinary monks, too, the disposal of the body was just a matter of course, e.g., bringing a fellow monk to the charnel ground? This practice would not require regulations as it did not cause any change in the social environment. This will suffice as a summary of the dispute over the 'missing section' in the Pāli Vinaya.

Worship of the relics. Passages dealing with worship and offerings to *stūpas* and to (or on behalf of) the departed will be discussed in the context of giving merit, but one legend is worth relating here: the self-sacrifice of King Aśoka on the occasion of the completion of 84,000 *stūpas*. It is related in the Mahāparinibbāna Sutta, how Mahākassapa decided to house all the relics in one *stūpa* until a future time when King Aśoka would build 84,000 *stūpas* for the relics. The story of his self-sacrifice is related in the Lokappaññatti and translated by Strong (1994, 119):

> On the seventh day, King Aśoka, desirous of paying pūjā to the great *stūpa*, had his own body wrapped in cotton up to his neck and his limbs up to his wrists, and had himself soaked with five hundred pots of scented oil. Then, standing facing the Mahāstūpa, making añjali, his head anointed with oil, and mindful of the Buddha, he had his body set on fire; and the flames rose up in the air to a height of seven persons.[184]

Strong (1994, 120) points out that this legend not only attributes supernatural powers to Aśoka, but also—by recalling the *cakkavatti's* cremation—turns Aśoka into a *cakkavatti*.[185]

Summary

What little information on funeral customs can be gained from the canonical texts is found almost entirely in the Mahāparinibbāna Sutta or in the context of the death of eminent disciples. These particular circumstances cannot be taken as generally representative of the funeral practice at the time. One important exception is the Udāna, where the Buddha reportedly gave instructions on how to deal with the remains of an ordinary monk.

The commentarial literature, on the other hand, is full of references to funeral rites (*śarīrakicca*), but once again, few details. Some interesting glimpses of cremations of less privileged people, which are quite different from the grand, cosmic cremations found in the canonical sources, are gained from stories in the Dhammapada-aṭṭhakathā. The Jātakas add another dimension of stories of the cremation of the Bodhisatta in his animal incarnations (as monkey or horse). Overall, the tension between veneration and fear with regard to the departed that characterizes the Vedic material and the contemporary Sri Lankan practice is not found in the Pāli sources.

Archaeological evidence

A study of Buddhist funerals is not complete without at least attempting to paint a picture of early Buddhist mortuary monuments and cemeteries. The suttas and commentaries do mention the building of *cetiyas* for someone's remains, but give very little information about what these *cetiyas* might have looked like.[186] It seems, therefore, necessary to consult archaeological and inscriptional material. Not being an archaeologist, I will mainly rely on Schopen's articles (1997 and 2004), as well as Coningham (2001) for this part.[187]

Schopen has looked behind (and beyond) the great *stūpas* that were built for the Buddha's relics, and drew attention to the small monuments that might have housed the mortuary remains of ordinary monks. His work is, however, mainly based on inscriptions and Vinaya texts. Coningham, on the other hand, provides a wealth of archaeological detail regarding the Buddhist sites and structures.

Stūpas

The structure. Schopen 1997, 179 states that small *stūpas* do not differ structurally from larger *stūpas* that were associated with the Buddha. This is, according to Schopen (1997, 119), the reason why they have frequently been interpreted as votive *stūpas*. Before going into the details of the finds I wish briefly to summarize (following Roth 1980, 84ff.) the main structural elements of Buddhist *stūpas*.

The ground plan of the *stūpa* is a circle drawn around a centre point, which represents a wheel (with four or eight spokes) laid out in accordance with the cardinal directions. Four terraces form the foundation for the dome, which can assume various shapes, and contains the relics. On top is a quadrangular superimposed structure (*harmikā*), which frequently contains caskets with precious stones, etc., and the highest part of the building is a pole with one or more umbrellas, according to the rank of the person. A pole (*yaṣṭi*), which runs through the centre of the *stūpa*, is sometimes interpreted as the *axis mundi* or connecting link between heaven and earth. Irwin (1980, 15) identifies it with the Vedic sacrificial pole (*yūpa*), and with Indra's peg (*indrakīla*). Snodgrass (1985, 221) describes the three main types of the *stūpa* as follows: first, dome *stūpas* which are found all over Sri Lanka, Thailand and Burma and the prototype of which is the great *stūpa* at Sāñchi; second the terrace *stūpa* which is found in Tibet, Nepal,[188] Burma, etc. (the most famous example of this type being Borobudur), and thirdly the tower *stūpa* which is represented in Bodhgaya as well as by the pagodas of China and Japan. While differing considerably in shape and size, they still share the main structural elements.

Individual stūpas (*Amarāvatī, south*). Fragmentary finds in Amarāvatī will help to build up a clearer picture of what the small *stūpas*, which are interpreted either as mortuary or votive, might have looked like. The find of a small *stūpa* with a lower portion still encased in a sculptural slab (as described by

Rea (1909, 118–119)) is particularly important as a number of dislodged slabs were discovered, some of which were inscribed.[189] Other finds in Amarāvatī provide further clues as to the shape of these small *stūpas*, and a circular stone slab is described by Burgess (1882, 49):

> A circular slab 2 feet 1 inch in diameter . . . with a mortise hole in the centre surrounded by a lotus, and this again by a sunk area carved with rays. The outer border is raised . . . a well-cut inscription. . . .[190]

This slab is referred to in an inscription, which runs along its edge as an 'umbrella' (*chata, chattra*) and considering its relatively small size might have belonged to one of the smaller *stūpas*. Small clay pots in the dome of some of the *stūpas* were found to contain human remains, which proves that at least some of the small *stūpas* were actually mortuary in character. These *stūpas* come in various sizes and the ones excavated at Amarāvatī were made for a particular individual. Longhurst (1936, 14) observes:

> [T]he *stūpas* erected over the remains of ordinary members of the Buddhist community were humble little structures. The ashes of the dead were placed in an earthenware pot and covered with a lid, and the humble little *stūpa* erected over it. Plenty of Buddhist *stūpas* of this class may still be seen in the Madras Presidency and also in Ceylon.[191]

To sum up: a number of small *stūpas* were found in the vicinity of a big *stūpa* associated with the Buddha. Carved slabs of stone formed their base, and a circular stone slab, which was called an 'umbrella', was attached to at least some of the *stūpas*. The base and the umbrellas of some of these slabs had been engraved with inscriptions typically stating for whose benefit and by whom the *stūpa*, or the umbrella, had been donated. Schopen points out that the names identified from these inscriptions were predominantly monastic.

Groups of individual stūpas *in caves (Sudhagarh, northwest).* Schopen (1997, 182) describes the occurence of groups of small *stūpas* of varying size and belonging to different periods in the Western Caves.[192] Both caves are dated around the same period: Sudhgar from 200–150 BC (Kail 1966, 188) and Nadsur at around 200 BC (Cousens 1891, 10).[193] It would be interesting to know if there were other, surrounding caves and for what purpose these might have been used.

Coningham (2001, 77) comments on the difficulty of determining whether caves are actually Buddhist:

> Whilst there is little doubt that *chaitya-griha* 19 in Ajanta in Western India was dedicated to the *Buddha*, the attribution of Buddhism to

many other rock-cut and natural caves in the region is in doubt as indicated by Mitterwallner's research in south-west India (1981). In Goa she surveyed a series of caves, devoid of evidence, and found it difficult to interpret one as either a Hindu swami's cell for yogic exercise or as a Buddhist monument and debated whether another was 'the initiative of the Saivas, Jainas or Buddhists?'

Collective stūpa *Nāgārjunakoṇḍa (South).* Other *stūpas* housed the remains not of an individual, but of one or more groups of individuals. Longhurst (1938, 20–21) describes his finds in the foundations (between the 'spokes') of two *stūpas*:

> Twelve water pots covered with inverted food bowls . . . together with six large begging-bowls . . . placed on the floor of the chamber near the other vessels. The pots were in small groups of three or four and filled with a mixture of bone ash and fine red earth.[194]

Longhurst concludes from this (and similar finds in another *stūpa*) that it was 'built to contain the remains of twelve monks and the ashes of some important divine'. This raises a number of questions: did the monks die at the same time? Were they connected in some other way, e.g., by teacher lineage? Were they deposited in a collective *stūpa* straightaway or at some later stage and possibly by later generations?

Schopen (2004, 371f.) points out another rather peculiar find at Nāgārjunakoṇḍa: deposits of bones of large animals (such as an ox, deer and hare) in otherwise empty *stūpas* and a burnt pea-fowl in a heap of ashes in another *stūpa*.[195] He comments that this is reminiscent of finds in megaliths at the site and sees here a continuation of pre-Buddhist practice:

> The Buddhist deposits, then, would probably best be explained as a reflection of the incorporation or continuation of elements of local megalithic practice in Buddhist mortuary rites. But if this is true, it would mean that the Buddhist community not only was aware of the nature of the megalithic monuments they encountered and built upon, but had actually continued some of the practices associated with these monuments—at least in Nāgārjunikoṇḍa.

The question is what Schopen means by 'Buddhist deposits'? Does he imply that the deposit of animal bones was made by people who would consider themselves to be 'Buddhist' or that it is a specific Buddhist activity? From the contemporary Buddhist context I see no problem here. It is not a great secret that even 'Buddhists' occasionally engaged in 'non-Buddhist' activities and vice versa. There is also evidence that Buddhists do not necessarily agree on what a 'Buddhist' activity is. To quote but one example: a pious laywoman at the temple in our village told me rather excitedly that she was planning an alms giving for the benefit of beloved pets. She clearly regarded this as a Buddhist activity, even though other people I talked to were rather appalled at the thought. But to what degree can a religious identity be assumed for the time in which these deposits were made? The question has been discussed above and I would agree with Coningham (2001, 90) who says:

> Perhaps the need to allocate discrete categories of religious jurisdiction owe more to the concepts of a British census rather than responding to actual practice.[196]

Besides, considering that Schopen had earlier pointed out the overlap between the megalithic and early Buddhist period and the similarity of megalithic structures and *stūpas*, one needs to ask if these *stūpas* were 'Buddhist' at all.[197] Coningham (2001, 73) gives three examples of the difficulty of determining if a *stūpa* is Buddhist or not. The first is the example of '17 square brick *stūpas*' at Sagarhawa, which were originally interpreted as Buddhist, but later this interpretation was challenged and the possibility was raised that they might be Hindu temples and not *stūpas* at all. The second example regards an Aśokan inscription in Nigali Sagar recording the enlargement of a *stūpa* in honour of Buddha Konakamana. Here Coningham (2001, 74) points out that without the inscription this *stūpa* might have been recognized as Buddhist, but it would have been virtually impossible to determine which Buddha it was dedicated to. His third example from an early historic site at Sirkap illustrates the difficulty of distinguishing between Jain and Buddhist *stūpas*.[198] This will suffice to show that there is good reason to be careful in judging a building (or practice) to be Buddhist unless inscriptional evidence is adduced.

Stūpas *in monks' cells (Taxila, Kālawān, Moḥra Morādu, north west).* Schopen (1997, 185) presents us with another rather interesting piece of information on monastic mortuary rites:

> In *vihāras* at Taxila, Kālawān and Moḥrā Morādu, Marshall found small *stūpas* built in what originally could only have been the living quarters of individual monks. He suggested that these *stūpas* were funeral monuments intended 'as memorials to signalise the sanctity of the cell where some specifically holy *bhikshu* had lived and died', that these *stūpas* 'probably' contained the ashes of these monks, or 'doubtless contained the bodily relics' of a former resident.[199]

Unfortunately, this is all we learn from Schopen about this highly interesting find, and, again, many questions remain unanswered: how many of the cells were 'occupied' in this way? Were neighbouring cells still being lived in? Could these small *stūpas* have been moved into these cells after the monastery had been half, or totally, deserted?

Interestingly Coningham (2001, 78), based on the same archaeological report by Marshall (1951), describes the find at Mohra Moradu very differently:

> The courtyard was reached by a northern gateway and was bounded by 27 cells, each of which opened onto a verandah—Cell 15 also led to a first floor, whilst 7 led to the Western rooms. The cells, some 3.6 m high, varied between 6–15 m^2 in area and were provided with small alcoves and, in some cases, high ventilation slits (ibid.: 360). Although largely empty, some cells contained store jars and water vessels and one had been converted into a sanctuary complete with 3.6 m high votive stupa. Alcoves and plinth in the portico and the courtyard were also provided with small clay figures of the *Buddha, Bodhisattvas*, attendants, the god Indra and donors.

Not only is it clear from this description that only one of the cells contained a *stūpa*, but Coningham takes it that the nature of the *stūpa* is votive rather than mortuary.

Burial grounds

It is now time to step back and take a look at the bigger picture, i.e., the location where the small *stūpas* were found. Schopen (1997, 185) points out that the list of places where there is evidence for the treatment of the 'local monastic dead':

> contains several of the earliest sites that we have certain knowledge of (Sāñcī, Sonārī, Andher, Bhājā, Bhojpur, Pitalkhorā); it includes some of the main Buddhist sites referred to in *nikāya/āgama* literature (Śrāvastī, Kauśāmbī); it includes sites from the South (Amarāvatī, Guṇṭupalle, Nāgārjunikoṇḍa), from the West (Bedsā, Kānheri, Sudhagarh, Nadsur, etc.), from the Northwest (Taxila, Kālawān, Mohṛā Morādu), from Central India (Sāñcī, Sonārī, etc.) and from the Buddhist heartland. In short, this list testifies to a preoccupation with permanently housing or enshrining the local monastic dead that was very early and very widespread geographically.

Small *stūpas*, some of which house human remains, occur in great numbers in the vicinity of important *stūpas*, which are associated with a relic of or a visit by the Buddha. Schopen points out that a pattern can be observed: around a large *stūpa* a great number of smaller *stūpas* are jumbled. These were added at different times and some of these *stūpas* were actually portable.

Further away from the main *stūpa* smaller *stūpas* are found arranged in neat rows. Schopen (1997, 122) names, amongst others, famous Buddhist sites such as Dharmarājikā at Taxila (NW, second century B.C.E.); Jauliāñ and Mīrpūr-Khas (fourth and fifth centuries C.E.); Ratnagiri (tenth and twelfth centuries C.E.) as examples for this archaeological pattern.[200] Cunningham (1892, 82) describes how the many layers of these small *stūpas* actually raised the ground level near the famous temple at Bodhgayā considerably.[201] Schopen (1997, 180) points out that the earliest of these small *stūpas* are contemporary with the main *stūpa* of the respective sites (such as Bārhut, Bhājā, Bedsā, etc.). And Schopen (1997, 118) goes one step further in claiming that even the pattern of crowding and jumble of *stūpas* in the vicinity of a main *stūpa* was established within a century:

> The Dharmarājikā *Stūpa* in Taxila is a good, early example. Although, as Marshall himself admits, there is no surviving evidence to actually prove that the main *stūpa* is Mauryan, it is unlikely that it is much later; a second century B.C.E. date is not unlikely. Within a century this main *stūpa* was surrounded by a tight circle of smaller *stūpas* crowding around it, some of which can be dated by coin finds more specifically to the first century B.C.E.

Based on the same source (Marshall 1951) Coningham (2001, 86) paints a somewhat different picture again. While confirming the pattern of small *stūpas* around a bigger *stūpa* associated with the Buddha, Coningham only speaks of votive *stūpas* and image shrines, there is no mention of any mortuary *stūpas*.

Schopen (2004, 361–366) points to another curious fact: ancient Buddhist sites such as Amarāvatī, Nāgārjunikoṇḍa, Mohenjo-Daro, Kusinārā, Lumbinī, etc., were built either near, or actually on top of, pre-historic megalithic burial sites. Schopen (2004, 374f.) concludes:

> It would appear that immigrant Buddhist monastic communities, when they settled in many 'foreign' areas of what we call India, intentionally and knowingly chose to establish their monasteries and *stūpas* in, near, or on sites already occupied by proto-historic cemeteries or burials. . . . Their choice of such sites would have placed the Buddhist complex at an already established focal point in the local landscape and in the local community. It would have established the Buddhist monastic community as the keepers, the guardians of the native dead, and claimed thereby an important function for the newly arrived monks.

There seem to be several problems with this conclusion: first, does Schopen want to imply here that these foreign immigrant monks forcefully took over the burial sites? Second, in what sense were the burial grounds 'focal points in the local community'? The Mahāparinibbāna Sutta locates the hall where the cremation is to take place to the east of the city rather than in the centre. If contemporary Sri Lanka is anything to go by, burial grounds are outside the villages and not places of great activity but positively avoided.[202] And finally, what would the 'important function as keepers and guardians of the native dead' consist of? The image that Schopen conjures up is more akin to a Christian churchyard with well-kept graves in the village centre than anything I have seen in India or Sri Lanka, or are we to understand that the monks took over the function of burning the bodies?

Schopen does not touch upon the question of different patterns of patronage (Coningham 2001, 81) nor does he take into account that the developments of Buddhism in different parts of the country were neither uniform nor centrally regulated. Buddhism was never a 'church' as Dutt (1962, 28) puts it.

Inscriptions

Schopen (1997, 126ff.) also refers to a number of inscriptions as evidence that the relics of the Buddha were actually thought of as a 'living presence'. To quote but two of his examples: 'the relic of the Blessed One Śākyamuni which is endowed with life'[203] (second century B.C.E.); and in a Karoṣṭhī inscription the relics are described as 'infused with morality, infused with concentration, wisdom'[204] (early first century C.E., 25 to 26 C.E.), etc. He also quotes a number of passages from the Buddhacarita, Milindapañha and Mahāvastu, to further prove the point.[205] Schopen (1997, 125) then goes one step further and points out some of the implications that a 'living presence' of the Buddha might have:

> In other words, death at Bodh-Gayā and *burial ad sanctos* at Carthage and Kōyasan have exactly the same result, although the heaven in each case is somewhat differently appointed. In fact, the key concept in this old text—only very slightly extended—is probably able to account by itself for what is seen in the archeological record of several Buddhist sacred sites in India. The extension would only be from *death* to *deposition of the already dead* in close physical proximity to that actual presence.

But are the relics 'alive' because they are relics of the Buddha or is some quality of life thought to be inherent in all mortuary remains? The practice of *burial ad sanctos* (as manifest in the small *stūpas* crowded around a large *stūpa*) seems to imply that there is some connection between the remains, or more specifically the bones, and the person.

Most of the *stūpas* dedicated to Gotama Buddha have inscriptions stating this fact and—according to Schopen (1997, 180)—in these inscriptions the

Buddha appears in the genitive (*bhagavato*) as the owner or inhabitant of the *stūpa*. Schopen further observes that the *stūpas* for the 'local dead' not only resemble the *stūpas* for the Buddha structurally, but their inscriptions, at least what little we have of them, display a similar syntax (indicating ownership).[206] They typically give the name of the dead person (usually a local monk) in the genitive ('for' or 'of') and sometimes the name of the donor as well. Schopen (1997, 179) quotes one such inscription:

> Of the lay-sister Cadā, the mother of Budhi, together with her sons, together with her daughters, to the shrine of the Venerable Luminary from Utayi, the umbrella is a gift.[207]

There are essentially two questions here: whose (if anybody's) remains were buried in these *stūpas* and who were the donors? According to Schopen (1979, 187–188), the overwhelming majority of the recipients (i.e., the dead mentioned in these inscriptions) are monks, but the titles mentioned in these inscriptions (*bhikṣu*, *vinayadhara*, *ācārya*, etc.) are neither particularly prestigious ones nor linked to spiritual achievement.[208]

When it comes to the donors, Schopen (1997, 190)—due to the absence of conclusive evidence—speculates that '*stūpas* in the monastic cemeteries at both Bhājā and Kānheri could have been erected . . . and maintained only by the monks' and extends the same logic to other Buddhist sites. And elsewhere (1997, 190) he concludes:

> Even in the case of un-inscribed *stūpas*, it is difficult to avoid the conclusion that the monks themselves were responsible for the deposit of the remains of what appear to be local monastic dead.

This statement, which expresses a recurrent theme of his article ('An Old Inscription'), is somewhat puzzling. First, if not the monks themselves, who should take care of their dead? Contemporary Buddhist practice in Sri Lanka shows that it is understood as the filial duty of monks to make the funeral arrangements for their departed teacher. Second, Schopen emphasises repeatedly that these smaller *stūpas* house the remains of the 'local monastic dead', but why should that be remarkable or controversial? The question is not so much why *stūpas* of (and for) monks were found near a big *stūpa*, but why there were not more *stūpas* of (and for) laypeople or nuns.

Summary

The early Buddhist sites have a number of things in common: they have been built near or on existing proto-historic funeral sites; they started with a *stūpa* which was associated with the Buddha and then attracted very quickly great numbers of smaller *stūpas* of, possibly, mortuary function. Schopen adduces evidence that the relics of the Buddha were considered 'alive' in some way, and burial in the vicinity of such a 'live' relic was regarded as auspicious and beneficial with regard to the next rebirth. Some of these smaller *stūpas* were actually portable and might have been brought there from quite a distance. They also resemble the larger *stūpas* for the Buddha, and even their inscriptions show similar syntax. A majority of inscriptions testify that the recipient of the *stūpa*, the dead person, was a monk, which does not necessarily mean that only monks' remains were treated in that way, as Schopen seems to suggest. These small *stūpas* came in various sizes, containing the remains of an individual person or of a group of individuals. Some *stūpas* were found in caves, others in monks' cells in a monastic complex. The nature of these small *stūpas* is not undisputed, and some refer to them as votive *stūpas*, others call them mortuary *stūpas*.

III

POST-FUNERARY RITES

Contemporary Sri Lankan practice

Baṇa

A laywoman's baṇa

1. It is the sixth day after the death. It is almost dark when we arrive. Today we bring a bunch of bananas. This time we are greeted with big 'hellos' instead of formal *āyubōvan*. The family members are again dressed in white. A big crowd of 70–80 people has gathered at the house. The place is very alive and busy with familiar faces. In the garden a square of 1m to 1.5m is fenced off with poles and ropes. Young coconut leaves hang from the rope like a curtain. Inside the square a bamboo pole has been stuck in the ground. No one is around and there are no lights in the garden. The metal roof and chairs of the funeral society are still there. The front room is empty of furniture. In a corner is a single chair covered with a white piece of cloth. A small table is covered with a white cloth. A tray of betel leaves and a large alarm clock are on the table. A white piece of cloth has been tied to the ceiling above the chair and table. We walk through to the kitchen and put the bananas on the table. Everywhere are plates with cookies and traditional Sri Lankan sweets. Women are rushing in and out. In the garden several fireplaces are set up with big clay pots. There are a great many different dishes. White plain rice and yellow fried rice are prepared. Various vegetable dishes, cashew curry and chicken curry are in different stages of completion. Papadams and small fish fried in oil are drying on newspaper. There are plastic bowls with sweet and sour pickles. Small green leaves are finely cut for a salad. Tomatoes and cucumbers are arranged on plates. There are platters with pineapple, mango and even a couple of apples. Clay pots of curd and bottles of treacle are on the table. The women are busy cooking and keeping the children away from the sweets. The granddaughters walk around offering tea and cookies to the guests.

2. At about 7.30 p.m. the son-in-law comes into the kitchen.[1] He brings a cone made of banana leaves sewn together. The daughter fills it with rice and curries, salads and papadam. A small plate with cookies, a banana and betel is placed on top. The son-in-law makes sure nothing is forgotten. Filled to the brim the cone is taken to the square in the garden. The son-in-law places the cone in the bamboo stand. The grandson holds the torch. He fetches various utensils of the dead woman from the house. Her sleeping mat is spread out in the square. The pillow, a glass of water and an oil lamp are placed on the mat. Only two or three men stand by to watch. Finally the son-in-law steps into the square. He lights the oil lamp and stands facing the pillow and food stand. He makes the gesture of formal greeting (*āyubōvan*) and calls the spirit of the dead mother:

> Mother! Mother! Mother! Now it is seven days since you left us on a day like today. We, all the children and relations of yours, have gathered here and make [the monk] preach [the *baṇa*] tonight. Mother, you too must come and listen to the *baṇa*. We will give alms to the great *saṃgha* tomorrow. All of us, the children and the assembly of relations, make the [earnest] wish that you may obtain all the merit resulting from that *sāṃghika* almsgiving, and obtain the good happiness of Nirvāṇa from where you are [now]. Please, come and listen to the *baṇa*, please![2]

His voice begins to shake and he has to start again. After a few minutes the son-in-law and the other men go back to the house. The food and the burning oil lamp are left behind.[3]

3. At about 7.45 p.m. the monk who had performed the funeral arrives in a three-wheeler. People stop chatting and gather in front of the house. At the entrance the monk takes off his slippers and steps onto a mat. A man pours a cup of water over his feet and pats them dry with a towel. The monk sits down on the prepared seat. The front room quickly fills up. Most of the people have to sit outside in front of the house. The ceremony begins with the salutation to the Buddha, etc. The monk then chants:

> *dhammassavanakālo ayaṃ bhadantā!*[4]
>
> This is the time to listen to the Dharma, honourable ones!

People say, '*Sādhu, sādhu, sādhu!*' The monk begins his sermon. He emphasises the meritorious character of the occasion. He mentions that the merit is for the benefit of the dead mother. The virtues of a mother and the importance of filial respect are extolled. The dead parents are said to be watching from the other world. They can still exert a positive influence over their children and grandchildren. But if the children neglect their duties, they may turn into troublesome spirits. After this general introduction he begins the *dharma* talk with a Pāli verse:

Aciraṃ vat' ayaṃ kāyo paṭhaviṃ adhisessati
chuddho apetaviññāṇo niratthaṃ va kaliṅgaraṃ.[5]

Soon this body will lie on the ground, thrown away, deprived of consciousness, like a useless piece of wood.

Throughout his talk he repeatedly makes reference to this verse. Different causes of death are explained. The image of an oil lamp is evoked. The lamp cannot burn without oil or without a wick. A lamp can be blown out by a sudden gush of wind. He moves on to the topic of illnesses. A story from the Pāli scriptures is related: the monk Pūtigattatissa suffers from a very unpleasant illness. The Buddha heals him. The *dharma* is his medicine. The sermon concludes with an admonition. Giving merit is only part of the filial duty. The other part is leading a religious life. The giving of merit ceremony follows.[6] The monk formulates the religious wish for the dead mother: 'By the power of this merit may she be reborn in good existences! May she attain *nirvāṇa* under the future Buddha Maitreya!' The giving of merit to the gods follows: 'May the gods obtain this merit! May the gods make our activities successful! May the gods, too, attain *nirvāṇa*!' Finally everyone present is included in the wish: 'May the family and everyone present attain well-being! May everyone present attain *nirvāṇa!*' After each of the three wishes the monk addresses the audience: 'With this in mind make a religious wish (*prārthanā*)'. People respond by saying *sādhu, sādhu, sādhu!* There is a moment of silence. The monk is given a glass of water. A parcel wrapped in brown paper is carried around. People touch the parcel and then their foreheads with both hands. The parcel containing an umbrella is offered to the monk. The monk chants:

Ākāsaṭṭhā ca bhummaṭṭhā devā nāgā mahiddhikā
Puññan taṃ anumoditvā ciraṃ rakkhantu sāsanaṃ
. . . ciraṃ rakkhantu desanaṃ
. . . ciraṃ rakkhantu tvaṃ sadā.[7]

May the gods of the ether and the earth and the powerful snakes
rejoice in the merit and long protect the dispensation!
[May they] . . . long protect the teaching!
[May they] . . . long protect you always!

The religious wish for everyone present is repeated. The sermon did not exceed one hour. The monk exchanges a few words with the family. The three-wheeler is waiting. He leaves at about 8.45 p.m. taking the parcel with him.

4. Preparations for the meal start straightaway. Plates and finger bowls are brought out. Some people are in a rush to get home. They are being served first together with the children. The invitation to the almsgiving on the following day is repeated. I am urged to bring my husband and son along. We inquire about our contribution for the next day. We are told ice-cream would be welcome. In true Sri Lankan style people leave straight after the meal. We are on our way by 9.45 p.m.[8]

A monk's baṇa

1. It is the sixth day after the death, the day following the cremation. We arrive slightly late at 7.45 p.m. The preaching hall is brightly illuminated with neon lamps. Mats are spread out in the preaching hall on the floor. At one end is a low stage where cushions are placed along the walls. Framed pictures of former abbots hang on the wall. In the centre is a small, brightly coloured Buddha statue on a shelf. A chair is placed to one side facing the lower level. It is covered with a white and orange check cloth. In front of it is a small table with a patterned tablecloth. A tray of betel, an alarm clock and a microphone are on the table. A big enamel spittoon and an electric fan are on the floor.[9]

2. The temple grounds are dark and deserted. No preparations are made for a meal or a *pūjāva*.[10] Except for a few late-comers there is no one outside. A big crowd of about 150 to 200 people has turned up. People have already settled on the floor mats inside the hall. About 20 to 30 monks of different ages and seniority sit on the upper level. The most senior monks are sitting near the chair. The preaching monk has taken his place.[11]

3. The ceremony starts with the salutation to the Buddha, etc. The speaker begins his sermon. He is holding a fan in his hand.[12] Respect for the parents is emphasised. This is followed by remarks on how to be a Buddhist. His sermon touches upon a number of other general topics loosely connected. People are listening attentively. After about 45 minutes merit is being dedicated. First, a religious wish for the benefit of the dead abbot is expressed: 'May he attain Nirvāṇa by the power of this merit!' Next come the gods: 'May they rejoice in the merit and give their support to us!' Finally everyone present is included: 'By the power of this merit may everyone be reborn in good existences! May everyone be reborn in the time of the future Buddha Maitreya and attain Nirvāṇa!' People respond with '*sādhu, sādhu, sādhu!*' after every wish. There is a short break now. A cup of plain tea and a glass of water are offered to the preacher. A young monk brings the dome-shaped parcel containing the eight requisites. The senior monks touch the parcel before it is presented to the speaker. The sermon is concluded with the chanting of the verses dedicating merit to the gods. Again people say '*sādhu, sādhu, sādhu!*'

4. The sermon lasted for exactly one hour. People get up and stand around in small groups. Some monks surround the speaker and talk to him. Others come down from the upper level and mix with the laypeople. The majority of the people are leaving now. Only laypeople involved with organizing the next day's alms giving stay back. Some vans and three-wheelers are waiting outside the temple gate. Most people have come on foot. Some from as far as our village, about five km away.[13]

Seventh-day matakadānaya

A laywoman's seventh-day matakadānaya

1. It is the seventh day after the death; the fourth day after the funeral. We take the nine o'clock train to the next town. Near the station we buy two huge tubs of vanilla ice cream. After a short bus and three-wheeler ride we arrive at the house. It is ten o'clock and beginning to get hot. There are fewer people, but more children than the previous night. Most faces are familiar by now. Bringing my husband and two-and-a-half-year-old son proves a success. The fenced square in the garden is empty now. Remains of the *pūjāva* have been cleared away. The front room is already prepared for the monks. A white piece of cloth covers the whole of the ceiling. Nine chairs along the walls are covered with white cloth. A tall table with an arch on top is wrapped in white cloth. The kitchen is as busy as the previous night and women are cooking on the fireplaces.[14]

2. At about eleven o'clock the grandson brings an ornamented brass bowl to the kitchen.[15] The bowl is filled with rice and curries. Sweets and fruits on a round shaped 'plate' cut out of a banana leaf follow. Finally bananas and betel are balanced on top. A king coconut is opened and the top loosely put back on. The son-in-law covers his head with a towel. He carries the bowl to the waiting three-wheeler. The grandson invites us to join him. We pile into the three-wheeler. The son-in-law hands the bowl to the grandson. The ride to the temple takes only five minutes. We leave our sandals in the three-wheeler and enter the shrine room. The grandson places the food items on a big table in front of the Buddha statue. A young monk comes over from the main building. We sit down on the floor and the ceremony begins with the salutation to the Buddha, etc. The monk chants eight Pāli verses. With each verse a food item is offered to the Buddha:

Nivedayāmi sambuddhaṃ vītarāgaṃ mahāmuniṃ/
nimantayāmi sugataṃ lokaseṭṭhaṃ narāsabhaṃ//

sugandhaṃ sītalaṃ kappaṃ pasannamadhuraṃ subhaṃ/
pānīyam etaṃ bhagavā patigaṇhātu-m-uttamaṃ//[16]

adhivāsetu no bhante bhojanaṃ parikappitaṃ/
anukampaṃ upādāya patigaṇhātu-m-uttamaṃ//

... *vyañjanaṃ parikappitaṃ*/
... *khajjakaṃ parikappitaṃ*/
... *rasavantaṃ phalāphalaṃ*/
... *parikkhāraṃ parikappitaṃ*/
... *sabbaṃ saddhāya pūjitaṃ*/

I address the Buddha, who is free of passion, the great sage.
I invite the well-gone, the most excellent in the world, the lord of men.

May the Blessed One accept the best, this water,
fragrant, cool, proper, clear, sweet and pleasant.
... this prepared food ...
... this prepared curry ...
... these prepared sweet meats ...
... these tasty fruits ...
... these prepared utensils ...
... all things offered in faith ...

The *pūjāva* takes about ten minutes. After a short chat with the monk we return to the house of the dead woman.

3. In the middle of the room a big white sheet has been spread out. Ten identical plates with food are placed on the sheet. The food is arranged on banana leaves in three layers on the plates. On a small table are a number of parcels wrapped in brown paper. Amongst them is one containing the eight requisites. At noon nine monks arrive in a van. The son-in-law covers his head with a towel and walks to the vehicle. The relic receptacle is passed to him from inside the van. It is covered with orange silky fabric. The monks line up and walk in a procession after the son-in-law. A layman holds a black umbrella over the receptacle. People pay their respects with joined palms saying, '*Sādhu! sādhu! sādhu!*' The son-in-law places the receptacle on the 'altar'. Two laymen pour water over the monks' feet and pat them dry with a towel. The monks enter the house walking on a strip of white cloth. The most senior monk sits next to the temporary 'altar'. The ceremony begins with salutation to the Buddha, etc. The most senior monk gives a short introduction in Sinhala. He then chants the appropriate Pāli verses, offering food items to the Buddha.[17] After that he continues his sermon introducing non-local monks.[18] They are said to be representative of the *saṃgha* (past, present and future). The senior monk formulates the religious wishes: 'By the force of the merit acquired on this occasion may the dead mother attain Nirvāṇa! May the gods attain Nirvāṇa! May everyone present attain Nirvāṇa!' People respond with *sādhu! sādhu! sādhu!* The monk begins to chant slowly, two or three words at a time. People repeat after him:

Saparikkhāraṃ sāṭṭhaparikkhāraṃ imaṃ bhikkhaṃ bhikkhusaṃghassa dema! (repeated twice)
Imaṃ tambūla-bhesajja-dānaṃ bhikkhusaṃghassa dema!

We offer this alms food to the community of monks together with the eight requisites and other utensils!
We give this gift of betel and refreshments to the community of monks!

After that the monk continues chanting without the participation of the people:

Icchitaṃ patthitaṃ tuyhaṃ khippaṃ eva samijjhatu
sabbe pūrentu cittasaṃkappā cando paṇṇaraso yathā//

āyu-r-ārogyasampatti sagga-sampatti-m-eva ca/
atho nibbānasampatti iminā te samijjhatu//

May everything whatsoever that is desired and wanted by you quickly come to be.
May all your wishes be fulfilled like the moon on the full-moon day.

May there be the attainment of long life and good health and of heaven and by this may you be successful in the attainment of Nirvāṇa![19]

Again the monk repeats the religious wishes and people respond with *sādhu, sādhu, sādhu!* Most people get up and leave. The front room is empty except for the immediate family.

4. The family begins to serve the food. One of the plates is put in front of the relic receptacle. The arched opening is closed with an orange cloth. Finger bowls are being brought in for the monks. The food plates are offered individually.[20] One of the sons goes around with a banana leaf in his hand. Every monk puts a small portion of food onto the leaf. The food is then taken outside into the garden and left under a tree.[21] The family members are busy doing rounds: vegetable dishes, fish and chicken, sambols and salads. Vegetable soup is served in cups. A couple of children are told off for staring at the eating monks. After the main course leftovers from the monks' plates are packed in a plastic bag. Fruit plates, ice cream, curd and treacle are served. Betel is offered and people come back to the front room. One of the sons offers the parcel with the eight requisites to the most senior monk. It is subsequently placed on the 'altar'. The family now invite other people to join in the distribution of the parcels. Every monk is handed one parcel.[22]

5. The immediate family members sit down on a mat in the middle of the room. A jug of water and an empty bowl is brought. The other people sit down on the floor. The most senior monk introduces a monk from a temple in a nearby town as the next speaker. Everyone says, '*Sādhu, sādhu, sādhu!*' The 'speech of appreciation after the meal' (*bhuttānumodanā*) begins with general remarks about rebirth.[23] Merit given is never lost. The benefits of offering the eight requisites to the community of monks in particular are extolled. These benefits are different for women and men. The monk and the family members chant:

Idaṃ me ñātīnaṃ hotu! Sukhitā hontu ñātayo!
May this be for my relatives! May my relatives be happy!

The family take hold of the jug and begin to pour the water. All the monks chant together:

Yathā vārivahā . . . (*as before*).

The bowl begins to overflow. The monks continue their chanting without a break:

Icchitaṃ patthitaṃ tuyhaṃ . . . (*as before*).

Everyone says, '*Sādhu! sādhu! sādhu!*' The monk utters a short invocation to the gods for support. This is followed by a long list of religious wishes for everyone present. People say *sādhu, sādhu, sādhu* after every wish. Again the monks chant together:

Sabbītiyo vivajjantu sabbarogo vinassatu
Mā te bhavatv antarāyo sukhī dīghāyuko bhava.

Bhavatu sabbamaṅgalaṃ rakkhantu sabbadevatā
Sabbabuddhānubhāvena sadā sotthi bhavantu te.
(repeated twice)[24]

May all misfortunes be averted, may all sickness be healed, may no danger befall you, may you live long and happily!

May all blessings accrue. May all *devas* protect.
By the glory of all Saintly Disciples may security ever be yours!

Abhivādanasīlissa niccaṃ vaddhāpacāyino
cattāro dhammā vaḍḍhanti āyu vaṇṇo sukhaṃ balaṃ.[25]

For one who is habitually respectful and always honouring elders
four things will increase: lifespan, beauty, happiness and strength.

People say *sādhu, sādhu, sādhu* and get up from the floor. The monk tells the son to pour the water onto a young papaya tree. The son-in-law carries the relic casket back to the van and people help to carry the parcels. At about 1.45 p.m. the monks leave.

6. The children run in and out of the kitchen. Plates are handed out and people help themselves to food. Everyone sits down wherever there are chairs, small walls and shadow. The daughter and granddaughters urge everyone to take seconds and thirds. Curd and treacle and ice cream are served in cups. Fruit platters are passed around. Food parcels are packed for people to take home for their families. People start leaving at about 2.30 p.m. We are offered a lift to the station.

A monk's seventh-day matakadānaya

1. It is the seventh day after the death; the second day after the cremation. We arrive at the temple at about 10.30 a.m. The preaching hall has been completely transformed. On the upper level along the wall are about thirty chairs covered with white cloth. In front of them are long, low tables with check table cloths. Underneath a small Buddha statue on the wall is a simple table covered with white cloth. On the lower level about eighty chairs covered with white cloth are arranged along the walls. The long tables in front of them are covered with newspaper. At the back of the hall are big tables. Two laypeople bring in huge clay and aluminium pots with cooked food. A monk is busy ladling curries into brand new, large, red plastic bowls.[26] More plastic buckets are brought for the great variety of dishes. Chicken curries, fried and cooked fish dishes, various vegetable curries, fried potatoes, sambols of finely chopped leaves, sweet and sour pickled vegetables. The monk has trouble keeping up. Buckets of bright yellow coconut sauce and vegetables in curried sauce follow. More than twenty bowls are filled and covered with sheets of newspaper. At another table clay pots full of curd are stacked up. There are five bottles of treacle and lots of small blue plastic serving dishes. At other tables more than a hundred small plastic plates are layed out to be filled. Monks and laypeople work hand in hand. They place two pieces of cake and some cookies for each plate. Nicely wrapped sesame sweets and a small banana complete the picture. A monk brings an armful of black umbrellas and puts them on a chair. Laypeople bring various parcels wrapped in paper, two of them in the characteristic dome shape. The number of people involved is difficult to judge, maybe about 20–30 laypeople and 30–40 monks. Some laypeople stand by watching the proceedings. All are dressed very smartly, but only the older laypeople wear formal white.

2. By midday still more people arrive. There are fewer laypeople present (about one hundred) than the previous night but far more monks. A brass bowl is being filled with different dishes. An elderly layman puts a towel on his head and carries it over to the shrine room. Another layman walks beside him holding an umbrella.[27] The shrine room is crowded with people. The brass bowl is carried around and people jostle closer to touch it. Shouts of *sādhu, sādhu, sādhu* follow. Finally the bowl is placed in front of the main Buddha statue. People sit down on the floor inside the shrine room and outside. There is a slight delay. The woman next to me points at my tape recorder. She assures me that she will chant extra loudly. Finally a cup of soup is brought and placed next to the bowl. The ceremony begins with the salutation to the Buddha, etc. A single monk is facing the statue; his back is turned to the people. He leads the chanting beginning with Sinhala. Two to three words at a time are repeated by everyone. The helpful woman is shouting into my ear. This is followed without pause by Pāli verses. The different food items are now dedicated to the Buddha.[28] Towards the end the monk speeds up. After the last verse everyone says *sādhu, sādhu, sādhu*. The monk now chants the Pāli verse of dedicating merit to the gods. Again the laypeople say *sādhu, sādhu, sādhu*. The monk retreats to the main temple building and people follow him. A handful of laymen rush back to the preaching hall for last minute preparations.

3. At the main building a big crowd of about one hundred laypeople has gathered. More and more monks come out of the different temple buildings. An elderly layman dressed in white appears. A neatly folded orange cloth covers his head. He receives the relic receptacle. The young man next to him holds a yellow umbrella over it. A procession forms: eight laymen hold up a white sheet tied to wooden poles. It is about two metres wide and ten metres long. The most senior monks and abbots walk underneath this canopy, followed by senior and junior monks. All in all about 120 monks take part in the procession. The layman walks straight into the preaching hall and places the relic receptacle on the 'altar'. The monks line up at the two entrances to the hall. Two laymen wash and dry their feet. The thirty most senior monks are seated on the upper level. Some chairs there remain empty. The eighty or so junior monks take their seats on the lower level. The laypeople sit down on the floor. A middle-aged monk begins the ceremony with the salutation to the Buddha, etc. After a few words in Sinhala the different food items are offered with Pāli verses. The laypeople repeat after him. The most senior monk walks over to the microphone and delivers a sermon in Sinhala.[29] Merit is dedicated to the dead monk, the gods and everyone present. Religious wishes are formulated. People are invited to join in and say *sādhu, sādhu, sādhu.* The monk begins to chant and people repeat after him:

Saparikkhāraṃ sāṭṭhaparikkhāraṃ . . . (as before).

After that the monk continues chanting without the participation of the people:

Icchitaṃ patthitaṃ . . . (as before).

Everyone says *sādhu, sādhu, sādhu* and gets up. Most laypeople leave the preaching hall now. Only about twenty laymen and monks remain.

4. A plate with food is placed in front of the relic receptacle. Finger bowls and plates are distributed. Laypeople and monks work together ladling food onto the plates. The monks indicate 'enough' by covering their plate with one hand. Now two laymen go around with a 'banana-leaf plate'. Most of the monks put a small amount of food onto the leaf.[30] The two laymen then leave the hall through a small door at the rear. The food is left there on a piece of waste land. After the main course finger bowls are distributed. Next the cakes, sweets, curd and treacle are offered. After the meal is over people return to the hall and sit down on the floor. The parcels with the eight requisites are offered to the most senior monks. The other parcels and the black umbrellas are distributed on the upper level. Monks and laymen are involved in their distribution.

5. Woven floor mats are being spread out on the upper level. A group of about ten monks and two elderly laymen sit down. A big, pink water jug and an empty vessel are brought. Senior monks deliver elaborate sermons in Sinhala. Eventually the giving of merit is performed. The monks chant:

> *Idaṃ me ñātīnaṃ hotu!* (*as before*)

The monks and the two laymen on the mat form a circle. They hold or touch the jug and begin to pour the water. This is accompanied by the other monks' chanting:

> *Yathā vārivahā . . .* (*as before*).

The bowl begins to overflow while the chanting continues:

> *Icchitaṃ patthitaṃ . . .* (*as before*).

The laypeople on the lower floor say, '*Sādhu! sādhu! sādhu!*' Once more one of the monks formulates the religious wishes. May the dead abbot attain Nirvāṇa. May the gods, too, join in the merit. May everyone present be included in the wishes. The ceremony ends with a concluding chant by all the monks.

> *Sabbītiyo vivajjantu . . .* (*as before*).

The great number of monks makes for impressive chanting.

6. People stand around in small groups and chat. Quite a few leave the hall to go home, others remain to help. It is afternoon by the time the ceremony is over. The serving of the 120 monks has taken a long time.

Our three-wheeler driver is getting impatient. It is well past the arranged pick-up time.

Excursus: treatment of the remains

When there is a burial the physical remains are disposed of on the funeral day itself whereas in the case of a cremation they are dealt with separately. I will first give a brief introduction to the 'collecting of the bones'. Then I will take a look at the secondary literature on the historical background (Buddhist and Hindu). Finally, I will give a brief description of the practice in contemporary Sri Lanka.

By drawing on different sources (philological, archaeological, anthropological) and religions (Buddhism and Hinduism) I intend to provide some parallels to the contemporary practice.

Terminology and the bone/ash distinction. The English term for the physical remains after cremation is 'ashes' and includes bones and other residue. According to an undertaker in Bristol it is common practice in Britain to send the physical remains through a 'crusher', as it might upset relatives to find pieces of bone when 'scattering the ashes' of a dead relative. In the contemporary Indian context, on the other hand, the natural term to use for the remains of a cremation seems to be 'bones', as Parry (1994, 188), points out. And from my understanding the connotation is 'bone' as opposed to other remaining matter. However, according to Firth (1997, 90), euphemisms such as 'picking flowers' are also used to refer to the collecting of the bones after cremation.

The situation in Sri Lanka is somewhat more complex. My informants used the terms *(minī)aḷu* or *bhaṣmāvaśeṣa*, both meaning 'ashes' and seem to positively avoid the Sinhala word for bones (*äṭa*) which is regarded as 'not respectful'. Even in the specific context of the actual 'collecting the bones' the preferred term was *bhaṣmāvaśeṣa ekatu karanavā* ('collect ashes') rather than the more specific *äṭa ekatu karanavā* ('collect bones'). Interestingly, my English-speaking informants did not display the same sensitivity to the word 'bones'. However, 'bones' and other remains, which I will refer to as 'ashes' for want of a better term, are perceived (and treated), differently. The distinction, though not always made by my informants and very rarely found in secondary literature, seems to be rather significant.

The remains in the Mahāparinibbāna-sutta. The well known and often quoted passage of the Mahāparinibbāna-sutta (D II 164) about the purity of the Buddha's remains has already been discussed:

> Now when the Blessed One's body burned, no cinders or ash at all were formed from what had been the layers of skin, flesh, sinews

> and oil of the joints, only the bones remained as relics. Just as when ghee or oil burns no cinders or ash at all are formed, in exactly the same way when the Blessed One's body burned, no cinders or ash at all were formed . . . only the bones remained as relics.
>
> (Gethin, unpublished; D II 164)

Here the term *sarīrāni* (the plural of *śarīra*, 'body, corpse') denotes 'relics, bones' and *chārikā* and *masi* denote 'ashes' and 'soot' respectively. This distinction is not mentioned in passing, but is repeated verbatim and illustrated with the simile of butter or oil burning down without leaving any kind of residue. The context here is not that of an ordinary cremation, but the cremation of a Buddha, and accordingly, his remains are not just pieces of bone, but relics. It would be interesting to investigate whether in the context of ordinary people, too, the term *sarīrāni* would be used, or if this term has acquired the connotation 'relics' rather than 'bones' (for which the Pāli would be *aṭṭhi*).[31]

Three interesting aspects emerge: first, bones and ashes are not only linguistically distinguished, but defined as essentially different ('ashes' are non-bone matter). Second, only the 'bone-matter' was distributed and venerated. Thirdly, much trouble is taken to assure the purity of the relics, which might suggest that 'ashes' were regarded as 'polluting' in some way.

Contemporary Hindu practice and anthropological interpretations. Let us do a leap in time (of about 2500 years) and change discipline (from philology to anthropology) and religion (from Buddhism to Hinduism). Firth (1997, 90), distinguishes between bones and ashes and describes their treatment as follows:

> In India the bones and ashes are usually collected on the third day, although in busy city crematoria, especially electric ones, they may be collected the same day. The term used is *phūl chānnā* (picking flowers). The bones are picked out, washed in water or water and milk and hung in a pot from a tree or from the roof of the house, or kept at the cremation ground until they can be taken to a sacred river. The ashes are thrown into the nearest river. . . . In Varanasi the ashes and bones are thrown into the river straight away; the holiness of the city and the river makes elaborate procedures unnecessary.

It is particularly interesting here, that the bones are washed and disposed of separately in a 'sacred river', whereas the ashes can be scattered into any river.[32] Parry (1994, 188) interprets the contemporary Hindu practice of treating ashes and bones separately as a distinction between flesh and bone:

> Bones, as we have seen, are the product of the father's semen; flesh is the product of the mother's milk and menstrual blood, and hair is the repository of sin. What cremation completely eradicates are the flesh and the 'body hairs' of the deceased—causing 'sin and expiation (*prayashchitt*) to fly about in the smoke' at Manikarnika *ghat*. The implicit logic seems to be that cremation destroys what has to be got rid of—sin and female flesh. By so doing it distills out a pure (masculine) residue of bone, which is not only the product of semen but which serves like semen as a source of future fertility when delivered into the (female) Ganges.

And (Barley 1995, 100) goes one step further and sees here a 'common Asian model', but he does not define the term further, and it is not quite clear if he is suggesting that this is a concept underlying the practice in Asia or an interpretation superimposed on this practice.[33] So far I have not been able to find evidence for the bone/male and flesh/female association or the connection of body hair and sin in Buddhist texts in general, or in the Sri Lankan cremation context in particular.[34] However, it cannot be dismissed out of hand that the different treatment of bones and ashes might in some way be connected with a bone–flesh divide and that different associations and concepts, be it male/female or polluting/pure, might be associated with it.

Treatment of the remains in Sri Lanka (historical). Robert Knox's description of the treatment of the remains is very brief:

> After all is burnt to ashes, they sweep together the ashes into the manner of a Sugar-loaf: and hedg (*sic*) the place round from wild Beasts breaking in, and they will sow Herbs there.
>
> (Knox 1681, 116 (1966, 219))

Interestingly he no longer distinguishes between noblemen and ordinary people in this context.[35] Forbes provides an account of the different treatment of the remains—divided into bones and ashes—of the king:

> The body of a Cingalese King was burnt with many ceremonies; and the fire, kept up until the tenth day, was then extinguished. The fragments of bones were next collected, and buried (together with certain offerings made during the ceremony) at the spot where the monumental dagoba was to be raised. The ashes, enclosed in an earthen urn, were consigned to a man dressed in black, wearing a mask, and mounted on an elephant: he then headed the procession, and was followed by all the chiefs and people in funeral array to the Mahawelli-ganga. On arriving at the river, the mask descended

> from his elephant; and bearing in one hand the urn, in the other a drawn sword, embarked in a double canoe ornamented with plantain-trees coconut flowers. The vessel having been towed into the middle of the river, the mask held up the urn, cut it in two with the sword, then dived into the river, and disappeared. The royal dust of the 'race of the sun' vanished in the waters; The frail and gaudy vessel drifted to destruction; the elephant, removed across the river, was never again to be used; and the people (who had collected the ashes), conveyed to the opposite side, had the penalty of death attached to their return.[36]
>
> (Forbes 1840, II 105)

This is the earliest, specific Sri Lankan reference I have come across describing the custom of 'collecting the bones'. Brief as it is, the three key elements of the contemporary practice are there: collecting the bone fragments, burial of these and building a monumental dagaba over the bones. However, his description of the disposal of the ashes is far more detailed and colourful. Here two points are of interest: first, the ashes are scattered into the river and second anyone who came in touch with the ashes was exiled, which supports the hypothesis that the ashes were regarded as polluting.

But again the cremation is that of an extraordinary person, and therefore not necessarily representative for the customs at their respective times. Tillakaratne (1986, 166) describes how the remains of ordinary people (at least there is no indication otherwise) are treated and disposed of on the seventh day:

> Early next morning the relatives of the deceased returned to the place of cremation and sprinkled water charmed by recitation of *pirit* over the ashes. This was done to prevent any vicious person from using the ashes for any offensive magic and also perhaps to prevent the ashes from being scattered by the winds until they were collected. Seven days after the cremation the ashes were scraped together by elderly members of the family and put into an earthen vessel. Perera says that the ashes were collected 'in the following day or a few days after'. According to Davy it was done after seven days. Forbes too states that ashes were collected seven days after the cremation. Sometimes these ashes were put into an earthen vessel and deposited near a Vihāra.[37]

This matches my own observations closely, apart from the fact that there is no mention of a distinction between bones and ashes.

Collecting of the bones in Sri Lanka (contemporary). Let me start with a brief description of one such event: We arrive at the arranged time (3.00 p.m.)

at the cemetery, only to find that the clay pot containing the fragments and pieces of bone is already closed. The son and a couple of his friends had set out for the cremation ground early in order to avoid the rain and were in the process of mixing some concrete.

The son walks with us to the back of the small cemetery, where the remains of the funeral pyre are. The corner posts, hardly even charcoaled, still stand, half melted sheets of white plastic are hanging down the sides. The floor is littered with partially burnt planks of wood and an area of about ten square metres is covered with ashes about twenty centimetres deep. The son then gives us a rather matter-of-fact demonstration of how to distinguish the white bone fragments from charcoaled pieces of wood, etc. He is searching through the ashes with a coconut ladle and continues to find small pieces of bone, which he picks out and shows us. I am told that the idea is to find 'important bones', such as parts of the spine or skull. He also tells us, that on the previous day he had sprinkled some *pirit* water on the ashes, but he does say why he had done so.

In the meantime, at the other end of the cemetery, near the roadside, the clay pot is lowered into a hole and covered with earth and fresh concrete into which the day's date is scratched. This will form the base for a small 'monument' to be built later, but the son does not seem in a particular rush. Before we leave the cemetery, the son's friends cover the fresh concrete with a plastic sheet to protect it from the rain. The remains of the funeral pyre are left and presumably the next funeral party will have to clear up.[38]

This description requires some remarks. At some point after the cremation *pirit* water, or even pork fat,[39] is sprinkled on the remains to render the bones useless for purposes of black magic to members of the family or to anyone else. The 'collecting of the bones' is done on the seventh day after the death by the son or other male family members in a very matter-of-fact, unsentimental way. Monks do not play any part in it; no one is invited to attend; there is neither chanting of verses nor any other ritualized activity.[40]

Cemeteries are often located next to a temple and are fairly deserted places, without clear boundaries or fences, with a few cows roaming and grazing between the gravestones.[41] Along the coast and in the hills one can also find individual or small groups of graves located in beautiful spots, overlooking the sea or a valley. It is not very common to look after the grave and only very occasionally—mostly on *pōya* days and on the death anniversaries—can one see people lighting oil lamps on the graves. This custom might well be due to Western influence and, generally speaking, is not an important part of post-funerary rites, which consist mainly of alms givings.

Summary. Three points seem worth mentioning: first, a distinction between bones and ashes, although not always expressed linguistically, is noticeable in the different treatment. The bones are disposed of separately either by immersion in a more sacred river (Hindu) or in a small 'monument' (Buddhist).

The ashes are either scattered in a less sacred river (contemporary Hindu) or carefully removed, along with everyone who came in contact with them (historical royal cremation Sri Lanka) or simply left at the place of cremation together with half-burnt firewood, etc. (contemporary Sri Lanka). Anthropologists see a bone/flesh division reflected in this practice and this is interpreted in various ways as male/female, pure/polluting, etc.

Second, the Mahāparinibbāna Sutta asserted that only the bones of the Buddha constitute relics. Special importance is given to identifiable bones, which indicates a close connection with the dead person. Furthermore, there is the notion that bones are in some way charged and have to be desacralised either by way of immersion in the Ganges (Hindu) or sprinkled with *pirit* water or pork fat (contemporary Sri Lanka).

Thirdly, the notion that non-bone corporal remains were seen as polluted and polluting—at least at some point in history and with regard to the special case of the king—is confirmed by Forbes's colourful description. According to Hindu customs the bones are washed in water or water and milk, which points into the direction of pollution or possibly danger.

Two examples of later **matakadānas**

A three-month matakadānaya *at home*

1. We start out early in the morning in a hired van. At about 11.00 am we arrive in a commuter town South of Colombo. The house is easy to spot. Vans and three-wheelers are parked in the street. Metal chairs are arranged on the patio. About forty to fifty people have gathered. They are mainly family and close friends. Tea and cookies are passed around. The children are quieter than usual. No strict dress code is observed. The house is big and modern. Fifteen armchairs are arranged alongside the walls in the front room. Chairs and ceiling are covered with white cloth. A temporary altar is set up in one corner. An impressive cupboard dominates one wall. Behind the glass doors are several laminated death notices. A framed photo of the deceased is decorated with a white flower garland. A long corridor leads to the busy kitchen at the back. A long table is covered with bowls and plates of food.

2. There is a brass bowl to be filled with food. A man prepares a tray with betel and king coconut. These are carried through the house to the waiting van. People touch the trays as they pass. The brother of the deceased summons a couple of friends. They get into vans and drive off to the temple.[42] We stay behind at the house, eating more cookies.

3. About half an hour later drumming can be heard in the distance. Inside the house hectic last preparations are made. The procession comes up the road led by two drummers in sarongs and vests. Neighbours come out of their houses to watch.[43] The brother of the dead person carries the relic receptacle on his head.[44] Someone holds a yellow, frilly umbrella over it. The monks walk behind him holding black umbrellas and fans. The children briefly get excited watching the spectacle. The relic receptacle is placed on the 'altar'. The monks line up to have their feet washed. A strip of white cloth is spread across the patio. One by one they take their seats. The drumming continues for a few minutes. People crowd in and sit down on the floor. The ceremony starts with the refuges and precepts. Two monks deliver short sermons. The names of the dead man and his widow are mentioned frequently. Occasionally everyone says, '*Sādhu, sādhu, sādhu*'.

4. It is fast approaching midday. Finger-bowls are brought in for the monks. The brother places a plate of food in front of the relic receptacle. The altar is covered with a white cloth. Most people have by now cleared out of the front room. An endless succession of dishes is brought through from the kitchen. Men do the rounds and serve the monks. A man comes forward with a banana leaf in his hand. Every monk puts a small amount of his food on the banana leaf. The food is taken outside into the courtyard. The chickens enjoy the feast. Eventually the plates are cleared away. In the kitchen a girl scrapes leftover food from the monks' plates into a plastic bag. Desserts are served next: fruit salad and ice-cream or curd and treacle. The children are sent out of the kitchen to play. Finally, trays of betel are offered to the monks.

5. Small parcels wrapped in brown paper are brought in. Two have the characteristic dome shape. The widow's elderly parents offer the requisites to the most senior monks. The front room gets very busy now. Men and women are invited to join in the offering of the parcels. The smaller parcels contain milk powder and exercise books. Then a mat is spread out in the centre of the room. A jug of water and an empty bowl are brought. The widow and the two daughters sit on one side. The brother and the two nephews sit on the other side. One of the monks delivers a sermon. All the monks join in the chanting of the verses. The family very slowly pours the water. The older nephew is crying quietly. People join in the chanting.[45] The widow takes the bowl outside and pours the water onto a plant in the front garden. The brother carries the relic receptacle to the vans. The monks take their parcels, fans and umbrellas. Someone brings the plastic bag with leftovers for the stray dogs in the temple.

6. It is about 1.30 p.m. and very hot now. The children get their lunch in the kitchen. The food is being served buffet style. People help themselves, sit down and eat. Immediately after the meal the first people start leaving. They are given parcels with cookies to take home. We leave at about 2.30 p.m. to avoid the rush hour in Colombo.

A ten-year matakadānaya *at the temple*

1. My interview with the abbot of the town temple is over. He invites me to come along to a ten-year *matakadānaya.*[46] The ceremony is scheduled for about 11.30. We walk across the temple ground to the small hall. Along one wall is a long desk and bench-like seats. A big wardrobe is squeezed into a corner. A large table occupies the centre of the hall. It is covered with food containers filled with a variety of dishes. There are bunches of bananas and other fruits. An elderly couple, a young man, two children and a teenage girl are waiting.

2. A *buddhapūjāva* was probably conducted before the ceremony. I arrive at the hall with the abbot. There is no chance to inquire about this.[47]

3. The abbot enters the hall with three junior monks. They take their seats behind the desks. The relic receptacle is not brought to the hall.[48] The family greets the monks one after the other. A mat has been spread out in front of the desk. A jug of water and an empty vessel are brought in. The ceremony starts with the three refuges and five precepts. The abbot delivers a short sermon. The name of the dead person for whom the ceremony is conducted is mentioned at certain intervals. The abbot keeps forgetting the name of the departed. This is followed by another sermon.

4. The food is offered by the elderly man. The monks acknowledge the offering with a short sermon.[49]

5. A small parcel wrapped in brown paper materialises and is offered to the abbot. The family once more sits down on the mat. They recite the appropriate verses. The family members all hold the jug and the monks begin to chant. The water is poured very slowly into the bowl. The people join in parts of the chanting. Somewhat abruptly the ceremony is over. The monks get up and leave the hall to return to the main building. The water bowl is still on the mat.[50]

6. The family gets ready to go home. No outsiders were invited. No food is provided other than that for the monks.

Excursus: other options (questionnaire D.1–3)

To observe the differences between *matakadāna*s it would be necessary to spend at least one year, preferably even more, revisiting the same houses where a funeral has been held and interviewing the families involved in these occasions. Unfortunately, I was not able to do so as my fieldtrip was restricted to six months. Instead I took the opportunity to describe two follow-up ceremonies in a different social setting: a three-month *matakadānaya* in a relatively well-to-do family in a commuter town south of Colombo and a ten-year *matakadānaya* held at the town temple in our village.

Three-month *matakadānas* in the home are always very costly affairs and one cannot avoid the impression that one of their many functions is to assert the social status of the family. As a general rule they are preceded by *baṇa*s the previous night, which are generally even better attended than the *dāna*s on the following day. All this adds to the already considerable financial strain on the family.

A ten-year (or in fact any) *matakadānaya* conducted at the temple, on the other hand, is a relatively simple affair. The fact that no *baṇa* takes place the previous night and food is only provided for the monks makes it much more economical. In fact, it comes very close to the everyday practice of taking food to the temple.

It is common for laypeople to provide meals (usually breakfast or lunch) for a certain number of monks on a set date every month for an unlimited period of time. The food containers (tiffin style) and a bucket for rice are provided by the temple.[51] When a *matakadānaya*, whether in the home of a layperson or at the temple, is scheduled for a particular day the temple will inform the family whose turn it is that no (or less) food is needed.

Apart from the traditional *matakadāna*s there are in fact other options: such as giving a donation to or providing a meal for a home for elderly people or an orphanage, etc. A widower in the village told me that he was going for one of these options instead of the traditional three-month *dānaya* for his departed wife. He was adamant that there was no difference in merit between giving to the monks or to orphans. Unfortunately, this was to take place two weeks after my departure.

This was not the first time I heard about a *dānaya* without monks, but I could not establish how recent or widespread this development is. Besides, my informants spoke about these alternatives only in the context of a three-month *matakadānaya* (or even an annual *dānaya*), but not the seventh-day *dānaya*. To decide against a traditional *matakadānaya* is something of a public statement and seems to express a general feeling of disillusion with the temple and monks.

Generating and giving of merit is not only the essential part of the post-funerary rites but also one of the main topics of sermons. I therefore included a set of three questions in my questionnaire with the aim of finding out more about the scale of values of the villagers:

> Questionnaire D.1: What do you think constitutes an act of merit or demerit? How would you define *pin* and *pav*?
> Questionnaire D.2: Is it a more meritorious act to give a *dānaya* to the monks than to give food to beggars?
> Questionnaire D.3: Is it possible to do meritorious deeds even though one never goes to the temple, or gives a *dānaya*, etc., just by being a good, helpful and generous person? Do we need to go to the temple to do meritorious deeds?

The monks defined merit and demerit very much in terms of *lobha*, *dosa*, *moha* and their counterparts or, more generally, as *puñña*/*pāpa* and *kusala*/*akusala*. The notion that the underlying thought or intention determines merit and demerit was mentioned. One monk said that merit is actually happines (*satuṭa*) resulting from a good deed such as offering flowers, holding one's parents in high esteem, etc. The monks unanimously agreed that more merit results from a donation to beings of higher moral quality, but that one can do meritorious deeds without going to the temple. The essential factor is to keep the five precepts and practise *maitrī*, *karuṇā*, *anukampā*, etc. On the other hand, the temple as a place where the *dharma* is taught was seen as conducive to gaining merit by way of happiness (*satuṭa*).

As for the laypeople, the definition of merit and demerit was mostly based on the five precepts; in one case reference was also made to the noble eightfold path and the ten *pāramī*s. People also talked more generally about good and bad deeds, giving examples such as helping others who are ill, doing *pūjās* and helping to build a *caitya*.

Interestingly, a very knowledgeable elderly person, distinguished *pina* and *kusala*. He defined *pina* as a store of merit that sustains gods in a *devaloka*, for example, until it runs out, whereas he explained that *kusala* was acquired by way of meditation (*bhāvanā*) and was conducive to *nirvāṇa*.

It was frequently stressed that merit and demerit is in the mind. It seems rather significant that a clear link was made between merit and joyful states of mind (*satuṭa*) and two people actually defined merit as joy (see below for *anumodanā*).

The last two questions were deliberately formulated in a provocative way, but people seemed to enjoy the opportunity to speak frankly about monks and temples. Only two people said that more merit results from a donation to monks than from a donation to a beggar. One argued that both depend on others for sustenance, but monks cannot ask for food, etc. The majority of people said either that there is no difference or that it is in fact more meritorious to give to a beggar, as the monks' bowls are always full. It was also stressed that even giving to animals is meritorious. The concept that the resulting merit increases with the virtue of the receiver was not generally accepted. Besides, it was pointed out that monks are not necessarily more virtuous than laypeople. Some people took the chance to complain about the decline in moral standards of the "Colombo monks". It was unanimously agreed that to do meritorious deeds is a way of life. It was striking how adamant people were on this point. However, it was conceded that the atmosphere at the temple was more conducive to contemplation than a home with its domestic struggles. Generally it was striking that the laypeople gave far less importance to the *saṃgha* and the temple than the monks did.

Before moving on, there remains one curious incident to be related. While the alternative options mentioned here such as orphanage, etc., differed from the traditional *matakadānas* with regard to the recipient of the donation, I came across a *matakadānaya* which differed with regard to the recipient of the merit. On one occasion the abbot of the local temple introduced me to an elderly laywoman, mentioning in passing that I was doing research into funeral rites. She got very excited and invited me cordially to a *matakadānaya* for beloved pets, which was to take place in the temple the following day. She assured me that it was going to be a proper *sāṃghika dānaya* with subsequent giving of merit by way of 'pouring the water'. The abbot was quiet throughout and only when prompted by me actually admitted that this *matakadānaya* was indeed for the benefit of dead pets. When I got there with the tape recorder the next day well in time at 7.00 am the ceremony was already over. I suspect the abbot had rushed the proceedings to finish before my arrival. So all I could do was discuss the idea with my friends, who speculated how the monks would have phrased the giving of merit to 'beloved dogs and cats, etc.' On the whole they were quite dismissive of the idea and said they had never heard of anything that 'stupid' (*pissu väḍa*). They blamed the elderly woman rather than the monk, and interestingly were most appalled not by the idea of giving merit to animals, but by the fact that spoilt pets were singled out to receive merit. They then told me that on Vesak days some people cook big pots of food for wild animals: crows, squirrels, stray dogs, cats, etc. But this was only about feeding the animals directly, not giving merit to them.

Commentary to the practice

Food offerings

To the Buddha(s)

Food offerings, along with other offerings such as flowers, etc., are a very common, everyday religious activity. They can be observed at the temple, in front of a Buddha image, relic receptacle, *bōdhi* tree or *cetiya* or even in people's homes as most Buddhist households have a small shrine.

At the seventh-day *dānaya*, in fact, two offerings were made: one in front of the main image in the local temple and the second in the house in front of the *dhātukaraṇḍuva*. The offering of food and the chanting of certain non-canonical Pāli verses are essentially the same in both cases.[52]

The Buddha *pūjāva* in the *vihāra* is done three times a day by the laypeople who provide the meals for the monks. If there is a *matakadānaya* at home, a special brass bowl from the temple is filled with food which has been prepared for the monks and taken back to the temple. Sometimes a monk is asked to chant the Pāli verses accompanying the Buddha *pūjāva*, sometimes the food is just placed on the table in front of the main Buddha image.[53]

On very special occasions a family, or a group of friends, might decide to do a more elaborate *pūjāva* for the twenty-eight Buddhas. I was invited by a friend to take part in such a *pūjāva*, where twenty-eight identical plates of food were prepared and offered in the *vihāra* of a temple south of Colombo. The *pūjāva* was organized by one family for a specific purpose, but they invited their friends to join in.

Gombrich (1988, 384) mentions the *buddhapūjāva* for the twenty-eight Buddhas in the context of his discussion of *bōdhipūjāva*, a particular type of *buddhapūjāva*, which was devised and made popular in the early seventies by Ven. Ariyadhamma. Gombrich (1988, 395) points out with reference to the *bōdhipūjāva* in general that unlike the *pirit* ceremony, it aims at creating a fund of merit that can be called on at need and is done with a special purpose in mind. A *pūjāva* conducted with a specific purpose in mind comes close to offerings done at Hindu temples or at the shrines devoted to gods in Buddhist temples (such as *Kataragama deviyō*, Ganesha, Lakṣmī, etc.).[54] But unlike food offerings to gods, which are subsequently —at least in part—consumed by the donor, the food items offered to the Buddha image (or relic receptacle) are regarded as *sāṃghika* and not later consumed.[55]

To return to the seventh-day *dānaya*, the *dhātukaraṇḍuva* is then carried back to the house by the same people who performed the Buddha *pūjāva* and a second food offering is made in the house on the prepared altar, which takes the position of the most senior monk.[56] Gombrich (1991, 143) comments on the use of these non-canonical verses (*Adhivāsetu no bhante . . .*), which are used both in the temple and in someone's home, when offering food to the Buddha:

> The crucial aspect in which modern practice seems to have changed from that commended by Buddhaghosa is the recitation of the verse quoted above, in which the Buddha, being asked to accept the food, is addressed as if he were alive. This looks like a break through of what I shall show to be the affective attitude to the cognitive level: feelings that the Buddha is a living presence here seem to find expression in words.

However, the fact that Buddhaghosa does not mention these verses does not exclude the possibility that some (if not necessarily the same) verses were recited on those occasions.

This brings us to the question of the Indian background to *buddhapūjāva* and the *dhātukaraṇḍuva*. Gombrich (1991, 143) disputes Hindu influence on the grounds that these offerings are already mentioned by Buddhaghosa (Samanta-pāsādikā III 2264–5):

> But the offering of food to the Buddha need not be explained by a diffusion of Hindu practices in Ceylon. Buddhaghosa says that wise men before a meal offer food and drink to an image or casket (*cetiya*) containing a relic, which they place before them.

This might prove that the influence is not post-Buddhaghosa, but does not exclude the possibility that these offerings are part of the Indian heritage (not necessarily exclusively brahmanical) that found its way into Buddhist practice.

Again it is illuminating to look into the contemporary Hindu practice for clues and a better understanding of the diverse nature of *pūjā*. Fuller (1992, 69) says:

> Certainly, the idea that the deities are royal guests is important, especially in major temples where they are proclaimed as sovereign rulers. On the other hand, . . . Hindu worship has a personal and homely aspect too. . . . Gods and goddesses are often the honored guests of humble worshippers, and the offerings and services of *puja* closely resemble the acts that ordinary people perform for each other or their guests at home.

Fuller's point about *pūjā* as 'hospitality to honoured guests' can easily be applied to the Sri Lankan context, the *buddhapūjāva* at the temple and particularly the food offerings to the *dhātukaraṇḍuva* in someone's home. Here the image or relics are treated on the same terms as the other monks, who are, without doubt, 'honoured guests'.[57]

To departed: more on prētas

I will start with offerings, which are made routinely, such as the personal food offering to the spirit of the dead person (*maḷagiyaprāṇakārayā*) and also the general food offerings to the *prētas*/crows.[58] Second, I will describe offerings, which are made in special cases, such as offerings aimed at pacifying or catching a troublesome *prēta*. I will then look into the Indian background and transition from Skt *preta* to *pitṛ*.

Offerings made routinely. To start with personal food offerings, an offering is made to the spirit of the dead person (*maḷagiyaprāṇakārayā*) on the evening of the sixth-day *baṇa*. It is personalized in that the sleeping mat and pillow of the departed are arranged in the garden.[59] A relation, usually the son of the dead person, calls the dead person by the normal mode of address ('Mother', 'Father', etc.). The departed is not conceived of as a hungry ghost, and whenever I questioned people about this custom the word *malagiyaprāṇakārayā* (spirit of the departed) was used and the term *prēta* was positively avoided.

Very little is found on this in secondary literature. Wirz (1941, 210) describes a similar offering as taking place in connection with the *baṇa* preaching, but the description reads rather like a compilation of various customs. A monk is invited to the house on the third day after the death after dark to preach for one hour and is given small presents before he leaves. If in the night noises or other signs indicate the presence of a *prēta*, a specialist (*ädurā*) is called who prepares offerings for the *prēta* (*prēta-pindenna*), including the favourite dishes of the departed which are left for a while in an empty room. If the food is undisturbed this is taken as a sign that the *prēta* has gone to hell and is beyond help. Finally, the food is taken outside for the crows and dogs.

There are certain similarities with the offering made on the *baṇa* day as described above: it is a fixed day after the death, in the evening. A monk preaches and the favourite food of the departed is offered. There are, however, significant differences: the offering was only done after the presence of a *prēta* was established by signs[60] ('our' departed is precisely not regarded as *prēta* but referred to as *maḷagiyaprāṇakārayā*). Besides, offering was done by a 'professional' and is an exclusively male affair (in our case the daughter of the dead woman prepared the food). Wirz's description seems like a compilation of three different offerings: to the spirit of the departed (*maḷagiyaprāṇakārayā*); to a troubled (or troublesome) ghost (*prēta*); to *prētas*/crows (*kākkā*).

There are, however, also collective food offerings to *prētas* and crows. The custom of putting small amounts of food outside for the *prētas* (or crows) is impersonal and not intended for anyone in particular. After the monks have been served, a layperson collects a small portion of rice from every monk on a banana leaf, which is subsequently placed outside in the garden. These small offerings appear a very small gesture, but they nevertheless form an integral part of all the ceremonies I attended.[61]

Tillakaratne (1986, 168f.) also describes a food offering taking place after the seventh-day *dānaya*:

> As soon as the alms-giving was over a little of the food was put into a small basket (*goṭuva*) and kept on a tree or at a meeting of roads (*mansandiya*) with a vessel of water and a burning lamp by its side. It was believed that the spirit of the departed would accept this offering; and further, to induce him to do so, the following Pāli stanza was recited while incense was burnt:
>
> > *gandhaṃ dīpoñ* (sic) *ca dhūpañ ca pāniyaṃ bhojanaṃ pi ca*
> > *patigaṇhantu santuṭṭhā ñāti-petā idam baliṃ*
> >
> > May the departed relatives accept this offering consisting of scent, lamps, fragrant smoke, water and food with pleasure.
>
> If a crow or any other bird ate of the offering, the omens were considered to be favourable. But if that did not happen it was taken as a sign, which indicated that the dead person had been reborn as a *prēta*.

This description shares certain features with the *pūjāva* for the spirit of the departed, but the use of the Pāli verse gives the impression that the offering is of a general rather than personal nature. The ambiguity of the

Pāli term *peta* ('dead' as well as 'hungry ghost'), allows two interpretations for *ñāti-petā*: 'dead relatives' or 'relatives who are *peta*s'. There seems to be a curious fusion here of personal and general offering, as well as of crows and *prētas*, and it is difficult to determine with any certainty where this offering fits in with the food offerings I observed.

In the context of the general offerings, which are made in connection with *dānas*, too, people said they were meant for *prētas* (not for *malagiya prāṇakārayā*) or crows. The latter is, according to Gombrich (1991, 275), a rationalization. This is, however, not entirely satisfying and does not acknowledge the many interesting parallels between *prētas* and crows (*kākkā*). There is a curious belief in Sri Lanka that both are unable to keep food in their stomachs or (in the case of crows) do not even have a stomach and digestive system at all. It is regarded as a meritorious deed to feed crows, and frequently it was mentioned that the only way to satisfy their perpetual hunger, at least temporarily, is to give them small pieces of cloth soaked in coconut oil or ghee.[62] Interestingly, two interviewees, both monks in their early thirties belonging to the Siam Nikāya, actually identified *prētas* and crows. Even though I was unable to determine how widespread the idea is, it is striking how similarly they seem to be perceived. The key to this curious fusion might be that according to the Sanskrit Dictionary (MW) crows are associated with Yama, who 'presides over the Pitṛis and rules over the spirits of the dead' and are also called Yama's messenger (*yamadūta*).[63]

Offerings made in special cases. If a dead relative turns into a troublesome ghost, special treatment is called for. Apart from *pirit* chanting, which is a rather all-round solution for a variety of problems, there are more specific solutions depending on the type of ghost and the trouble caused. It seems appropriate to include the methods of pacifying and getting rid of troublesome ghosts in this chapter, because in one way or another all of them (except the *pirit* chanting) include special food items.

First let us consider offerings which are intended to pacify. One method of dealing with troublesome ghosts is to play tapes of monks chanting or to invite monks to chant *pirit* in the house. This can be either *mahāparitta*, which principally consists of the three main *suttas* or, in more severe cases (and provided the family can afford it), all night chanting. Interestingly, *pirit* ceremonies might differ in length, but the choice of *suttas* is always the same and is not specifically geared to the occasion (house warmings, birthdays, ghosts, etc.). There is, however, one *sutta* most suitable for dealing with ghosts, the Āṭānāṭiya Sutta.

One of my informants told me that it is only if the chanting fails that the *ädurā* will be called in to make an offering to pacify the *prētas*. It seems, however, that the choice of method is at least partly due to personal inclination, background (urban or village) and possibly financial considerations. Someone might dismiss a *yakädurā* as a charlatan and only turn to monks, another person might call a *yakädurā* first. Wirz (1941, 212) too acknowledges the coexistence of various methods for dealing with non-humans as he relates a case of an outbreak of a disease in a village when monks were called in for *pirit* chanting after the other methods failed. Illnesses in Sri Lanka are more often than not regarded as being caused by demons.

This leads us to pacifying the ghosts by way of food and other offerings. The type of ghost (*prētayā* or *yakā*) and the appropriate method has to be decided on by a *yakädurā* (exorcist) who invites the spirit with *mantras* to use his body and act through it.[64] He then prepares fried foods (eggs, etc.), called *doḷa*, on a fire made of special firewood, which can take place at night on the burial ground. The food is looked at by the spirit/*yakädurā* and at the end the spirit leaves the *yakädurā* and, providing the ritual is done in the correct way, stops causing disturbances.

Wirz (1941, 204–207) gives a detailed account of such a *prēta-pindenna* ceremony, lasting all night and involving a great number of offerings to the *yakku* (Maha-sohona, Hiriyakka and Sūniyam) as well as to the *prētas*. The food offering is geared to the likings of *prētas* in general or specific types of *prētas* and disposed of after the ceremony by taking it to the cemetery. Wirz lists which offerings are regarded as suitable for the different types of *prētas* (*ñata-prēteo* and *mala-prēteo*).[65] This *prēta-pindenna* shares common features with the first *prēta-pindenna* (see Wirz 1941, 210): both are prompted by certain signs, food items are left in a closed room and at intervals examined for 'disturbance' (taken as a sign that a *prēta* was present), and finally the food is taken outside. There are, however, significant differences. It seems that the first one is a personalised offering for the spirit of the dead person and motivated by the idea of preventing it from descending into hell.[66] In the second *prēta-pindenna*, on the other hand, the emphasis has shifted and the spirit of the dead person is now treated like a fully-fledged *prēta*, belonging to a particular class of 'hungry ghosts'. The motivation is now mainly to stop the *prēta* from troubling his family by haunting the house, etc.

Second, there are offerings, which are intended as bait. If the *pirit* chanting or *prēta-pindenna* fails to keep the spirit away, the *yakädurā* has to be called again, this time to perform a ceremony called 'binding/tying the *prēta*' (*prēta-bandīma*).[67] Unfortunately I was not able to witness any of those rituals and my information comes exclusively from interviews. I was told that a *prēta* (or even a *maḷayakā*) can be lured into a bottle by way of certain fried foods or *mantras* chanted by the *yakädurā*. The bottle can be encased in concrete before it has to be thrown into the deep sea.

One interviewee, however, provided me with an actual example of this practice. He told me, almost jokingly, of an incident that happened in his wife's family 'many, many years ago'. A young man, who was married but childless died suddenly and became a *maḷayakā*. After some time his mother urged the young widow to remarry which made the *maḷayakā* very angry. He caused various disturbances in the house including putting chillies into the water, which the mother took to the toilet. A *yakädurā* was called, a fee agreed, the necessary ritual performed and the spirit caught in a bottle, which he took home with half the payment they had agreed. When the family failed to pay the balance the *yakädurā* released the spirit who promptly started his disturbances again. Finally the proper sum was paid, the spirit was recaptured and thrown into the deep sea.

Let us turn once more to Wirz (1941, 208f.) for more details of the various methods of disposing of a *prēta*. Preceding the ceremony offerings are made to Sūniyam-yakā, Aimānā (the leader of the *prētas*), the *prētas*, and the five gods (Viṣṇu, Īsvara, Kataragama-dēviyo, Saman-dēviyo and Nāta-dēviyo). Wirz (1941, 208f.) describes two different methods of catching *prētas*. The first method is to attach one end of a piece of string (*nūla*) with loose knots in it to the *taṭuva*. The *yakädurā* then catches the *prēta*, who was attracted by the offering and called by means of a *mantra*, by pulling the string and tightening the knots. The *nūla* with the *prēta* is then put into a small metal tube. Another method involves a small metal box with metal pins and cotton thread (with nine knots), which is left open while *mantras* are chanted. Throughout the night in regular intervals the box is checked. If a small insect, spider, etc., is found this is assumed to be the manifestation of the *prēta* and the box is quickly closed. Finally the metal tube or box is taken away by the *yakädurā* who has to cross water and three roads.[68] He searches for a 'useless' tree (Wirz names *kaduru* and *mendorang* trees) makes a small hole in which he deposits the metal tube or box. Alternatively, the tube can be hidden under a big stone.

Whatever the method of disposal, my informants assured me that the *prēta-bändīma* is not taken light-heartedly and is seen as a last resort to restore peace in the house. The people involved feel remorse at having inflicted suffering on the spirit and it is felt to be against the spirit of Buddhism. Furthermore, they might live in fear that the ghost might escape to haunt the family with renewed vengeance either in this or any future existence.

Hindu offerings to the departed. Food offerings to the departed are a pre-Buddhist, ancient Indian ritual and still constitute an important part of Hindu death rituals today. These offerings, called *śrāddha* are made in three stages: for the first ten days after the death rice balls (*piṇḍas*) are offered daily to create a new body for the *preta* which is the size of a thumb. On the eleventh day the departed receives for the first time the 'rites for a single deceased person' (*ekoddiṣṭa*). The next stage lasts up to one year, but can be condensed to twelve days (symbolic year). During this stage the departed needs offerings to strengthen him for the passage through the kingdom of Yama. The last of these (*sapiṇḍīkaraṇa*) completes the transition from departed (Skt *preta*) to ancestor (*pitṛ*) and marks the end of the preliminary stage. The *śrāddhas* offered after the *sapiṇḍīkaraṇa* are to ancestors in general, especially to the three generations of father, grandfather and great-grandfather.[69] The transformation from *preta* to *pitṛ* constitutes the core of the *śrāddha* ritual.

In Sri Lanka the giving of merit takes centre stage in the post-funerary rites, but in the present context I shall concentrate on the various food offerings.[70] The offerings made routinely are, in my opinion akin to and probably derived from the *śrāddha* offerings. The personal offerings (favourite food items such as a sleeping mat, etc.) made on the sixth day are reminiscent of the offerings made to the newly dead before he joins the ancestors. It was apparent from interviews in Sri Lanka that most people assumed the existence of an intermediate state and the presence of the spirit of the dead (*maḷagiyaprāṇakārayā*). The latter has many features in common with the *preta* before he becomes the *pitṛ*: he is in need of provision and is rather helpless. In Sri Lanka, however, the term *prēta* is avoided in the first seven days, due to the change in the connotation from Skt *preta* (Pāli *peta*) to Sinhala *prētayā/perētayā*.

The impersonal offerings (a small food deposit in the garden) are—in my opinion—a barely noticeable reminder of the offerings to ancestors. They are unspecific and said to be for the 'hungry ghosts' (or crows) and the term *prēta* is used freely. There is clearly a change from the somewhat elaborate personal offering on the sixth day to the token offering on the seventh day, and this is supported by a change in terminology from *malagiyapāṇakārayā* to *prēta*. Even though no formal ritual marks the end of the preliminary stage it appears that in Sri Lanka the seventh day *matakadānaya* fulfills that function (like the *ekoddiṣṭa* and *sapiṇḍīkaraṇa*). But while the *śrāddha* consists of food offerings throughout, there is another subtle shift in the Sri Lankan ritual from food cum merit (sixth day) to merit cum food (seventh day), which is where Buddhism made its own particular mark on ancestor worship.[71]

To a specific being or to all beings present

Dānas are not just about giving of merit, but also about feeding beings: from a fixed number of monks to *prētas*/crows, stray dogs and cats, and just about everyone present, and in that order. Family, friends and neighbours are involved in the massive task of organizing and preparing a meal to feed any number of people from fifty to well over a hundred and the cost of such a feast is considerable.[72] There might also be an element of asserting one's social status by preparing a great feast, but it would be unjust to overestimate this element. Sri Lankans are, in my experience, exceptionally hospitable people, and the tradition of feeding seems deeply ingrained in the culture.

Every *dānaya* starts with the invitation of a fixed number of monks—laypeople are not supposed to specify who is invited. On the appointed day the monks come in the morning at around 11.00 or 11.30 am bringing with them the *dhātukaraṇḍuva*, which adds 'one person' to the number of monks to be fed. Besides food the monks are also given parcels with utilitarian items ranging from a set of eight requisites for monks (*aṭapirikara*, Pāli: *aṭṭaparikkhāra*) to simple household items.

These offerings to the monks were at an earlier stage (as reflected in the *Petavatthu* for example) meant to benefit the dead. This can be explained in two ways: either the monks act as mediators or the offerings create a stock of merit which transforms into food and clothing in the realm of the *petas*. The similarity between monks and brahmins with regard to their role in ritual has been pointed out frequently in secondary literature.[73]

Parry (1994, 142) observes contemporary Hindu practice and provides us with an interesting clue:

> The fact that bargaining on the *ghats* is mainly over gifts makes it very different from the kind of bargaining described in the literature in another important aspect. The Mahabrahman stands in for the *pret*-ghost; the *panda* for the ancestral *pitr*. The gifts they receive are gifts both to, and for, the deceased: food that he might eat, a lamp that he might see, clothes in which to dress. The whole ideology is one of unstinting liberality. . . . He gives as much as he can afford, not as little as he can get away with. The proper objective of bargaining is not to obtain 'a bargain' but to ensure—for the sake of the soul of the departed—that the limits of the donor's capacity have really been reached.

The point that the 'gift' (*dāna*) really accrues to the departed is still tangible in Sri Lanka, and people often go to the limit of their capacity to cater for their departed.

There is also an aspect of 'payment' for the services of a monk/priest, which is referred to as *dakṣiṇā* in the Hindu context. In Sri Lanka, too, a monk who comes to a house for chanting or preaching never leaves empty-handed and there seems to be an unspoken understanding about which services require more substantial donations than others.[74] However, I am not aware of any 'bargaining' going on between monks and laypeople over the 'payment' for their services. Besides, donations are always given to the *saṃgha* not to an individual, which is stressed in sermons and has been pointed out to me repeatedly by monks and laypeople.[75]

The food offerings to the *prētas*/crows have been extensively discussed in the previous chapter and are only mentioned here to complete the account of feeding. Next leftover food is packed in plastic bags to be taken to the temple for the usual crowd of stray dogs and cats found at most temples in Sri Lanka. Some animals are brought there by people, who found them in the streets, others come on their own accord, attracted by the 'free meals' provided by the monks. I suspect that the food of the *buddhapūjāva*, too, is fed to them, as it is not regarded as proper for people to consume what had been offered to the Buddha.[76]

Strong (1992, 51) talks of a 'commensal community' going back to Buddhist monasteries in 'ancient India':

> It is clear from I-ching's text that crows, pigs, dogs, and other animals abounded in Buddhist monasteries in ancient India, especially around mealtimes, and that although monks avoided them while eating, it was considered legitimate to give them any leftovers. . . . More generally we may say that all these examples point to the existence in Buddhism of what might be called a 'commensal community'. Larger than the bounds of the everyday Sangha (which comprises only novices and monks), it is nonetheless clearly hierarchical. It includes in its upper reaches the Buddha and the figure of certain *arhats*, such as Piṇḍola, who are thought to be invisibly present and protecting the assembly. At its lower end, it includes certain kinds of laypersons (degwads, devout elders), monastery animals, and, in ritual contexts, demons and demonesses (such as Hārītī) and spirits of the dead (such as the hungry ghosts).

After the monks have left family, friends and neighbours who had come to help are served food from the same clay pots as the food for the monks and there is no difference in quality or number of dishes. The monks' food only becomes 'special' by formally offering it to the *saṃgha*. Tillakaratne (1986, 169f.) refers to a custom of holding a great feast in the memory of the dead person:

> In addition to the alms-giving to the monks described above it was also the custom to hold a feast a few weeks after a death to which many people of the village were invited. . . . This feast was sometimes called *mataka bata kāma*, 'the eating of rice in memory (of the dead)'. According to Perera all signs of sorrow were banished from the day this feast was held (Perera, *Glimpses of Sinhalese Social Life*, p. 4). Most of the post-funeral ceremonies described above have persisted up to the present day. However, the custom of holding a feast 'a few weeks after a person has died' is practically non-existent.

It is, however, conceivable that the three-month *matakadānaya* grew out of this feast for a village as it is a much more elaborate affair than the seventh-day *dānaya*. Gombrich (1991, 269) observes:

> The *dānēs* for the dead vary in character. The seventh day *dānē* is a private affair for the family and maybe close friends. It is preceded by a sermon (*baṇa*) late on the previous evening. The three months *dānē* (*tun māsa dānē*) on the other hand is an occasion for conspicuous consumption, and is usually preceded by *pirit*, to which all acquaintances are invited—though in the village explicit invitation is generally unnecessary.

But the feeding does not even stop with catering for everyone present at a *matakadānaya*. As people are leaving, food parcels are packed. The host might remember that the mother of one guest will need lunch, or the children of another guest will be coming home from school soon, and so on. These food parcels are so common that on the occasion of a sixth-day *baṇa* the host family felt the need to explain to me apologeticaly that 'it is not good to take food from a funeral house before the seventh-day *dānaya* is over'. The food parcel I was given the next day more than made up for it. Of course, one could argue that on such occasions there are bound to be large left-overs, which are difficult to keep in the tropical heat, but that does not do justice to the genuine generosity on these occasions, which is, of course, the original meaning of the Pāli term *dāna*.

Feeding in the funeral context links in with a wider, cultural context of food exchange. The custom to provide a bereaved family with food until the seventh day is an unspoken reciprocal arrangement. When invited to a *baṇa* it is customary to bring a packet of milk powder or sugar, which are useful on the day but which also keep. Good friends and neighbours might ask the bereaved family directly what contribution they could make to a *dānaya*. Tillakaratne (1986, 162) shows that this goes back to at least the thirteenth century:

> The *Saddharmālaṅkāraya* testifies to the fact that this custom was prevalent in Sri Lanka even in the earlier times:
>
> *apagē daruvan maḷa kalhi apa depakshayehi*
> *nǟyan hā sesu yahaḷu mitrayō epavat asā apa*
> *samīpayaṭa enakala yamtam vī namut kana bona*
> *deyak äragena ennāhumaya.*
>
> When our relatives and friends hear that our child is dead, they are sure to visit us bringing with them at least something to eat.

Outside the funeral context, too, the exchange of food items is common in Sri Lanka, as indeed it is in many cultures. When invited to a house, or just visiting a friend, it is customary to bring a tin of cheese biscuits, some bananas or a pineapple, etc. Again, in 'exchange' the host might pack a few home-made cookies to take home. A special occasion for the exchange of food is the Sinhala New Year (13th and 14th of April) when neighbours exchange small plates of food as a sign of goodwill. This is done quite unceremoniously by sending a son or daughter over, or even by passing the food over the wall.

Giving of merit

The practice of giving of merit, much like *pirit* chanting (see above), is extremely popular in contemporary Sri Lanka and one could almost say that no religious event is complete without it. The umbrella term giving of merit comprises a variety of rituals, motives, Pāli stanzas, etc., and it seems advisable to treat the different contexts separately.

To gods

Unlike *prētas*, gods are in 'no hurry' to gain merit, but they have no, or only limited, occasion to generate merit. In order to extend their lifespan in heaven, they depend on humans for merit and reward them generously (see Vessavaṇa below). The giving of merit to gods takes place at the end of almost every religious ceremony, including funerals and *matakadānas*, and is performed by chanting the verse:

> *Ākāsaṭṭhā ca bhummaṭṭhā devā nāgā mahiddhikā*
> *Puññan taṃ anumoditvā ciraṃ rakkhantu sāsanaṃ.*

> May the gods of the ether and the earth and the powerful snakes,
> rejoice in the merit and long protect the dispensation!

According to the occasion, the last *pāda* of the verse varies and *sāsanaṃ* can be (and often is) replaced by *desanaṃ* (the teaching), *tvaṃ/te sadā* (you always), etc. This shows that the donor of the merit expects something in return, either for the wider community or for himself. Sometimes the preaching monk expresses in a sermon the wish that the gods may support the donors in their everyday activities, such as agriculture, business etc.

According to Malalasekera meritorious deeds are performed especially in order to give the merit to the gods and with regard to a specific request. A variation of this is to pledge the observation of a vow after a successful completion of an enterprise. Malalasekera (1967, 88) comments:

> Of late, the practice of attempting to gain favor of the gods in order to achieve various personal ambitions has grown tremendously. It is evident, for instance, in political elections where rival candidates are seen going to the same famous shrine to win the goodwill of the presiding deity. Vows are made, promising that various meritorious deeds will be done in the name of the deity so he would enjoy the benefits thereof.

It should be noted, however, that the custom of giving merit to the gods has not completely replaced 'direct' offerings such as fruits, coconuts, etc. The worship of gods (*devas*) can be observed everywhere in Sri Lanka. It is practised either in the grounds of a Buddhist temple, where there are small statues of Viṣṇu (seen as protector of Buddhism in Sri Lanka) and Kataragamadeviyō, or more elaborately in the form of a pilgrimage to a specific temple or temple complex such as the one in Kataragama. The latter typically constitutes the fulfillment of a vow in return for successful (personal) accomplishments.

To the departed

The giving of merit to the deceased also takes place on the funeral day and on the sixth day after the death, but on these two occasions it is just one of a number of activities. On the seventh day, however, the giving of merit becomes the core and main focus marginalising all other activities. I was told that occasionally people are prompted by a dream, but more often than not these *matakadānas* are done routinely, irrespective of any indication of the present situation of the dead relative.[77] The *matakadānas* are popular not only with laypeople, but monks as well, and, according to one of my informants, they make for ninety percent of all *dānas*. It is therefore surprising that not much is found in the secondary literature on modern Sri Lankan practice other than stock descriptions.

The procedure of how the merit is generated and given can be summed up as follows: a certain number of monks are served food and given presents (such as sets of the eight requisites for monks, etc.). The verse (*Idaṃ me ñātīnaṃ hotu . . .*) dedicating the merit to relatives[78] and the monks' chanting (*Yathā vārivahā . . .*) are accompanied by the water pouring ceremony. Kariyawasam (1995, 45) comments:

> The context shows that the pouring of water in this manner is a ritualistic act belonging to the field of sympathetic magic, symbolizing the beneficial inheritance of the merit transferred by the living to the dead, as a kind of *dakkhiṇā* or offering. The entire ritual is hence an act of grace whereby merit is transferred to the departed so that they may find relief from any unhappy realm wherein they might have been reborn.

Unfortunately, I did not come across any clues as to how old this custom of pouring the water is.[79] Dickson (1884, 234) relates that the custom of *matakadānaya* and giving of merit (no mention of chanting or water) takes place 'about a month or six weeks after a man's death'.[80] He adds, that on this occasion the Tirokuḍḍasutta is read from 'a sinhalese book, called the Prēta-kathāvastu-pota'. I never came across this custom in the area where I conducted fieldwork and it appears that a change of customs took place from Dickson's time to modern Sri Lanka.[81]

From food (cum merit) to merit (cum food). On the sixth day after the death, a personal offering (meal, water, sleeping mat, pillow) for the spirit of the departed is made which is followed by a sermon. The subsequent giving of merit (without water pouring ceremony) seems to be rather formulaic and almost like a 'supplement' to the food offering.

However, this situation is reversed on the seventh day, when the emphasis clearly shifts from food to merit. The end of the preliminary stage is thereby not marked by way of a formal ritual (such as its brahmanical counterpart the *sapiṇḍīkaraṇa* ceremony) but by subtle changes in the nature of the offerings. On and after the seventh day the food items and utensils are given not to the departed, but to the monks, and giving of merit becomes the main feature of the *matakadānas*.[82] Nevertheless, it seems quite significant that the small, impersonal deposit of food for the *prētas* or the crows in the garden, which appears to be a simple gesture, has not disappeared altogether but supplements the merit.

Feeding ghosts or worshipping ancestors? The main motif of both laypeople and monks for the giving of merit (or offerings) to the departed seems to be filial duty. Tillakaratne (1986, 169f.) states:

> As has already been mentioned spirits of the departed were not considered very difficult to please. And they were less feared than the demons or gods. Moreover they were not regarded as necessarily malevolent. On the contrary, they were sometimes supposed to take an interest in their descendants' material well being. But if neglected they were believed to show their displeasure by withdrawing the help or even becoming aggressive. This belief was often so firmly held that the Sinhalese went to great length to pacify the spirits of the departed. What the *prētas* needed most was merits. And at the end of any religious ceremony they transferred a share of the merits thus acquired to them. The fact that this practice is sometimes mentioned in Sinhalese inscriptions makes it clear that this was the position in Sri Lanka even in early times.

Tillakaratne's use of the term *prētas* and 'spirits of the departed' as synonyms is rather interesting. It does not point to the notion of *prēta* as a particular form of existence (*gati*), but conjures up the image of ancestors instead, even though the word is not used. Premasiri (2001, 151–158) is another example of the point I am trying to make. He goes into detail about the connotation of the term *peta* as meaning 'hungry ghost' only to happily switch to 'ancestors' or even 'ancestral *petas*' on the next page. On a conscious level *prēta/peta* is understood as a particular being belonging to a specific *gati*, but on a practical, emotional level, the categories of 'hungry ghost' and 'ancestor' merge. This fusion is tangible not only in secondary literature but also in interviews despite the fact that my informants were clearly aware of the different categories of beings. I would therefore argue that the giving of merit at *matakadānas* is still very much about ancestors and filial duties, despite the fact that a Buddhist twist (in the form of giving of merit) was added to the ancient *śrāddha* ritual.

To a specific being or to all beings

Other than in the above two cases, the giving of merit to gods and to the departed, there is no special occasion or formula to give merit to a specific human being or all beings. However, certain ceremonies are done on behalf of or for the benefit of someone, who is unable to participate personally in a meritorious act conducted for his benefit. These seem to come close to giving of merit, even though, to my knowledge, they are not talked about in those terms. I will take only three examples to illustrate the role of merit and merit creating activities on behalf of someone else and place them in the context of giving of merit.

The first example: it was not uncommon in the past that parents took a vow on behalf of their son to become a monk, and I personally know of at least one case some forty years ago. A small boy fell seriously ill and a vow was made that he should become a *śrāmaṇera* if he recovered from his illness. Joining the *saṃgha* is a highly meritorious act and it was hoped that the boy's situation would improve in some way by the power of that merit. However, certain conceptual questions arise from this. Does the merit accrue from the act of becoming a monk at some future day, when the boy has recovered and is old enough? This would mean that a 'loan of merit' is taken out by the parents on behalf of the child. Or does the merit accrue from the parents' undertaking of the vow? In this case, the merit would presumably accrue to them and the question is how can the parental merit be beneficial to the boy and improve his state of health? Another interesting question is, would demerit arise if the vow was not fulfilled and if so for whom, the boy or his parents? The only problem is that none of these questions, interesting as they might be, were 'natural', and my strong suspicion is that the concept of vows originates from an altogether different context which has little to do with *puṇya*.

The second example is a *bōdhipūjāva* in the village performed on behalf of an ill family member who is living abroad in Europe. The *bōdhi* tree in the premises of the older of the two local temples in our village was a popular location for *bōdhipūjās*. These are to be perfomed over seven consecutive days in the evenings: at first a small offering of flowers is made at the *cetiya*; then a more elaborate *pūjāva* is performed at the *bōdhi* tree and finally another small offering of flowers and incense is made in front of the Buddha image in the shrine room. Other *bōdhipūjās*, which I observed at the temple were also performed by laypeople (two to five people) and were fairly low-key affairs.[83] Sometimes laypeople request a monk to come to the *bōdhi* tree after the offering is over and chant in Pāli and Sinhala for about twenty or thirty minutes (normally on the first or on the seventh day). The name of the ill person for whose benefit the *pūjā* was performed was not mentioned, nor was there a special stanza or formula to give merit. However, there was no doubt, and people freely mentioned, that the *pūjāva* was performed on behalf of a sick relative.[84]

Again the question arises of how a *pūjāva* performed at the *bōdhi* tree of a village temple in Sri Lanka could benefit someone who is 6,000 miles away and, in our case, unaware that a *pūjāva* is performed on his behalf.

According to Gombrich and Obeyesekere (1990, 392–95), the *bōdhipūjāva* has taken over the functions of white magic and is used for specific purposes, such as protection from sorcery, evil influence of the planets, etc. And there is even mention of a *bōdhipūjāva* performed on behalf of someone else:

> [A] woman had seen in her daughter's horoscope that the daughter was about to pass through an unlucky period, so to avert misfortune she had watered a Bodhi tree with milk perfumed with turmeric and sandal every day for a week and given the merit to her daughter. This again illustrates the mechanism by which the Bodhi pūjā is deemed to work: its performance creates good karma, a fund of merit that can be called on at need.

It would be interesting to know what precisely is meant by 'given the merit to her daughter' and if a Sinhala speaker would have used the expression *pin denavā* or *anumōdan karanavā*. However, the *bōdhipūjāva* seems to be instrumental in an attempt to exert influence over someone else's destiny (in this example the daughter's). The text of the *bōdhipūjāva* Gombrich and Obeyesekere (1990, 400) quote includes a wide range of issues besides illnesses caused by planets, and the chanting concludes with the wish that all beings may be happy and well.

The third example is the religious wish (*prārthanā*), which is loosely connected with the *bōdhipūjāva* by the idea of a store of merit that can be drawn on. A common occasion for a *prārthanāva* is a *dānaya*, when it is expressed by the following verse, chanted by the monks either before or after the meal:

> *Icchitaṃ patthitaṃ tuyhaṃ khippam eva samijjhatu*
> *Sabbe*[85] *pūrentu attasaṃkappā cando pannarasī yathā.*
>
> May what you wish and desire very soon be successful; may all your wishes for yourself be fulfilled like the full moon.[86]

Gombrich (1991, 255ff.) says:

> [T]raditionally . . . the form of such a wish is for the monk to hope that the donors, or all present, or those for whose sake the ceremony is taking place, may in their future lives enjoy human and divine bliss

(i.e., be reborn as well-off men or gods) till they are reborn in the time of Maitrī, and *then* attain *nirvāṇa*. All then say 'Sādhu', and by their assent make this *prārthanāva* for themselves.[87]

It should, however, be noted that this is only one interpretation, and that the wording of the verse ('May what you wish or desire very soon be successful') is open to other interpretations as well. Such a *prārthanāva* can be done for one's own sake and need not even be expressed verbally or directed towards Nirvāṇa. To my knowledge, no systematic research has been done so far into the contents of these *prārthanās* and there is nothing to suggest that a *prārthanāva* cannot be (and is not) done on behalf of someone else (like a *bōdhipūjāva*, for example). Gombrich (1991, 258) points out:

> The donor makes a wish and the monk hopes it will be fulfilled. This is not strictly in contradiction to *karma* theory, because it can be said that the merit gained just before a *prārthanā* is made should ensure this. However, there is little doubt that affectively the donor feels he is achieving a certain result by a certain action in an automatic, magical way.

This seems to indicate that merit is, from an emic point of view no part in the process.

In search of a possible interpretation of the three examples let us turn to the tradition itself. All cases seem to exclude the possibility of giving of merit in the Abhidhamma sense of creating the opportunity for rejoicing in a meritorious deed as that would require the presence of the recipient.

On the other hand, the concept of influencing another being's mind by the power of one's own mind is not particularly uncommon in Buddhism and is more or less taken for granted in Sri Lanka. The classic, canonical, example is the use of certain *sūtras* as snake charms, which work by sending out *mettā* to pacify wild animals (particularly snakes). The question now is how does merit come into it, why is merit necessary at all to influence someone else's mind? A virtuous mind is stronger, more powerful than a non-virtuous mind, just as an important truth of moral significance is ritually more effective. In this sense the meritorious acts in our examples make the mind more powerful and enable it to exercise positive influence over someone else's mind. An expression frequently used in Sinhala sermons is *puṇyaśaktiya*, the power or force of merit. In fact, two of the monks I interviewed asserted that one can indeed influence other beings by way of the power of the mind (like an electrical current).

The question remains as to how this positive influence of the mind might improve the situation of someone who is ill. Let us briefly revisit the Abhidhamma explanation of *pirit* chanting at the sick bed: by listening to *pirit* the patient himself purifies his thought and as a result his own good *karma* comes to fruition. This does not mean that bad *karma* is annihilated; it may still show an effect at some later stage, but it is temporarily suppressed. My cautious guess would be that the same can be achieved by way of positive thoughts for someone else. The patient's mind is purified by the power of good, beneficial thoughts directed towards him and as a result his good *karma* comes to fruition. Abhidhammically speaking, nothing is added to his stock of merit, as that would not be possible. This might be an explanation for the three examples discussed above: the parents, relatives or friends recharge their minds (to stay with the imagery of electricity) by way of meritorious deeds and then charge someone else's mind with this power. Besides, as in the contexts of *pirit* chanting and *bōdhipūjāva*, there might be an element of ritual efficacy involved, which is, as Schmithausen (1997) shows, not a new invention.

To sum up: Buddhist funerals are only one of the contexts for the practice of giving of merit, even though a very important one. Merit generated by acts of *dāna*, *sīla* and *bhāvanā* is given not only to the departed, but subsequently to the gods. Everyone present is invited to partake by way of *prārthanās*, usually pre-formulated by a monk. Besides giving of merit there are other ceremonies on behalf of someone else (such as *bodhipūjās*) which combine merit generating activities with an element of ritual efficacy.

Excursus: anumodanāva *(questionnaire A.1–3)*

In order to establish a somewhat clearer picture of people's beliefs with regard to the beneficiary of the giving of merit a set of three questions was included in the questionnaire.

> Questionnaire A.1: At the moment when the water is poured and the merit is given, how can the departed person receive the merit? How can a meritorious deed performed by one person benefit another person?
> Questionnaire A.2: What is the meaning of the words '*anumōdan karanavā*' and '*anumōdan venavā*'? Is there a difference to the expressions '*pin dīma*' and '*pin läbenavā*'?
> Questionnaire A.3: Who can benefit from giving of merit? Can a departed relative benefit from giving of merit even after one year or five years, etc., and after he is reborn somewhere else, for example as an animal, god, human being or in hell?

Question A.1 raises the problem of the actual process of how merit is acquired and given, while question A.2 investigates what an impact Abhidhamma interpretation might have on people's beliefs and finally, question A.3 is concerned with the problem of who can benefit. As these questions are closely linked and overlap they will be treated together and, as before, the monks' answers will be discussed first. Their explanations were very much in line with the Theravāda Abhidhamma interpretation of giving of merit as a two-way process of offering merit on the side of the donor and (joyful) consent on the side of the recipient. Frequently reference was made to the ten meritorious acts (*dasapuññakiriyā*) which include *pattidāna* and *pattānumodanā* to denote the giving of and rejoicing in merit. Furthermore, the recipient is described as expecting or hoping for (*balāporottu venavā*) merit and accepting it by being glad and/or saying *sādhu* to express consent. Again, when asked explicitly about the meaning of *anumodanā* (one of the keywords in Sinhala sermons) the unanimous answer was in line with the original Pāli meaning of 'rejoice, be happy'. The rejoicing (Sinhala *satuṭa*) on the side of the recipient was taken as the *conditio sine qua non* for a successful giving of merit. One interviewee went one step further in claiming that the actual presence of the recipient is required. Another interesting point brought forward by two of the interviewees is the possibility of rejoicing in bad actions committed by somebody else (*pāpānumodanā*) which in itself constitutes a bad deed (*pāpa*). In so far as it is a negative mental act on the side of the person who rejoices in the bad deed it is said to create bad karmic influence.[88] One interviewee even suggested that one can actually harm people by way of negative thoughts. He compared the power of good or bad thoughts, or as he put it 'offering energy', to electricity which seems to move away from the concept of giving of merit as a two-way process (see above).

When asked who can benefit from the giving of merit, my informants named first one of the four classes of *petas*, the *paradattūpajīvin* ('those sustained by what is given by others').[89] Most of the interviewees then quoted the Bimbisāra story, which does not name *paradattūpajīvins* but only mentions *petas* in general.[90] *Prētas* were further defined as miserable, rather than evil, beings whose physiognomy (big bellies and long thin necks) is an outward sign of their inability to partake of food.

Rather reluctantly, and after further probing, gods were said to be another class of beings who are able to benefit from the giving of merit. They are, so to speak, on the other end of the scale, certainly not suffering but enjoying a rather pleasant lifestyle. Like *prētas*, however, they cannot do meritorious deeds themselves and totally depend on humans for merit. While the merit given to *prētas* transforms into food, clothing, etc., merit given to gods serves to prolonge their lifespan in *devaloka*. Another common characteristic, according to at least one interviewee, is their ability to be physically present where merit is given. This was explained to me as a prerequisite for the receiving of merit. Applied to a *matakadānaya*, the implication is that those dead relatives who have taken rebirth in a womb or in one of the hells are unable to be present and benefit from merit given to them. All interviewees were adamant that even in the case of relatives being reborn as, say, a human or animal, the merit would not go to waste but 'return' to the donor.[91] Also opinion was undivided in that there is no time limit for giving of merit due to the (very long) lifespan of the gods and *prētas* who are the recipients. This means that, provided the departed has taken rebirth in the *petaloka* or a *devaloka* and is present and appreciative, merit can be successfully given to him or her even ten or twenty years after his or her death. The picture we get from the replies by the monks is, with minor variations, more or less undivided and largely consistent with Theravāda doctrine.

The picture is somewhat more diverse when it came to laymen. The explanations given by religiously educated people and the older generation in general—particularly *upāsaka-ammās*[92]—were again largely in line with the Theravāda doctrine if somewhat less technical. It was frequently mentioned that the departed hope for merit (*balāporottu venavā*) and that merit cannot be 'given' without the recipient's consent or against his will. It has been suggested that merit is 'given' by way of making a religious wish (*prārthanāva*) and that the act is symbolized by pouring water from a jug into a vessel.

Furthermore, the recipient of the merit was frequently said to appreciate the giving by saying *sādhu* or being happy (*satuṭu vīma*) which indicates that, despite the fact that the literal meaning of *anumodanā* did not seem to be widely known, a link (in some cases even an equation) was made between merit and happiness (*satuṭa*). The terms *pin anumodan karanavā* and *pin anumodan venavā* were paraphrased by all the interviewees (except for one who had a degree in Pāli) as 'giving merit' and 'receiving merit' (*pin denavā* and *pin läbenavā*). One person suggested that the former is a more formal terminology, used by monks or on formal occasions.[93]

About one third of the interviewees, the older and more religiously educated, said that only (*paradattūpajīvin*) *petas* and gods (earth and tree deities, *bhūtas* and *yakku* were mentioned) can benefit. Some people were rather hazy and unspecific as to the question who can benefit.[94] Again about a third of the people stated that the dead can only benefit from the merit 'given' to them as long as they are not reborn yet. Opinions on the duration of this intermediate state differed, but the interviewees agreed that once the departed is reborn, the giving of merit should be regarded merely as a sign of respect for the dead person. Finally, one (younger) person was adamant that all giving of merit is a mere token of respect (*salakanavā vitarayi*). Still this custom was to be encouraged, as it increases the donor's merit and reduces his greed (*taṇhāva*). This position seemed to be singular in its radical dismissal.

Some historical roots: giving of merit

Buddhist religious activity can be described in terms of *dāna*, *sīla* and *bhāvanā*, which are traditionally regarded as the three pillars of meritorious deeds.[95] Any religious ceremony, such as giving alms to the monks includes activities from all three categories: the laity present take the three refuges and the five precepts, and thereby act in accordance with morality (*sīla*); the presenting of food (and/or presents) to the monks constitutes an act of generosity (*dāna*); and finally the listening to a sermon falls under the category meditation (*bhāvanā*).

The performance of any religious activity, provided it is done with a positive mental attitude, contributes to an individual store of merit. This merit can, according to the widespread belief not only of Sri Lankan Buddhists, be given to or shared with other living beings. There is, however, no single Pāli equivalent of the terms 'transference (or transfer) of merit' or *Verdienstübertragung*, which are so widely used in secondary literature. Furthermore, the Pāli terminology seems to change from the early Nikāyas to later canonical texts and commentaries.

Wezler (1998, 578) warns against subsuming a great variety of cases under the broad umbrella term of 'transference of merit or demerit'. Schmithausen (1987 210–216) introduces subcategories such as 'voluntary' and 'involuntary transference', but still judges it a not altogether satisfying solution. With the exception of some passages from the earlier material (Nikāyas) when I render the verb *ā √dis* as 'dedicate' or 'assign', I use the term giving of merit throughout. I thereby follow the commentarial tradition, which speaks of 'giving [of merit]' (*pattidāna*), and the Sri Lankan expression (*pin denavā*).[96] While still a broad umbrella term, giving of merit nevertheless has the advantage of being a 'real' Buddhist term (albeit a later one) and, considering the nature of sources (mainly Pāli commentaries, Abhidhamma and modern Sinhala interview material), I felt it was an adequate, even though not ideal, rendering.

As before, the giving of merit will be discussed separately according to the recipients of the merit (gods, departed relatives and specific human beings or even all living beings)—first, because it makes it possible to single out passages relevant to the funeral context; second, because attempts have been made to establish one or the other of these contexts as the 'original context' of the notion of giving of merit and finally, because the motivations for giving of merit seem to differ greatly.

The present chapter attempts to provide some historical roots for the contemporary practice in Sri Lanka and is not intended as an exhaustive study of the phenomenon of giving of merit. The first part tries to establish the textual evidence for the giving of merit (early stage, late stage and Abhidhamma); the second part presents archaeological evidence, and the last part discusses proposed origins of this practice.

The early stage: assigning merit

To gods and demons

The earlier canonical passages dealing with offerings to gods or the departed, mainly use the expression *dakkhiṇā* in combination with the verb *ādis* ('to dedicate'). The problem is what is *dakkhiṇā*?[97] Schmithausen (1986, 210) points out that:

> *dakṣiṇā/dakkhiṇā* primarily means the *gift* given to a person to be honoured, originally to a priest as reward for his sacrificial service, but in Buddhism, of course, to the Buddha or to the Order or to monks. This being the case, it seems difficult to exclude *a priori* the possibility that, at least at an earlier stage, the expression *dakkhiṇaṃ ādis-* simply meant that a *gift*, though presented to the monks, is *assigned* to divine beings (or deceased persons), the monks somehow acting as their representatives or as mediators.

Bearing this in mind one has to distinguish between passages merely suggestive of merit and passages where the context is such that merit can safely be assumed.[98]

In the *Mahāparinibbānasutta* the Buddha is reported to have spoken the following three verses showing his appreciation (*anumodanā*) after receiving a meal:

> Wheresoe'er the prudent man shall take up his abode
> Let him support the brethren there, good men of self-control,
> And give the merit of his gifts to the deities who haunt the spot.
> Revered they will revere him: honoured, they will honour him again;
> Are gracious to him like a mother to her own, her only son.
> And the man who has the grace of the gods, good fortune he beholds.[99]
> (Rhys Davids (1910) 1989, II 93f; D II 88)

These three verses contain some important features found also in other passages dealing with offerings to gods: the wise man is encouraged not only to give to the ascetics, but to dedicate *dakkhiṇā* ('gift' or with Rhys Davids 'merit') to the local gods, who are presumably present, and finally it is said the gods in return will honour him and as a result (reward?) he will find good fortune. Buddhaghosa glosses *dakkhiṇā* as *patti* ('acquisition, merit'), but does not provide any additional information as to what those gods' reaction might have been.[100]

Gombrich (1991, 267) takes this passage as proof that the 'transfer of merit to the gods is canonical'. Schmithausen (1986, 210), however, is much more cautious:

> It should, however, be borne in mind that this passage can be taken as proof of merit transference only if it could be demonstrated that, in the expression *dakkhiṇaṃ ādis-*, *dakkhiṇā* invariably and from the very beginning has the meaning of 'reward (for one's gift)'.

According to Schmithausen there are, however, at least two unambiguous passages where *dakkhiṇā* is used in the sense of merit or result of a gift rather than the gift itself. At M III 255 fourteen offerings (*dāna*) are graded according to the recipient from the Tathāgata down to animals, and a distinction is made between the actual gift (*dāna*) and its reward (*dakkhiṇā*). There is, however, no mention of dedicating or assigning of these rewards. The context of the second passage (A IV 63ff.) is particularly interesting: Vessavaṇa asks a laywoman to prepare a meal on his behalf for some monks and to assign the *dakkhiṇā* to him. After serving the meal to the monks she relates the event to Sāriputta who does not object to the proposed dedication of merit. She therefore declares, 'Sir, may the merit, the benefit which is in this gift bring happiness for the great king Vessavaṇa'[101] and is (according to the commentary) subsequently rewarded by him with ever-filled stores of rice. The terms *dakkhiṇā* and *puñña* are linked here by way of context: Vessavaṇa asks for *dakkhiṇā*, but receives merit (*puñña*) and he is obviously satisfied, because he rewards the laywoman afterwards. One gets the impression that the emphasis of his request is less on the resulting merit than on the wish of the god to pay his respect to the monks.[102]

The common features of the above mentioned passages from the Aṅguttaranikāya and Dīghanikāya are: *dakkhiṇā/puñña* is assigned while the god or gods are present and the donor is being rewarded by them. Nothing is said about how the gods actually receive the *dakkhiṇā* and of what benefit it might be for them.

To the departed

In the case of offerings to deceased relatives, the situation is equally confused, if not more so. There are no unambiguous passages in which *dakkhiṇā* can only be understood as merit, but there are passages that suggest that actual food is given to the *petas* either directly or indirectly (by way of monks as mediators). Donations (*dakkhiṇā*) to deceased relatives are mentioned in the Sigālovādasutta in the context of the five duties of a child to his parents.[103] Again we are faced with the problem of how to understand *dakkhiṇā*, because there is no context that would allow us to exclude the possibility that actual, material donations are being given. Since it is part of the Sigālovādasutta, we can conclude, however, that donations to departed parents are regarded as a positive practice, which is to be encouraged. Buddhaghosa's commentary on this passage again glosses *dakkhiṇā* as *patti*, but nothing is said about the actual procedure of giving merit (*pattidāna*) or about the reaction of the recipient of the merit (*patti*).[104]

At A V 269ff. a brahmin asks the Buddha directly about the efficiency of the brahmanical ritual for the departed (*śrāddha/saddha*) and if it is possible that donations (*dāna*) given for the deceased (*peta*) can actually be enjoyed by them.[105]

The Buddha's reply is that only ghosts (*petas*) can enjoy (food) offerings, but not beings in hell, animals, humans, or gods.[106] As Gombrich (1991, 272) and Schmithausen (1986, 211) observe, there is no hint that this might refer to giving merit rather than food offerings. Besides, the question remains as to whether the offering can be enjoyed by the *petas* directly or only with mediation of some kind.

A similar question is posed in a later, paracanonical text, the Milindapañha, where the situation is initially very similar. Offerings (*dāna*) are given for the benefit of the deceased, but then the terminology changes; it then says their result (*vipāka*) is gained (*paṭilabh*) by the deceased. The reply is reminiscent of A V 269 in that it excludes beings in hell (*nirayūpapannā*), in heaven (*saggagatā*), and animals (*tiracchānayonigatā*), as well as three of the four classes of *petas* (*vantāsika, khuppipāsino, nijjhāmataṇhikā*) from the benefit of the offering (humans are not mentioned here). The only beings who are said to benefit are the *petā paradattūpajīvino* ('those living off what has been given by others'). Another striking parallel between those two passages (Mil 294ff. and A V 269ff.) is that both state that even if it were possible that no relative happened to be reborn in the realm of *petas*, a gift or donation made for the deceased is never without reward for the donor himself. But whereas the latter deals with actual donations, the former now goes on to discuss the qualities of good (*kusala*) and bad (*akusala*). Interestingly, the Milindapañha explicitly excludes the possibility of giving *akusala*.

Again, a Kathāvatthu discussion (see Kv 346ff. = Kv. VII.6 and its commentary) is also relevant to the problem of what is being given. While some modern interpreters say this discussion is early evidence for the acceptance of the idea of giving of merit,[107] Schmithausen (1987, n. 70) has suggested otherwise. The Kathāvatthu commentary says that some non-Theravāda schools (such as the Rājagiriyas) held the view that donations of actual food and clothes are passed on to and enjoyed by the *petas* directly, and it seems that a giving of merit is actually excluded. Schmithausen (1987, n. 70) asks of the wording of the Kathāvatthu itself:

> Wouldn't it be more natural to understand it in the sense of some mysterious, invisible handing over of food or clothes to the *pretas*, perhaps through mediation of monks?

Even in the Petavatthu we can still find both possibilities: the first ten verses of the Tirokuḍḍapetavatthu seem to imply a real giving of food, whereas only the last verse suggests the mediation of the monks. Schmithausen (1987, 211) comments on this as follows:

> The first pattern would correspond to the Brahmanical offering of rice-balls and water to the recently deceased (*preta*) as well as to the *piṇḍapitṛyajña* where rice-balls, etc., are offered to the *manes*

> (*pitṛ*) and directly eaten by them, whereas the second pattern reflects the situation of the Brahmanical *śrāddha* rite (the connection with which is explicit at A V 269) where the rice-balls, water, clothes, etc., meant for the *manes* are at least partly consumed or taken by the *Brahmins* who act as their representatives.

It should be noted, however, that the Tirokuḍḍapetavatthu constitutes an exception in that the other stories of the Petavatthu explicitly deny the possibility of giving food.

To sum up, there seem to be three possibilities: First, actual food, clothes, etc., are given directly to the *petas* and enjoyed by them; second, food and clothes, etc., (*dāna*) are given to the monks, who act as some kind of mediators in the process and thirdly, merit is generated by way of an offering of food, clothes, etc., to the monks and benefits the *petas* in the form of *phala* and *vipāka* which, interestingly, again transforms into food and clothes for the *petas*.

To a specific being or to all beings

A curious case of dedication of *dakkhiṇā* to a (living) relative is found in the Therīgāthā where a wife (Cāpā) asks her husband (Upaka) to dedicate *dakkhiṇā*:

> You should utter (my) greeting now to the unsurpassed protector of the world; and having circumambulated him you should dedicate (my) gift.
>
> (Norman 1969, II 32; Thī 307)

However, a problem with Norman's translation is that there is no actual gift of hers mentioned before nor does it say to whom it should be dedicated. This makes the interpretation of Dhammapāla's commentary more plausible, which takes *dakkhiṇā* as the husband's merit resulting from the meritorious act of greeting and circumambulating the Buddha.[108]

Milindapañha (Mil 295ff.) proposes the possibility of sharing the 'stored beneficial potency' (*kusala*) with the 'world with its gods' (*sadevakaṃ lokaṃ*).[109] This would, of course, strictly speaking include departed relatives who are reborn as humans, animals or gods, even though no differentiation is made (nor intended) as to the possible status of these beings as former relatives. However, particularly interesting here is the water image for *kusala* (an overflowing well is filling up again and again and cannot be exhausted). It is customary in Sri Lanka for the head of the household to make a jug of water overflow to symbolize the act of giving merit.

A rather curious case of dedication of merit to all beings is found in the Buddhāpadāna, which Bechert (1976, 48) places as late as the first or beginning of the second century A.D. It relates the story of the Bodhisattva, who dwells in a Buddhafield (*buddhakṣetra/buddhakkhetta*), in a palace, with past Buddhas and their disciples, from where merit (*puṇya/puñña*) is dedicated to all beings. The terminology is, again, changed from *dakkhiṇā* or *kusala* to 'fruit of/which is merit' (*puññaphala*). In a brief summary of the content of the Buddhāpadāna Bechert (1976, 44) says of the relevant verses that they serve to connect the Buddhafield with the world of humans, etc.

The later stage: giving merit

In later texts we find the terms *patti* (lit. acquisition [of merit]) and *pattidāna* (giving of the acquisition [of merit]) on the one hand and *anumodanā* (rejoicing) and *pattānumodanā* (rejoicing in or joyful consent to a gift [of merit]) on the other hand. The latter terms provide some clue as to how the giving of merit from donor to recipient might take place.[110] In defining *patti* we are again faced with the problem that its primary meaning is not 'merit' (see PED) but merely 'acquisition' or 'profit'. We will, however, concentrate here on the passages where the context suggests merit. Similarly the term *anumodanā* seems to have undergone a change in connotation and usage. The verb *anu* √*mud* and the noun *anumodanā* is frequently met with in the Nikāyas referring to a little speech or verses spoken by the Buddha or a monk as a sign of appreciation and gratefulness after receiving a meal.[111] In the Abhidhamma texts it seems to have acquired a more technical meaning of 'appreciation' or 'joyful consent' which constitutes a prerequisite for the successful giving of merit.

Agasse (1978, 319 ns. 42 and 43) gives some interesting 'statistics' based mainly on the Petavatthu (with its commentary) and the Dhammapada-aṭṭhakathā. He shows that the merit-generating deeds are almost exclusively done by human beings. The amount of merit generated by way of donations increases with the virtue of the recipient of these donations. At M III 255 it is said that a gift to an animal brings about a hundredfold result, a gift to a human being a thousandfold, etc., with the Tathāgata being the most worthy recipient of a gift.[112] This hierarchy is reflected in the stories of the Dhammapada-aṭṭhakathā where most frequently donations to a Buddha, Pratyekabuddha, or monks are related and only occasionally donations to ordinary laymen and animals (e.g., fish) as well.[113] As far as the recipients of the merit are concerned, the emphasis seems to have changed compared to the earlier material of the Nikāyas.[114] The gods/deities still feature as recipients of merit but are by far outnumbered by *petas* and human beings. An additional problem is the definition of the category of '*petas*'. In the Petavatthu the word *peta* is no longer used as a general (plural) term for the deceased but almost exclusively for a specific class of beings (hungry ghosts), or to be precise, for a specific member (singular!) of that class. So the new category would be *peta/petī* (hungry ghosts) who, in most cases, happens to be a former relation of the donor.

The following selection of examples and stories is not meant to be an exhaustive investigation into the problem but merely as an illustration of the two terms *patti(dāna)* and *anumodanā* and their possible relationship.

To gods and demons

In a story in the Dhammapada-aṭṭhakathā a man is desperate to find some water lilies, etc., in order to satisfy the king. On his way to the lake he gives a portion of rice to a traveler and another portion to some fish and his generosity results in merit a thousandfold and a hundredfold respectively (see the above discussion of M III 255). 'Armed' with this merit he arrives at the lake and offers it to the mighty serpent (*nāga*), who accepts it in exchange for water lilies, etc.[115] The interesting aspect in this story is that *patti* seems to serve here as a kind of currency. One gets the impression that a straight-forward business deal has taken place and the *nāga* king accepts and hands over the 'goods'.

Dhp-a IV 18f relates the story of a female demon (*yakkhinī*) who benefits from merit (*patti*) which was meant for someone else. The novice Sānu dedicates the merit resulting from his recitation of the Dharma to his parents who are unaware of this. Incidentally, the *yakkhinī*, who was the novice's mother in a previous existence, overhears this and expresses her appreciation (*anumodāmi*), whereby she gains great respect amongst other *yakkhas*. This story is interesting for two reasons: first, it implies that without the knowledge (and presence?) of the receiving party a successful giving of merit cannot take place, and second, because it relates the *yakkhinī's* reaction (*anumodāmi*).[116] The latter could be seen in the context of this story as a confirmation that the novice had unwittingly dedicated his merit to a different mother from the one he's thinking of.

Unlike the Nikāya passages in which the gods reward the donor of the merit, the first story of the *nāga* reports a straightforward business deal, and in the second story only the *yakkhin*ī benefits, but not the novice.

To the departed: yet more on prētas

The principal source of information for the giving of merit to *petas* is, of course, the Petavatthu (which, according to Norman (1983, 71), was compiled approximately 300 BC). Even though the Petavatthu is regarded as canonical and the terminology used in the Petavatthu to denote what is being given is still mostly *dakkhiṇā* rather than *patti*, the stories are taken here as belonging to the 'later stage'.[117] The reason for this is that the efficacy of the giving of merit seems (with one exception) to be taken for granted throughout the Petavatthu, and the possibility of giving donations to *petas* directly is explicitly denied.[118] Furthermore, in some cases the giving of merit occurs not in the verses of the Petavatthu but is 'added' in the frame story related in Dhammapāla's commentary.

The title *Petavatthu* has usually been translated as 'stories of the departed', but in fact deals with only one particular class of 'departed' (*peta*): those who happen to have been reborn in the realm of the 'hungry ghosts' (*peta*). Therefore it can be said that the prevalent connotation in the stories of the Petavatthu is that of a (hungry) ghost (*peta/petī*) in desperate need of help from humans, who reveals himself/herself to be a former relative, a fact, which is almost incidental to the story.[119] And according to Holt (1981, 17), the general motivation is not one of gratitude and duty, as one might expect in case of a deceased parent, etc., but one of 'compassion and selfless giving, motivations which agree much more easily with the karmic theory of action'.[120] The Tirokuḍḍasutta constitutes an exception here in that it contains a verse emphasizing the importance of giving to the departed (*petā*, plural!) out of gratitude and in memory of what they had been or done.[121] Holt (1981, 18) comments on this as follows:

> In this passage, which on the whole constitutes a theoretical anomaly in the Petavatthu, we find the same motive for merit transfer amongst Buddhists as we did for Śrāddha amongst Brāhmaṇical counterparts. Just as Brāhmaṇical family survivors fulfilled their dharmic obligations out of gratitude for the deceased family member, so are Buddhists here enjoined to do the same.

I agree with him, as far as the motivation in the Tirokuḍḍapetavatthu is concerned, but this is not where the anomaly ends. Most of the Tirokuḍḍapetavatthu still assumes actual food donations rather than merit, as has been pointed out by various scholars.[122] It does not appear at all impossible that these two aspects are connected and that the Tirokuḍḍapetavatthu marks a transition from actual food offerings given to ancestors (or deceased relatives, etc.) out of gratitude to giving merit to ghosts motivated by compassion. The verses and the different versions of the frame story of King Bimbisāra, which is often seen as the origin of the Sri Lankan *matakadānaya*, needs to be considered in somewhat more detail.

The commentary to the Petavatthu relates the famous story as follows: King Bimbisāra invites the Buddha and the *saṃgha* for a meal but fails to give donations to the *petas*. Greatly disappointed they make themselves heard to Bimbisāra by making a loud noise in the night. The next day the king asks the Buddha about the noise and is told about its cause. Accordingly, Bimbisāra invites the monks again and this time remembers the *petas*, whose situation improves instantly. Another version of the verses of the Tirokuḍḍapetavatthu is found in the Khuddakapāṭha under the title Tirokuḍḍasutta. The commentary to the Khuddakapāṭha, the Paramatthajotikā (usually ascribed to Buddhaghosa), also relates the story of King Bimbisāra and still explains his offerings to the *petas* as actual food, etc. Yet another version of the Bimbisāra story is found in the

Dhammapada-aṭṭhakathā (Dhp-a I 103–4), but the situation is changed in that it is now merit that is being offered to the *petas*, and the merit is subsequently transformed into divine food, clothes, etc. This version of the Bimbisāra story is, therefore, as far as the giving of merit is concerned, much more in line with the rest of the Petavatthu stories than the actual Tirokuḍḍapetavatthu. Holt (1981, 11) says of the stories of the Petavatthu:

> Although veneration of the dead and grieving over their departure from life is firmly discouraged in at least six of the fifty-one tales, the ancient Brāhmanical belief that the living in some way benefit the dead in their afterlife existence persists. The new means by which this is accomplished is through the transfer of merit, a practice advocated in eighteen stories.

He further explains (n. 47) that '[t]he pattern here is that if the story is to include giving of merit, the *peta* almost always appears to surviving kin'. The pattern of these stories is very fixed: due to an evil deed someone is reborn as a *peta*/*petī* in great suffering; he/she appears to a human being (former relative) and tells his/her story (whereby karmic retribution is demonstrated); finally a request for merit is fulfilled by way of a donation to the *saṃgha* and subsequent giving of merit, motivated by compassion for the *peta*. The result is an instant improvement in the conditions of the *peta*/*petī*. But, as Schmithausen (1986, 212) points out, this does not result in a change to a higher form of existence but leads only to a 'drastic change of status *within* their existence as *pretas* by being, through the gift, raised to the rank of powerful and blissful divine *pretas*'.

In some cases the verses end with the description of the *peta's*/*petī's* suffering (much like the stories that do not contain a giving of merit) and the giving of merit is found in the commentary only. It has been pointed out that in some cases the merit has been generated and given to the *peta*/*petī* by a monk, even though this is not generally the case in the stories of the Petavatthu.[123] Occasionally, but not always, it is said that the *peta*/*petī* is happy about the offering which is then mostly expressed in the stock phrase *dānena modāmi* (Pv 19, 21, 24) or simply *modāmi*, or *sukhita*. This suggests that *anumodanā* is not a *conditio sine qua non* for the successful giving of merit.

One story, however, seems to give emphasis to *anumodanā* (Pv 21–37 commentary): A tailor is too poor to give donations to beggars and ascetics coming to his house, but he gladly points with his right hand the way to a rich man's house. As a result he is reborn as a *yakkha* with a golden hand, which bestows gifts. The rich man's employee who is in charge of charity, on the other hand, is not in favour of these donations and makes faces at the beggars. Due to his bad behaviour he is reborn as a *peta*. Interesting here is that the (uninvited) rejoicing in generosity practised by someone else (*parassa dānaṃ anumodamāno*; Pv 33, verse 20) results in a rebirth particularly favourable to engaging in charity (golden hand).

To a specific being or to all beings

As mentioned above *patti* can be equated to money or in certain contexts even serve as a 'currency'. A frequently quoted example in this context is found in the Dhp-a IV 200: Two brothers jointly own a sugarcane field and the younger one goes there to fetch two sticks of sugarcane. On his way back home he meets a *pratyekabuddha* and offers him first one stick (his share) and then the other stick (his brother's share). While offering the second stick of sugarcane he reflects that he will have to pay back his brother either in money (*mūla*) or in merit (*patti*) resulting from his generosity. His brother, like any good business man would, inquires what exactly the *pratyekabuddha* said (presumably to find out which of the options would be most profitable) and decides in the end to take the merit.

Hayashi (1999, 34) relates a very interesting, albeit, late incident of giving merit, a 'royal exchange of *patti*':

> In Sri Lankan chronicle literature we find instances of exchange of *patti* or *pattidāna* by royal letters (*rājasaṃdesa*) to promote amity between two kings, Kittisirirājasīha (AD 1747–1781) of Ceylon and Dhammika of Siam.[124]

In the last example merit is treated like a present of goodwill, possibly even accompanied by material presents. The recipient would be expected to reciprocate, as it would possibly be regarded as a great offence not to reply with a similar message of merit.

There are other examples equating merit (*patti*) with money (*mūla*) to illustrate the pricelessness of merit: at Dhp-a I 269 and Dhp-a II 197–98 large sums are offered to someone for items needed for a meritorious deed (roof pinnacle and honey). In both cases the offer of money, even though it exceeds the value of the respective goods by far, is declined and a share in the merit is demanded instead as 'payment'.[125]

Yet another example from the Dhammapada-aṭṭhakathā further illustrates the investment character of merit. A rich man called Sumana tries to persuade his poor employee called Annabhāra to sell him his share of alms (*piṇḍapāta*) to a *pratyekabuddha*. When Annabhāra refuses, Sumana tries to persuade him to sell the merit (*patti*), which he gained by way of the *piṇḍapāta*. The meaning of this distinction between a share in the *piṇḍapāta* already given and a share in the merit resulting from the *piṇḍapāta* is not quite clear to me. Perhaps by sharing the cost of the *piṇḍapāta* the merit would be shared (i.e., cut in half), whereas by sharing the merit resulting from the *piṇḍapāta* both would actually get the full benefit. However, Annabhāra decides to consult the *pratyekabuddha*, who illustrates with the example of the oil lamp that merit given away is not lost to the donor but merely multiplies.[126] Annabhāra decides now to give the merit away out of faith (*saddhāya*) without compensation and is subsequently rewarded by the rich man. The king, too, on hearing this story asks Annabhāra for merit, and again Annabhāra is rewarded generously. Even though there are still all the signs of a proper business deal (and in fact Annabhāra is doing quite well out of it) the merit is now 'given away' rather than sold, and the recipients of the merit show their appreciation by way of presents (no mention of *anumodanā*).

Yet another example for the giving of merit to a fellow human is related in the Jātakas (J IV 15–22): a generous brahmin is planning to embark on a sea journey in order to generate more wealth for his good deeds. His generosity is such that even on his way to the harbour he gives his shoes and a sunshade to a *pratyekabuddha*, who had foreseen that the brahmin will be in need of that merit later. When he is shipwrecked a deity who searches the seas for virtuous men in need of rescue spots him and grants him a wish. Interestingly the brahmin first questions the deity which of his many meritorious deeds resulted in his good luck and is reminded of the gift to the *pratyekabuddha*. He wishes for a new ship, which the deity makes appear for his rescue, but she overlooks his attendant who is swimming in the sea. The brahmin generously gives merit (*pattiṃ adāsi*) to him, the attendant rejoices (*so anumodi*) and is rescued as well. This passage is interesting for two reasons: the origin of the merit is established and both the giving of merit and the reaction of rejoicing is recorded.

A story from the Vimānavatthu (Vv 44.9) goes one step further in suggesting a direct connection between rejoicing (here stressed as *suddhanumodanā* 'pure rejoicing') in the merit and and the result (being reborn in the realm of the Thirty-Three). The commentary to this story uses the terms: *pattidāna* ('giving of the acquisition [of merit]') on the side of Visākhā and *anumodanā* ('appreciation or joyful consent') on the side of laywoman. With the introduction of *anumodanā* as a technical term the emphasis shifts from donor to recipient.[127]

An interesting episode relating to the giving of merit to all beings is found in the Dhammapada-aṭṭhakathā. Hayashi (1999, 31) sums up this incident:

> In Dhp-a IV 76, when Sakka requests the Buddha to bestow the merit of the discourse of the Dhamma, the Buddha himself proclaims to the order: 'Monks, from today you should give merit to all beings after arranging the great audience of the *dhamma* (*mahādhammasavana*), the ordinary audience of the *dhamma*, the informal discourse, or even after rejoicing (*anumodanā*).' A curious configuration here is, that while merit is usually the domain of the giver, even a monk who receives a gift and utters *anumodanā* assigns his merit of that to others.

Here various aspects are of interest: first, the Buddha himself reportedly encouraged his monks to engage in the giving of merit. Second, *anumodanā* constitutes a meritorious activity in its own right—just like preaching *dhamma*—and the merit resulting from rejoicing (*anumodanā*) [in somebody else's meritorious deed], can, consequently, be given as well, which is, of course, consistent with the Abhidhamma interpretation of *anumodanā*.

The Abhidhamma interpretation

Dickson quotes and translates as a starting point for his account of religious ceremonies in Ceylon a Pali verse enumerating the ten good deeds:[128]

> *Dānaṃ sīlañ ca bhāvanā*
> *Patti pattānumodanā*
> *Veyyāvacca-apacāyañ ca*
> *Desanā sutti* (sic) *diṭṭhi-ju*[129]

> 1. Charity; 2. piety; 3. meditation; 4. the giving of merit; 5. sharing in the merits of another; 6. helping the helpless; 7. showing respect; 8. preaching; 9. listening; 10. rejecting heresy.
>
> (Dickson 1884, 203)

An almost identical list with slight variations occurs in the Abhidhammāvatāra where *pattidāna* is found instead of *patti* and *anumodanā* instead of *pattānumodanā*.[130] Interesting here is the concept that the list of ten is regarded as an elaboration of a list of three good deeds (*dāna*, *sīla*, *bhāvanā*), which are the first three in our verse, or as the following two verses of the Abhidhammāvatāra explain it, the other seven can be seen as included in the first three. And again in the Abhidhammatthasaṅgaha, we find a classification of good *karma* as three-, eight-, or tenfold, the last of those being:

> It is also tenfold according to (i) generosity, (ii) morality, (iii) meditation, (iv) reverence, (v) service, (vi) transference of merit, (vii) rejoicing in [others'] merit (viii) hearing the doctrine, (ix) teaching the doctrine, (x) and straightening one's views.
>
> (Nārada Mahā Thera 1956, I 241; Abhidh-s 25)[131]

Of these ten, vi and vii are included in generosity (*dāna*), iv and v in morality (*sīla*), viii, ix and x in meditation (*bhāvanā*). The commentary to the Abhidhammatthasaṅgaha explains *pattidāna* and *pattānumodanā* as follows:

> The volition that wishes for the merit that occurs in one's own [mental] continuity to be common to others is called giving of good fortune.

> The volition that, free of the stain of miserliness, etc., rejoices in merit whether given or not given by others is called rejoicing in good fortune.[132]
>
> (Wijeratne and Gethin 2002, 186; Abhidh-s-mhṭ 135f.)

Various interpretations of giving merit are found in secondary literature: Agasse (1978, 320) concludes, mainly on the basis of the stories in the Dhammapada-aṭṭakathā, that *pattidāna* always takes place in the presence of the being or beings (visible or invisible) for whose benefit it is meant, and implies that *pattidāna* can only take place together with *pattānumodanā*, or at least with the knowledge of the beneficiary (Dhp-a IV 18). This, of course, would make the concept of giving merit to all beings problematic unless it is implied that 'all beings' is to be understood as 'all beings who are present and who consent'. Malalasekera (1967, 85f.) on the other hand, says about *pattidāna*:

> The doer of the good deed has merely to wish that the merit he thereby gained should accrue to someone in particular, if he so wishes, or to all beings. The wish may be purely mental or it may be accompanied by an expression in words. This could be done with or without the particular beneficiary being aware of it.

This would bring the concept of *pattidāna* very close to the concept of well-wishing (*prārthanāva*) and might reflect a modern Sri Lankan interpretation, rather than the Abhidhamma one. With his next statement that '*anumodanā* can take place with or without the knowledge of the doer of the meritorious act' he is again completely in line with the Abhidhamma interpretation. As we just saw, the definition of *pattānumodanā* in the commentary of the Abhidhammatthasaṅgaha was that rejoicing in merit can take place even if it is not 'given' (*adinna*). Accordingly the practice of reciting a verse or formula on the occasion of a giving of merit is interpreted in modern Sri Lanka not as actual offering of merit but as an act merely meant to draw attention to the merit. There is, however, the problem of how this 'modern' position (and the Abhidhamma explanation) can be reconciled with the Bimbisāra story (and in fact the rest of the Petavatthu stories), which explicitly required the act of offering to the *petas*.

The key seems to lie in the fact that in most of the Tirokuḍḍapetavatthu (and Tirokuḍḍasutta including its commentary) the offerings to the dead were actual food, etc. On the other hand we find that in the other stories of the Petavatthu the possibility of handing over food, etc., directly to the *petas* is explicitly denied and giving of merit has replaced the food offerings. The *petas* still had to wait until the merit is actually offered, just as in the case of actual food, etc. (Tirokuḍḍapetavatthu), but the giving of merit, being a mental act, was more open to various interpretations. In some of the cases discussed above (see Dhp-a II 1; IV 200, etc.), the giving of merit was still reminiscent of a material exchange of goods, the connotation of 'handing over or exchanging merit' is still tangible. The 'royal exchange of merit' in the eighteenth century indicates either a return to this mentality, or it might be taken as evidence that merit never really lost its commodity character totally. Other stories (Dhp-a IV 18, 122; Vv-a 188) emphasise the aspect of merit as a 'spiritual gift' to be appreciated, and eventually *anumodanā* in the (technical) Abhidhamma interpretation came to be the *conditio sine qua non* for the successful giving of merit.[133]

Gombrich (1991, 277ff.) postulates that the term *anumodanā* has actually undergone a shift in meaning from 'thank' to 'rejoice'. This seems to me somewhat contrived for various reasons: first, the Sanskrit root *mud* only means 'be merry or glad or happy, rejoice' (see MW) and it seems rather unlikely that in Pāli the original meaning was 'thank' which was, due to doctrinal problems, later interpreted 'rejoice'. Second, the distinction between 'to thank' and 'to rejoice' seems rather artificial in the Indian context. The natural way to express gratefulness in Sri Lanka or the Indian subcontinent is by body language (smiling, shaking of the head, etc.) conveying joyfulness rather than shaking hands and saying 'Thank you!'[134] And thirdly, Gombrich bases his argument on the assumption that one can only 'thank' if something material has been handed over, but 'rejoice' in the case of a mental act, which seems unconvincing.

Schmithausen (1986, 214) does not seem to support the theory that a radical reinterpretation of the concept of giving merit took place in early Buddhism. On the contrary, he shows that on the more popular level of religions different strata can coexist without 'a need for complete systematical consistency'. He continues:

> In popular religious practice and doctrine the notion of individual responsibility and the notion of merit transference could thus be alternatively emphasized according to the situation, without any conflict being felt.

He further states that even on a more dogmatic and philosophical level there was no attempt made in Buddhism to actually put a stop to the practice of giving merit, in the way it was done in Jainism.

To sum up, the giving of merit seems to have posed certain doctrinal problems (as can be seen at Kv 347–49), in that it contradicted the individual responsibility. The Abhidhamma solution to the problem of individual responsibility was to reinterpret the giving of merit as a two-way mental process and at the same time shift the emphasis from the act of giving to the act of rejoicing, which is karmically a positive mental attitude. It is no longer the giving away of merit that improves the situation of the recipient but his/her positive mental attitude, the rejoicing (*anumodanā*) in a meritorious act performed by someone else, which brings about the karmic changes. In fact one might argue that the expression 'transference of merit' is misleading for the Abhidhamma interpretation as a two-way mental process. It has to be borne in mind, however, that the material looked at here (with the exception of the late, but canonical example of Vv-a 188, and possibly Dhp-a IV 18) does not provide evidence that the success of the giving of merit solely depended on the recipient's reaction of *anumodanā*; in fact in most cases it is mentioned not at all or only in passing.[135]

Inscriptions

The aim of this section is to introduce the relevant (Sri Lankan) epigraphical material, which is often overlooked or neglected in the discussion of giving merit. This material is treated separately for various reasons: first, it differs greatly in content and style from the literary Pāli sources. Second, I have to rely entirely on secondary literature since a detailed investigation into the inscriptions would go beyond my expertise. Thirdly, the donations documented in the inscriptions are mainly objects of worship (*stūpas*, images, caves, etc.) and by nature very different from a meal or utensils given to the *saṃgha* which makes comparison with contemporary Sri Lankan practice problematic.

Schopen's extensive research based on epigraphical material provides us with interesting information regarding ancient Buddhist practice.[136] One of the practices documented in the inscriptions is the giving of merit to (deceased) parents and to a specific individual or even all beings or a combination of both.

Schopen (1997, 38–39) distinguishes between Hīnayāna and Māhāyāna inscriptions and demonstrates certain patterns: the beneficiaries in 'Hīnayāna inscriptions' range from individuals and parents to all beings and the goals are either not specified or intended to grant health, long life or even Nirvāṇa to an individual. 'Mahāyāna inscriptions' on the other hand nearly always mention all beings as beneficiary first and might then go on to name an individual and the specific goal is supreme knowledge (*anuttarajñāna*). It should be noted, though, that his basis for classifying an inscription as Hīnayāna seems to be the mention of a Hīnayāna school (Mahāsāṃghikas, Sarvāstivādins, etc.) in the inscription itself. However, these names, as Bechert (1976a, 36) rightly points out, refer to an ordination lineage and do not necessarily provide any information about the doctrinal inclination. Of interest to us are, in particular, two Ceylonese inscriptions. Paranavitana (1970, 3 and 27) places the first one (dedicating merit to parents) around 210–200 B.C. and the second one (dedicating merit to all beings) possibly even slightly earlier.[137]

To the departed

In the first inscription the merit resulting from the donation of a cave is given to parents:

> The cave of princess (Abi)Tissā, daughter of the great king Gāmaṇī-Uttiya, is given to the Saṅgha of the ten directions, for the benefit of the mother and the father.[138]
>
> (Paranavitana 1970, 3. Nr. 34 (1))

It is not mentioned in this inscription if the parents are deceased or still alive, but this might be of little importance, as far as the giving of merit is concerned. Schopen points out that the objects mentioned in the inscriptions are mostly used for worship and in providing them the donors provide countless opportunities for generations of people to generate merit, which would thereby again increase the 'original merit' that was given (in this case to the parents). So unlike a *matakadānaya*, which is usually repeated in certain intervals for the deceased, the donation of an object of worship, such as a *stūpa*, etc., once given, continues, as long as it lasts or is 'in use', to produce merit on behalf of the beneficiary. Schopen (1997, 67) concludes:

> And it was no small matter to transfer such an act to the donor's parents. By doing so, the donor denied to himself but provided for his parents a source of merit, which would continue and be maintained long after the donor himself was dead. This, it would seem, is true filial piety.

Even though this intriguing idea seems difficult to prove, it does not appear to be entirely implausible. In the light of the Indian love for numerical evaluations and 'quantitative determination of the result of religious acts'[139] it is quite possible that in giving objects of worship the resulting merit was considered as increasing with the repeated use of the object, or even to multiply. On the other hand, there does not seem to be any conclusive evidence that the people involved in these activities indeed held such a specific belief, and did not simply have the vague notion of giving something longer-lasting and more substantial than, say, a meal for the monks, or the donation of robes to the *saṃgha*.

To all beings

The second inscription mentioned above is actually a set of four identical inscriptions, recording the giving of merit to all beings:

> Princess (Abi)Anurādhi, daughter of king Nāga and wife of king Uttiya, and king Uttiya, caused this cave to be established, for the Saṅgha of the four quarters, as comfortable abode of all that are come, and for the welfare and happiness of beings in the boundless universe.[140]
>
> (Paranavitana 1970, 27. Nr. 338 (–341))

The fact that the giving of merit to all beings is documented for such an early date in Sri Lanka seems significant. Schopen (1997, 68) further quotes a number of Indian 'Hīnayāna inscriptions' where a donation is given for the benefit of all beings.[141] These inscriptions are particularly important, since the textual evidence for this practice is not strong.[142]

It is impossible to judge exactly how widespread and popular the practice of giving merit to all beings was. Cousins (2003, 20) says:

> Moreover, the emphasis on all beings is already there in the Kuṣāṇa version of the formula. While we might expect such a development to be attractive to Mahāyānists, it may long precede the formation of anything distinctively Mahāyānist.

Schopen (1997, 252) shows (based on epigraphical material (though not Ceylonese)) that monks and nuns, too, were involved in the practice of giving merit (mostly for the benefit of their parents):

> The actual monk, unlike the textual monk, appears to have been deeply involved in religious giving and cult practice of every kind from the very beginning. He is preoccupied not with *nirvāṇa* but above all else with what appears to have been a strongly felt obligation to his parents, whether living or dead. He is concerned as well, for example, with the health of his companions and teachers. He appears, in short, as very human and very vulnerable.

However, Schmithausen (1986, n. 95) has already pointed out that there are hints already in the Pāli literature (Pv II.2; III.2) as to the involvement of monks in the practice of giving merit, which makes the dichotomy between 'actual' and 'textual' monk appear rather false.

Proposed origins of the notion of giving of merit

Various scholars have in the course of the last thirty or so years developed different theories regarding the origin of the practice of giving merit. Their investigations are based on more or less the same set of passages from the Nikāyas and commentaries (and partly inscriptions) that has been introduced here. Some of these theories shall be briefly summarized.

Brahmanical ritual for the dead (śrāddha). The most popular theory is probably that the practice of the giving of merit has its origin in the brahmanical ritual for the dead (*śrāddha*).[143] Already in the canon itself (at A V 269ff.) a connection is made between the brahmanical *śrāddha* ritual and the offerings of food, etc., for the dead in the Buddhist context. However, it is still one step to go from offerings of actual food to giving merit, and second, the question remains, if this is where the origin of the giving of merit lies and how other instances of this practice fit in.

Holt goes into great detail to point out the parallels between the brahmanical *śrāddha* ritual and the Buddhist practice of *dāna* and subsequent giving of merit. Holt (1981, 10) states that 'ethical action has replaced ritual technique' and demonstrates how the Buddhist monks replaced the brahmins in their ritual function. This fact has been pointed out by various scholars, but Holt (1981, 19f.) takes this one step further in claiming that the monks took on the function of the ancestors (*pitaras*) as well. However, Holt's topic is not giving merit in general, but 'assisting the dead'. He therefore concentrates on the brahmanical *śrāddha* ritual and its 'Buddhist transformation' (mainly relying on the Petavatthu) without referring to other instances of this practice, such as giving merit to gods.

Malalasekera (1967, 87) relates the story of Bimbisāra as the 'classic example' of giving merit and calls the Tirokuḍḍa Sutta the 'counterpart of the Hindu custom . . . (generally called *śrāddha*)'. His suggestion on the following page that the practice of giving of merit to gods somehow followed from this, however, remains very vague:

> As time went on, this transference of merit was extended in various ways. One of the most interesting of these developments is its introduction into the worship of *devas* or superhuman beings.

Gombrich (1971, 206) agrees with Malalasekera at least on two points: the giving of merit originated in the *śrāddha* ritual for the dead, and this practice was later extended to the *devas*. His argument is based on Buddhaghosa's commentary to the Mahāparinibbānasutta (D II 88) where *dakkhiṇā* is being offered to the local gods. Buddhaghosa not only glosses *dakkhiṇā* (at Sv II 542) as merit (*patti*), but according to Gombrich (1991, 267),

> significantly continues: '"When worshipped they worship": they think, "These people are not even our relatives, and even so they give us the merit."'

Gombrich then continues:

> Though the commentator is much later than the text, I think he is right about the implied origin of merit transference. We come here to a complex of ideas centring on those funeral feasts for dead relatives, which are common to so many cultures.

The main problem with this position seems to be that one would like to find more evidence than a single passage from a later commentary (Sv II 542), to establish that the giving of merit to the departed was indeed the origin of the practice of giving merit in general and that the giving of merit to the gods is secondary to or even derived from it.

Mahāyāna influence. Bechert (1992, 43), too, sees a problem with explaining the notion of giving merit as solely originating from offerings to the dead ('Totenopfer'). He proposes instead that the Mahāyāna concept of giving merit to all beings was, at least partly, responsible as well. To summarize briefly his position, which is not always clear to me, he argues that on the one hand the possibility of giving merit is explicitly denied in the Kathāvatthu, on the other hand the (later) Buddhāpadāna contains both the concept of giving merit to all beings as well as the notion of buddhafields (*buddhakṣetra*). This would, according to Bechert (1992, 102), qualify the Buddhāpadāna, which was accepted by the Mahāvihāra tradition as canonical, as a 'full-fledged Mahāyāna text'. He then attempts to date the influx of Mahāyāna ideas (such as giving merit) into the tradition of the Mahāvihāra between the second century B.C. (after the strict orthodoxy of the Kathāvatthu relaxed) and the third century A.D. (when according to the Sinhalese chronicle, the Mahāvaṃsa, any trace of Mahāyāna was suppressed). To sum this up, Bechert seems to want to trace the origin of the concept of giving merit in the Theravāda Buddhism of Sri Lanka back to certain Mahāyānistic tendencies in the Mahāvihāra tradition, which found their expression in the Buddhāpadāna, which was, according to Bechert, composed in the first or beginning of the second century A.D. It is not quite clear why he sees the need to introduce Mahāyāna concepts at all to explain the origin of giving merit, after quoting *nikāya* passages to show its early presence. Furthermore, his textual ground for attributing the concept of giving merit in Theravāda Buddhism to the influx of Mahāyānistic tendencies seems to be one single Buddhāpadāna passage.

Schopen's (1997, 43) criticism points in a similar direction:

> If then, in the end, Bechert wants the doctrine of the transference of merit to be a 'Mahāyāna idea' in the Theravāda Buddhism of Ceylon, there appear to be only two problems. The first is that this ignores the early and massive presence of the doctrine in Hīnayāna inscriptions. The second is that he does not give us the means by which we could know where what he presents as the 'Mahāyāna idea' of the transference of merit actually comes from. His references are always in the form 'in den Mahāyāna-Texten,' but those texts are never cited nor are we ever given specific references. Moreover, the implication here is that there is a single, unified, and unchanging conception of the 'idea' in Mahāyāna texts.

Schopen, on the other hand, is adamant that epigraphical evidence (mention of Hīnayāna schools in inscriptions) shows the giving of merit to be a popular practice of the Hīnayāna.

Inclusivism. Attempts to single out one of the above-mentioned contexts (gods, departed, all beings) as the original context or prototype, from which the others somehow followed, are not convincing. Schmithausen, on the other hand, refrains from such attempts and points to the broader principle of inclusivism. The inclusivist nature of Buddhism can be demonstrated not only for the case of Sri Lanka but for other countries as well (Tibet, Japan, etc.). Schmithausen (1986, 213) points out that giving of merit in Buddhism was:

> developed, or somehow adapted from Hinduism, in the context of integrating, into a framework of the karma doctrine, such deep-rooted popular practices as presenting gifts to protective deities or for the benefit of deceased relatives.

Buddhist monks not only replaced the Brahmins in their ritual function as mediators (see above) but actively participated and took a leading role in the practice of giving merit. This seems a much more convincing working hypothesis because it is broad enough to include various contexts for the giving of merit (such as *petas*, gods, etc.) found in the canonical and post-canonical Pāli texts.

To go one step further, one might suggest that there are cross-cultural (even though not universal)[144] needs that independently find similar expressions in different religions. One such need might be to give something to one's departed relatives (especially one's parents) as a token of gratitude or out of a feeling of obligation.

CONCLUSIONS

In Part I we have seen that every effort is made to ensure that the time of death is not disturbed by negative feelings, particularly greed and hatred (to avoid rebirth as hungry ghost (*prēta*) or animal, etc.). With the help of flowers, images of a *stūpa*, or chanting of protective Suttas (*pirit*), relatives try to direct the attention of the dying person towards the Buddha, Dharma, or meritorious deeds.

The concept of good death and bad death is found in the Pāli material as well. We find Suttas describing how a particular rebirth may be achieved by cultivation of an earnest wish, and the commentaries contain a wealth of stories relating how a good person was reborn in a bad existence (and vice versa) due to the quality of his last conscious moments. These stories serve a dual purpose: a warning to evil-doers as well as encouragement to keep striving till the end. In the Abhidhamma we find the attempt to reconcile the concept that the last conscious moments of one's life are crucial in determining the next rebirth with the law of *karma*.

The idea of making a conscious wish for a particular form of rebirth has a precedent in the Upaniṣads and Brāhmaṇas, where we find that 'rebirth according to one's wish' (*kāmacāra*) was a goal people aspired to. This concept experienced a revival in the Mahāyāna and is still tangible in modern practice.

In Part II the actual practices surrounding the disposal of the body were investigated. The presence of the spirit of the deceased is tangible in a number of customs in modern Sri Lanka and interviews confirmed that the belief in an intermediate state was widespread despite the Theravāda doctrine of instantaneous rebirth. The relationship with the spirit of the deceased (*malagiyaprāṇakārayā*) is ambivalent: it is sometimes prevented from returning; other times it is invited back to the house for food, drink and merit. The actual funeral (which can be a burial or cremation) is devoid of elaborate ritual. The offering of a white piece of cloth (*mataka-vastra*) to the monks, the chanting and the speeches follow a fixed pattern, which is the same for monastic and non-monastic funerals.

Apart from the description of the most famous Buddhist funeral, the cremation of the Buddha, which is found in the Mahāparinibbāna Sutta, and a few other rather high profile cremations, we find very little in the suttas. Some few details of cremations of ordinary people can be gleaned from the commentaries. It is possible that taking the bodies to a charnel ground was the common way to dispose of the dead at the time of the Buddha and that cremations were reserved for special groups of society (e.g., Brahmins).

The Vedic ritual assumes cremation, but the basic stages of preparation of the body, the mourners, the procession, the lighting of the pyre and purificatory rituals read like a more elaborate version of the modern practice, with one important difference: the Sri Lankan Buddhist ritual has totally disposed of animal sacrifices in the funeral context. But the underlying motifs of keeping the spirit of the dead from returning as well as the need to provide food and utensils for the spirit are all there.

The archaeological material indicates that Buddhist sites in India show a certain pattern: clusters of small *stūpas* surrounding a large *stūpa*, which is associated with the presence of a Buddha. Schopen has interpreted the pattern as 'burial *ad sanctos*' and concludes on the basis of inscriptions that monks and lay people alike were involved in this popular practice. This might be an indication that cremation had become the predominant form of disposal of the dead in India.

In Part III two main ceremonies featured. At the sixth day *baṇa* a personal food offering is performed for the spirit of the deceased, which is 'supplemented' by merit at the end of the monk's sermon. At the seventh day *dānaya*, emphasis has shifted to the offering of merit to the deceased and only scraps of food are offered in the garden for the hungry ghosts or the crows (to supplement the merit?). The pattern for this, as well as the following *matakadānas* (after three months, one year, etc.), is very fixed and goes back to the Bimbisāra story (Petavatthu). There is also an element of ritual efficacy as the monks serve as mediators receiving food and other material goods on behalf of the deceased. The accruing merit then transforms back into the equivalent goods in the world of the hungry ghosts/ancestors.

The inquiry into the historic background showed that giving of merit goes back to the Nikāyas and it is not confined to the funeral context at all. Merit serves in some contexts rather like a currency; in other contexts it seems to assume the joyful consent of the recipient. The giving of merit to gods, deceased, and everyone present takes place at the end of every meritorious activity in Sri Lanka. Some scholars attempted to identify a particular one of these contexts (gods, deceased, all beings) as the original context for the giving of merit, but it seems more plausible to assume that a broader principle (inclusivism) is at work here.

The material presented in the ethnographic sections ('A Laywoman's Burial', etc., and 'A Monk's Cremation', etc.) is meant to provide examples.

Additional material including transcripts and translations related to a set of ceremonies ('A Laywoman's Burial', 'A Laywoman's *baṇa*', 'A Laywoman's *dānaya*') as well as photographs, etc., is available on the website of the Department of Theology and Religious Studies at the University of Bristol (*http://www.bris.ac.uk/thrs/*); follow the link to Centre for Buddhist Studies.

Brief outline of conclusions: The concept that the last conscious moments of one's life determine the quality of one's rebirth is both old and resilient and sometimes takes the form of an earnest wish on the death bed. There is some evidence (e.g., Mahākammavibhaṅga Sutta) that this concept was seen as conflicting with or contradicting the laws of *karma*. The Abhidhamma attempts to reconcile the two and discusses extensively the hierarchy of *kammas* (i.e., which *kamma* takes precedence) at the time of death. However, the very idea that the frame of mind at the time of death directly influences the next rebirth takes away some of the rigor of karmic retribution and accommodates people's deep-felt wish to help a dying relative. This might be the key to the longevity and popularity of the concept.

A comparison of the Vedic and contemporary Sri Lankan funeral rites shows that in fact surprisingly little change has taken place on a practical level even though changes on the doctrinal level are considerable. Now, as then, a recurring motif is the fear of and for the spirit of the deceased. This manifests itself in a number of customs during the first seven days, despite the Theravāda doctrine of instantaneous rebirth. This suggests a certain reluctance to let go of a custom or ritual in the death context.

Hacker coined the term *inclusivism* to describe the appropriation of existing customs into a new system (in this case Buddhism) by way of subordination. The alms givings on behalf of the deceased (*matakadānaya*) and the subsequent giving of merit are a prime example. The existing brahmanical custom of providing the deceased with food and utensils was adapted so that the emphasis shifted to offering merit. However, giving merit did not simply replace the material offerings to the ancestors and deities, but both types of offering coexist and complement each other depending on the context.

In the Hindu ritual the transformation from ghost to ancestor becomes manifest in a change of name: the newly dead spirit (*preta*) is transformed into a proper ancestor (*pitṛ*). In Sri Lankan Buddhism the situation is somewhat more complex. The Sinhala term *prēta* seems to have lost the connotations 'dead' (Skt *preta*) or 'ancestor' (Skt *pitṛ*) and refers solely to a particular type of *gati*, the hungry ghosts (Pāli *peta*). However, there is little doubt that ancestor worship is alive in Sri Lanka, even though it might not find linguistic expression, and the ancestors do not feature as a distinct group in the Sinhala cosmological system. The *matakadānas* are held in honour of and for the benefit of a specific relative, and the doctrinal explanation that in fact only ghosts or gods (*prētas* or *devas*) can benefit from the given merit does not alter that fact.

CONCLUSIONS

It is generally accepted that exploring the historical roots of contemporary practice is conducive to a better understanding of it. I would like to propose that the reverse is true. Acquainting oneself with contemporary Buddhist culture and practice can only enhance one's understanding of the texts. Of course great care has to be taken to avoid unfounded assumptions about the past on the basis of contemporary practices. However, by looking at past and present, textual and epigraphical sources as complementing each other, one gains a richer and more colourful picture of both present and past.

NOTES

INTRODUCTION

1 Primarily the Pāli canon and its commentaries. Cf also Collins (1998, 40–89) who, reflecting on the inside and outside of texts, has coined the term 'Pali imaginaire'.
2 Bechert 1978, 6.
3 I refer the interested reader of Sinhala to a dissertation by Sandhya Piyaruvan Kahandagamage (Colombo University 1998), which has an extensive bibliography. I am very grateful to her for letting me photocopy her dissertation. See also Senaratne 2000 and Siripala 1997.
4 Norman 1983, 9. And Collins (1990, 102) points out 'the text oriented self definition' of the Mahāvihārin lineage.
5 Cf. Obeyesekere and Gombrich 1988, 202–40.
6 The figures one finds in different books vary little if at all. Barlas and Wanasundera (1992, 24) seem to give slightly more differentiated figures: 74% Sinhalese; 18.1% Tamil (out of which 12.6% Jaffna Tamils; 5.5% Indian Tamils); 7.1% Muslims; 0.2% Burghers; the rest are Veddhas, Malays, Parsis and Europeans.
7 As to the history of the Nikāyas in Sri Lanka see Gombrich 1991, 40 and 359.
8 See also Disanayaka 1998, 95–114.
9 My then two-year-old son and husband joined me for the field trip. Having a child in the local nursery made integration into village life very easy.
10 The problem of translating certain terms or concepts into English made it necessary to frequently double check Sinhala terminology underlying an English term or word in order to avoid misunderstandings.
11 As far as I know there is no Sinhala term or equivalent for 'last rites' other than *avasāna kaṭayutu* ('last duties') which is sometimes used in a non-technical sense.
12 Ven. D, a Sri Lankan monk resident in Berlin, had flown in to help organise the cremation and follow-up events for his departed teacher. As his German was by far superior to my Sinhalese it seemed the natural choice of interview language.
13 I did not conduct interviews with terminally ill, dying, or recently bereaved people. I do not think it generally unethical to do so, provided the interviews are conducted in a sensitive manner, but it did not seem essential to my research topic.
14 Gombrich 1991, 286f.

I DEATH AND DYING

1 A *bodhipūjā* is essentially paying respects to the Bodhi-tree (involving pouring a libation of water seven times and circumambulation of the tree), which is sometimes followed by pacificatory rituals for the planets (*navagrahapūjā*).

2 The latter is documented for mediaeval Ceylon by Ariyapala 1968, 360.
3 Mahāvaṃsa XXXII. 25ff. Walpola Rahula 1966, 254 mentions this custom and adds, 'There is no reference to suggest that any *bhikkhu* had a "Merit-Book". Monks were interested in their spiritual development, and there was no way of recording this in a book. The "Merit-Book", therefore, served no useful purpose for monks while it was a valuable treasure for laymen.' See also Tillakaratne 1986, 161.
4 Cf. Tillakaratne 1986, 161: 'This was considered an important rite. In fact a common form of curse among the Sinhalese is, "may there be no person near you to put a little water into your mouth in the hour of death".'
5 See Dubois 1906, 482 and Firth 1997, 66.
6 Forbes (1840, I 334) mentions the custom of turning the bed of a dying person in the East-West direction (head to the East), but none of my informants mentioned this.
7 Here the term *jīvadāna* is used as a technical term referring to a *dāna* given by or on behalf of someone still alive, as opposed to a *matakadānaya* which is given on behalf of the dead. See also Gombrich 1991, 268 and n. 24.
8 This is, of course, Abhidhamma terminology and will be discussed in more detail in the context of Pāli material relating to the moment of death.
9 See also Maithrimurthi 1986, 40 and 53, on releasing animals.
10 See Schmithausen 1985, n. 119.
11 Ven. Wetara Mahinda, oral communication. None of my informants used the term *jīvadāna* in that meaning.
12 von Rospatt, oral communication.
13 Cf. A V 342, Vism IX 75 (PTS ed., p. 314).
14 MV chapter XXXII. The monk passed over the detail that, according to the Mahāvaṃsa story, the king was told by Arahats that he had in fact only killed one and a half human beings. See Geiger 1950, 178 and Bretfeld 2001, 125.
15 The term *gilaṃpasa* (Pāli: *gilānapaccaya*, 'support or help for the sick' (PED) or in its full form *gilāna-paccaya-bhesajja-parikkhāra*) refers to one of the four main requisites of a monk, the others being *cīvara* (robe), *piṇḍapāta* (alms bowl), and *senāsana* (lodging). The usage of the Sinhala term *gilaṃpasa*, however, is more general in the sense of *dāna* given in the evening to the Buddha or monks which usually consists of soft drinks which are permitted after midday.
16 See also Rastrapal 2000.
17 Unfortunately I was unable to locate this story.
18 M II 97ff. This example seems somewhat ill-chosen as illustration of a good death moment, as Aṅgulimāla became an *arahat* during his lifetime and so did not take rebirth after he died.
19 See also the Cūḷakammavibhaṅga Sutta (M III 202–207) and the Mahākammavibhaṅga Sutta (M III 207–215).
20 The technical Abhidhamma term for any *kamma* that does not come to fruition (because it is too 'weak' for example) is *ahosi-kamma*, and one informant actually used the term in this context. It is not quite clear to me why Gombrich (1991, pp. 253, and 300) claims that the example of King Duṭṭhagāmaṇi is the only case of *ahosi-kamma* besides those related of *arahats*. See also Bhikkhu Bodhi 1993, 205.
21 The interview was conducted in English and when I asked her to repeat this sentence in Sinhala she replied, '*Märena velāvedi apiṭa hoňda sitivili pahala venna kiyalā api hämadāma prārthanā karanavā*.'
22 According to Wirz (1941, 203), who confirms this hierarchy, *prētas* follow certain powerful *yakṣas*, and their leader, Aimāna, is in fact both *prēta* and *yakā* at the same time.

23 Furthermore, he mentions yet another category, that of *holman*, which I did not come across in my interviews other than as the verb *holman karanavā* ('to haunt', i.e., a person or a house). Wijesekera (1949, 202, n. 1) defines *holman* as 'haunting, unseen appearances, unusual sounds, weird noises'.
24 A *prētayā* (Sinhala) is not the same as Skt *preta* (or *pitṛ*) or Pāli *peta.*
25 According to MW, the *pitaras* (plural of *pitṛ* (m.)) are 'fathers, forefathers, ancestors, esp. the Pitṛis or deceased ancestors' (see MW s.vv. *preta, pitṛ*).
26 s.v. *prēta*: ghost, goblin, sprite, an evil being especially animating the carcasses of the dead; manes of the deceased ancestors, dead, extinct, expired; disembodied.
27 See also Langer 2005.
28 In the stories of the *Petavatthu* they might have further unpleasant, physical attributes (such as foul-smelling breath) due to certain deeds or behaviour (such as bad or malicious speech) which led to their present state.
29 See Tambiah 1970.
30 See also Wirz 1941, 201.
31 Wirz 1941, 204; Terwiel 1994, 236.
32 Dickson (1884, 232) mentions the custom of calling a monk to the deathbed to chant *pirit* and distinguishes it from the *jīvadāna* in that there is no mention of offerings or gifts to the monks in the context of the former.
33 For *pirit* thread see Gombrich 1991, 240, referring to J I 399; for *pirit* water see Rahula 1966, 277, referring to Sn-a 204f. A story in the Mahāvaṃsa (VII 8 and 9) relates how on his deathbed the Buddha orders the god Sakka to go to the island of Lanka and protect Vijaya who is just arriving there. Sakka hands Vijaya a vessel with water and some string (to wear around the hand) for protection. Even though the water and the string are not actually said to have been chanted over by the Buddha, it is nevertheless clear from the context that some connection is made between the Buddha and the two items. Cf. Geiger, 1908, 62f.
34 M II 98ff.
35 Schmithausen (1997, 45 n. 95) defines *satyakiriyā* in the context of *mettā* as follows: 'I.e., if the efficacy of the declaration of (unbroken) friendship or friendliness is (also) due to the fact that it 1. formulates a truth which is unverifiable by ordinary means of knowledge (Thieme 1952, 109), 2. concerns the person who announces the declaration and his/her fundamental duties or qualities . . . and 3. is closely connected with the effect aimed at (Hacker 1959, 97)'. Cf. Also Maithrimurthi 1999, Index sv 'Wahrheitsmagie'.
36 Cf. also: Kariyawasam 1995, 33.
37 I am grateful to Dr. Mürmel (University of Leipzig) who pointed out to me that the term magic is somewhat problematic since Frazer (*The Golden Bough*) defined the term 'magic' as opposed to 'religion'. As this usage is not intended here, I take up Dr. Mürmel's suggestion to speak of 'ritual efficacy' rather than 'magic quality' of truth utterance and *pirit* chanting. See also Spiro 1982 chapter 6 who calls this the apotropaic aspect.
38 But see also Pj I 232ff. (*Illustrator of Ultimate Meaning* 266ff.) where the Buddha teaches a group of monks the Metta Sutta so they won't be disturbed by earth *devas.*
39 Lokuliyana (1993, xv) suggests that these *suttas* are used successfully for healing. See also de Silva 1993, p. 31.
40 See Strong 1995, 234ff.
41 Gombrich 1990, 5–20 (p. 11): '[S]ome of my colleagues are finding inconsistencies in the canonical texts which they assert to be such without telling us how the Buddhist tradition itself regards the texts as consistent—as if they were not important.'

42 None of my informants named Nirvāṇa as the immediate goal or aim. Cf. also Gombrich 1991, 338.
43 See Dhp-a II 235 (*Āyuvaḍḍhanakumāravatthu*) where a little boy, who was promised to a *yakkhinī* as a boon, was saved by the Buddha and a group of monks by seven days of *paritta* chanting. The threat to the boy's life was posed by non-human beings and it is not mentioned that the chanting would have protected the boy from other threats to his life, such as accidents.
44 The interpretation of this Aśokan edict was questioned by Norman (1975, 16–24) who claims that capital punishment had been abolished and that this edict speaks of 'beating' or 'striking'. I would, however, agree with Guruge, that this edict indeed deals with capital punishment. For the text of pillar edict IV see Janert 1972, 133.
45 Cf. also Vibh-a 159.
46 M. Maithrimurthi (oral communication).
47 While I managed to locate a number of other stories quoted by Aggacitta Bhikkhu in the Dhammapada-aṭṭhakathā, I did not succeed with this one.
48 W.Y. Evans-Wentz who produced the first translation into English in 1927 was often criticised for his choice of title, 'The Tibetan Book of the Dead', which is regarded as somewhat ill-suited and misleading.
49 Sogyal Rinpoche 1992, chapter VII.
50 None of my Sri Lankan informants talked about 'changing' *kamma*, nor is this concept found in the Visuddhimagga.
51 Cf. also Cohen 1976, 317–327.
52 Cf. also Stevenson 1995, 592–602.
53 For an overview of various other beliefs and religions, see Edgerton 1927, 219–249.
54 For the interaction between future parents and the being to be conceived, see also BĀU 6.4.1–22, AKBh III.15, and Doniger O'Flaherty 1980, 34.
55 For the older Sanskrit material found in the Vedic texts, I rely mainly on secondary sources.
56 Halbfass 1980, 268.
57 See also Frauwallner 1926, 134.
58 Edgerton 1927, 223; Frauwallner 1953, 65 and n. 23; Horsch 1971, 131; Schmithausen 1995, 70, and nn. 130–32.
59 Caland (1896, 166), however, questions the validity of passages like ṚV X.18, 10–13, which had been taken as proof for burials in Vedic time, but claims to have found 'traces' of the custom of burial in ritual texts.
60 Obeyesekere 1980, 140. Cf. also v. Fürer-Haimendorf 1953.
61 Horsch (1971, 107) suspects that this question ultimately led to the concept of the two paths.
62 O'Flaherty 1980, 3; Halbfass 1980, 269.
63 Cf. Maitrāyaṇī Saṃhitā 1.8.6.
64 JUB 3.28.4. In the course of time human existence itself became a place of retribution, which it had not been to start with (Vetter 1998, 22).
65 Schmithausen 1995, 60.
66 Cf. Bodewitz 2002, 11f.
67 ChU 3.13.7–8 and BĀU 5.9.
68 My brackets.
69 My brackets. Cf. also ChU 3.14.1 and BĀU 4.4.4.
70 To add to the confusion, Eggeling translates *dakṣa* in the second passage as 'will'.
71 In SāmavBr 3.8.1 (*atha yaḥ kāmayeta punar na pratyājāyeyam iti*) we read that even those who do not wish any rebirth are given a chant to achieve as they

wish. We are not told what happens to the ones who do not know either chant. Winternitz 1909, I 239 calls the Sāmavidhāna Brāhmaṇa a 'Zauberhandbuch' which, despite its name, belongs with the Sūtra literature.

72 As quoted in Horsch 1971, 144, n. 57. My brackets. The text of SāmavBr is unfortunately not available to me at present.

73 It looks as if *etam* is used with regard to the heavenly world (in contrast to *iha*), in the same way as *etad* and *atra* are contrasted in the sentence 5.

74 My brackets. JUB 3.28. Cf. also Fujii 1997.

75 See also GB 1.1.15.

76 Cf. also Horsch 1971, 144.

77 Olivelle 1998, 120 and 208.

78 Schmithausen 1995, 55.

79 Olivelle 1998, 120f. and 208f.

80 In ChU 3.14 the topic is the union of *ātman* and *brahman*, which comes about purely as the result of man's resolve (*kratu*).

81 Vibh 137; Vism 571. See also Wijeratne and Gethin (2002, 290). This might be secondary and caused by the need to integrate *karman*, as the word *bhava* does not lend itself naturally to this interpretation.

82 AKBh 333, 10.

83 Cf. Jurewicz (2000, 77–103), who goes much further in trying to establish a connection between Vedic cosmogony and the Buddha's teaching of the *pratītyasamutpāda* formula.

84 The term *punarbhava* does not appear to be found in the early and middle Vedic material.

85 There is, however, also evidence of another concept, where the sun is the heavenly world in the sense of a permanent place, and no mention is made of a Brahma world above. JUB I 17–18 and I 50. Cf. Bodewitz 1973, 54f. and 116.

86 Cf. BĀU 5.10.1.

87 Schmithausen 1995, 55.

88 *Cittaṃ hīne 'dhimuttaṃ* ('a mind which is inclined to or set on a low level') is given as alternative (Burmese) variant in the PTS edition. Cf. also a modern Sinhala edition (possibly influenced by the Burmese manuscripts), *Dīgha-Nikāyo: The First Book of the Suttanta-Pitaka* (Colombo: P.De. S. Manatunga Publications, 1954), p. 562, which reads *hīne 'dhimuttaṃ* and gives *hīne vimittaṃ* as an alternative reading. Buddhaghosa's commentary (Sv III 1045) does not clarify the situation either and *adhimuttaṃ* makes more sense not only in this context, but there are precedents in the Pāli texts for the confusion of the two terms (due to similarities between *-v-* and *-dh-* in the Sinhala and Burmese scripts). Cf. Maithrimurthi and Rospatt, 1998, 177, n. 21.

89 M I 289f, M III 99ff, S IV 302, S III 243, S III 244, S III 247, S III 248, S III 250, S III 251.

90 Possibly Saṅkhārupapatti; Vetter (2000, 45) suggests-*uppatti* derives from the commentary (*saṅkhārānaṃ yeva up*[*a*]*patti*), which seems to have taken the compound as a Tappurisa with a genitive relation in the first part, rather than instrumental, as would have been expected.

91 The same list of qualities is found in S V 369ff.: Mahānāma is worried that he might lose his concentration of mind on the way home from the temple. Now if, by accident, he were to be run over by a horse or ox cart, his dying moment would not be conducive to a better rebirth. This is interesting for two reasons: first, at the time of the compilation of this *sūtra* Kapilavastu was quite a busy town; second, the moment of death was a matter of genuine concern for people.

92 For this set of six Saṃyutta Suttas (two almost identical Suttas each for *nāgas*, *supaṇṇas*, and *gandhabbas*) I will add the chapter and paragraphs in brackets where they differ and where only one of the two are referred to in order to avoid confusion and facilitate the search.
93 Sinhala/Sanskrit: *prārthanāva* or *prārthanā* is very commonly used in Sri Lanka, especially at the end of merit-making activities.
94 The commentary Ps IV 146f explains mutual dependency of the five conditions (*saddhā*, *sīla*, *suta*, *cāga*, *paññā*) and *patthanā*.
95 There is an additional explanation given here in M III 100: 'These aspirations and this abiding of his, thus developed and cultivated, lead to his reappearance there.' It is interesting that *saṅkhāra* is used in the title and text of this *sutta* (Saṅkhāruppatti Sutta) as a quasi-synonym of *patthanā* (cf. also Bhikkhu Ñāṇamoli and Bhikkhu Bodhi 1995, 959 and n. 1132).
96 Chinese understands 'due to the purity of his *sīla*' (Schmithausen, oral communication).
97 We are not told precisely what one has to donate in order to be reborn, say, amongst the Tusita *devas*, but nevertheless, one gets the impression here that generosity is the entitlement, a currency with which to buy one's self a good rebirth in return.
98 Walshe (1995, 505 and n. 1117) likens the 'pure-minded aspiration' to 'a declaration of truth' (D III 259). A bit further on (D III 260), in the context of discussing the various gods, the formula is changed to 'effective through liberation from passion'. The term *vītarāga* is normally applied to people.
99 See also Collins 1982, 218–224 (vegetation imagery).
100 The concept of the Bodhisattva making a firm resolution and decisions regarding the time and place, etc., of his descent from Tusita is, of course, well known. Cf. also Mahāvastu I 1; Ja I 48; Lalithavistara (*adhyāya* 3).
101 Geiger 1921, xxxvii.
102 Cf. also the thirteenth major rock edict, in which Aśoka expresses his regret for killing 100,000 people in a military campaign.
103 Maithrimurthi 2005, 37 translates the last line as: 'so the unpitiful became pitiful face to face with death', to convey the two connotations of '*soka*': objective (that he is to be pitied) and the subjective (he himself feels pity).
104 Cf. Also Aggacitta Bhikkhu 1999, 1. Unfortunately, I was unable to find textual evidence for this story.
105 Geiger 1921, xxxvii.
106 For Pāli text see Geiger 1908, 264. Cf. also Mp II 213. See also Collins 1998, 355.
107 I am grateful to Dr Mürmel for drawing my attention to yet another version of the story in the Saddharmālaṅkāraya (translation in Reynolds 1970, 252ff). Unfortunately the book is not available to me at present.
108 At the conference 'Buddhism and Conflict in Sri Lanka' held at Bath Spa University College, 28–30 June 2002, a number of Sri Lankan and non-Sri Lankan scholars alluded to this story. For papers of the conference see *Journal of Buddhist Ethics*, Vol. 10 (2003) online (http://-jbe.gold.ac.uk/bath-conf.html) without pagination and Maithrimurthi 2005.
109 Cf. also Kulke 2000, 129 and 134, n. 65.
110 Paramatthadīpanī-anudīpanī (p. 153: Chaṭṭhasaṅgāyana CD-Rom Version 3). See Maithrimurthi 2005, 38ff.
111 There are other, unobservable acts of merit, such as the gladness or appreciation of good deeds. Expressions of the king's joy are frequent in chapter 32 (in verses 9, 16, 24, 25, 47, 56, for example).
112 Geiger 1912, 222. Mv 32.25.

113 At M II 184ff. Sāriputta employs a similar technique in counselling Dhanañjāni, a ruthless tax collector, on his death bed, but was later criticised by the Buddha for not guiding him beyond the Brahma world. See also de Silva 1993 for more examples of counselling the ill (A III 295ff, S v 344, etc.).

114 Gethin (2004, 12) makes a rather subtle point that when the monks spoke in praise of death, they did not realise their own underlying intention of wanting the monk to be dead (so the suffering would stop), which in itself is *akusala* and cannot occur at the same time as the *kusala dhamma* of compassion.

115 A Sri Lankan monk told me that monks are not allowed to 'preach' at the deathbed, only to 'chant'. So far I have not been able to find evidence in the Vinaya for any such rule, but it is possible that passages like Sp 464 might be the basis for such a statement.

116 See also Dhp-a I 25ff. which relates how dying with a joyful heart weighs more than meritorious deeds.

117 Pun with the two meanings of *aṭṭhi*, one being 'bones' (i.e., as object of meditation) and the other being 'kernel' (which would be what parrots live off).

118 Burlingame 1921, I 172. Dhp-a I 47f.

119 Dhp-a I 47f.

120 Dhp-a III 119f.

121 Dhp-a III 120. According to Aggacitta 1999, 67, her rebirth in Tusita heaven is due to her 'reserve *kamma*', as there was no opportunity for creating one of the other three types of *kamma* while in hell.

122 This is, of course, reminiscent of the story of Bhṛgu: the trees he cut in this world take revenge on him by chopping him up in the other world (ŚB 11.6.1). Cf also Schmithausen 1991, 97.

123 Cf. also Aggacitta 1999, 48–55. On the importance of confession see also the Sāmaññaphala Sutta (D I 85).

124 Cf. Also Aggacitta 1999, 43.

125 There are two alternative readings: *sarañjita* ('decorated with or full of arrows') and *śarajita* ('overpowered/conquered by arrows') which might be ambiguous enough to serve as a qualifier for both heaven and hell. Besides, both readings are confirmed by the Chinese parallels (Schmithausen, oral communication).

126 Maithrimurthi 2005, 36 draws attention to another interesting aspect of the story: '[the soldier is] more worried about being misled by his teachers and teachers' teachers in this way, than by being killed in battle and consequently going to hell'.

127 Cf. also S IV 310 (for elephant-warrior and cavalry warrior).

128 This is reminiscent of Doniger O'Flaherty's (1980, p. 13) above quoted definition of *karma* in the Purāṇas as a 'straw man . . . set up to be knocked down'.

129 Ps V 19.

130 M III 72 (for *sammādiṭṭhi* as opposite), and Vibh 392 (for *micchādiṭṭhi*). For a comprehensive study on views, see Fuller 2005.

131 The Chinese parallels understand 'instantly, like the bending and stretching of an arm he falls into *niraya*' (Schmithausen, oral communication).

132 My brackets. Cf. also It 12 and M III 163ff. (Bālapaṇḍita Sutta).

133 Cf. Mp V 83. See Maithrimurthi 1999, 63, for a discussion of the soteriological aspect of *mettā*.

134 Hare 1934, III 69ff. Cf. also A III 142.

135 See e.g., Collins 1998 and Southwold 1983.

136 See Gethin 1998, 215ff. and Collins 1982, 240ff. In this chapter, as in all questions regarding Abhidhamma, I am indebted to Rupert Gethin for his time and patience in explaining to me repeatedly what I should have understood from reading his articles.

137 Vism XIV 110–24, XVII 120–45, XX 43–5; As 266–87; Abhidh-av 49–59; Abhidh-s 17–21.
138 Gethin 1994, 20.
139 See also Collins 1982, 240ff.
140 Abhidh-s 15, 27; Abhidh-s-mhṭ 100, 144; cf. Gethin 1994, 23. The term 'concept' (*paññatti*) here refers to the objects of the form-sphere *jhānas* and the first and third formless attainments: the *bhavaṅga* of beings reborn in the Brahman world takes as its object the object they experienced during the attainment of *jhāna*.
141 King Duṭṭhagāmaṇi's last worship of the (almost) completed Mahāstūpa while on his deathbed might have been an attempt to prompt a *kammanimitta*.
142 See also Vism 549 [from one happy destiny to another].
143 Cf. also Vibh-a 159.
144 One might assume that it is best to avoid bringing objects that are particularly dear to the dying person to his attention so as not to trigger greed, but this is not stated anywhere.
145 One of my interviewees said the lack of a 'dying thought' due to a sudden death causes people to have to remain in an intermediate state for an unspecified time.
146 Cf Abhidh-k-bh (Pradhan, 477, 20–24), which gives three kinds of *kamma: guru, āsanna* and *abhyasta*.
147 Vibh-a 408 states that *kamma* done in dreams, even though it has results, is too weak to effect rebirth.
148 Gethin 1994, 24.

II THE FUNERAL

1 The occurrence of a death, be it at home or in hospital, makes people refer to a house as a 'funeral house' (*malagedara*) even before the coffin is brought back into the house from the undertakers or from the hospital. See Disanayaka 1998, 87f.
2 These 'posters' serve as sympathy messages and are sent by organizations and companies rather than private persons, thereby asserting a certain social status.
3 The metal chairs (in this case ca. 50–70) were provided by the 'funeral aid society' (*maraṇādhāra samitiya*), which is run by laymen and has a president and an accountant. Families who are members meet once a month at the local temple to pay a monthly fee of about RS 30 (30 pence). In return they receive a lump sum of RS 2000 (£20) to help cover the substantial costs of the funeral in case a family member dies.
4 Chewing betel seems very popular at funerals with laymen as well as monks. This is probably due to the fact that in the funeral house itself no food, snacks or biscuits can be offered until after the ceremony. In Sinhala there are two words for betel: when it is bought and consumed by laypeople it is called *bulat*, and when offered to monks, *dähät*. Presenting betel leaves is also a traditional way of inviting someone to carry out an honorary service.
5 The coffins in Sri Lanka are made of wood and designed in such a way that all four sides (lined with white cloth) fold out flat.
6 See Ariyapala 1968, 359.
7 The traditional (evening) funeral meal (*malabata*) is prepared outside (see below) and consists of four dishes: pumpkin, plantains, fried, dried fish and red lentils and is served on banana leaves.

8 Ven. Mahā Lao, Birmingham (personal communication) tells me that in Thailand at least four monks are required for the funeral rites. Maithrimurthi (oral communication) confirms that in Sri Lanka, too, four monks are normally required for a *sāṅghika* ceremony, but even one single *śrāmaṇera*, provided he is authorized by his superior, can act on behalf of the *saṃgha* and conduct ceremonies.

9 The funeral conductor is either a neighbour or a friend of the family, or the president or secretary of the 'funeral society'.

10 D II 157, D II 199, et al.

11 The first half of this verse is found in Pv 8, Pv-a 23, but also in the commentary to other stories of the Petavatthu.

12 The order of the two verses is reversed compared to the Tirokuḍḍapetavatthu (Pv 4, verses 7 and 8). See also Malalasekera 1967, 87.

13 The coffin bearers change twice on the way to the cemetery. Initially, close family members carry the coffin, then members of the extended family take over and finally, for the last part of the way, it is handed to friends and neighbours.

14 Description based on a different funeral as I had followed the procession to the cemetery on this occasion.

15 The digging of the grave (always east-west direction) is an honorary service for which neighbours are invited by way of a present of betel-leaf. It has to be dug on the funeral day itself and should not be left unattended at any time.

16 All the decorations are in orange at a monk's cremation in keeping with the colour of monks' robes. The colour of monks' robes ranges in fact from bright orange to dark brown and dark red (as in Tibet) and the Pāli term (*kāsāya*) seems to denote the whole range of shades.

17 The funeral pyre looks very similar (not grander, as might have been expected in case of a monk's cremation) to the funeral pyres for laypeople.

18 I had been told that a funeral pyre, like an open grave, should not be left alone.

19 They were not used in any part of the ceremony. In the Hindu funeral rites the fence marks off the sacred space and the eight pots mark the directions, which are identified with respective deities. The breaking of a pot is an important part of the Hindu funerary rite and symbolises the breaking of the cranium of the corpse, which is regarded as necessary to release the *ātman*. See: Parry 1994, 177 and Firth 1997, 78.

20 I was told that when a death occurs in a temple the big temple bell is rung (even at night) to inform the *dāyakas* that they are needed. See Schopen 1997, 207f. See Gombrich 1991, 77 for definition of the term *dāyaka* (in contrast to *upāsaka*).

21 During the last two days before the funeral, his disciples, two at a time, have to remain standing near the coffin holding a fan. Their robes are wrapped in a special way with the piece of cloth serving as a belt (one of the eight utensils allowed for monks; Pāli *kāyabandhana*, Sinhala *baňdapatiya*). This 'ceremonial' way of wearing the robe is peculiar to the monks of the Siam Nikāya (Maithrimurthi, personal communication).

22 I was told that in the case of monks there is no astrologically determined moment for the coffin to be carried out of the temple, nor is there a milk boiling ceremony or any other cleansing rituals performed in the temple.

23 The long poles with ornamented discs at the top, which are carried by the young men walking in front of the procession are called *sēsat* (sg. *sēsata*; Sanskrit *śvetacchatra*), which literally means 'white umbrella'.

24 The technical term for the spreading out of the white cloth is *pāvāḍa elīma*. It was the usual practice at every funeral in the past to employ members of the (very low) washer caste to perform this service. See Disanayaka 1998, 89.

25 Monks of the different ordination lineages (*nikāyas*) can be distinguished by certain signs such as different ways to wear the robes, different umbrellas and eating utensils. See Gombrich 1991, 358 on the history of and differences between the different ordination lineages.
26 The procession consists of between 120 and 150 monks and about 350 to 400 laypeople and is almost part of the funeral ceremony itself.
27 The disciples of the dead abbot, his 'spiritual sons', fulfil their filial duty.
28 I was told that the head cloth was meant as a reminder of an accident the deceased had had as a young monk (*śramaṇera*) in this very temple.
29 At another cremation I had a chance to take a closer look inside the pyre before a lorry arrived loaded with coconut shells and old tyres.
30 The funeral pyre is traditionally lit by two nephews of the dead, who could be paternal or maternal. The procedure is no different in the case of monks.
31 Cf. Forbes 1840, 334. See Disanayaka 1998, 88 and Wijesekera 1949, 97.
32 See Tillakaratne1986, 162.
33 See Wijesekera 1949, 97.
34 Geiger 1953 xv gives the dates of King Sri Vijaya Rājasiṃha's reign as 1739–1747.
35 Unfortunately I do not have access to the quoted work (*Budusamaya hā samāja-darśanaya*, p. 141).
36 In S I 211 it is mentioned that Anāthapiṇḍika went to the 'gate of a charnel ground' (*sīvathikadvāra*), which suggests that bodies far from being dumped in the forest, were actually taken to a defined (and possibly fenced) space.
37 It is also commonly used in the commentary to gloss *sīvathika*. I am grateful to Dr. Kieffer-Pülz for sending me a copy of her unpublished MA dissertation (*Das Leichenfeld in der kanonischen und frühen nach-kanonischen Pāli-Literatur*, Göttingen 1983), which contains a great number of interesting details, references and stories.
38 It is also possible that there was a division on the grounds of class: a cemetery for the privileged people (used predominantly for cremation) and a paupers' cemetery (used as a charnel ground).
39 D II 295. See Vism 178ff., Bhikkhu Ñānamoli 185ff., etc.
40 The fact that the 'burnt' corpse was added later to the list of corpses in various stages of decomposition would support this hypothesis. See Schmithausen 1982, 71 (n. 66) and Lamotte 1970, 1313.
41 See Forbes 1840, I 334 and Tillakaratne 1986, 164. See also Ariyapala 1968, 308.
42 Unfortunately, I was not able to follow up Tillakaratne's source (H.W. Condrington, *Ancient land tenure and revenue in Ceylon*).
43 During my fieldwork I observed one burial, one 'deposit in a concrete underground chamber' (it was pointed out to me by various people as rather unusual) and three cremations.
44 See Wijesekera 1949, 199. Terwiel (1994, 232) documents similar restrictions concerning cremations in modern Thailand.
45 In the Indian context there are, of course, bad days for dying and funerals. Five days in the lunar month are regarded as inauspicious, even dangerous for dying and cremation. cf. Firth 1997, 79.
46 Seven of the planetary deities, *navagraha*, own a day of the week each, which determines its quality, e.g., Śani for Saturday.
47 Maithrimurthi (private communication) calls these *kemmura* rather than *kemvara*; however, as I refer here to Gombrich, I will stick to *kemvara* in this paragraph.
48 See Wirz 1954, 21.
49 This links into the wider discussion of religious syncretism/inclusivism, which I have touched upon elsewhere (Langer 2002).

50 Godakumbura (1996, 31) says with regard to the dating of this work, 'The oldest Sinhalese work whose date can be fixed with certainty is the Dhamapiyā-Aṭuvā-Gäṭapadaya, a glossary to the Pali Dhammapadaṭṭhakathā compiled by King Kassapa V (A.D. 913–923)'.
51 I am grateful to Dr. Mürmel (Leipzig University) for pointing out that this distinction is not very helpful.
52 At Thai Buddhist funerals it is customary to put incense on the coffin. See also Terwiel 1994, 235.
53 See also Parry 1994, 174 and 177.
54 Disanayaka 1998, 92 mentions that the close relatives circumambulate the coffin three times.
55 See Disanayaka 1998, 92.
56 For contemporary Hindu context see Parry 1994, 175.
57 See Disanayaka 1998, 89.
58 Hindu funeral processions are remarkably similar, but here certain offerings are made on the way (Firth 1997, 75).
59 The Theravāda monks in Nepal do walk in the procession (v. Rospatt, oral communication).
60 Parry (1994, 215) makes a distinction between accidental and innate states of pollution. See Weightman 1978, 19f.
61 According to Disanayaka (1998, 92) the milk is sprinkled in the house as well.
62 See also Disanayaka (1998, 89), who ascribes special power to the lime tree.
63 Parry 1994, 187; Firth 1997, 75; Ghosh 1989, 143.
64 Ja VI 479–593. See Collins 1998, 497–554.
65 Other methods include removal of the coffin through a hole in the wall or even through the roof (Maithrimurthi, oral communication). See Terwiel 1994, 231f. and Spiro 1982, 251 for Thai and Burmese practices respectively. Interestingly, the same reason is given by Firth 1997, 73 for the Hindu custom to bind together the two big toes after death occurred.
66 Ghosh 1989, 144; Pandey 1969, 234.
67 See also Parry 1994, 176.
68 This aspect is described in the *Tibetan Book of the Dead*, which contains admonitions for the departed during the first three days after death.
69 See Ghosh 1989, 154.
70 It is possible that the concept that the danger is greatest for close blood relations might have exerted a certain influence in Sri Lanka as well. At least it would provide a certain rationale to the custom that it is precisely not the sons of the departed (as in India) but his nephews who light the funeral pyre.
71 Hindus cremate normally within twenty-four hours after death, whereas in Sri Lanka the cremation or burial usually takes place on the third day or even later.
72 *Visabīja* is not a religious term and does not have the connotation of spiritual pollution (*kili*).
73 Ñānasīha 1962, 56.
74 Terwiel 1994, 231 and Spiro 1982, 249. The word *dähät* only applies to betel when offered to monks or at a *buddhapūjāva*; in everyday language the word *bulat* is used.
75 See also Disanayaka 1998, 90. For Thailand see Terwiel 1994, 234.
76 Bizot 1981.
77 The bibliographical details of the edition Ariyapala quotes are not available to me.

78 Particularly interesting is his mention of a dispute between washer men and lower caste people in a twelfth-century inscription (*Epigraphia Zeylanica*, Vol. III, p. 307). The men of the washer caste refused to perform the service of providing the cloth for the men of the blacksmith caste, whom they considered lower than themselves in the caste hierarchy. The dispute was settled in favour of the blacksmiths whose right to the service was upheld.
79 Regarding ascetic practices see Dantinne 1991, 10, and Wijayaratna 1983, 50f.
80 Vin I 280 (Mahāvagga VIII.1.34f).
81 Vism II 4 (Warren 1950, 48).
82 According to Buddhaghosa, *paṃsukūla*-monks practising the mild form are allowed to pick up clothes left for them 'by people seeking merit', etc. (Vism II 24 in Warren 1950). There is no mention of formal offering.
83 See also Dickson 1884, 226.
84 In a similar way, a white cloth is offered to the mother of the bride by the groom as a mark of his gratitude and viewed as a 'payment' for the bride.
85 Mahāvaṃsa (X 102; see also Geiger 1964, 75 and Malalasekera 1988, 113) mentions that King Paṇḍukābhaya (377–307) cared for a great variety of religious individuals and groups which indicate that before the introduction of Buddhism by King Devānampiya-Tissa (247–207) there was already a rich and varied religious climate on the island. And, most importantly for the Vedic connection, brahmins are mentioned explicitly.
86 Caland (1896, 163) alludes to various attempts at reconstructing the actual funeral rites purely on the basis of the Vedic hymns by a number of scholars such as V. Roth, Kägi, Monier Williams, Lefmann and Zimmer.
87 For more specific attempts of dating of particular *sūtra*s see also Gonda (1977, 477, n. 35). For Dharmasūtras see Olivelle 1999, xxvff. (esp. xxxii–xxxiv).
88 For details see Gonda 1977 chapter IV (616–628) and Caland 1896, iii–xiv (Einleitung).
89 Other sacrifices such as the *agnihotra* (daily oblations into the sacred fire), too, exist in a *śrauta* and *gṛhya* version (Gonda 1977, 468). See also Gonda 1980, 441.
90 Evison 1989, 195; Mylius 1983, 155.
91 See Firth 1997, 32.
92 See Caland 1896, 168–171.
93 See Caland 1896, iii–xiv. On the whole one gets the impression that his choice of material was determined by availability rather than any other criteria.
94 I will rely mainly on Gillian Evison's unpublished dissertation for this. I am very grateful to her for making her thesis available to me.
95 Based on Caland 1896, 12–18.
96 Based on Caland 1896, 81.
97 In Sri Lanka the corpse is turned around so that the head is to the west.
98 There is a notion in Sri Lanka, and presumably in India as well that hair and nails can be used by sorcerers for black magic.
99 See the chapter on *matakavastra*.
100 Based on Caland 1896, 19–23.
101 According to the GP the body has to be tied to the bier for fear that flying demons might snatch it (UttK 35: 41–41 in Evison 1989, 212). This adds yet another dimension. Not only is the dead person dangerous, but also in danger from other spirits. Evison (1989, 214) also speaks of offerings to the crows, which represent spirits and which may impede the progress of the procession.
102 Caland (1896, 23) uses the term 'Stadt' (town). It would be interesting to know from what period we have towns with gates in India.

103 In Sri Lanka the corpse has to be taken out at a particular moment (determined beforehand by an astrologer) to ensure that the spirit of the dead will not return. The concept of auspicious and inauspicious moments seems, to a degree, to have replaced the concept of auspicious directions in some instances.

104 Caland (1896, 171) offers an interesting interpretation: the fanning, which was in later sources interpreted as honouring the dead, was originally an act of shaking the spirit of the dead out of the folds of one's garment where he might try to hide. But unfortunately Caland does not give any reference as to where that idea comes from.

105 In one of the two cemeteries in the village in Sri Lanka, I noticed broken claypots on the grave, but could not get any information as to why or by whom they might have been placed there.

106 Based on Caland 1896, 30–54.

107 According to the GP *piṇḍas* are offered to the spirits of the cremation ground so that they will leave the corpse alone (UttK 35: 33–34 in Evison 1989, 216).

108 Based on Caland 1896, 55–72.

109 There is no mention here (nor in GP according to Evison 1989, 214) of the breaking of the skull, which is such an important part of contemporary Hindu cremation.

110 Based on Caland 1896, 73–79.

111 Based on Caland 1896, 99–112.

112 In the case that I observed in Sri Lanka, the bones were collected and buried on the seventh day after the almsgiving (*matakadānaya*) for the monks.

113 Based on Caland 1896, 81–82.

114 GP is somewhat more elaborate here, but no less confusing. It is said that on the first three days only milk and water are to be offered as the spirit is still airborne and begins to inhabit the (still incomplete) *piṇḍa* body only afterwards (UttK 15:59 and 34: 12–13 in Evison 1989, 232). These first offerings are technically known as the sixteen impure offerings, as they take place during the period when the family is still impure.

115 According to GP there are 16 *piṇḍa*s to be offered to the deceased and deities; and these are refered to in GP as the middle sixteen (UttK 5:38 in Evison 1989, 239). See Buss 2005.

116 According to Garuḍa Purāṇa household items which the deceased might need on his way to the Yamaloka are given to the priest (UttK 18:16 in Evison 1989, 243).

117 Evison 1989, 253 also mentions caste feasts that seem to be held after the deceased has become an ancestor. According to the Sāroddhāra (Sār 13:56, 94–5), which is a summary of the GP, Caṇḍālas were invited to these feasts.

118 The translation of this, as well as the following passages from the Mahāparinibbāna Sutta are quoted (and sometimes adapted) from an as yet unpublished anthology of Buddhist Suttas by Rupert Gethin.

119 D II 134. His birth, too, was reported to have taken place between towns.

120 Cf. D II 107. Earthquakes also occur on the occasion of arahants' *parinibbāna* (Thī-a 151).

121 It is in this context that we find the god Sakka's well-known verse '*aniccā vata saṃkhārā* . . .'.

122 D II 157.

123 D II 158. Cf. Waldschmidt 1951, 406 (§ 45.7) where the Skt reads *antarhitaḥ*.

124 Thī-a 154. Pruitt 1998, 197.

125 J v 126. Francis 1895, 65.

126 Pruitt 1998, 223. Thī-a 174.

127 Dhp-a III 176. Burlingame 1921 III, 18. See Also Dhp-a I 152.

128 Pv-a 162. Masefield 1980, 168.
129 Hare 1934, 48. A III 57.
130 D II 158.
131 D II 159.
132 Cf. also Spk III 221 for a seven-day pre-cremation celebration in honour of Sāriputta.
133 Thī-a 155. Pruitt 1998, 199. Also Pv-a 76 for a pre-cremation celebration of unspecified length in honour of 500 *paccekabuddhas*.
134 Ja III 434.
135 D II 160.
136 D II 161. Caland (1896, 174) says that originally the west was thought of as the region of the dead, but this was replaced by the south. In Sri Lanka, west is still associated with the dead.
137 D II 161. According to Manu V 92 only Brahmins are carried out of the east gate, whereas Kṣatriyas are carried out of the north gate.
138 Nothing is said about the starting point, i.e., the place where the Buddha passed away, in relation to the village. Hsüan-tsang locates the sāl grove and the place where the Buddha passed away to the northwest of the city Kusinārā beyond a river (Beal 1884, II 32).
139 This is reminiscent of Vedic schools who also differ in their opinion on matters of direction.
140 D II 160.
141 Another example of reinterpretation of funeral rites is the respectful fanning of the corpse which was, according to Caland, originally intended to shake the soul out of the folds of one's clothes.
142 See also Ps V 63.
143 Ja III 374.
144 D II 161.
145 Sv II 583.
146 See also Bareau 1970–71 II 43–44 and Strong 2004, 106.
147 See also Strong 2004, 106–110.
148 An example of gentle decomposition is wood charcoal, which is sometimes beautifully preserved and even shows traces of the original wood grain, whereas a log of wood in a fireplace pretty much dissolves into ashes and carbon dioxide. I am grateful to my brother, Dr Thomas Langer, who explained to me the chemical reactions which take place during combustion and the effect that a lack of oxygen has on the procedure.
149 Hare 1934, 48. A III 58.
150 Pollock 1986, 213 (Ayodhyākāṇḍa, Sarga 60, 12). See also Caland 1896, 87.
151 Pollock 1986, 232 (Ayodhyākāṇḍa, Sarga 70, 4–5).
152 Strong (2004, 109) suggests that previous discussions of this issue place 'too much emphasis on the burning process and not enough on the symbolic, precursorial, role of the *taila-droṇī*'.
153 D II 163.
154 Note that the circumambulation is in the auspicious direction, not in the inauspicious one (*apradakṣiṇā*) as prescribed in the Vedic sources.
155 An 2003, 204. Sv II 603. See also Strong 2004, 113f.
156 See Oldenberg 1897, 428; Rhys Davids 1910, II 154; Gombrich 1988, 119–124; etc.
157 See also Silk 2006.
158 See also Spk II 380.
159 Maybe the Bodhisattva's advice to the king not to perform a *yañña* (Ja III 434) actually referred to animal sacrifice.

160 Dhp-a III 342, however, suggests that the person who attends on the dying person is entitled to the inheritance.
161 Dhp-a II 100. See also Strong 2004, 112f.
162 D II 164. See also Strong 2004, 103f. on the Buddha's 'autocremation'.
163 Caland 1896, 58–59.
164 See Also Ud 181 (Ven. Dabba's pyre self-ignited).
165 See also Mp I 282 and Spk III 221 (Sāriputta's cremation), which adds that a bundle of fragrant roots (*usīrakalāpaka*) is used to light the pyre.
166 Burlingame 1921, I 186. Dhp-a I 70. The religious identity of the woman is not indicated, but there is no evidence that there were special Buddhist cremation customs.
167 This change from Vedic family rituals to delegation of duties to specialists is also found in other areas of life and ritual activity. To name but one example, provision of meat (for example for sacrificial purposes) was delegated to specialists (*sūkarika*, *goghātaka*, etc.) in special slaughterhouses (*sūna*).
168 The bamboo structure (*kambalakūṭāgāra*) might refer to the kind of structure similar to the ones used in Sri Lanka today.
169 At Spk III 221 we read that after Sāriputta's cremation there was a night of *dhamma* preaching before Anuruddha finally extinguishes the pyre with scented water.
170 The only suggestion of a collection of relics that I have found is the case of Cunda putting Sāriputta's relics in his waterstrainer to take them to Sāvatthi, where the Buddha was staying at the time (Spk III 221).
171 The assertion that everthing was burnt except for the bones is also found in connection with other eminent personalities such as Mahāpajāpatī (Thī-a 156) and Ven. Dabba (Ud 93).
172 Schopen 1997, 99–113 seems to be consistent in his interpretation of *sarīrāni* (plural) as 'relics', rather than 'bones'.
173 D II 164. A seven-day worship of the Mahāmoggalāna's relics (*dhātu*) is also mentioned at J V 127.h.
174 The pot in which the bones were collected is considered polluted in the Vedic context and smashed to pieces. Sv II 609 reports that Doṇa manages to snatch one of the teeth while dividing the relics and would have succeeded if it had not been for the god Sakka.
175 D II 166.
176 The translation 'distributed' for *vippakiriṃsu* is doubtful. What is meant here by the expression '*dhātūnaṃ vikiraṇaṃ*' (Sv 604) is the breaking up of the relics into minute pieces in order to allow as many people as possible to receive a piece which they could worship. This was instigated by the Buddha himself when he was still alive by way of an act of will. The *ṭīkā* comments on the state of the seven relics mentioned here: 'they remained as they were' (*sarūpen' eva ṭhitā ti attho*), that means they alone did not break into minute pieces.
177 Adikaram 1946, 139. He names in a footnote Papañcasūdanī (Sinhala edition 882) as his source. See also Ps IV 115; Mp I 91; Mp II 10.
178 See Dhp-a III 29. See also Bareau 1962 who examined the Vinaya Piṭakas of the various schools and who suggests that some schools (e.g., the Mahāsāṃghikas) distinguish between *stūpa* (as housing relics) and *caityas* (not housing relics) whereas other schools (such as Mūlasarvāstivādins) do not make this distinction.
179 See also: A II 245.
180 An translates 'remarkable', for 'rare' (cf. von Hinüber, 1994, 17f.). See also Mp III 219 and Masefield, 1986, 22.
181 Mp I 282.

182 See Kottkamp 1992, 3 (n. 2). Deeg (2004, 3) sees this as the 'pragmatic background' of the legend of King Aśoka building 84,000 *stūpas*.
183 Sri Lankan commentaries suggest that it was indeed uncommon to build a mortuary *stūpa* for the remains of ordinary monks (see Masefield 1986, 23), and Schopen does not present evidence for the building of mortuary *stūpas* in Sri Lanka.
184 Strong refers to it as the 'Lokapaññatti, written in Burma in the 11th century' but does not give a more specific reference to the passage he tranlates. See also Strong 2004, 103f.
185 See also Trainor 1997, who sets out to 'rematerialize the Sri Lankan Theravāda tradition'.
186 Schopen does not distinguish between *cetiya* and *stūpa*, but seems to prefer *stūpa*. Goswamy (1980, 2) ascribes structural and architectural significance to the term *stūpa*, and a more extended sense and a religious observance aspect to the term *cetiya*. I shall use the term *stūpa* in this chapter.
187 I have drawn on material from several of Schopen's articles, mainly 'An Old Inscription from Amarāvatī and the Cult of the Monastic Local Dead' (Schopen 1997, 165–203) and 'Burial ad Sanctos' (Schopen 1997, 114–147), and 'Immigrant Monks and the Proto-historical Dead: The Buddhist Occupation of Early Burial Sites in India' (Schopen 2004, 360–381). There is a substantial overlap in sources used as well as subject matter discussed in those articles.
188 See v. Rospatt 1999 for the construction of *stūpas* in Nepal.
189 See Schopen 1997, 169.
190 Quoted after Schopen 1997, 167.
191 Quoted after Schopen 1997, 96, note 19.
192 Schopen quotes as his sources: Kail 1966/67, 184–189 (for Sudhagarh) and Cousens 1891, 3–4 (for Nadsur).
193 References taken from Schopen 1997, 200 fns 76 and 77.
194 Quoted after Schopen 1997, 184.
195 Coningham talks about 'faunal remains at Buddhist sites' in the context of Buddhist diet (2001, 88) and articulates the problem that sometimes animal bones are simply thrown away at archaeological sites in Sri Lanka, as they do not fit the contemporary view of monks' diet.
196 He further quotes a number of inscriptions from twelfth-century Polonnaruva recording donations to Buddhist sites made by Tamils, the donation of Sri Lankan Buddhist caves by Brahmins, etc.
197 Schopen 2004, 370.
198 Goswamy (1980, 2) relates an amusing story of King Kanishka (reigned ca. A.D. 78–144) accidentally venerating the wrong (i.e., Jain) *stūpa* instead of a Buddhist *stūpa*, which might be taken as further proof that even in the first century A.D. the *stūpas* looked rather similar.
199 Schopen (1997, 118) quotes as his source Marshall 1951, 246, 335 and 361; and Marshall 1931, 120–121.
200 For more examples, see Schopen 1997, 183.
201 Quoted after Schopen (1997, 118), who gives as reference: Cunningham, *Mahābodhi*, 46–49.
202 One of my informants told me that no one likes to live on land near a cemetery and that for this reason plots of land near a cemetery are sometimes donated to the *saṃgha*.
203 Schopen names as his source: Sirkar, *Select Inscriptions*, 105.
204 Quoted after Fussman 1984, 38.
205 See also Trainor 1997, particularly chapters four and five.

206 Schopen (1997, 179) further concludes that there is no essential difference between the remains of a Buddha and those of an ordinary person. Ñāṇasampanno (2003, 401), however, describes how relics collected from the funeral pyre of an arahant had transformed into crystals. See also Strong 1992 and Trainor 1997.

207 Schopen (1997, 167), who names as his sources Lüders 1912, no. 1276; Franke 1896, 600 and Sivaramamurti 1942, 295, no. 92.

208 Schopen (2004, 329–359) explains the absence of *stūpas* for nuns rather unconvincingly on the basis of a single (admittedly rather curious) Pāli Vinaya passage as a tale of suppression and ritual murder of nuns by monks.

III POST-FUNERARY RITES

1 All ceremonies were conducted by the son-in-law even though the sons of the dead woman were present, which proves a certain degree of flexibility with regard to the 'chief mourner'. See also Parry 1994, 183.

2 In Sri Lanka every elderly woman would be addressed as '*ammā*'. However, on another *baṇa* occasion a son called his father's spirit '*tāttā*' and the only natural way to understand this invocation is that the son was calling his own father. Kinship terms with regard to a dead family member are, according to Parry 1994, 174, strictly avoided in the Hindu funeral context. For similar customs in Burma and Thailand see Spiro 1982, 249f., and Terwiel 1994, 230 respectively.

3 In this case the ritual, which is generally referred to as *pūjāva*, took place before the monk arrived, in the other two cases I observed (both in our village) it was performed after the monk had arrived and taken his seat, but without his participation. The food is later either fed to the animals, or thrown away.

4 This stanza is usually preceded by a verse inviting the gods to listen to the preaching, which runs as follows: *Samantā cakkavāḷesu atrāgacchantu devatā/saddhammaṃ munirājassa suṇantu saggamokkhadaṃ*. However, according to Ven. R. it is not usual practice to invite the gods to a funeral house before the seventh-day *dānaya*, as it is regarded as an unclean place. See also Palihawadhana 1997, 509.

5 Cf Dhp-a I 321 for the story of Pūttigatatissa including this verse. *Kaliṅgara* is often used as a metaphor for something useless, therefore, the interpretation as firewood (*dara*) seemed inappropriate at first sight. However, the commentary to the verses explains that these pieces of wood might be useless as timber but can still be useful to make small parts of furniture, to serve as fire wood, etc., which makes them superior to a corpse. Cf Carter/Palihawadanas 1987, 129.

6 This was carried out only verbally without the water-pouring ceremony. There is no distinction in Sinhala (*anumodan karanavā/venavā*) between giving of merit with, or without the water pouring ceremony.

7 Nārada Mahāthera 1975, 29–30 gives *anumodantu* with a footnote, that usually in recitation *anumoditvā* is used, as in this case.

8 I am told apologetically that it is not good to take food away from the funeral house before the seventh-day alms-giving is over.

9 Besides the *cetiya*, the *bodhi*-tree, the shrine room (*vihāraya*) and the living quarters for the monks, most temples have a big hall (*dharmasālāva*) used for functions such as ordinations, teaching, sermons on full moon days (*pōya*), etc.

10 One of the organizer of the ceremonies confirmed that neither food offerings (*pūjāva*) nor calling of the spirit (*prāṇakārayā*) had been performed outside the hall before the start of the *baṇa*. He further added that this is only done by and for laypeople.

11 As we arrived late I did not observe if the speaker was received in the customary way by washing his feet and, if so, who would have performed that service.

12 The function of the fan in preaching was traditionally to serve as a screen between the preaching monk and the audience, shifting the emphasis from the monk to the sermon. See Maithrimurthi 1988, 121–126.
13 As the ceremony takes place in the temple no meal or refreshments are offered to the people.
14 Alms in Sri Lanka are not vegetarian affairs and often fish, chicken or mutton are given. It is, however, noticeable that beef, pork or egg dishes are avoided. There is a general tendency for laypeople to avoid cooking beef or pork in their homes, as it is regarded as impure, *kili* (presumably due to Hindu and Muslim influence). Eggs, too are avoided by pious Buddhists particularly on *pōya* days, as they are regarded as 'alive', and breaking an egg constitutes an act of direct killing. Cf. also Gombrich 1991, 305, and Maithrimurthi 1986.
15 The brass bowl, which is used every day for the *buddhapūjāva* at around noon, had been collected earlier from the local temple.
16 The variant *uttama* (vocative) also exists (Maithrimurthi, oral communication).
17 There are only minor variations in the verses for offering the food at the Buddha *pūjāva*. Sometimes the verses mention all the individual items, sometimes a 'summarised version' is chanted. Cf. also Gombrich 1991, 135 ff., esp. 141.
18 The local abbot was unable to attend and it was noticeable how much effort was made to assure the family of the legitimate status and rank of the monks present. There are two possible reasons for this: first, according to canonical texts (M III 255), the worthier the recipient, the greater is the amount of merit accruing from an offering, and second, there is an element of social status attached to inviting high ranking well-known monks.
19 This is a variation of the verses chanted at the funeral (see above).
20 Siam Nikāya monks are served their food on plates, whereas the Rāmañña Nikāya monks bring their alms bowls. Except for very few places such as Ambalangoda (South-west coast), it is not common practice in Sri Lanka for monks to go on alms round. See also Carrithers 1983.
21 I was told that collecting a small portion of food from the monks is peculiar to the Siam Nikāya, otherwise food is taken straight from the kitchen.
22 Presents for the *saṃgha* can range from exercise books (for novices in a temple school) to household goods (brooms, rakes, etc.). It is, however, customary to give at least one full set of the eight requisites for monks (robes, alms bowl, etc.). These are purchased in special shops for monks' requisites where there is a great choice of products and qualities. Two former monks told me that the average temple receives by more sets than can possibly be made use of and subsequently sells them back to the shop.
23 The tradition of the 'speech of appreciation after the meal' (*bhuttānumodanā*) goes back to canonical times.
24 From the Abhayaparittha or Mahājayamaṅgala gāthā (verse 12), Nārada Mahāthera 1975, 51 reading variate 'te' instead of 'me'. I have so far not been able to locate this gāthā.
25 Dhp 109. Cf. Skilling 1994, 748.
26 In an interview a close disciple of the departed emphatically stated that it is important for monks to occasionally organise and arrange alms givings in order to set an example for lay people. He explained that monks earn money as teachers in schools or at universities, etc., and are in a position to do so. The convention is, however, that the laypeople provide the 'gift of food' and the monks the 'gift of the teaching' (*dhammadāna*).
27 The two men involved in the *buddhapūjāva* were laypeople representing the village, not blood relations of the dead abbot.

28 The chanting is more elaborate than the small *Buddhapūjāva* described above (twenty verses instead of eight).
29 The ceremony is essentially the same but more elaborate than the 'Laywoman's Seventh-day *matakadānaya*' described above.
30 On this occasion even the Rāmañña Nikāya monks ate from plates, but they were not approached by the layman, who collected food from the other monks.
31 Schopen 1997, 99–113, discusses the terms *sarīra* and *śarīrapūjā* at length and seems to be consistent in his interpretation of *sarīrāni* (plural) as 'relics', rather than 'bones'.
32 Parry (1994, 187f.) elaborates on the function of the Ganges 'to sacralise' (for example the corpse and chief mourner) as well as to 'serve as an agent of desacralisation, returning both persons and things charged with sacredness to a more ritually neutral state'.
33 Barley 1995, 100 and 107: 'Moreover, the normal scheme can be reversed. Among the matrilinear Khasi of India, people are held to be composed of the bone from the mother, while the soft, fleshy parts come from the father. So in the initial, polluting, fleshy stages of death, it is primarily men who handle the corrupt body and pass the clean bone to women.'
34 However, it is interesting that Sri Lankans avoid accidentally burning hairs, as the smell might attract demons (*yakku*), who think that a corpse is being cremated (Maithrimurthi, oral communication).
35 Cf. Forbes (1840, I 335), who adds that collection of bones takes place on the seventh day after the death.
36 Something similar is practised in Nepal, where a Brahmin has to consume part of the dead king's brain and is exiled subsequently (v. Rospatt, oral communication).
37 Reference is to Perera 1904 and Davy 1821.
38 I did not have the opportunity to observe the collecting of the bones following the monk's cremation, but I do not have any reason to suspect it differed in any meaningful way from what is described here.
39 Kahandagamage 1998, 133f.
40 Terwiel (1994, 233ff.) states that in rural Thailand the bones are arranged in the shape of a miniature human body and a second cremation ritual is performed, which shows all the main features of a funeral ceremony (monks, the chanting of *aniccā vata saṅkhārā* . . . and the offering of a piece of cloth).
41 In our village there were two cemeteries: one next to the so-called 'town temple' and another, smaller one, located right outside the village on the main road.
42 The Buddha*pūjāva* received little attention in the context of organizing transport for fifteen monks.
43 Hiring drummers for a ceremony is an indication of social status and attracts a certain amount of attention.
44 In this case acting as head of the family involved rather more than leading a procession. He was the youngest in the family and still single; he had lost both his brothers in the space of six months and was not only faced with the costs for the funeral ceremonies but also with the responsibility for their young families.
45 The giving of merit was emotional at this *matakadānaya:* the widow and young daughters were still very much in a state of shock and grief, and the nephews, who joined in the giving of merit, had themselves lost their father only some months previously.
46 A ten-year death anniversary is treated as any other anniversary.
47 A *Buddhapūjāva* is always performed and not only on the occasion of *matakadānaya*, but in fact every time someone brings food for the monks to the temple. When four or more families share the responsibility for one meal there will be four or more *Buddhapūjāva*s that day, and the food is later given to beggars or animals.

48 It appears that the presence of the relic receptacle is not necessary as the ceremony takes place on the temple premises in close vicinity to the main *vihāra*.
49 The monks later ate together with the younger monks from the monks' training college (*pirivena*).
50 The actual ceremony differs in no respect from the ceremonies which I observed in peoples' houses.
51 At that time there were about twenty-five resident monks in the town temple and on average four families shared the responsibility for a meal each providing food for six to seven monks.
52 Apart from Gombrich (1991, 140–144), surprisingly little is found on *buddhapūjāva* or the food offerings to the *dhātukaraṇḍuva*.
53 Southwold (1983, 168) offers an interesting interpretation of the *buddhapūjāva*.
54 Already in the Veda, purpose or aim are connected with the sacrifice. The purpose can be an individual or a communal one (such as preservation of the world). The latter might have been the primary purpose and the former secondary.
55 Cf. also Gombrich 1991, 140.
56 See Dickson 1884, 208.
57 This is reminiscent of the Vedic concept of the sacrifice as a feast for the gods (Gastmahl). Cf. Thieme 1984, I 343–370 (343–361).
58 Some of my informants spoke in the context of these offerings of *pretas* and others of crows.
59 See Wijesekera 1949, 98.
60 Wirz does not clarify if this *prēta-pindenna* is similar to the one described in detail under the heading 'Die pirit-Zeremonie' (Wirz 1941, 204ff.). Because of substantial overlap I suspect that both are compilations and I will refer to both ceremonies as *prēta-pindenna*.
61 Cf. Schmithausen and Maithrimurthi 1998, 185, note 44, for the parallel of Buddhist and non-Buddhist ascetics sharing their food with animals. Cf. Wezler, 1976, 82.
62 See also Maithrimurthi 1986, 36.
63 Sanskrit Dictionary (MW).
64 Wirz 1941, 203.
65 Besides food items, these include flowers, gold and silver ornaments, copper coins, a white piece of cloth and a new plate. The mention of a new plate is especially interesting here, as I was told several times on the occasion of the sixth-day offering that old items which had been used by the dead person (pillow, sleeping mat, etc.) are presented to the spirit.
66 Wirz 1941, 210.
67 Terwiel (1994, 237) describes for modern Thailand a practice of catching the spirit of the dead child in a vessel (in cases of miscarriage or still birth).
68 The crossing of water ditches also features in the Vedic post-funerary rites when the funeral party returns home from the cremation ground.
69 This summary is based on Knipe 1977.
70 Such a distinction is, of course, artificial. According to Doniger O'Flaherty (1980, 10f.), it is not just food that is exchanged, but food served as a vehicle for merit already in the time of the Veda. Doniger O'Flaherty (1980, 12) explains: 'The *piṇḍa* offering is a simultaneous transfer of flesh and merit, substance-code, to appease potentially angry and harmful ancestors, like the offerings to demons or the *prasāda* offerings to malevolent gods.'
71 See also Kazama 1965 (particularly interesting for Buddhist view on Chinese filial piety).
72 A friend of mine spent Rs 7000, nearly twice her monthly salary, on fish alone on the occasion of a *matakadānaya* for her mother.

73 Holt 1981, 19. Vetter (1998, 20) goes one step further and states that the monks took over the roles of 'best field of merit' and sole mediator between the living and the dead and that they used promises, threats, and devaluation of other customs in doing so.
74 A young monk chanting for half an hour at a *bōdhipūjāva* might be given a couple of exercise books, while a group of monks performing overnight chanting will receive more substantial donations.
75 It happens, of course, that individual monks approach laypeople with personal requests (i.e., for a TV, mobile phone, etc.) and I have, on occasions, heard laypeople complain about it, but this should not be seen as 'payments' to monks.
76 In this respect the Buddhist attitude to and treatment of 'sacred food' is the opposite of the Hindu attitude, where it is part of the ritual and regarded as auspicious to eat some of the food that had been accepted by the deity (*prasāda*).
77 See also Gombrich 1988, 405.
78 It is clear that the beneficiaries are only dead relatives, even though this is not explicitly said in the verse.
79 A IV 210 there is, however, a story involving the pouring of water to seal a solemn act of handing over one's wife to another man.
80 A caesura in the death rituals after seven weeks is known in many cultures. Dickson as well as Tillakaratne (1986, 169) seem to refer to roughly the same time frame.
81 See also Gombrich 1991, 273 n. 30.
82 The funeral day represents an exception, in that it usually falls into the preliminary seven-day stage, but nevertheless contains the full-blown merit-giving ceremony symbolised by water pouring.
83 Grander occasions described by Gombrich and Obeyesekere 1990, 384–410.
84 I do not know for what purpose other *bōdhipūjās* I witnessed were conducted.
85 '*Sabbe*' appears to be an addition which does not fit the metre.
86 Gombrich 1991, 257. Dickson (1886, 209) gives a different reading of the verse: *Icchitaṃ patthitaṃ tuyhaṃ khippam eva samijjhatu/pūrentu cittasaṃkappā cando pannarasi yathā.* I came across yet another version of this verse as chanted at one of the ceremonies: *Icchitaṃ patthitaṃ tuyhaṃ sabbam eva samijjhatu/pūrentu cittasaṃkappā maṇi jotiraso yathā.*
87 He claims further down that 'only modernist monks confine themselves to the bald wish that all may attain *nirvāṇa*'. However, in the context of funerals the wish that the departed may attain Nirvāṇa is common and Gombrich compares the use of this formula with the Christian *Requiescat in pace*.
88 At Ap I 299 we find the story of the Buddha getting headaches because in a previous life as a fisherman's son he rejoiced in watching fish being caught.
89 Both Dickson (1884, 223) and Gombrich (1991, 271) report that it is believed by people that only a man reborn as one specific type of *peta* (*paradattūpikapeto* and *paradattūpajīvin* respectively) can actually benefit from giving of merit. In cases of a different rebirth the given merit goes back to the donor (see Mil 294).
90 Dhp-a I 103f.; Pv-a 19ff.
91 A V 269ff. and Mil 294ff.
92 Elderly women who spent religious days at the temple keeping the ten precepts and listening to sermons.
93 Prof. Wijayawardhana confirmed my observation that the literal meaning of the term *anumodan*, though frequently used in sermons, is not generally known.
94 When I asked a friend of mine if it was possible to give merit to an ill family member who was unable to attend a ceremony personally, he replied that he thought it was a 'very good idea'. Hayashi (1999, 34) relates a case of royal exchange of merit by letter.
95 See Bond 1988, 152.

96 See the discussion above of *anumodan karanavā* and *anumodan venavā*.
97 For a more detailed investigation see Schmithausen 1986.
98 Dhirasekera 1984, 279 distinguishes two meanings: '(i) *dakkhiṇā* is an offering of food, and perhaps clothing too, made to *śramaṇas* and *brāhmaṇas*, i.e., men of religious orders both Buddhist and non-Buddhist, as part of one's social and religious obligations, (ii) *dakkhiṇā* is the benevolent force which arises out of giving (*dāna*) to persons of virtue and pity . . .'.
99 Cf. Ud 89 with almost identical wording. Maitrimurthi (1999, 54) comments on *anukampā* as motherly care for someone weaker.
100 Sv II 542.
101 *Yad idaṃ bhante dāne puññaṃ hitaṃ Vessavaṇassa mahārājassa sukhāya hotū ti.*
102 This story seems to assume that gods cannot generate their own merit by giving donations.
103 D III 189. See also A III 43.
104 Sv III 953.
105 This passage is quoted in Pv-a 27 where the phrase '*mayam assu, bho gotama, brāhmaṇā nāma. dānāni dema, saddhāni karoma* . . .' is changed and *saddhāni* is substituted by *puññāni*. Nanayakkara 1979, 195 interprets this as 'deliberate attempt to elevate this commemorartive rite from the level of sympathetic magic to that of an ethical duty'.
106 It should be noted, that Pāli *peta* does not distinguish between *pretas* and *pitṛ*, as has been pointed out by various scholars. This is particularly tangible here, where it is said that only *petas* (departed) who are reborn as *petas* (ghosts) can benefit from gifts given to them.
107 McDermott 1975, 431; Bechert 1992, 41.
108 Pruitt 1998, 287. The situation recalls Vessavaṇa's request of merit at A IV 63f.
109 This understanding of the term *kusala* is borrowed from Schmithausen, '*Kuśala*: Good or Skilful or What? Reconsidering the Meaning of *kusala/kuśala* in Buddhist Texts', unpublished paper delivered on the occasion of the annual meeting of the United Kingdom Association of Buddhist Studies (UKABS) 6/7/98, 14.
110 Agasse (1978, 311–332) is an excellent source for references.
111 Weeraratne 1965, 747 refers to an interesting incident in the Vinaya (Vin II 212) where it is related that laypeople complained about monks not performing an *anumodanā* and in consequence the Buddha laid down a rule that monks should do so.
112 No absolute quantity is named, i.e., it is not explained what the hundred- or thousandfold refer to. Wezler (1997, 569) describes a similar phenomenon in the context of Hinduism.
113 Agasse 1978, 319, nn. 42 and 43.
114 Agasse 1978, 320, nn. 44–50.
115 Dhp-a II 1.
116 See also Dhp-a 62f. where a thief accidentally overhears a conversation in which a rich man relates to the Buddha the evil deeds done to him by the thief and his (the rich man's) transfer of merit to him (the thief). However, this does not prompt a joyful reaction (*anumodanā*) in the thief but the fear of being caught out and reported to the king, which makes him confess his evil deeds to the rich man. We learn later in the story, that the thief was reborn in the Avīci hell due to his evil deeds (and lack of *anumodanā*?).
117 See also Gehman 1923, 410–421 and 1924, 73–75.
118 Schmithausen 1986, 212.
119 With one exeption: in Pv 23 (*Nandāpetavatthu*) Nandasena, touchingly, invites the *petī* (after she revealed her identity as his former wife Nandā) to come home with him so that she can obtain clothes, food and drink and see their children.

120 Endo (1987, 96) on the other hand, sees gratitude as the main motivation in the stories of the Petavatthu.

121 Pv 4 (verse 22). Two other stories (Pv 82 v. 701 and Pv 92 v. 798) tell of a daughter who, presumably out of a sense of gratitude and duty to her parent, gives alms to a bhikkhu on behalf of her departed father without knowing his present state of being.

122 Schmithausen 1986, 212; Holt 1981, 17; Gombrich 1991, 275.

123 Cf. Pv 15ff, 17ff. (Ven. Sāriputta) and Pv-a 144 (Ven. Revata); cf. Agasse 1978, 316 n. 27; Schmithausen 1986, 213 and n. 95.

124 See also Dietz 1984, 92–113.

125 See also Vv-a 288f.

126 Dhp-a IV 123. cp. Mil 295.

127 For more examples see Hayashi 1999, 34f.

128 See also Malalasekera (1967, 85) and Gombrich (1991, 87).

129 This should probably read *diṭṭhi 'ju* (*uju*) for 'right view'. Gombrich (1991, 87) gives as an alternative for the last two lines: *desanā savaṇaṃ pūjā, veyyavaccaṃ pasaṃsanā.*

130 Abhidh-av 3 verse 21.

131 For Pāli text see: Saddhātissa 1989, 135.

132 Wijeratne and Gethin 2002 184f translate *patti* as 'good fortune' to distinguish it from *puñña.*

133 Hayashi (1999, 43) quotes a modern Burmese commentary as evidence that *anumodanā* still plays an important role and is emphasised in modern Theravāda writing.

134 In fact in modern Indian languages the words for 'thank you' such as *istutiyi* (Sinhala) or *dhanyawād* (Hindi) are somewhat artificial and not used in a natural conversation.

135 Hayashi (1999, 44) points out that in a number of stories in the Dhammapada-aṭṭhakathā mindfulness rather than *anumodanā* seems to be the prerequisite.

136 I will utilise mainly three of Schopen's articles for the following discussion: 'Two Problems in the History of Indian Buddhism: The Layman/Monk Distinction and the Doctrine of Transference of Merit' (Schopen 1997, 23–55), 'Filial Piety' (Schopen 1997, 56–71), and 'On Monks, Nuns, and "Vulgar" Practices' (Schopen 1997, 238–257).

137 For the dates of the inscriptions see: Schopen 1997, 42 and footnotes 101 and 102 and Falk 1993, 205–18.

138 *Gamaṇi-Uti-maharajhaha(jhita Abi-Ti)śaya leṇe daśa-diśaśa sagaye dine* (Symbols 3a and (1) (2)) *mata-pitaśa aṭaya.*

139 Wezler 1998, 569.

140 *Rajha-Naga-jhita rajha-Uti-jhaya Abi-Anuradi ca rajha-Uti ca karapita śe ima leṇa catudiśaśa śagaya agat-agatana paśu-viharaye aparimita-lokadatuya śatana śita-śukaye.*

141 On the problem of Hīnayāna and Mahāyāna see also Cousins (2003, 18), who draws a lively picture of what Buddhist monasteries in India might have been like in the second century A.D.

142 The spirit of a wish for the benefit of all beings (*sabbe sattā . . .*) is, of course, tangible in texts such as the Karaṇīyamettasutta (Sn 145–147).

143 Cf. Doninger 1991, especially chapter III.

144 Barley (1995, 16) warns against claims of universality.

APPENDIX

Questionnaire: English and Sinhala

A. Giving of merit – *pin dīmalanumōdanāva*

A.1. At the moment when the water is poured and the merit is given, how can the departed person receive the merit? How can a meritorious deed, performed by one person benefit another person? *(pän vaḍalā pin dīpuhāma malagiya ayaṭa mē pin läbenne kohomada?)*

A.2. What is the meaning of the words '*anumōdan karanavā*' and '*anumōdan venavā*'? Is there a difference between the expressions '*pin dīma*' and '*pin läbenavā*'? (*anumōdan karanavā anumōdan venavā kiyana ekē tēruma mokakda?*)

A.3. Who can benefit from giving of merit? Can a departed relative benefit from giving of merit even after one year or five years, etc., and after he is reborn somewhere else, for example as animal, god, human being or in hell? *(pin dunnāma ē pin kāṭat labāganna puluvanda, udāharanayak häṭiyaṭa satek velā ipadunāma hari manussayek velā hari deviyek velā hari? märilā avurudu dahayak pahalovak giyāṭa passet pin anumōdan venna puluvanda?)*

B. Immediately after a death has occurred – *märunāṭa passe palaveni davas hata*

B.1. Why is the light kept on in the house and why are people always awake in a funeral house until after the seven–day *dānaya? (malagedara davas hatak dorajanel vahanne nätte hari layiṭ ōf karanne nätte hari nidāganne nätte hari äyi?)*

B.2. Are people reborn immediately after death, or later, after seven days or more? *(märunu aya samaharak märunat ekkama āyet vena lōkeka upadinavāda? samaharak ekkō davas hatakaṭa passe nätinam huṅga davasakaṭa passe upadinavāda?)*

B.3. If people are not reborn immediately, do they exist as a kind of ghost and what would they be called, *perētas* or something else? *(märunu kenā ē ekkama ipadunē nätnam eyā perētayekda ehema nätinam eyāṭa kiyana visēsa namak tiyenavāda?)*

C. Customs connected with imminent death in the house – *märena mohota*

C.1. What do people do if someone is about to die in the home? Are there special customs? *(kenek märenna laṃ venakoṭa gedara aya monavada karannē?)*

C.2. Is it better to die with a clear mind? What happens if someone dies with an angry mind or in a sudden accident? *(hoňda sihiyen märena eka väḍiya hoňdada? taraha hiten hari äksiḍanṭ velā hari märunāma mokada venne?)*

C.3. Can a bad person go to a good place because he had a good thought at the moment of death, or can a good person go to a bad place because of a bad thought at the moment of death? *(hoňda hiten märunot naraka kenekuṭa vunat hoňda tänaka upadinna puluvanda? naraka hiten märunot hoňda kenek vunat naraka tänaka upadinna venavāda? ē mokada?)*

D. Merit and demerit – *pin/pav*

D.1. What do you think constitutes an act of merit or demerit? How would you define *pin* and *pav*? *(pin kiyalā kiyanne monavāda? pav kiyalā kiyanne monavāda?)*

D.2. Is it a more meritorious act to give a *dānaya* to the monks, than to give food to beggars? *(hāmuduru namakaṭa dānē dunnāmada pin väḍi, hiňgannekuṭa dunnāmada?)*

D.3. Is it possible to do meritorious deeds even though one never goes to the temple, or gives a *dānaya* etc., just by being a good, helpful and generous person? Do we need to go to the temple to do meritorious deeds? *(kavadākavat paṃsal nogihillat anit ayaṭa udav karalā vitarak hari hoňda minihek velā hari piṃ karanna puluvanda? ē kiyanne pin karanna paṃsal yanna ōnämada?)*

BIBLIOGRAPHY AND ABBREVIATIONS

1. Abbreviations and Primary texts

A	Aṅguttara-nikāya. Edited by R. Morris and E. Hardy, London, PTS, 1885–1900.
AKBh	Abhidharmakośa-bhāṣya. Edited by P. Pradhan. Patna: Kashi Prasad Jayaswal Research Institute, 1967.
Abhidh-av	Abhidhammāvatāra. Edited by A.P. Buddhadatta, London, PTS, 1915–1928.
Abhidh-s	Abhidhammatthasaṅgaha; see Abhidh-s-mhṭ.
Abhidh-s-mhṭ	Abhidhammatthasaṅgaha-mahāṭīkā (Abhidhamatthavibhāvinī). Edited by Hammalawa Saddhātissa, Oxford, PTS, 1989.
As	Atthasālinī. Edited by E. Müller, London, 1979. PTS.
BĀU	Bṛhadāraṇyaka Upaniṣad; see Olivelle 1998.
ChU	Chāndogya Upaniṣad; see Olivelle 1998.
D	Dīgha-nikāya. (1) Edited by T.W. Rhys Davids, et al., London, 1890–1911. PTS. (2) Edited by Somalokatissa Nayaka Thero. Maradana, Colombo, 1954.
Dhp	Dhammapada. Edited by K.R. Norman and O. v. Hinüber, Oxford, PTS, 1994.
Dhp-a	Dhammapadaṭṭhakathā. Edited H.C. Norman, London, PTS, 1906–15.
Dīp	Dīpavaṃsa. Edited by Hermann Oldenberg, London, 1879.
EB	*Encyclopaedia of Buddhism* (4 vols). Edited by G.P. Malalasekera, Colombo, 1961–.
ERE	*Encyclopaedia of Religion and Ethics* (12 vols). Edited by James Hastings with the assistance of John A. Selbie and other scholars. Edinburgh: T. & T. Clark, 1908–1926.
GP	Garuḍa Purāṇa. Edited by Jivananda Vidyasagar, Calcutta Sarasvati Press. 1890.
GRETIL	Göttingen Register of Electronic Texts in Indian Languages.
It	Itivuttaka. Edited by E. Windisch, London, PTS, 1899.

It-a	Itivuttaka-aṭṭhakathā. Edited by M.M. Bose, London, PTS, 1934–36.
Ja	Jātaka. Edited by V. Fausbøll, London, PTS, 1877–97.
JB	Jaiminīya Brāhmaṇa. See Bodewitz 1973.
JUB	Jaiminīya Upaniṣad Brāhmaṇa. See Oertel 1894.
KauśU	See Bodewitz 2002.
Khp	Khuddakapāṭha. Edited by H. Smith, PTS, 1915.
Kv	Kathāvatthu. Edited by Arnold C. Taylor, London, PTS, 1894–97.
M	Majjhima-nikāya. Edited by V. Trenckner and R. Chalmers, London, PTS, 1888–1902.
MBh	Mahābhārata. Muneo Tokunaga's digital edition available via GRETIL (www.sub.uni-goettingen.de/).
Mahāparinirvāṇasūtra	*Das Mahāparinirvāṇasūtra: Text in Sanskrit und Tibetisch, verglichen mit dem Pāli nebst einer Übersetzung der chinesischen Entsprechung im Vinaya der Mūlasarvāstivādins.* Edited by E. Waldschmidt, Berlin, 1951.
Mil	Milindapañha. Edited by V. Trenckner, PTS, London, 1880.
Mp	Manorathapūraṇī. Edited by E. Hardy and M. Walleser, London, PTS, 1924–56; 2nd ed. 1967–73.
Mv	Mahāvaṃsa. (1) Edited by Wilhelm Geiger, London, PTS, 1908, 1958. (2) Extended Mahāvaṃsa, edited by G.P. Malalasekera, Oxford, PTS, 1988.
MW	Monier-Williams, Monier, Sir. *A Sanskrit-English dictionary: etymologically and philologically arranged with special reference to cognate Indo-European languages*, Oxford: Clarendon Press, 1899.
PraśU	Praśna Upaniṣad; See Olivelle 1998.
Ps	Papañcasūdanī. Edited by J. Woods, D. Kosambi, I.B. Horner, London, PTS, 1922–38.
PTS	Pali Text Society.
Pv	Petavatthu. Edited by N.A. Jayawickrama, London, PTS, 1970.
Pv-a	Petavatthu-aṭṭhakathā (= Dhammapāla's Paramattha-Dīpanī, III). Edited by E. Hardy, London, PTS, 1894.
Rāmāyaṇa	Muneo Tokunaga's digital edition available via GRETIL (www.sub.uni-goettingen.de/).
Saddharmaratnāvaliya	Edited by D.B. Jayatilaka, Colombo, 1945.
S	Saṃyutta-nikāya. Edited by L. Feer, London, PTS, 1884–98.
SāmavBr	Sāmavidhānabrāhmaṇa. See Burnell 1873.
ŚB	Śatapatha-Brāhmaṇa. Edited A Weber, Varanasi, 1964. Originally published, Berlin, 1855.
Sn	Suttanipāta. Edited by Dines Andersen, and Helmer Smith, London, PTS, 1913.
Sp	Samantapāsādikā. Edited by J. Takakusu and M. Nagai, London, PTS, 1924–47.

Spk — Sāratthappakāsinī. Edited by F.L. Woodward, London, PTS, 1929–37.
Sv — Sumaṅgalavilāsinī. Edited by T.W. Rhys Davids, London, PTS, 1886–1932.
Sv-pṭ — Sumaṅgalavilāsinī-purāṇa-ṭīkā (= Līnatthappakāsinī). Edited by Lily De Silva, London, 1970. PTS.
Th — Theragāthā. Edited by H. Oldenberg, London, PTS, 1883; 2nd revised edition by K.R. Norman and L. Alsdorf, London, PTS 1966.
Th-a — Theragāthā-aṭṭhakathā. Edited by F.L. Woodward, London, PTS, 1940–52.
Thī — Therīgāthā. Edited by R. Pischel, London, PTS, 1883; 2nd revised edition by K.R. Norman and L. Alsdorf, London, PTS 1966.
Thī-a — Therīgāthā-aṭṭhakathā. Edited by E. Müller, London, PTS, 1893.
Ud — Udāna. Edited by P. Steinthal, London, PTS, 1885.
Ud-a — Udāna-aṭṭhakathā. Edited by F.L. Woodward, London, PTS, 1926.
UttK — Uttarakhaṇḍa of the Garuḍa Purāṇa (also referred to as Pretakalpa or Pretakhaṇḍa).
Vibh — Vibhaṅga. Edited by C.A.F. Rhys Davids, PTS, London, 1904.
Vibh-a — Vibhaṅga-aṭṭhakathā (= Sammohavinodanī). Edited by A.P. Buddhadatta, PTS, London, 1923.
Vin — Vinaya. Edited by H. Oldenberg, London 1879–83.
Vism — Visuddhimagga. (1) Edited by C.A.F. Rhys Davids. London, PTS, 1920–21. (2) Edited by H.C. Warren and D. Kosambi, Harvard, 1950.

2. Secondary Literature (including Translations)

Abegg, E. 1921. *Der Pretakalpa des Garuḍa-Purāṇa*, Leipzig.

Adikaram, E.W. 1946. *Early History of Buddhism in Ceylon or 'State of Buddhism in Ceylon as Revealed by the Pāli Commentaries of the 5th Century A.D.'*, Dehiwala: Buddhist Cultural Centre.

Agasse, J.-M. 1978. 'Le Transfer de mérite dans le Bouddhisme Pali classique', *Journal Asiatique* 266, 311–332.

Aggacitta, Bhikkhu 1999. *Dying to Live: The Role of Kamma in Dying and Rebirth*, Taipei: Sukhi Hotu.

An, Yang-Gyu (trans.) 2003. *The Buddha's Last Days: Buddhaghosa's Commentary on the Mahāparinibbāna Sutta*, Oxford: Pali Text Society.

Ariyapala, M.B. 1968. *Society in Mediaeval Ceylon: The State of Society in Ceylon as Depicted in the Saddharma-ratnavaliya and Other Literature of the Thirteenth Century*, Colombo: Department of Cultural Affairs.

Assmann, J., Maciejewski, F. and Michaels, A. (eds.) 2005. *Der Abschied von den Toten: Trauerrituale im Kulturvergleich*, Göttingen: Wallstein Verlag.

Aung, Shwe Zan and Mrs. Rhys Davids (trans.) 1915. *Points of Controversy or Subjects of Discourse: Being a Translation of the Kathā-Vatthu from the Abhidhamma-Piṭaka*, Oxford: Pali Text Society.

Bareau, A. 1957. *La Vie et L'Organisation des Communautés Bouddhiques Modernes de Ceylan*, Pondicherry: Institut Français d'Indologie.

Bareau, A. 1962. 'La construction et la culte des *stūpa* d'aprés les Vinayapiṭaka', *Bulletin de l'École Française d'Extrême-Orient* 50, 230–74.

Bareau, A. 1970–71. *Recherches sur la biographie du Buddha dans les sūtrapiṭaka et les vinayapiṭaka anciens: II. Les derniers mois, le parinirvāṇa et les funérailles*, 2 vols. Paris: Bulletin de l'École Française d'Extrême-Orient.

Barlas, R. and N.P. Wanasundera 1992. *Culture shock! Sri Lanka: a Guide to Customs and Etiquette*, London: Kuperard.

Barley, N. 1995. *Dancing on the Grave: Encounters with Death*, London: John Murray.

Basham, A.L. 1967. *The Wonder that was India*, London: Sidgwick and Jackson.

Beal, S. (trans.) 1884. *Si-Yu-Ki: Buddhist Records of the Western World: Translated from the Chinese of Hiuen Tsiang (A.D. 629), 2 vols*, London: Kegan Paul, Trench, Trübner & Co.

Bechert, H. (ed.) 1973. *Wilhelm Geiger: Kleine Schriften zur Indologie und Buddhismuskunde*, Wiesbaden, Franz Steiner Verlag.

Bechert, H. 1976. 'Buddha-Feld und Verdienstübertragung: Mahāyāna-Ideen im Therāvada-Buddhismus Ceylons', *Bulletin de l'Académie royale de Belgique* 5, 27–51.

Bechert, H. 1976. 'R.F. Gombrich, Precept and Practice: Traditional Buddhism in the Rural Highlands of Ceylon (Oxford 1971)', *Indo-Iranian Journal* 18, 145–149.

Bechert, H. 1976a. 'Mythologie der Singhalesischen Volksreligion' in Haussig 1976, 511–656.

Bechert, H. 1978. 'The Beginnings of Buddhist Historiography: *Mahāvaṃsa* and Political Thinking' in *Religion and Legitimation of Power in Sri Lanka*, edited by B.L. Smith, Chambersburg: Anima Books, 1–12.

Bechert, H. 1987. *Zur Schulzugehörigkeit von Werken der Hinnyāna-Literatur: Zweiter Teil Symposien zur Buddhismusforschung, III, 2*, Göttingen: Vandenhoek.

Bechert, H. 1992. 'Buddha-Field and Transfer of Merit in a Theravāda Source', *Indo-Iranian Journal* 35, 95–108.

Bhikkhu, Bodhi (trans.) 1978. *The Discourse on the All-Embracing Net of Views: The Brahmajāla Sutta and its Commentarial Exegesis*, Kandy: Buddhist Publication Society.

Bizot, F. 1981. *Le don de soi-meme: Recherches sur le bouddhisme khmer III*, Paris: École française d'Extrême-Orient.

Blackburn, A.M. 2001. *Buddhist Learning and Textual Practice in Eighteenth-Century Lankan Monastic Culture*, Princeton: Princeton University Press.

Bodewitz, H.W. (trans.) 1973. *Jaiminīya Brāhmaṇa I, 1–65*, Leiden: Brill.

Bodewitz, H.W. (trans.) 2002. *Kauṣītaki Upaniṣad: Translation and Commentary with an Appendix Śāṅkhāyana Āraṇyaka IX–XI*, Groningen: Egbert Forsten.

Bodewitz, H.W. 1996. 'Redeath and its Relation to Rebirth and Release', *Studien zur Indologie und Iranistik* 20, 27–46.

Bodhi, Bhikkhu (trans.) 2000. *The Connected Discourses of the Buddha: A New Translation of the Saṃyutta Nikāya*, Oxford: Pali Text Society in association with Wisdom Publications.

Bodhi, Bhikkhu et al. 1993. *A Comprehensive Manual of Abhidhamma: The Abhidhammattha Sangaha of Ācariya Anuruddha*, Kandy: Buddhist Publication Society.

Bond, G.D. 1988. *The Buddhist Revival in Sri Lanka: Religious Tradition, Reinterpretation and Response*, Columbia: University of South Carolina Press.

Bretfeld, S. 2001. *Das Singhalesische Nationalepos von König Duṭṭhagāmaṇī Abhaya*, Berlin: Dietrich Reimer Verlag.

Buddruss, G. (ed.) 1984. *Thieme: Kleine Schriften*, Wiesbaden, Franz Steiner Verlag.

Buitenen, J.A.B. van (trans.) 1973. *The Mahābhārata 1: The Book of the Beginning*, Chicago: University of Chicago Press.

Buitenen, J.A.B. van (trans.) 1975. *The Mahābhārata 2–3: The Book of the Assembly Hall; The Book of the Forest*, Chicago: University of Chicago Press.

Buitenen, J.A.B. van (trans.) 1978. *The Mahābhārata 4–5: The Book of Virāṭa; The Book of the Effort*, Chicago: University of Chicago Press.

Burgess, J. 1882. *Notes on the Amaravati Stupa*, Madras.

Burlingame, Eugene Watson (trans.) 1921. *Buddhist Legends: Translated from the Original Pāli Text of the Dhammapada Commentary*, Oxford: Pāli Text Society.

Burnell, A.C. (trans.) 1873. *The Sāmavidhānabrāhmaṇa (being the Third Brāhmaṇa) of the Sāma Veda: Edited Together with the Commentary of Sāyaṇa, an English Translation, Introduction, and Index of Words*, London: Trübner & Co.

Buss, J. 2005. 'Gieriger Geist oder verehrter Vorfahr? Das "Doppelleben" des Verstorbenen im Newarischen Totenritual' in Assmann, Maciejewski and Michaels 2005, 181–198.

Caland, W. 1896. *Die Altindischen Todten- und Bestattungsbräuche*, Wiesbaden: Dr. Martin Sändig.

Carrithers, M. 1983. *The Forest Monks of Sri Lanka: An Anthropological and Historical Study*, Oxford: Oxford University Press.

Carter, J.R. 1993. *On Understanding Buddhists: Essays on the Theravāda Tradition in Sri Lanka*, Albany: State University of New York.

Clough, Rev. B. 1892. *Clough's Sinhala English Dictionary*, New Delhi.

Cohen, A.P. and Rapport, N. 1995. *Questions of Consciousness*, London: Routledge.

Cohen, M. 1976. 'Dying as Supreme Opportunity: A Comparison of Plato's *Phaedo* and *The Tibetan Book of the Dead*', *Philosophy East And West* 26, 317–327.

Collins, S. 1982. *Selfless Persons: Imagery and Thought in Theravāda Buddhism*, Cambridge: Cambridge University Press.

Collins, S. 1990. 'On the very Idea of the Pāli Canon', *Journal of the Pali Text Society* XV, 89–126.

Collins, S. 1998. *Nirvana and Other Buddhist Felicities: Utopias of the Pāli Imaginaire*, Cambridge: Cambridge University Press.

Cone, M. 2001. *A Dictionary of Pāli: Part I a–kh*, Oxford: Pali Text Society.

Coningham, R. 1998. 'Buddhism "Rematerialized" and the Archaeology of the Gautama Buddha. Review: Relics, Rituals and Representation in Buddhism: Rematerializing the Sri Lankan Theravada Tradition by Kevin Trainor', *Cambridge Archaeological Journal* 8, 121–126.

Coningham, R. 2001. 'The Archaeology of Buddhism' in Insoll 2001, 61–95.

Coningham, R. and N. Lewer 1999. 'Paradise Lost: The Bombing of the Temple of the Tooth: A UNESCO World Heritage Site in Sri Lanka', *Antiquity* 73, 857–866.

Coningham, R. and N. Lewer 2000. 'The Vijayan Colonization and the Archaeology of Identity in Sri Lanka', *Antiquity* 74, 707–712.

Cousens, H. 1891. *An Account of the Caves at Nadsur and Karsambla*, Bombay: Government Central Press.

Cousins, L.S. 2003. 'Śākiyabhikkhu/Sakyabhikkhu/Śākyabhikṣu: A Mistaken Link to the Mahāyāna?', *Nagoya Studies in Indian Culture and Buddhism: Saṃbhāṣā* 23, 1–27.

Cowell, E.B. et al. (trans.) 1895–1907. *The Jātaka or the Stories of the Buddha's Former Births*, London: Pali Text Society.

Cunningham, A. 1892. *Mahābodhi or the Great Temple under the Bodhi Tree at Buddha-Gaya*, London: W.H. Allen.

Dallapiccola, A.L. and S. Zingel-Avé Lallemant (ed.) 1980. *The Stūpa: Its Religious, Historical and Architectural Significance*, Wiesbaden, Franz Steiner.

Dantinne 1991. *Les Qualités de l'ascète (Dhutaguṇa)*, Bruxelles: Edition Thank-Long.

Davy, J. 1821. *An Account of the Interior of Ceylon*, London: Longman.

De Silva, Lily 1993. 'Ministering to the Sick and Counselling the Terminally Ill' in Wagel and Watanabe 1993, 29–39.

Dhammajoti, Bhikkhu Kuala Lumpur et alia (ed.) 1997. *Recent researches in Buddhist Studies: Essays in Honour of Professor Y. Karunadasa*, Colombo, Y. Karunadasa Felicitation Committee.

Dhirasekera, J.D. 1984. 'Dakkhiṇā', *EB* IV, fasc. 2, 279–81.

Dickson, J.F. 1884. 'Notes Illustrative of Buddhism as the Daily Religion of the Buddhists of Ceylon and Some Account of their Ceremonies before and after Death', *J.R.A.S. (Ceylon Branch)* 8, 203–36.

Dietz, S. 1984. *Die buddhistische Briefliteratur Indiens*, Wiesbaden: Harrassowitz.

Disanayaka, J.B. 1998. *Understanding the Sinhalese*, Colombo: Godage Poth Mendura.

Doniger O'Flaherty, W. (ed.) 1980. *Karma and Rebirth in Classical Indian Traditions*, Berkeley, University of California Press.

Doniger O'Flaherty, W. 1980. 'Karma and Rebirth in the Vedas and Purāṇas' in Doniger O'Flaherty 1980, 3–37.

Doniger, Wendy (trans.) 1991. *The Laws of Manu*, London: Penguin Books.

Dubois, Abbe J.A. 1906. *Hindu Manners, Customs and Ceremonies*, Oxford: The Clarendon Press.

Dutt, S. 1962. *Buddhist Monks and Monasteries of India*, London: George Allen & Unwin.

Edgerton, F. 1927. 'The Hour of Death', *Annals of the Bhandarkar Institute* 8, 219–249.

Edgerton, F. 1953. *Buddhist Hybrid Sanskrit Grammar and Dictionary*, New Haven: Yale University Press.

Eggeling, Julius (trans.) 1966. *The Śatapatha-Brāhmaṇa: According to the Text of the Mādhyandina School (Part II, Books III, IV)*, Delhi: Motilal Barnarsidass; originally published Oxford: Clarendon Press, 1885.

Eggeling, Julius (trans.) 1966. *The Śatapatha-Brāhmaṇa: According to the Text of the Mādhyandina School (Part IV, Books VIII, IX, X)*, Delhi: Motilal Barnarsidass; originally published Oxford: Clarendon Press, 1897.

Endo, T. 1987. *Dāna: The Development of Its Concepts and Practice*, Colombo: Gunasena.

Evans-Wentz, W.Y. (trans.) 1957. *The Tibetan Book of the Dead: or the after-death experiences on the Bardo Plane*, London: Oxford University Press.

Everding, U. and A. Tilakaratne (ed.) 2000. *Wilhelm Geiger and the Study of the History and Culture of Sri Lanka*, Colombo, Goethe Institute & Postgraduate Institute of Pali and Buddhist Studies.

Falk, H. 1993. *Schrift im Alten Indien*, Tübingen: Gunter Narr.

Fernando, M.S. 2005. *Rituals, Folk Beliefs and Magical Arts of Sri Lanka (New, updated and Expanded Version)*, Colombo: Susan International.

Firth, S. 1997. *Dying, Death and Bereavement in a British Hindu Community*, Leuven: Peeters.

Fleet, J.F. 1906. 'The Tradition about the Corporeal Relics of the Buddha', *Journal of the Royal Asiatic Society* 655–71, 881–913.

Flood, G. 1996. *An Introduction to Hinduism*, Cambridge: Cambridge University Press.

Forbes, Major 1840. *Eleven Years in Ceylon: Comprising Sketches of the Field Sports and Natural History of that Colony, and an Account of its History and Antiquities*, London: Richard Bentley.

Francis, H.T. (trans.) 1895. *The Jātaka or Stories of the Buddha's Former Births V*, Oxford: The Pali Text Society.

Frauwallner, E. 1926. 'Untersuchungen zu den älteren Upaniṣaden', *Zeitschrift für Inologie und Iranistik* 4, 1–45.

Frauwallner, E. 1953. *Geschichte der indischen Philosophie Vol. 1: Die Philosophie des Veda und des Epos, Der Buddha und der Jina, Das Samkhya und das klassische Yoga-System*, Salzburg: Otto Müller.

Freiberger, O. 1998. 'The Ideal Sacrifice: Patterns of Reinterpreting Brahmin Sacrifice in Early Buddhism', *Bulletin D'Etudes Indiennes* 16, 39–49.

Fujii, M. 1997. 'On the Formation and Transmission of the Jaiminīya-Upaniṣad-Brāhmaṇa' in Witzel 1997, 89–102.

Fuller, C.J. 1992. *The Camphor Flame: Popular Hinduism and Society in India*, Princeton, New Jersey: Princeton University Press.

Fuller, P. 2005. *The Notion of Diṭṭhi in Theravāda Buddhism*, Abingdon: RoutledgeCurzon.

v. Fürer-Haimendorf, C. 1953. 'The Afterlife in Indian Tribal Belief', *Journal of the Royal Anthropological Institute of Great Britain and Ireland* 83, 37–49.

v. Fürer-Haimendorf, C. 1982. *Tribes of India: The Struggle for Survival*, Berkeley: University of California Press.

Fussman, G. 1984. 'Nouvelles inscriptions śaka (II)', *Bulletin de l'Ecole francaise d'Extrême Orient* 73.

Gehman, H.S. 1923. 'Ādisati, anvādisati, anudisati, and uddisati in the Peta-vatthu', *JAOS*, Vol. 43, 410–421.

Gehman, H.S. 1924. 'A Palism in Buddhist Sanskrit', *JAOS*, Vol. 44, 73–75.

Geiger, Wilhelm (trans.) 1912. *The Mahāvaṃsa or The Great Chronicle of Ceylon*, London: Pali Text Society.

Geiger, Wilhelm (trans.) 1964. *Mahāvaṃsa: The Great Chronicle of Ceylon*, London: Pali Text Society.

Gethin, R. 1992. *The Buddhist Path to Awakening: A Study of the Bodhi-Pakkhiyā Dhammā*, Leiden: E.J. Brill.

Gethin, R. 1994. 'Bhavaṅga and Rebirth According to the Abhidhamma' in Skorupski 1994, 11–35.

Gethin, R. 1997. 'Cosmology and Meditation: From the Aggañña-Sutta to the Mahāyāna', *History of Religions* 36, 183–217.

Gethin, R. 1998. *The Foundations of Buddhism*, Oxford: Oxford University Press.

Gethin, R. 2004. 'Can Killing a Living Being Ever be an Act of Compassion? The Analysis of the Act of Killing in the Abhidhamma and the Pali Commentaries', *Journal of Buddhist Ethics* 11, 167–202.

Ghosh, Shyam 1989. *The Hindu Concept of Life and Death (As Portrayed in Vedas, Brāhmaṇas, Āraṇyakas, . . .)*, New Delhi: Munshiram Manoharlal.

Glasenapp, H. v. 1960. *Glaube und Ritus der Hochreligionen in vergleichender Übersicht*, Frankfurt a. Main: Fischer Bücherei.

Glasenapp, H. v. 1985. *Die Philosophie der Inder*, Stuttgart: Alfred Kröner Verlag.

Godakumbura, C.E. 1996. *Sinhalese Literature*, Colombo: Department of Cultural Affairs.

Goldmann, R.P. et al. (trans.) 1984. *The Rāmāyaṇa of Vālmīki: an Epic of Ancient India*, Princeton, N.Y.: Princeton University Press.

Gombrich, R. 1971. '"Merit Transference" in Sinhalese Buddhism', *History of Religions* 11, 203–19.

Gombrich, R. 1972. 'Feminine Elements in Sinhalese Buddhism: "Buddha Mother"', *Wiener Zeitschrift für die Kunde Südasiens* XVI, 67–78.

Gombrich, R. 1981. 'A New Theravādin Liturgy', *Journal of the Pali Text Society* 9, 47–73.

Gombrich, R. 1988. *Theravāda Buddhism: A Social History from Ancient Benares to Modern Colombo*, London and New York: Routledge.

Gombrich, R. 1990. 'Making Mountains without Molehills: The case of the missing *Stūpa*', *Journal of the Pali Text Society* XV, 141–143.

Gombrich, R. 1990. 'Recovering the Buddha's Message' in Skorupski 1990, 5–20.

Gombrich, R. 1991. *Buddhist Precept and Practice: Traditional Buddhism in the Rural Highlands of Ceylon*, Delhi: Motilal Banarsidass.

Gombrich, R. and G. Obeyesekere 1988. *Buddhism Transformed: Religious Change in Sri Lanka*, Princeton: Princeton University Press.

Gonda, J. 1977. *The Ritual Sūtras*, Wiesbaden: Otto Harrassowitz.

Gonda, J. 1980. *Vedic Ritual: The non-solemn Rites*, Leiden: E.J. Brill.

Gooneratne, D. De S. 1865. 'On Demonology and Witchcraft in Ceylon', *Journal of the Royal Asiatic Society (Ceylon Branch)* 4, 1–117.

Goswamy, B.N. 1980. 'Introductory Speech: The *Stūpa*—Some Uninformed Questions About Terminological Equivalents' in Dallapiccola 1980.

Guruge, A.W.P. 1997. 'The Evolution of Emperor Aśoka's Humanitarian Policy: Was Capital Punishment abolished?' in Dhammajoti 1997, 258–275.

Guruge, Ananda W.P. (trans.) 1989. *Mahāvaṃsa: The Great Chronicle of Sri Lanka*, Colombo: Associated Newspapers of Ceylon.

Hacker, P. 1959. *Prahlada: Werden und Wandel einer Idealgestalt*, Wiesbaden: Akademie der Wissenschaften und der Literatur in Mainz.

Hacker, P. 1978. *Paul Hacker, Kleine Schriften*, Wiesbaden: Steiner.

Halbfass, W. 1980. 'Karma, Apūrva, and "Natural" Causes: Observations on the Growth and Limits of the Theory of Saṃsāra' in Doniger O'Flaherty 1980, 268–302.

Hallisey, C. 1990. 'Apropos the Pāli Vinaya as a Historical Document: A Reply to Gregory Schopen', *Journal of the Pali Text Society* XV, 198–208.

Hare, E.M. (trans.) 1932. *The Book of the Gradual Sayings (Anguttara-Nikāya) or more numbered Suttas*, Oxford: Pali Text Society.

Hare, E.M. (trans.) 1934. *The Book of the Gradual Sayings (Anguttara-Nikāya) or more numbered Suttas*, Oxford: Pali Text Society.

Härtel, H. (ed.) 1981. *South Asian Studies*, Berlin, Dietrich Reimer.

Haussig, H.W. (ed.) 1976. *Wörterbuch der Mythologie*, Stuttgart, Klett Verlag.

Hayashi, T. 1997. 'Death and Rebirth in Theravāda Buddhism—Some Problems of Mental Objects', *Ronshū* 24, 69–89.

Hayashi, T. 1999. 'Preliminary Notes on Merit Transfer in Theravāda Buddhism', *Ronshū* 26, 29–55.

Hazra, R.C. 1975. *Studies in the Purāṇic records on Hindu Rites and Customs*, Delhi: Motilal Barnassidas.

v. Hinüber, O. 1996. *A Handbook of Pāli Literature*, Berlin: Walter de Gruyter.

v. Hinüber, O. 1990. 'Khandhakavatta: Loss of text in the Pāli Vinayapiṭaka?', *Journal of the Pali Text Society* XV, 127–138.

Holt, J.C. 1981. 'Assisting the Dead by Venerating the Living: Merit Transfer in the Early Buddhist Tradition', *Numen* XXVIII, 1–28.

Horner, I.B. (trans.) 1938–1966. *The Book of the Discipline*, Oxford: Oxford University Press.

Horner, I.B. (trans.) 1954–1959. *Middle Length Sayings*, London: Pali Text Society.

Horner, I.B. (trans.) 1963–1964. *Milinda's Questions*, London: Luzac & Co.

Horsch, Paul 1971. 'Vorstufen der indischen Seelenwanderungslehre', *Asiatische Studien* XXV, 99–157.

Insoll, T. (ed.) 2001. *Archaeology and World Religion*, London, Routledge.

Irwin, J. 1980. 'The axial Symbolism of the Early *Stūpa*: an Exegesis' in *The Stūpa: Its Religious, Historical and Architectural Significance*, in A.L. Dallapiccola, 1980, 12–38.

Jaini, P.S. 1980. 'Karma and the Problem of Rebirth in Jainism' in Doniger O'Flaherty 1980, 217–238.

Janert, K.L. (ed.) 1972. *Abstände und Schlussvokalverzeichnungen in Aśoka-Inschriften: mit Editionen und Faksimiles in 107 Lichtdrucktafeln*. Wiesbaden.

Juo-Hsüeh, Shih 2000. *Controversies over Buddhist Nuns*, Oxford: Pali Text Society.

Jurewicz, J. 2000. 'Playing with Fire: The *pratītyasamutpāda* from the Perspective of Vedic Thought', *Journal of the Pali Text Society* XXVI, 77–103.

Kahandagamage, Sandhya Piyaruvan 1994. 'Maraṇaya, susāna bhūmiya āśrita sāhityayika saṃskṛtika adhyayanayak', unpublished PhD dissertation, Colombo University.

Kail, O.C. 1966/1967. 'The Buddhist Caves at Sudhagarh', *Journal of the Asiatic Society of Bombay* 41/42.

Kalalalle, S. 1998. *Early Buddhist Sanghas and Vihāras in Sri Lanka (up to the 4th century A.D.)*. Campbell, CA: Rishi Publications.

Kalupahana, D.J. (ed.) 1991. *Buddhist Thought and Ritual*, New York, Paragon House.

Kane, P.V. 1941–1953. *History of the Dharmaśāstra*, Poona: Bhandarkar Oriental Research Institute.

Kapferer, B. 1991. *A Celebration of Demons: Exorcism and the Aesthetics of Healing in Sri Lanka*. Providence, R.I., USA: Berg.

Kapferer, B. 1995. 'From the Edge of Death: Sorcery and the Motion of Consciousness', in Cohen and Rapport, 1995, 134–52.

Kapferer, B. 1997. *The feast of the Sorcerer: Practices of Consciousness and Power*. Chicago: University of Chicago Press.

Kariyawasam, A.G.S. 1995. *Buddhist Ceremonies and Rituals of Sri Lanka*, Kandy: Buddhist Publication Society.
Kazama, T. 1965. 'Ancestor worship, India' in *EB* 1, fasc.4 583–93.
Keyes, C.F. 1983. 'Merit-Transference in the Kammic Theory of Popular Theravāda Buddhism' in Keyes and Daniel 1983.
Keyes, C.F. and E.V. Daniel (ed.) 1983. *Karma: An Anthropological Inquiry*, Berkeley: University of California Press.
Knipe, D.M. 1977. 'Sapiṇḍīkaraṇa: The Hindu Rite of Entry to Heaven' in Reynolds and Waugh 1977, 111–124.
Knox, R. 1681. 'An Historical Relation of the Island Ceylon in the East-Indies Together with an Account of the Detaining in Captivity the Author and divers other Englishmen now living there, and of the Author's Miraculous Escape: Illustrated with figures and a map of the Island' in Saparamadu 1966, 1–356.
Kottkamp, H. 1992. *Der Stupa als Repräsentation des buddhistischen Heilsweges: Untersuchungen zur Entstehung und Entwicklung architektonischer Symbolik*, Wiesbaden:
Kulke, H. 2000. 'Sectarian Politics and Historiography in Early Sri Lanka: Wilhelm Geiger's Studies of the Chronicles of Sri Lanka in the Light of Recent Research' in Everding and Tilakaratne 2000, 112–136.
Kyaw, U Ba (trans.) 1980. *Elucidation of the Intrinsic Meaning: so named The Commentary on the Peta-Stories (Paramatthadīpanī nāma Petavatthu-aṭṭhakathā) by Dhammapāla.*
Lamotte, E. 1970. *Le Traité de la grande vertu de Sagesse de Nāgārjuna (Mahāprajñāpāramitāśāstra) avec une nouvelle Introduction*, Louvain: Université de Louvain.
Langer, R. 2001. *Das vijñāṇa als lebenstragendes Prinzip im Pālikanon*, Wiener Studien zur Tibetologie und Buddhismuskunde. Wien: Arbeitskreis für tibetische und buddhistische Studien der Universität Wien.
Langer, R. 2002. 'Synkretismus und Inklusivismus am Beispiel der buddhistischen Beerdigungsriten im zeitgenössischen Sri Lanka' in *Buddhismus in Geschichte und Gegenwart IV*, Hamburg: Universität Hamburg 2002, 48–64.
Langer, R. 2005. 'Von Göttern, Geistern und Krähen: Buddhistische Bestattungsriten in Sri Lanka' in Assmann, Maciejewski and Michaels 2005, 125–149.
de La Vallée Poussin, Louis 1911. 'Death and Disposal of the Dead, Buddhist' in *ERE* 4, 446–449.
Legge, James (trans.) 1886. *A Record of Buddhist Kingdoms*, Oxford: Clarendon Press.
Lienhard, S. and I. Piovano (ed.) 1997. *Lex et Litterae: Studies in Honour of Professor Oscar Botto*, Alessandria, Edizioni dell'Orso.
Lokuliyana, L. (ed.) 1993. *The Great Book of Protections: Sinhala Maha Pirit Pota*, Singapore, Singapore Buddhist Meditation Centre.
Longhurst, A.H. 1936. *The story of the Stūpa*, Colombo: Ceylon Government Press.
Longhurst, A.H. 1938. *The Buddhist Antiquities of Nāgārjunakoṇḍa, Madras Presidency*, Delhi: Manager of Publications.
Lopez, Donald S. (ed.) 1995. *Buddhism in Practice*, Princeton, Princeton University Press.
Lüders, H. 1912. 'A List of Brahmi Inscritions from the Earliest Times to About A.D. 400 with the exception of those of Aśoka', *Epigraphia Indica* 10.

Maithrimurthi, M. 1986. 'Das Verhalten der ceylonesischen Buddhisten gegenüber Tieren und Planzen', unpublished MA dissertation, University of Hamburg.

Maithrimurthi, M. 1988. 'Die Fächer der buddhistischen Mönche in Sri Lanka', *Mitteilungen aud dem Museum für Völkerkunde Hamburg* 18, 121–126.

Maithrimurthi, M. 1999. *Wohlwollen, Mitleid, Freude und Gleichmut: Eine ideengeschichtliche Untersuchung der vier apramāṇas in der buddhistischen Ethik und Spiritualität von den Anfängen bis zum frühen Yogācāra*, Stuttgart: Franz Steiner Verlag.

Maithrimurthi, M. 2004. 'The Buddha's Attitude Towards Social Concerns as Depicted in the Pāli Canon', *Buddhist Studies Review* forthcoming.

Maithrimurthi, M. and A. v. Rospatt 1998. 'Review: Richard F. Gombrich: How Buddhism Began: The Conditioned Genesis of the Early Teachings', *Indo-Iranian Journal* 41, 164–179.

Malalasekera, G.P. 1967. '"Transference of Merit" in Ceylonese Buddhism', *Philosophy East and West* XVII, 85–90.

Malalasekera, G.P. 1974. *Dictionary of Pāli Proper Names*, London: Pāli Text Society.

Marshall, J. 1931. *Mohenjo-Daro and the Indus Civilisation: Being an Official Account of Archaeological Excavations at Mohenjo-Daro Carried out by the Government of India Between the Years 1922 and 1927*, London: Arthur Probstain.

Marshall, J. 1951. *Taxila. An Illustrated Account of Archaeological Excavations Carried out at Taxila Under the Orders of the Government of India Between the Years 1913 and 1934*, Cambridge: Cambridge University Press.

Masefield, Peter (trans.) 1994. *The Udāna Commentary (Paramatthadīpanī nāma Udānaṭṭhakathā) by Dhammapāla*, Oxford: Pali Text Society.

Masefield, Peter (trans.) 1994. *The Udāna: Translated from the Pāli*, Oxford: Pali Text Society.

Masefield, Peter (trans.) 2000. *The Itivuttaka*, Oxford: Pali Text Society.

McDermott, J.P. 1980. 'Karma and Rebirth in Early Buddhism' in Doniger O'Flaherty 1980, 165–192.

Mettanando, Bhikkhu and O. v. Hinüber 2000. 'The Cause of the Buddha's Death', *Journal of the Pali Text Society* XXVI, 105–117.

v. Mitterwallner, G. 1981. '2 Natural Caves and 11 Man-Made Cave Excavations of Goa' in *South Asian Studies*, in Hartel 1981, 469–99.

Münch, P. and Walz, R. (ed.) 1998. *Tiere und Menschen: Geschichte und Aktualität eines prekären Verhältnisses*, Paderborn: Schoeningh Ferdinand GmbH.

Mylius, K. 1983. *Die Geschichte der Literatur im alten Indien*, Leipzig: Verlag Philipp Reclam.

Ñāṇamoli, Bhikkhu (trans.) 1991. *The Dispeller of Delusion (Sammohavinodanī)*, London: Pali Text Society.

Ñāṇamoli, Bhikkhu (trans.) 1997. *The Minor Readings (Khuddakapāṭha)*, Oxford: Pali Text Society.

Ñāṇamoli, Bhikkhu 1956. *The Path of Purification (Visuddhimagga) by Bhadantācariya Buddhaghosa*, Colombo: R. Semage.

Ñāṇamoli, Bhikkhu and Bhikkhu Bodhi (trans.) 1995. *The Middle Length Discourses of the Buddha: A New Translation of the Majjhima Nikāya*, Boston: Wisdom Publications.

Ñāṇasampanno, Ācariya Mahā Boowa 2003. *Venerable Ācariya Mun Bhūridatta Thera: A Spiritual Biography*, Thailand: Wat Pa Baan Taad.

Ñāṇasīha, H. 1962. *Maharahatan Vahansē*, Colombo.
Nanayakkara, S.K. 1979. 'Commemoration of the Dead', *EB* IV, fasc. 1, 193–96.
Nārada Mahāthera 1956. *A Manual of Abhidhamma*, Bangalore: Power Press. (repr. Kandy: Buddhist Publication Society).
Nārada Mahāthera and Kassapa Thera (ed.) 1975. *The Mirror of the Dhamma*, Colombo: Lake House Printers.
Neufeldt, R.W. (ed.) 1986. *Karma and Rebirth: Post Classical Developments*, Albany: State University of New York Press.
Norman, K.R. (trans.) 1969–1971. *Elders' Verses*, London: Pāli Text Society.
Norman, K.R. 1975. 'Aśoka and Capital Punishment', *Journal of the Royal Asiatic Society* 16–24.
Norman, K.R. 1983. *Pāli Literature*, Wiesbaden: Harrassowitz.
Oberhammer, G. (ed.) 1982. *Epiphanie des Heils: Zur Heilsgegenwart in indischer und christlicher Religion*, Vienna:
Oberhammer, G. (ed.) 1995. *Im Tod gewinnt der Mensch sein Selbst: Das Phänomen des Todes in asiatischer und abendländischer Religionstradition*, Vienna: Verlag der Österreichischen Akademie der Wissenschaften.
Oberhammer, G. and E. Steinkellner (ed.) 1982. *Erich Frauwallner: Kleine Schriften*, Wiesbaden: Franz Steiner Verlag.
Obeyesekere, G. 1970. 'Religious Symbolism and Political Change in Ceylon', *Modern Ceylon Studies* 1.
Obeyesekere, G. 1980. 'The Rebirth Eschatology and its Transformations: A Contribution to the Sociology of Early Buddhism' in Doniger O'Flaherty 1980, 137–164.
Obeyesekere, G. 1981. *Medusa's hair: an essay on Personal Symbols and Religious Experience*, Chicago.
Obeyesekere, Ranjini (trans.) 1991. *Jewels of the Doctrine: Stories of the Saddharma Ratnāvaliya*, Albany: State University of New York Press.
Oertel, Hanns (trans.) 1894. *The Jaiminīya or Talavakāra Upaniṣad Brāhmaṇa: Text, Translation and Notes*, Yale: The American Oriental Society.
Oldenberg, H. 1897. *Buddha: Sein Leben, seine Lehre, seine Gemeinde*, Berlin: W. Hertz.
Oldenberg, H. 1971. *Buddha: His Life, His Doctrine, His Order*, Delhi: Indological Book House.
Olivelle, Patrick (trans.) 1998. *The Early Upaniṣads: Annotated Text and Translation*, New York: Oxford University Press.
Olivelle, Patrick (trans.) 1999. *Dharmasūtras*, Oxford: Oxford University Press.
Palihawadana, M. 1997. 'Pali Sajjhāya and Sanskrit Svādhyāya: An Inquiry into the Historical Origins of the Parittāna Recitation' in Dhammajoti 1997, 493–515.
Pandey, R.B. 1969. *Hindu Saṃskāras: Socio-Religious Study of the Hindu Sacraments*, Delhi: Motilal Barnasidass.
Paranavitana, S. (ed.) 1970. *Inscriptions of Ceylon: Vol I Containing Cave Inscriptions From 3rd Century B.C. to 1st Century A.C. and Other Inscriptions in the Early Brahmi Script*, The Department of Archeology Ceylon.
Parry, J.P. 1994. *Death in Banaras*, Cambridge: Cambridge University Press.
Perera, A.A. 1904. *Glimpses of Singhalese Social Life*, Bombay: Bombay Education Society's Press.
Pieris, R. 1956. *Sinhalese Social Organization: the Kandyan Period*. Colombo: Ceylon University Press Board.

Pollock, S. (trans.) 1986. *The Rāmāyaṇa of Vālmīki: an epic of ancient India, vol. II, Ayodhyākāṇḍa*, Princeton, N.J.: Princeton University Press.

Premasiri, P.D. 1991. 'Significance of the Ritual Concerning Offerings to Ancestors in Theravāda Buddhism' in Kalupahana 1991, 151–158.

Pruitt, W. (trans.) 1998. *The Commentary on the Verses of the Therīs (Therīgāthā-Aṭṭhakathā Paramatthadīpanī VI) by Ācariya Dhammapāla*, Oxford: Pali Text Society.

Przyluski, J. 1918–20. 'Le Parinirvāṇa et les Funérailles du Buddha', *Journal Asiatique*

Rahula, W. 1966. *History of Buddhism in Ceylon: The Anuradhapura Period 3rd Century BC–10th Century AD*, Colombo: M.D. Gunasena & Co. Ltd.

Rajapakse, V. 1990. 'Review: Gombrich, R.F. and Obeyesekere, G.: Buddhism Transfomed: Religious Change in Sri Lanka', *Journal of the International Association of Buddhist Studies* 13, 139–51.

Rastrapal, Mahāthera 2000. *Five Visions of a Dying Man*, Kandy: Buddhist Publication Society.

Rea, A. 1909. 'Excavations at Amarāvatī', *Annual Report of the Archaeological Survey of India 1905–06.*

Reynolds, C.H.B. 1970. *An Anthology of Sinhalese Literature up to 1815*. London: Allen & Unwin.

Reynolds, Frank and Earle H. Waugh (ed.) 1977. *Religious Encounters with Death, Insights from the History and Anthropology of Religions*, Pennsylvania: Pennsylvania State University Press.

Rhys Davids, T.W. (trans.) [n.d.]. *Buddhist Birth Stories (Jataka Tales)*.

Rhys Davids, T.W. and C.A.F. Rhys Davids (trans.) 1910. *Dialogues of the Buddha*, London:

Rhys Davids, T.W. and William Stede 1921–25. *Pali-English Dictionary*, London: Pali Text Society.

Rocher, L. 1986. *The Purāṇas*, Wiesbaden: Harrassowitz.

Rospatt, A. v. 1995. *The Buddhist Doctrine of Momentariness: A Survey of the Origins and Early Phase of this Doctrine up to Vasubandhu*, Stuttgart: Franz Steiner Verlag.

Rospatt, A. v. 1999. 'The Conception of the *Stūpa* in Vajrayāna Buddhism: The Example of the Svayambhūcaitya of Kathmandu', *Journal of the Nepal Research Centre* XI, 121–147.

Roth, G. 1980. 'Symbolism of the Buddhist *Stūpa* according to the Tibetan Version of the Caitya-vibhāga-vinayodbhāva-sūtra, the Sanskrit Treatise *Stūpa*-lakṣaṇa-kārikā-vivecana, and a Corresponding Passage in Kuladatta's Kriyāsaṃgraha' in Dallapiccola and Lallemant 1980.

Ryan, B.F. 1953. *Caste in Modern Ceylon: the Sinhalese System in Transition*. New Brunswick: Rutgers University Press.

Saddhatissa, H. (trans.) 1985. *The Sutta-Nipata*, London: Curzon.

Saddhātissa, H. 1989. *The Abhidhammatthasaṅgaha of Bhadantācariya Anuruddha and the Abhidhammatthavibhāvinī-ṭīkā of Bhadantācariya Sumaṅgalasāmi*, Oxford: Pali Text Society.

Saparamadu, S.D. (ed.) 1966. *An Historical Relation of Ceylon by Robert Knox: Text of the First Edition 1681 Together with the Introductory pages of the Autobiography Written by Knox in June 1696*, Dehiwala: Tisara Prakasakayo.

Schalk, Peter 1972. 'Der Paritta-Dienst in Ceylon', thesis, Lund.

Schischkoff, G. (ed.) 1991. *Philosophisches Wörterbuch*, Stuttgart: Alfred Kröner Verlag.

Schmithausen, L. 1982. 'Versenkungspraxis und erlösende Erfahrung in der Śrāvakabhūmi' in Oberhammer 1982, 59–85.

Schmithausen, L. 1983. 'Buddhism in Ceylon and Studies on Religious Syncretism in Buddhist Countries: Report on a Symposium in Goettingen', *Mundus* 19, 191.

Schmithausen, L. 1986. 'Critical Response' in Neufeldt 1986, 203–230.

Schmithausen, L. 1987. 'Beiträge zur Schulzugehörigkeit und Textgeschichte kanonischer und postkanonischer buddhistischer Materialien' in Bechert 1987.

Schmithausen, L. 1991. *The Problem of Sentience of Plants in Earliest Buddhism*, Tokyo: The International Institute for Buddhist Studies.

Schmithausen, L. 1994. 'Review: 'Herman W. Tull, The Vedic Origins of Karma. Cosmos as Man in Ancient Indian Myth and Ritual. State University of New York Press, Albany 1989, X, 181 pp.', *Indo-Iranian Journal* 37, 151–158.

Schmithausen, L. 1995. 'Mensch, Tier und Pflanze und der Tod in den älteren Upaniṣaden' in Oberhammer 1995, 43–76.

Schmithausen, L. 1997. *Maitrī and Magic: Aspects of the Buddhist Attitude Toward the Dangerous in Nature*, Vienna: Verlag der Oesterreichischen Akademie der Wissenschaften.

Schmithausen, L. and Maithrimurthi, M. 1998. 'Tier und Mensch im Buddhismus' in: P. Münch 1998, 179–224.

Schopen, G. 1984. 'Filial Piety and the Monk in the Practice of Indian Buddhism: A Question of "Sinicization" Viewed from the Other Side', *T'oung Pao* 70, 110–26.

Schopen, G. 1985. 'Two Problems in the History of Indian Buddhism: The Layman/Monk Distinction and the Doctrines of the Transference of Merit', *Studien Zur Indologie und Iranistik* 10, 9–47.

Schopen, G. 1987. 'Burial Ad Sanctos and the Physical Presence of the Buddha in Early Indian Buddhism: A Study in Archaeology of Religions', *Religion* 17, 193–225.

Schopen, G. 1988. 'On Monks, Nuns, and "Vulgar" Practices: The Introduction of the Image Cult into Indian Buddhism', *Artibus Asiae* 49, 153–68.

Schopen, G. 1989. 'The *Stūpa* Cult and the Extant Pāli Vinaya', *Journal of the Pali Text Society* XIII, 83–100.

Schopen, G. 1991. 'Monks and the Relic Cult in the Mahāparinibbānasutta: An Old Misunderstanding in Regard to Monastic Buddhism' in Schopen and Shinohara 1991, 187–201; reprinted in Schopen 1997, 99–113.

Schopen, G. 1995. 'Death, Funerals, and the Division of Property in a Monastic Code' in Lopez 1995, 473–502; reprinted in Schopen 2004, 91–121.

Schopen, G. 1996. 'Immigrant Monks and the Protohistorical Dead: The Buddhist Occupation of Early Burial Sites in India' in Wilhelm 1996, 360–381; reprinted in Schopen 2004, 215–238.

Schopen, G. 1996. 'The Suppression of Nuns and the Ritual Murder of Their Special Dead in Two Buddhist Monastic Codes', *Journal of Indian Philosophy* 24, 536–592.

Schopen, G. 1997. *Bones, Stones, and Buddhist Monks: Collected Papers on the Archaeology, Epigraphy, and Texts of Monastic Buddhism in India*, Honolulu: University of Hawai'i Press.

Schopen, G. 2004. *Buddhist Monks and Business Matters: Still more Papers on Monastic Buddhism in India*, Honolulu: University of Hawai'i Press.

Schopen, G. and K. Shinohara (ed.) 1991. *From Benares to Beijing: Essays on Buddhism and Chinese Religions,* Oakville: Mosaic Press.

Seligmann, C.G. and Seligmann, B. 1911. *The Veddas*. Cambridge: The University Press.

Selkirk, J. 1844. *Recollections of Ceylon*, London: J. Hatchard and Son.

Senaratne, P.M. 2000. *Shree Lankāvē Avamangalya Cāritra*, Colombo: M.D. Gunasena.

Seneviratna, A. (ed.) 1994. *King Aśoka and Buddhism: Historical and Literary Studies*, Kandy: Buddhist Publication Society.

Seneviratne, H.L. 1999. *The Work of Kings: The New Buddhism in Sri Lanka*, Chicago: The University of Chicago Press.

Silk, J.A. 2006. *Body Language: Indic* śarīra *and Chinese* shèlì *in the* Mahāparinirvāṇa-sūtra *and* Saddharmapuṇḍarīka, Tokyo: The International Institute for Buddhist Studies.

Siripala, B.D. 1997. *Jatika Sirit Virit Sangrahaya*, Nugegoda: Dipani Ltd.

Sirr, H.C. 1984. *Ceylon and the Cingalese: their History, Government, and Religion, the Antiquities, Institutions, Produce, Revenue, and Capabilities of the Island, with Anecdotes Illustrating the Manners and Customs of the People*. Dehiwala, Sri Lanka: Swarna Hansa Foundation.

Sivaramamurti, C. 1942. *Amaravati Sculptures in the Madras Government Museum*, Madras: The Superintendent, Government Press.

Skilling, P. 1992. 'The Rakṣā Literature of the Śrāvakayāna', *Journal of the Pali Text Society* XVI, 109–182.

Skilling, P. 1994. *Mahāsūtras: Great Discourses of the Buddha Vol. I*, Oxford: Pali Text Society.

Skilling, P. 1997. *Mahāsūtras: Great Discourses of the Buddha Vol II*, Oxford: Pali Text Society.

Skorupski, T. (ed.) 1990. *The Buddhist Forum, Vol. I Seminar Papers 1987–88*, London: School of Oriental and African Studies.

Skorupski, T. (ed.) 1994. *The Buddhist Forum, Vol. III Seminar Papers 1991–93*, London: School of Oriental and African Studies.

Snodgrass, A. 1985. *The symbolism of the stūpa*, Ithaca: Cornell University.

Sogyal, Rinpoche 1992. *The Tibetan Book of Living and Dying*, San Francisco: Harper Collins Publishers.

Southwold, M. 1983. *Buddhism in Life: The Anthropological Study of Religion and the Sinhalese Practice of Buddhism*, Manchester: Manchester University Press.

Spiro, M.E. 1982. *Buddhism and Society: A Great Tradition and its Burmese Vicissitudes*, Berkeley: University of California Press.

Stache-Rosen, V. 1968. *Dogmatische Begriffsreihen im älteren Buddhismus II: Das Sangitisutra und sein Kommentar Sangitiparyaya*, Berlin: Akademie Verlag.

Stevenson, D. 1995. 'Death-Bed Testimonials of the Pure Land Faithful' in Lopez 1995, 592–602.

Stevenson, D. 1995. 'Pure Land Buddhist Worship and Meditation in China' in Lopez 1995, 359–79.

Strong, J.S. (trans.) 1983. *The Legend of King Aśoka*, Princeton: Princeton University Press.

Strong, J.S. 1992. *The Legend and Cult of Upagupta: Sanskrit Buddhism in North India and Southeast Asia*, Princeton, New Jersey: Princeton University Press.

Strong, J.S. 1994. 'Images of Aśoka: Some Indian and Sri Lankan Legends and Their Development' in Seneviratna 1994, 99–125.

Strong, J.S. 1995. *The Experience of Buddhism: Sources and Interpretations*, Belmont, California: Wadsworth, Inc.

Strong, J.S. 2004. *Relics of the Buddha*, Princeton: Princeton University Press.

Tambiah, S.J. 1970. *Buddhism and the Spirit Cults in North-East Thailand*, Cambridge: Cambridge University Press.

Terwiel, B.J. 1994. *Monks and Magic: An Analysis of Religious Ceremonies in Central Thailand*, Bangkok: White Lotus.

Thieme, P. 1952. 'Bráhman', *Zeitschrift der Deutschen Morgenländischen Gesellschaft* 102, 91–129.

Thieme, P. 1984. 'Indische Wörter und Sitten' in Buddruss 1984, 343–370.

Tillakaratne, M.P. 1986. *Manners, Customs and Ceremonies of Sri Lanka*, Delhi: Sri Satguru Publications.

Trainor, K. 1997. *Relics, Rituals and Representation in Buddhism: Rematerializing the Sri Lankan Theravada Tradition*, Cambridge: Cambridge University Press.

Trenkner, V., et al. 1924. *A Critical Pali Dictionary*, Copenhagen: Royal Danish Academy.

Vetter, T. 1988. *The Ideas and Meditative Practices of Early Buddhism*, Leiden: Brill.

Vetter, T. 1998. 'Tod im Buddhismus' in *Buddhismus in Geschichte und Gegenwart, I*, 12–35 (also in Barloewen 1996. 296–330).

Vetter, T. 2000. *The 'Khandha Passages' in the Vinayapiṭaka and the Four Main Nikāyas*, Vienna: Verlag der Österreichischen Akademie der Wissenschaften.

Waldschmidt, E. 1934. 'Das Paritta', *Baessler-Archiv* 17, 139–50.

Walshe, M. (trans.) 1995. *The Long Discourses of the Buddha: A Translation of the Dīghanikāya*, Boston: Wisdom Publications.

Wagle, N.K. and Watanabe, F. (eds) 1993. *Studies on Buddhism in Honour of Professor A.K. Warder*, Toronto: University of Toronto.

Weeraratne, W.G. 1965. 'Anumodanā', *EB* I, fasc.4, 747–750.

Weightman, S. 1978. *Hinduism in the Village Setting*, Milton Keynes: The Open University Press.

Wezler, A. 1976. *Die wahren Speiseresteesser*, Wiesbaden: Akademie der Wissenschaften und der Literatur.

Wezler, A. 1983. 'Inklusivismus: eine indische Denkform' in *Publications of the De Nobili Research Library*, edited by G. Oberhammer, Vienna: Institut für Indologie der Universität Wien.

Wezler, A. 1997. 'On the Gaining of Merit and the Incurring Demerit Through the Agency of Others: Deeds by Proxy' in Lienhard 1997, 567–589.

Wijayaratna, M. 1983. *Le moine bouddhiste: selon les textes du Theravāda*, Latour-Maubourg: Les Éditions du Cerf.

Wijayaratna, M. 1990. *Buddhist Monastic Life: According to the Texts of the Theravāda Tradition*, Cambridge MA: Cambridge University Press.

Wijeratne, R.P. and Rupert Gethin (trans.) 2002. *Summary of the Topics of Abhidhamma (Abhidhammatthasaṅgaha) by Anuruddha and Exposition of the Topics of Abhidhamma (Abhidhammatthavibhāvinī) by Sumaṅgala being a commentary to Anuruddha's Summary of the Topics of Abhidhamma*, Oxford: Pali Text Society.

Wijesekera, N.D. 1949. *The People of Ceylon*, Colombo: M.D. Gunasena & Co.

Wijesekera, N.D. 1984. *Anthropological Gleanings from Sinhala Literature*, Colombo: M.D. Gunasena & Co.

Wijesekera, N.D. 1990. *The Sinhalese*, Colombo: M.D. Gunasena & Co.

Wilhelm, F. (ed.) 1996. *Festschrift Dieter Schlinghoff zur Vollendung des 65. Lebensjahres dargebracht von Schülern, Freunden und Kollegen*, Reinbek.

Williams, P. 2000. *Buddhist Thought: A Complete Introduction to the Indian Tradition*, London: Routledge.

Willis, M. 2000. *Buddhist Reliquaries from Ancient India*, London: British Museum Press.

Wiltshire, M.G. 1990. *Ascetic Figures before and in Early Buddhism*, Berlin and New York: Mouton de Gruyter.

Winternitz, M. 1909. *Geschichte der indischen Literatur: Einleitung; der Veda; Die volkstümlichen Epen und Purāṇas*, Leipzig: Amelang.

Winternitz, M. 1920. *Geschichte der indischen Literatur: Die Buddhistische Literatur und die heiligen Texte der Jainas*, Leipzig: Amelang.

Wirz, P. 1941. *Exorzismus und Heilkunde auf Ceylon*, Bern: Verlag Hans Huber.

Wirz, P. 1954. *Exorcism and the Art of Healing in Ceylon*, Leiden: E.J. Brill.

Witzel, M. 1997. *Inside the Texts; Beyond the Texts: New Approaches to the Study of the Vedas*, Cambridge MA: Harvard University Press.

Woodward, F.L. (trans.) 1917–1930. *The Book of the Kindred Sayings*, London: Pali Text Society.

Woodward, F.L. (trans.) 1936. *The Book of the Gradual Sayings (Anguttara-Nikāya) or more numbered Suttas*, Oxford: Pali Text Society.

GENERAL INDEX

abbot 64
abhayadāna (giving of fearlessness) *see* animals, releasing of
Abhidhamma 16, 21f., 54–61, 83, 162ff., 177–180, 188; chanting of 46
ādāhanaya see cremation
ädurā (ritual specialist) 148, 150ff.
Agasse 171, 178
Aggacitta Bhikkhu 24
Agni 96
akusala see kusala
alms 109, 131; food (*piṇḍapāta*) 175; giving *see dānaya/dāna*
altar 130, 131, 134, 141, 142, 147
amulet 78
An 103, 104, 110, 112, 113
Ānanda 44, 99–101, 104–106, 108, 109
Ānanda Maitreya 83
Anāthapiṇḍika 40
ancestors (*pitṛ*) 17ff., 79, 80, 96, 148, 150, 152f., 159, 169f., 173, 183, 187, 188, 192n25; offering for 98, 173, 182, 184; path of (*pitṛyāna*) 28; realm of 108
anger (*kēntiya*) 15, 18, 19
Aṅgulimāla 15, 20
animals 146, 155, 171; bones of 118, 205n195; incarnation as 45ff., 48, 49, 50, 56, 115, 169f., 186; pet 119, 145f.; releasing of 12, 14, 102, 191n9; sacrifice 94, 95, 96, 99, 102, 103, 108, 187, 203n159; wild 86, 87, 146
Annabhāra 175f.
anniversary 98
antarābhava see intermediate state
ānubhāva see ritual power
anukampā (sympathy) 145, 211n99
anumodanā see rejoicing
Anuruddha 100, 101
appreciation *see* rejoicing
arahat (saint) 15, 24, 42, 47, 50, 100, 102, 110, 155
arch 65, 96, 98, 129, 131
archaeology 6, 89, 115–124, 136, 166, 187
Ariyadhamma 147
Ariyapala 12, 70, 71, 85
ascetic 37; 13 practices (*dhutaṅga*) 86, 87
ash (*chārikā*) 97, 110, 111, 136–141
ashes *see* remains
Aśoka 2, 15, 23, 24, 41f., 115, 119, 195n102, 195n103, 205n182
astrology 63, 78, 79, 99
attachment 19, 42, 44, 49ff., 80
aṭṭhakathās see commentaries
Aung, Shwe Zan 48
auspicious/inauspicious 14, 75, 95, 124, 210n76
auto-cremation *see* cremation
aversion *see* hatred
Avīci 48; *see also* hell

bacteria (*visabījā*) 82
Bāhiya Dāruciriya 108, 109
baṇa 83, 125–129, 143f., 148, 149 (*see also* preaching; sermon); book of 12, 13
banana 143, 156; leaf cone 125f.; leaf plates 65f., 129, 130, 131, 135, 142, 149
Bareau 113f.
Barley 128

INDEX OF CITED PASSAGES, *SUTTAS* AND TEXTS

Lightning Source UK Ltd.
Milton Keynes UK
UKOW031444030512

191942UK00002B/32/P

9 780415 544702